—1001—
Answers to
Correspondents

Daily Mail

1001

Answers to
Correspondents

Andy Simpson & James Black

Robinson
LONDON

Dedication

*Andy Simpson and James Black would like
to dedicate this book to
The Great British Public, to everyone who asked a question,
everyone who came up with an answer and all who
contributed to the debate.*

Robinson Publishing Ltd
7 Kensington Church Court
London W8 4SP

First published in the UK by Robinson Publishing Ltd 1998

Volume copyright © 1998 Hazar Publishing
Text copyright © 1998 Associated Newspapers
Designed by John Dunne

A copy of the British Library Cataloguing in Publication data
is available from the British Library

ISBN 1-85487-579-5

Printed and bound in the EC

10 9 8 7 6 5 4 3 2 1

Introduction

Though up-to-date for the Internet Age this book
has a venerable pedigree.

A few years before Alfred and Harold Harmsworth changed
the face of the British newspaper industry by founding the
mould-breaking Daily Mail, they tapped into the insatiable
desire for knowledge among the British public with the
launch of Answers to Correspondents, a penny weekly which
sought to both inform and entertain.

It shocked and amused its way through late Victorian society
and paved the way for the kind of investigative journalism
which led eventually to the campaigning Daily Mail, launched
in 1896. By the time it disappeared in February 1956 it had
passed on a million pieces of interesting, extraordinary,
fascinating and entertaining information.

But the quest for knowledge lived on and, in 1993,
the Daily Mail revived its own progenitor and Answers to
Correspondents became a lively daily feature of the paper.

Since then the newspaper's researchers and readers together
have re-roasted a few old chestnuts, shot down some hardy
canards, scotched some old myths and disseminated a wealth
of information in entertaining and enlightening fashion, as
well as posing many of the questions about which we ponder
only after someone else has bothered to ask them.

In one of Burt Lancaster's last films,
Louis Malle's Atlantic City, Susan Sarandon pleads with him:
'Teach me things.' 'You want information,' he shrugs,
'or you want wisdom?' She, with a pout, replies,
'Both.' Read on...

ANDY SIMPSON, NORTHCLIFFE HOUSE, JULY 1998

1: How much does it cost to mint a £1 coin?

Like any other commercial enterprise, the Royal Mint is normally very cagey about revealing its specific production costs. To get a rough idea of the price of the £1 coin we have to go back to its introduction in April 1983. The accepted price per coin at the time was roughly 2.5p. Allowing for inflation in the last 13 years, new technology and the introduction of a semi-privatised regime, plus the effects of movements in metal prices, it's safe to assume that the coins can be produced for somewhere between 2p and 4p each. BASIL RAMPTON, BIRMINGHAM.

2: How did the expression 'put a sock in it' originate?

Emil Berliner produced the first record-playing gramophone in 1887, the sound from which emerged from a large horn, later substituted by a resonant box, to amplify the volume. Missing from this arrangement was any form of volume control and the most popular way of regulating the sound was literally to put a sock in it: a woollen sock was stuffed in the horn or resonance box to reduce the sound emitted. Gramophones were still being quietened in this way as late as the Thirties. COLIN CUTLER, BILLERICAY, ESSEX.

3: How many times has Norway scored no points in the Eurovision song contest?

Norway has finished bottom in the contest five times and in 1978 scored no points at all. However, Norway won the competition in 1985 with a Rolf Lovland song performed by girl duo Bobby Socks and scored well, without winning, with a song called Do-Re-Mi, sung by Jahn Teigen, in 1983. Teigen had also been the pointless singer in 1978, attributing his failure to the fact that his song's co-author was bald. Jokes about Norway's Eurovision Song Contest performance have worn a little thin since the country won the title again in 1995 with Rolf Lovland's Nocturne performed by Secret Garden. In 1996 a political element crept into the show when the Norwegian hostess accused their Swedish neighbours of failing to grant any votes to Norway, despite the Norwegians' regular support for Swedish entries. Norway finished second that year, way ahead of Sweden, while The Voice, written by Brendan Graham and sung by Eimear Quinn, made sure the Irish entry topped the poll for the fourth time in five years, making a record seven wins for the Emerald Isle. MIKE SPENCER, ROMFORD, ESSEX.

4: Why do Australians call us 'pommies'?

The oldest explanation is that POME stood for Prisoner Of Mother England but there's no documentary evidence that this acronym was ever used and the expression 'Mother England' isn't a normal or well-known construction. D. H. Lawrence, in his novel Kangaroo, claims Pommie was an abbreviation of pomegranate, rhyming slang for immigrant. British people newly arrived in Australia also tend to turn red in the sun, assuming the colour of a pomegranate. On her recent trip Down Under, my mother was told POM simply stood for Poor Old Migrant.

JOHN BURGESS, ORPINGTON, KENT.

The name Pommie is a derivative of the initials POHMIE printed on transported convicts' uniforms, standing for Prisoners Of Her Majesty In Exile.

DENISE BLAIR, WEST LOTHIAN.

5: Who devised the idea of sending Christmas cards in the UK?

In the 18th and early 19th centuries it became the tradition in the upper echelons of English society for people to have a form of greeting card, designed by an artist, to send to their friends. The circulation of these cards was extremely limited. The most significant event in the development of the Christmas card as we know it came exactly 150 years ago. In 1843 Sir Henry Cole, director of the Victoria and Albert Museum from 1853 and 1873, when it was known as the South Kensington Museum, wanted to contact a number of his friends at Christmas time but felt he didn't have the time to write a letter to all of them. So he had a card designed by the artist John Horsley. When all the cards had been sent, those that were left over were put on sale in a London shop at a cost of one shilling each. Over the next 20 years, the idea of sending Christmas cards was gradually picked up by others but generally progress was slow. Two later developments really stimulated what has now become a tradition all over the world – the introduction of the penny post and the fact that in the 1860s colour printing became cheaper and more accessible. It is now estimated that 1.6 billion Christmas cards a year are sent in Great Britain alone.

JOHN ROSCOE, GREETING CARD AND CALENDAR ASSOC, LONDON.

6: Why do you rarely see women serving in Indian restaurants?

Most of the early 'Indian' restaurants in Britain were opened by men coming from the Sylhet area of what used to be East Pakistan, now Bangladesh. Most of these men initially came to this country without their wives and the vast majority were Moslem so that, when their wives were eventually able to join them here, they were not permitted, under their culture, to serve other men.

YVONNE MALIK, RHODES, MANCHESTER.

The vast majority of the first wave of so-called 'Indian' restaurants in this country were owned and run by people who came from what used to be called East Pakistan, and is now Bangladesh. Most were Moslem, and in strong traditional Islamic culture it is not considered right for a woman to work away from home. Even among those who were of the Hindu faith, objections to women serving food at certain times of the month caused practical problems for women working as waitresses. In addition, when the first 'Indian' restaurants opened, many of the men that came to Britain from the Indian sub-continent left their wives and families behind, to join them at a later date. ZAHOOR KHAN, WALSALL.

7: Since Asil Nadir jumped bail and fled to Northern Cyprus in early 1993 all attempts to bring him to trial have failed. How many other countries have no extradition treaty with Britain?

Britain has extradition treaties with the 47 Commonwealth countries and with the 19 countries that have signed the European Convention on Extradition, including Spain – so the 'Costa del Crime' is no longer a safe refuge. Greece, Turkey and Cyprus are also in this group but Cyprus is regarded as entirely Greek. Nadir fled to the northern, Turkish part, which Britain doesn't recognise, so extradition is difficult if not impossible. We also have individual treaties with 28 countries ranging from Albania to the USA. However, in Parliamentary language 'not all of these treaties are currently operative' which means that a country with a military regime or totalitarian ruler might return a fugitive only if its rulers felt like it, or in return for some diplomatic or trade favour. Egypt, Libya and the USSR successor states have no extradition treaties with Britain.
D. SMITH, READING.

8: Which was the first invention patented?

The earliest of all known English patents was that granted by Henry VI in 1449 to Flemish-born John of Utyman for making the coloured glass for the windows of Eton College. The patent lasted for 20 years.
LAURENCE KING, MILBORNE ST ANDREW, DORSET.

The first invention patented after the establishment of the Patent Office in 1801 was the ring binder invented by its first chairman, Dr Ayfor, to file all subsequent patent applications. MR G. J. WRIGHT, PARKSHOT, SURREY.

9: What does the 'E' in E numbers stand for?

An E number signifies that the food additive referred to has been accepted as safe for food use throughout the European Union. At present, there are just over 300 listed additives and about 3,000 flavourings. E numbers are divided into five groups: colourings (E100-180), preservatives (E200-290), anti-oxidants (E300-321), emulsifiers (E322-494) and sweeteners (E420-421).   MARISA KERR, WANSTEAD, LONDON E11.

10: Which actor or actress has made the most film appearances in the history of the cinema?

Tom London (1883-1963) appeared in more than 2,000 films in a career which began with The Great Train Robbery in 1903. He was the leading man at Universal Films for very many years. Later in his career he specialised in B-movie Westerns, generally taking the part of the sheriff. He made his last film, The Lone Texan, in 1953.   COLIN CRUICKSHANK, EDINBURGH.

11: Do animals suffer jealousy?

Animals do appear to have jealous tendencies of a territorial and possessive nature which manifests itself mainly when a creature meets another in the company of its owner. There is no evidence that animals have the human capacity to covet another's property and, although they may fight over food, this is for self-preservation rather than for the acquisition of property.   BRIAN MALTBY, MANCHESTER HOME FOR LOST DOGS.

12: How did fishwives get such a bad press?

Before birth control and education for women, there were few avenues open to women to support themselves outside marriage. One job they were allowed to do in London from at least medieval times was the preparation and sale of fish. They were not permitted to keep permanent shops or stalls but walked the streets carrying their wares. Their headquarters was Billingsgate Market where their scolding and bad language became notorious. Billingsgate became synonymous with foul language and by the time of the Restoration (1660) the term 'fishwife' was used to describe anyone who swore.   E. GORDON, EDINBURGH.

13: Why 'mad as a hatter'?

In former times, hatters used to achieve the high gloss finish on top hats by polishing them over hot mercury vapour. When inhaled, mercury vapour attacks the brain cells, causing insanity and sometimes blindness. A large percentage of hatters suffered from this occupational malady. Early photographers who used hot mercury fumes to develop their plates were similarly affected.   CHRIS STEBBINGS, BOOKHAM, SURREY.

14: *How do we get exact measurements to the nearest stars?*

If you look at an object and move your head, it appears to change position against its background in an effect called parallax, notably more pronounced for close objects. Astronomers use parallax to measure the distance between the sun and nearby stars. As the Earth moves in its orbit around the Sun, nearer stars appear to move in relation to more distant ones. Over a six month period the Earth moves from one side of the Sun to the other, a distance of about 186 million miles. By making two measurements of a star's position, six months apart, it's possible to estimate its distance from the sun. A star whose position changes by 1/2600 of a degree (one second of the arc) is said to be one parsec away. Measuring these tiny angles is very difficult so the method is limited to stars within 100 parsecs. Apart from the Sun, our closest star is Proxima Centauri, 1.3 parsecs away.   BOB LANG, BRISTOL.

15: *How many people have stood on top of Everest?*

Between 400 and 500, according to the Alpine Club of Great Britain. It's impossible to be more accurate because the number increases with surprising regularity. The Guinness Book of Records records Sherpa Angrita as the man who has climbed Everest most often. He has scaled the highest summit on Earth eight times.   A. REED, MIDDLESBROUGH.

16: *Why do bras fasten at the back when the front would seem more sensible?*

This is a convention inherited from traditional corsetry. Front opening sportswear was first made available by American manufacturer Menzies in 1910. Some front-fastening bras were fashionable in the Twenties but they are now mostly confined to maternity wear. Back fastenings may have persisted because there is more scope for size adjustments in the back straps.   AVRIL HART, VICTORIA AND ALBERT MUSEUM, LONDON.

Bras fasten at the back because at one time all ladies would have been dressed by a maid and it would have been unseemly for the girl to be fastening hooks in her mistress's cleavage. Sadly nowadays, bras do not come with a maid.   HELEN BAILEY, NORTHWICH, CHESHIRE.

17: *Why is love traditionally associated with the heart?*

Until 1628 when William Harvey published his discovery of the circulation of the blood nobody knew exactly what function the heart performed. But from early times it was considered that the heart was the principal organ of the body and the seat of every human emotion, the part with which man loved, hated and grieved. The heart is referred to in early writings like the Bible as the centre of emotion. Though we now know this to be incorrect, we still speak of the heart as symbolising the extreme emotion of love.　　　　　M. COOMBS, BOURNEMOUTH.

18: How fast is The Starship Enterprise's Warp Factor 9?

Warp factor speeds are multiples of the speed of light, where Factor 1 is light speed itself, Warp Factor 2 is 10 times that, Warp Factor 3 is 39 times, Warp Factor 4, 102 times; Warp Factor 5, 214 times; Warp Factor 6, 392 times; Warp Factor 7, 656 times; Warp Factor 8, 1,024 times and Warp Factor 9, 1,515 times the speed of light. Warp Factor 10 is infinite speed which can never be reached.　　　STEPHEN STROUD, FALLOWFIELD, MANCHESTER.

19: Why seven years' bad luck for breaking a mirror?

It used to be believed that a person's reflection in a mirror was a representation of their soul, so the destruction of the mirror was the effective destruction of their soul, bringing upon them a curse in one of three forms; early death, banishment from heaven after death or a period of bad luck while still on earth. Throwing the shattered pieces of mirror into a fast-flowing river was held to negate the unlucky effects of the breakage.
　　　　　TOM CROCKER, SOUTHPORT.

The seven years' bad luck associated with breaking a mirror comes from the seven years it is supposed to take the body to regenerate all its cells.
　　　　　GAIL McDONALD, BRISTOL.

20: Why were police vans known as Black Marias?

Since most police vehicles are now white, or brightly coloured, this expression, redolent of the Fifties, is now little known but it is supposed to date from Maria Lee, a black lodging house keeper in Boston, Mass, in the 1840s. Either because of her massive size, with which she subdued troublemakers, or because patrol wagons were called so frequently to her disorderly house, her nickname Black Maria became slang for a police van. The name failed to stick in America, where it went on to describe a hearse, while police vehicles became known as 'paddy wagons' in honour of the numbers of drunken Irish immigrants rounded up in them. Having arrived in Britain via American cops-and-robbers movies, Black Maria hung on here to describe police vans until they started to appear in white.
　　　　　DAVID ELIAS, NOTTINGHAM.

21: From where does the term 'wally' originate?

The original Wally is said to have been a dog which strayed off from its owner at a Glastonbury Fayre Festival in the late Sixties. As the dog's owner wandered around calling for it, the huge crowd took up his cry of 'Wally!' while waiting for the next band performance. In the next few years the habit of calling 'Wally!' proliferated at rock concerts, much as people now perform the 'Mexican wave' when there's a lull in proceedings.

GORDON TAYLOR, ALVASTON, DERBYS.

'Wally' is northern slang for the last gherkin in a large jar in a chip shop.

IVAN MILLER, DERBY.

Dennis the Menace's adversary, the nerdish Walter from the Beano, cannot escape some of the blame for the pathetic image of all Wallies.

CARL POPE, LONDON NW5.

22: Who named our planet Earth?

A word for the world we inhabit evolved as soon as man began to communicate by speech. The ancient Greeks used *ge,* which has given us geology, geography and geometry. The ancient Romans called it *terra,* whence come the French *terre,* Spanish *tierra* and our 'terrestrial' and 'terrace.' To the Germanic peoples of northern Europe it was *erda* or *ertha,* giving the modern German *Erde,* Dutch *aarde* and, thanks to the 5th Century invasion of Britain by Angles and Saxons, our English word 'earth.' In most languages the name of the planet is also used for the soil which make life on it possible.

R. I. BROWN, CANTERBURY, KENT.

23: Who audits the Audit Commission?

The Audit Commission, which audits local and health authorities, is itself audited by The National Audit Office, which is also the auditor of central government departments and other public bodies. The NAO is in turn audited by accountants Clark Whitehill and there the process ends because, as a partnership rather than a company, they are not subject to compulsory audit.

CLIVE GORDON, SOUTHALL, MIDDX.

24: Why is bureaucracy known as red, not yellow or blue, tape?

This expression dates from Tudor times when mounted messengers delivered to people required in court summonses tied around with a red tape and sealed with red sealing wax. Today's lawyers still bind their documents together with red ribbon.

D. G. HARVEY, HAILSHAM, EAST SUSSEX.

25: Why do the Chinese eat with chopsticks?

Chopsticks originated in very ancient times when they were used to remove pieces of cooked meat from the fire without burning one's fingers. The Chinese refined this for everyday use, long before Western culture began using table cutlery. Knives and forks were not used in China because Confucius, who had a rule for every aspect of human existence, decreed that civilised people should not use instruments of slaughter at the dining table. MISS S. POWLING. LEAMINGTON SPA, WARWKS.

26: Who gets the revenue from a letter sent to Britain from abroad?

In the short term, the country where the letter is posted. But all countries belong to the Universal Postal Union, whose headquarters is in Berne, Switzerland. This regulatory body monitors the balance of revenue between member countries and redresses it by agreement so if, for instance, far more people in Zaire send mail to Britain than vice versa, the Zairian authorities make a payment to the Royal Mail. M. R. DAVIS, LLANDUDNO, NORTH WALES.

27: Why do women tend to live longer than men?

This isn't strictly true. There are instances of cultures in the Third World where the roles of men and women as we traditionally know them are virtually reversed or at least equal. In those countries, life expectancy follows different patterns from ours. An example is Nepal where the sex roles as we know them in everyday life are reversed and males there generally live longer lives. In this country, shorter life expectancy for men is generally blamed on the stresses and traumas of our present-day society. Male peer pressure is said to bear heavily on men, made worse by a general male inability to release problems by talking about them in the way females do. Over the next few decades, life expectancy for the sexes is predicted to even out as females move increasingly into traditionally male-dominated areas of work, leisure and sport. JANE KENTON, DIDSBURY, MANCHESTER.

It has been suggested recently that men die earlier deaths because of the stress involved in 'chasing' women, because the onus is on the male sex to find partners in life, but this is conjecture. In current decades it may simply be the preponderance of smoking among men which leads to an average earlier demise. P. RYAN, LONDON E6.

28: Amid all the celebrations for the 40th anniversary of the conquest of Everest, whatever happened to Sherpa Tensing?

Sherpa Tenzing Norgay, who stood on the top of Everest with Sir

Edmund Hillary on May 29, 1953, died in the Indian city of Darjeeling in May 1986 at the age of 72. He was awarded the George Cross and Star of Nepal for his part in the historic climb and lived most of the rest of his life in relative obscurity, teaching climbing at an Indian hill station. When he died, India's Premier Rajiv Gandhi hailed him as 'the tiger of the snows' and said the whole nation would mourn him.

DAVID EMBLING, BROMLEY, KENT.

29: After watching the film Groundhog Day, can anyone tell me what causes déjà vu?

The subject may have experienced the actual sensation before, long ago, perhaps in childhood and either forgotten or blocked out the memory for some reason. Or events in the subject's ancestry may have been somehow 'recorded' and passed down genetically from one generation to another, leading to a feeling of recognising things one has not personally experienced. But the most likely explanation is that when experiencing something the information somehow bypasses your short-term memory and moves directly to long-term memory, giving you the impression that you are repeating an experience from long ago.

DAVID BARNETT, EDGWARE, MIDDX.

This is best understood by imagining, if you can, the simultaneous co-existence of everything. Time, as we humans perceive it, is merely the convenient 'ruler' by which things are set in order for us. To achieve this, our brain acts as a kind of receiver, 'tuned in' to highly particular signals from the enormous masses going on around us, according to our unique position in life as a whole. Just occasionally, for some unknown reason, the message becomes scrambled and arrives in our conscious perception in an order which makes us believe something happened 'before' another event, when the correct imposition of a timescale to the two phenomena would have placed them the other way round.

DR PETER SMITH, LONDON N5.

30: Who lives in Downing Street other than Nos 10 and 11?

Number 10 Downing Street has been the official residence and office of the British Prime Minister since 1732, when the house was accepted from King George II by Sir Robert Walpole in his official capacity as First Lord of the Treasury. The present house is one of only three that remain from a street built by Sir George Downing who obtained a lease on the site, partly through royal favour, in 1680. His other two surviving houses are No 11, now the official residence of the Chancellor of the Exchequer, and No 12, the ground floor and basement of which house offices for the Government whips. The other Downing Street houses have been demolished over the years and all other buildings there now back onto the street.   DR JULIAN DANIELS, ANLABY, HULL.

31: Why can't you buy tinned bananas?

The normal canning process for fruit includes subjecting it to extreme temperatures in quick succession to achieve complete pasteurisation. This process would destroy the texture of a banana to a point where it would become almost unrecognisable. Meanwhile the banana would also become oxidised, causing unsightly discoloration and forfeiting valuable nutrients. Few customers would want to buy it in this state. It is possible to buy canned banana but it comes in puree form and is used mostly by the confectionery industry or as baby food.

DR LAWRENCE SWAN, FYFFES BANANAS, DUNDALK, IRELAND.

32: Why do people end a radio message with the name 'Roger'?

It has long been customary to use the word 'roger' for 'received' in radio procedure. The wartime Combined Operators' Phonetic Alphabet used 'roger' to clarify the letter 'R' on air but in the current international version 'R' is given as 'romeo' while 'roger' still stands for 'received.'

MR G. E. BELL, EX-ROYAL SIGNALS, SHREWSBURY.

33: Why are newspaper reporters sometimes known as hacks?

'Hackney', derived from the old French hauenee, an ambling horse, was used for a horse let out for hire. The term hackney carriage comes from the same root. 'Hackney,' shortened to hack, was applied to anyone whose services were for hire, particularly writers and journalists.

JANE WHITE, DUNFERMLINE, FIFE.

34: Why is it considered unlucky to walk under a ladder?

Apart from the immediate dangers of things falling on your head, there are two explanations for this superstition. A ladder resting against a wall forms a triangle which in medieval times was looked upon as a sign of the Holy Trinity. Walking under the ladder was held to show disrespect for the Godhead and misfortune was bound to follow. In the 18th and 19th centuries, a leaning ladder was a reminder of the gallows, where a ladder was propped up against the supporting beam to enable the condemned man to climb up to reach the noose.   DAVID EMBLING, BROMLEY, KENT.

35: Who was Gordon Bennett?

James Gordon Bennett (1841-1918) was a lavish spender, famous yachtsman, motorist and newspaper owner who never did anything by halves. His father, also called James Gordon Bennett, was born in Keith, Scotland, and emigrated to America at 19, where he founded and edited the New York Herald. Gordon Bennett junior inherited immense wealth and soon made his mark on the world. As editor of the New York Herald he funded Stanley's 1871 expedition to search for Dr Livingstone to Africa and reputedly spent more than $30 million of the paper's revenue on similar ventures. One story about his extraordinarily lavish lifestyle comes from France. While establishing the Paris edition of the New York Herald in 1887, he discovered one day that a favourite hotel couldn't find him a table for lunch, so he bought the hotel. His extravagant exploits made him a legend in the Western world and whenever anything exceptional occurred people dropped the familiar 'fancy that' in favour of the expletive 'Gordon Bennett!'   GRAHAM KERSALL, KINGS NORTON, WEST MIDLANDS.

36: Why do we call a drink of tea a cup of 'char'?

T'cha or *t'e* was the Chinese name for the beverage supposedly discovered by a Chinese Emperor more than 2,000 years BC, when a leaf from a tree fell into some boiling water. Brought to India by early European traders, its name was corrupted to 'char' and it was served by 'char wallahs' to British soldiers during the days of the British Raj.
                                      PETER BURGESS, HULL, HUMBERSIDE.

37: Why is a boxing ring always square?

The first boxing 'rings' were in the open and consisted simply of on-lookers formed in a rough circle around the participants in a bare-knuckle contest. As the sport became organised, stakes were driven into the ground with ropes to define the fighting area and the ring became a square, while the fighting itself was subjected to the Marquess of Queensberry's rules. Today's boxing ring must be a maximum of 20ft and minimum of 14ft square.   G. W. FARMER, NOTTINGHAM.

38: Why does the bridegroom have a 'best man' and why is he so called?

General lawlessness in medieval times meant noble bridegrooms often felt vulnerable when at their most romantic and least warlike. They were particularly concerned to defend the honour of their new brides who were often among strangers and would have been considered prize captures by their enemies. So the groom sought the 'best man' from among his entourage to protect him and repel any attack on his nuptials. The man was charged with sticking close to his boss throughout the proceedings and, in certain instances, commanded a small army of 'grooms' to assist in the wedding's defence. In later years the best man's duties descended to ensuring the groom's attendance.   C. S. WARD, SUTTON PARK, HULL.

39: We all like looking smart but why 'dressed up to the nines'?

This expression is said to derive from the old English saying 'dressed to the eyes' meaning pleasing to the eye. In Old English it would have been written '...to the eyne' which became '...to the nines.' The saying gained further currency in military circles around 1850 when an account of members of the Wiltshire Regiment, the 99th, noted that their elegant dress set a standard other regiments tried to emulate.

S. MELLORS, CRAMLINGTON, NORTHUMBERLAND.

40: Why do we have candles on birthday cakes?

The use of lighted candles on birthdays began with the ancient Greeks: moon-shaped honey cakes were lit with tapers and placed in the temple of Artemis. The candles were supposed to have a special magic to induce the goddess to grant wishes. In pre-Roman Britain, the custom of offering congratulations, presenting gifts and celebrating a birthday with lighted candles on a cake were supposed to protect the birthday celebrant from evil spirits and demons in the coming year. Christianity originally rejected elaborate birthdays as a pagan custom, before the 4th Century AD, when celebrations resumed.   KEVIN PRICE, PRESTON, LANCS.

41: Why do wheels in some old films appear to be going backwards?

Wheels appear to be going backwards if the speed of the film (in frames per second) is slightly faster than the speed of the wheels (in spokes per second). A spoke which is vertical in one frame of the film will have rotated to a point just short of the vertical in the next frame, deceiving your eye into thinking it is rotating in the opposite direction. This illusion is most common in Westerns where carriage wheels, unlike modern car wheels, have very pronounced spokes.   RONALD PETERS, BUCKINGHAM.

42: Is there any truth in the belief that people or animals can fall under the influence of the moon?

There is a limited amount of statistical evidence that people can be affected by the passage of the moon overhead – physically as well as mentally. In 1940, Chicago physician Dr William Peterson discovered that tuberculosis deaths rose significantly seven days before a full moon.

In the Fifties, a German doctor reported that births along the North Sea coast tended to increase just as the moon reached its zenith. And French astrologer Michel Gauquelin concluded that an unexpectedly large number of politicians were born during a full moon. The suggestion is that the moon can affect humans and animals by making small changes in the chemistry of the blood. HELEN DURNFORD, MANCHESTER.

43: Why is the Leader of the Orchestra always a violinist?

Originally it was the harpsichordist who was supposed to keep all the other members of the orchestra in time but as the use of that instrument declined around the 18th Century the role was passed to the first violinist. He/she combined the advantages of being in a front position and could even stand up during a performance so the movement of his/her bow could provide a clearly visible beat. By the mid 19th Century, orchestras acquired a conductor with a baton to lead them but the principal violinist is still known as 'leader' and can still dictate the pace of a performance, on occasion. POLLY FENN, EAST DEREHAM, NORFOLK.

44: Who was The Real McCoy?

The expression 'the Real McCoy' is a corruption of the earlier Scottish saying 'the real MacKay' – MacKay being a blend of whisky. An Irish-American boxer called McCoy found it useful to use the amended version in his publicity after a journalistic 'translation' of the original phrase. OLIVER DEANS, BELFAST.

45: Do crocodiles really shed tears?

The crocodile is said to fool its prey into presenting itself as the croc's next meal by emitting a piercing cry, easily mistaken for a human being in great pain or shock. Crocodiles may have learned this trick from the observations made when they took a human victim: the snack shrieked and, as if by magic, another one came running to the scene. LES ROBERTS, SWINDON, WILTS.

When crocodiles are basking out of the water, for respiratory reasons, they leave their jaw gaping wide open, opening their tear ducts. With the flow of tears and what appears to be a broad grin, people use the expression 'crocodile tears' when referring to someone who is feigning sadness when in fact they're happy. ALAN MARSTON, WELLINGBOROUGH, NORTHANTS.

46: Why is a 'wolf whistle' so called and where did it originate?

The slang term 'wolf' first became popular for a predatory womaniser in the U.S. in the Thirties and a wolf call was used as a somewhat basic way of attracting a woman's attention. The use of the two-note wolf whistle as a sign of admiration for a pretty woman developed rapidly among American servicemen during World War II.   DAVID ELIAS, NOTTINGHAM.

47: Why blue for a boy and pink for a girl?

This well-established tradition stems originally from the Middle East where male children were valued more highly than females. Blue was the colour of heaven, the sacred colour, and was assigned to beloved male offspring. Less welcome female babies made do with pink, the colour of the earthly activities of childbearing and rearing. The association of these colours has continued in our culture to the annoyance of feminists who mistakenly think it identifies boys with cold, hard blue and girls with soft, warm pink.   MRS K. M. PARDOE, CANVEY ISLAND, ESSEX.

48: What sport puts the greatest strain on the human body?

It is generally thought that the biathlon puts most physical and mental strain on its participants. No doubt the triathlon, which adds the discipline of cycling to the running and swimming events, is even tougher. The best sports for all-round fitness, using the most muscles, are swimming and amateur wrestling.   ANN McGUINNESS, MANCHESTER.

Largely unrecognised as a tough physical sport, Formula 1 motor racing places alarming amounts of stress on the body and a regime of high speed decision making wearies the mind. At speeds in excess of 200mph, the forces at work as the car rounds corners are about 4 to 5G, 3G when braking and 2G when accelerating. Added to the sheer danger of this sport, they produce about two hours of non-stop strain on a driver's body and brain during a race.   R. RIGBY, OCKBROOK, DERBYS.

49: How on earth do you weigh a ship?

The weight of a ship is measured by calculating the volume of the hull beneath the waterline when the ship is afloat. Archimedes' Principle, the discovery which is supposed to have made him shout 'Eureka!' while taking a bath, dictates that a floating body displaces its own weight in water. We know how much a cubic foot of seawater weighs so, by measuring the cubic footage of a ship below its waterline, we can calculate how much water it will displace and thereby what it weighs.

LT CMDR GEOFFREY CARR, C. ENG., MELKSHAM, WILTS.

A ship can be weighed by floating it into a calibrated dry dock, removing the water, then pumping back in a known amount of water (enough to refloat the boat) and reading off how far the water comes up the scale on the side of the dock. Archimedes' Principle is then used to calculate the weight. In the construction of the ill-fated Titanic every piece of construction material or interior fitting was weighed before being added to the ship and the total calculated for the whole ship. It proved remarkably similar to the weight calculated by the method above.

RONALD STIMSON, SUNDERLAND.

50: There are millions of birds in Britain. Why do we see so few dead ones?

Due to their light nature, dead birds' bodies decompose very quickly and a bird carcass becomes an instant meal for millions of insects and small animals. Many birds are migratory and die in their flights between countries, falling into the sea. Many spend much of their lives, and die, in areas far from human habitation. Any dead birds you do see are likely to have met with a sudden, unnatural death, in traffic, against a window, attacked by a domestic pet or killed by crop spray poison.

MR K. HENDERSON, BELFAST.

51: How did the practice of shouting 'Hip! Hip! Hooray!' come about?

Crusaders in the Middle Ages are supposed to have chanted 'Hip, hip hooray!' after a successful battle. It was their abbreviation of 'Jerusalem is lost to the infidel: we are on the road to paradise.' The first part came from the slogan *'Hieroslyma est perdita'* (Jerusalem is fallen), shortened by Germanic tribes to 'Hep.' The second part comes from the Slavic word *'Huraj',* to paradise. This chant was transposed to the English games field by classically educated schoolmasters and is now associated with good gamesmanship rather than a war cry.

MRS C. K. BRIDSON-JONES, TRURO, CORNWALL.

52: We can 'mong' war, iron or fish but what is a monger?

A 'monger' is a dealer or trader. The word comes to us through Old English *mangere* and Germanic *mangojan* from the Latin *mango*, a dealer. There is also 'costermonger' a polite word for a barrow boy. In principle we could have any kind of monger: how about 'moneymonger' for banker or 'frockmonger' for a dress shop owner? But 'monger' has come to be regarded as a term of derision and used in terms like 'warmonger' and 'scandalmonger.' There is no verb 'to mong' but Old English had the word *mangian*, to traffic.

PETER STANFORD, COLNE, LANCASHIRE.

53: Why are church weathervanes almost always in the shape of a cockerel?

Dark Age superstition had it that the early morning crow of the cockerel summoned all night-wandering spirits back to the confines of the grave. Witness the early scenes of Shakespeare's Hamlet, where the ghost of his father fades on the crowing of the cock. So early lore was, like so many other customs, passed on into early Christian belief and lingers on in the symbolic use of the cockerel as a church weathervane, forever vigilant against restless spirits as it revolves in the wind.

BETTY MORGAN, CWMBACH, MID GLAMORGAN.

A 9th century Papal decree said a figure of a cock should be set on all church steeples to warn of St Peter's thrice repeated denial of Jesus before the cock crowed. MRS M. E. CLARK, BOURNEMOUTH.

54: Two branches of the armed forces are called the Royal Navy and the Royal Air Force. So why not the Royal Army?

Unlike the Navy and Air Force, the Army is not a self-contained entity but an association of many separate regiments and units, each with its own traditions and history. King Alfred the Great recognised that the Navy needed to be organised as a standing force and took it under his royal patronage but land forces were mainly raised only in time of war, by noblemen who trained and equipped their 'yeomen,' led them in battle and disbanded them as soon as any threat had passed. Britain had a long history of mistrust of standing armies, right up to World War I. Although a regular army became necessary to police the Empire it maintained its tradition of being in effect several smaller armies working together, some of which, like the Royal Engineers and Royal Tank Corps, carry a royal name. The Royal Air Force began as one of these, the Royal Flying Corps, and passed on its royal patronage to the RAF on its formation in 1918. DAVID W. ESSEX, HADDENHAM, BUCKS.

55: Why do we roll out a red carpet for VIPs?

From earliest times, pure red dye for colouring cloth (or carpet) was the most difficult and expensive to obtain. Its rarity ensured that the colour red became central to British tradition and culture, signifying importance and dignity. Red Books are used for court guides, peerage lists, directories of state servants and official regulations. The Red Box is used by ministers to contain important official documents and red hat bands are worn by senior army officers to indicate their distinctive rank. We still celebrate 'red letter days' and tradition decrees that everything important and official needs the association of the colour red.

CHARLOTTE HUTTON, BISHOP'S STORTFORD, HERTS.

In Ancient Greece around the 6th Century BC, red dye could be obtained only by crushing murniex sea shells or porphyra shellfish. Producing just a small quantity of dye meant crushing a huge amount of shells, making red dye highly expensive. Early Greek valuation of the colour red has led to its association with wealth and importance in our Western culture. MISS V. R. CONNER, SHERFIELD ON LODDON, HANTS.

56: Who invented the first ball game?

The first record of any ball games go as far back as 3100 BC in ancient Egypt where they seem to have been played mainly by children. Balls made of leather were stuffed with grain and kicked or thrown. Although these games are shown in many Egyptian tomb paintings we have no details as to the rules. MISS L. ILLINESI, WOKING, SURREY.

The first ball game to which we understand the rules was 'pok-ta-pok,' an ancient version of basketball played by the Aztecs around the 10th Century BC. As with other games played at that time, it was associated with fertility rites performed at religious festivals. RICHARD BROGAN, STRABANE, CO TYRONE.

57: Is the name John Smith really the most common in the country?

John Smith is indeed Britain's most common name. 'Smith' originally meant a foundryman or metalworker – as in blacksmith, ironsmith and coppersmith and evolved into a catch-all term like 'wright', meaning anyone who worked with his hands. In pre-industrial revolution Britain when the majority of families were peasant class, any cartwright, wainwright, cooper or other artisan who could not spell his name could conveniently call himself 'Smith.' TESSA KAMARA, EALING, LONDON.

The most recent published count showed 659,050 nationally insured Smiths in Great Britain, of whom 10,102 were plain John Smith. H. HODSON, BIRMINGHAM.

58: Why are royalty said to have 'blue blood'?

After the Moorish occupation of southern Spain when the invaders were finally driven out, questions arose as to who should inherit the various kingdoms. Those claiming 'pure' descent from the old royal houses could partly prove this by supposedly 'blue blood' showing through their veins. Those of mixed ancestry were in the main darker in skin colour and their veins didn't appear to be as blue as the paler skinned 'nobles'. Thus their claims of purity were rejected. JOHN DAVIS, FLEET, HANTS.

59: Why do we have '40' winks?

The number 40 appears frequently in the Bible and in the 17th Century port cities of Europe made ships anchor outside the harbour for 40 days before letting them dock to make sure no plague or sickness was onboard. This practice, based on Biblical precedent, began in Italy, and bequeathed us the Italian word for 40, *quaranta,* as our 'quarantine'. The number 40 became regarded as a magical figure which applied to a safe period of rest or sleep.   K. ROBINSON, INGATESTONE, ESSEX.

60: Why are there hundreds of little indentations on a golf ball?

Seeking to replace leather, feather-filled golf balls with something more durable, mid-19th century ball makers experimented with gum produced by Malayan trees. But these balls were smooth and ducked to earth after travelling only a short distance. They noticed that balls flew better after some use and concluded that cuts and bruises in the surface of the ball improved its efficiency through the air. Making artificial indentations was a natural development from this knowledge.

CHRIS THOMPSON, DROITWICH, WORCS.

Samuel Graham Ball was the first person to apply a scientific approach to the golf ball. He discovered that perfection lay in having exactly 332 dimples, each precisely .013in deep and his basic design has remained unchanged to this day. Ball died in 1991, aged 92, having worked for Dunlop in the physical research laboratory for 45 years.

JOYCE GARWOOD, HARLOW, ESSEX.

61: Who owns more paintings, the Queen or the nation?

The paintings in the hands of the monarchy number about 7,000, distributed throughout numerous royal establishments. Far more are in the possession of the nation. The National Trust alone has just over 8,000 in its 23 collections and thousands of other works of art are held by the National Gallery, English Heritage, government offices, town halls and galleries. It should be pointed out though that as the Queen is a representative of the nation and the nation theoretically represents the Queen, they own exactly the same things.   SIOBHAN EDWARDS, NATIONAL TRUST.

62: Why do women seldom go bald?

The answer lies in the balance between the oestrogen hormone, of which women have high levels, and testosterone, which is higher in men. Oestrogen has positive effects on hair growth on the scalp but a negative effect on other areas of body hair. Testosterone, on the other hand, can have a negative effect on hair growth on scalp and a positive effect on other areas. As the body ages, levels of these hormones change. This, combined with inherited genetic tendencies, influences whether a man will lose scalp hair. About 60 per cent of women experience a relatively small amount of hair loss after menopause. Three per cent of men and women lose hair at some time in their lives through alopecia arearta caused by stress. In nearly all cases this grows back.

TONY MALEEDY, THE TRICHOLOGICAL CENTRE, MANCHESTER.

63: Why is Hampshire illogically abbreviated to Hants?

Hampshire can trace its name back to Saxon times when the town known today as Southampton was called Hamtun, the town by the water meadow, and its surrounding area was the county of Hamtunscir. In the following centuries, the county name was abbreviated to Hamscir which in modern English became Hampshire, while the county town Hamtun gained the prefix 'south' to distinguish it from other towns of the same name. The letter 'n' from Hamtunscir survives in the abbreviation 'Hants' because it sounds better and is easier to say than 'Hampts.'

GRAHAM KINGSLEN, SOUTHAMPTON.

64: Where did the term 'red herring' originate?

This expression dates from the days when criminals were pursued across country by blood hounds. A common ploy by a pursued villain would be to wrap an old fish in a cloth bag and trail it behind him in the hope that its strong scent would confuse the dog's sense of smell. The best fish to use was one with an oily residue and strong odour such as a herring, whose oil and blood would soak the cloth, giving it a dark reddish appearance: hence the expression, now used for any false trail or misdirection.

R. W. STOKES, STRATFORD-UPON-AVON, WARKS.

65: Is it true that lightning never strikes twice in the same place?

The common claim that lightning never strikes twice in the same place is a fallacy. Many tall structures throughout the world are repeatedly hit. The huge bronze statue of William Penn, 548ft aloft on City Hall, Philadelphia, is struck about five times a year and the Empire State Building in New York gets a flash about ten times a year. On average there is one flash of lightning every six seconds somewhere in the world so mathematically lightning will often strike the same place more than once. Humans are not immune. Unlucky American Roy C. Sullivan, was hit on seven different occasions over a 35-year period, suffering relatively minor injuries each time before finally dying at his own hand by gunshot.

PATRICK KERRIGAN, ALDERSHOT, HANTS.

66: Why are the leading members of the Government called the Cabinet?

Before the 1660 restoration of the monarchy, most government business was carried out by the Privy Council, which was unwieldy and tediously slow. The new king, Charles II, was frustrated by this and slowly began to remove the political power of the council by doing more business with a small number of trusted advisers. At the end of the 17th century the political writer Trenchard said Charles had set up 'a cabal or cabinet council', cabal being an association of intriguers and cabinet a French word for a closet or small private room. Both terms were derogatory and illustrated the unease felt by many observers at this new political institution which vested real power in the hands of a small group of ministers. By the time the Government was drawn from the Houses of Parliament the name Cabinet remained, without its pejorative meaning.

DR JANET C. JENKINS, MAIDA VALE, LONDON.

67: Why is it that no matter how much I toss and turn when asleep, I never fall out of bed?

Mankind retains a residual level of awareness during sleep, which is a time of vulnerability. That is why only unusual noises wake us during the night, because they signify a potential threat. Tossing and turning during sleep represents a level of awareness of the need to change position and avoid discomfort. But this is not entirely instinct and to an extent has to be learned. Children sometimes fall out of bed but learn by experience to retain an awareness of their position during sleep.   NICK CLIFFE, BEESTON, CHESHIRE.

68: What is the origin of the phrase 'the full monty'?

This term originated in the dockland area of Salford, Lancashire, in the Forties when few men could afford to buy a full three-piece suit outright. Tailors Montague Burton allowed customers to contribute half-a-crown a week until they had saved up £5, enough to purchase 'the full monty' of suit, shirt and tie. The term gained extra impetus from the story that Field Marshall Montgomery of El Alamein fame, before his Operation Supercharge offensive, insisted on outnumbering Rommel's Africa Korps not by the two to one of conventional military thinking but by 'the full monty' of three to one.   MARK WRIGHT, AINTREE, LIVERPOOL.

69: Why are people from Newcastle called 'Geordies'?

The first recorded use of this term was in 1823 when local comedian Billy Parrs referred to a number of fellow citizens of his native Newcastle as 'Geordies', meaning they were foolish. 'Geordie' is a diminutive of the name George which came to mean stupid because of its association with George III, an unpopular King whose irrational behaviour led those around him to think he had gone insane. As the 19th Century progressed, well-to-do people who lived in and around Newcastle began to use 'Geordie' as a term of abuse for local mining workers, whom they disliked and feared. The name gradually ceased to be pejorative and came to describe anyone who lived in the Newcastle area.   H. SOULSBY, BIRTLEY, CO. DURHAM.

70: Why do we call the French 'frogs'?

Apart from the alliterative attractions, we call Frenchmen 'frogs' for much the same reason that they call us *Les Rosbifs* ('roastbeefs') because frogs' legs are a foodstuff we associate with them. The allusion to general sliminess helped fix the phrase while the French were our traditional enemies through hundreds of years of conflict. One 17th Century heraldist claimed that the French emblem, the fleur-de-lys was derived from an outstretched toad – but calling Frenchmen 'toads' never caught on.

ROGER MORGAN, FULMER.

71: Exactly how much rubbish have we dumped in space?

Since the first spacecraft, Sputnik I, was launched in 1957, the human race has managed to leave 21,533 trackable objects in orbit around our planet or in deeper space. Of these, 14,829 are large pieces like expired rocket stages and 6,704 are smaller bits, current or burned out satellites plus various kinds of spacecraft. There are also reckoned to be a few million smaller, untrackable pieces. The rubbish in space is being added to regularly as more countries join the space race. India, Pakistan and Indonesia have recently joined in. Reduction occurs only when bits of space junk eventually fall back towards Earth and either burn up in our atmosphere or crash.   GRAEME COBB, STEVENSTON, AYRSHIRE.

72: Why is a 99 ice cream called a '99'?

This ice cream got its name because the chocolate flake it carried was 99mm long. These flakes were specifically made for the ice cream trade, being more sturdy than the traditional, crumbly flake chocolate. The name became popular and is now used to describe any ice cream with a chocolate flake in it.   MICHAEL GEOGHEGAN, BOOTHSTOWN, MANCHESTER.

73: What does Formula One mean in motor racing?

Until 1906 international motor racing was open to all kinds of automobile.

As it became obvious that driving ability could not be tested fairly in widely differing cars, races were organised for cars with similar specifications. Types of vehicle were grouped into various formulas, each defined by characteristics of a car's performance. Various combinations of weight, cylinder capacity, fuel consumption, size of chassis, number of people carried, etc, developed at this time. The number of Formulas and the specifications that make them up have changed considerably since 1906. Present Formula One races are for cars weighing not less than 505kg, with a maximum width of 200cm, a four stroke engine with a maximum 12 cylinders, an engine capacity of 3500cc and no turbo-charger.

DAMON JENKISS, NORTHAMPTON.

74: How is the barcode for a product chosen?

All countries which use the barcode system for numbering products are affiliated to Electronic Article Numbering International, originally a European system, now broadened to comprise 62 countries worldwide. All countries have their own authority for numbering and each of these uses the first two or three digits for the 13-number sequence of a full barcode. In the UK the system is administered by the Article Number Association and all numbers issued have the prefix 50. When a company wants a barcode number for a branded product it is given a number beginning with 50, followed by five more digits. The company then allocates a further five numbers of their own, giving a total of 12. The 23th digit is a check, calculated from the other 12 to make sure the whole number is correct.

ANDREW OSBORNE, GENERAL SEC., ARTICLE NUMBER ASSOC.

75: When did the monarch first start sending telegrams on 100th birthdays?

The first congratulatory telegrams in Britain were sent by George V in 1917 and all monarchs have sent them since. Today, there is no telegram service but the Queen still sends a 'telemessage' to centenarians after someone writes to Buckingham Palace asking her to do so. In 1992 she sent a total of 4,804 messages and during her entire reign is estimated to have sent more than 150,000.

LINDY KERTON, BIRMINGHAM.

76: Everybody knows the exploits of the Eighth Army during World War Two, but what happened to the other seven?

There were in fact only seven British Armies during World War II: the 1st, 2nd, 8th, 9th, 10th, 12th and 14th. Intermediate numbers never existed except, possibly, in War Office records. The 1st Army, formed in

Britain to invade North Africa in 1942, subsequently took part in the campaigns in north west Europe. The 2nd Army was also formed in Britain and took part in north west European campaigns. The 8th Army was formed in Egypt in 1941 for the North African and subsequent Italian campaigns. The 9th Army was formed behind the 8th Army, in the Levant. The 10th Army was formed in Iraq in 1941 and controlled Syria, Persia and Iraq. The 12th Army was raised in Burma in May 1945 and joined the 14th Army, also raised there, in retaking Burma and Malaya. Army numbering always defied explanation and is generally considered yet another way to fool the enemy into thinking there were more fighting men than there actually were.   B. HUTCHINSON, NEWTON ABBOT, DEVON.

77: Why are women's shirts and blouses buttoned in the opposite way to men's?

A man's clothing buttons left over right and women's vice versa because in Georgian and Victorian times, gentlemen would be handed their clothing by a valet and dress themselves. Buttons on the right made this simpler for right-handed people. Ladies were dressed by their personal maids, for whom it was easier to have the buttons on the opposite side.
                                        GARY GLEGHORN, CAMBRIDGE.

78: Goalkeepers are moving out of their penalty areas more and more. Has any professional team ever operated a 'rush' goalie?

The nearest I can remember to a professional team employing a 'rush' or 'fly' goalkeeper occurred during a Division Three match between Reading and Halifax Town on August 31, 1961, before substitutes were allowed. Reading goalkeeper Arthur Wilkie injured his hands but wanted to play on. He could no longer keep goal so another team member took over between the posts while he played up-field. Reading won the match 4-2 and Wilkie scored twice, his two goals still standing as the most scored in a Football League game (with the exception of penalties) by a player who started the match wearing the number 1 shirt.
                              DAVID DOWNS, CLUB HISTORIAN, READING FC.

79: What are the origins of touching glasses when drinking a toast?

People who appreciated wine realised it satisfied only four of the five senses: the sight of the drink swirling round the glass, the scent of its bouquet, the sense of touch as the liquid passed over the lips and, of course, the taste of the wine. The one sense ignored was sound, and thus the fine glasses in which it was poured were gently clinked together as a way of completing the cycle of the senses.   BRYN WILLIAMS, ENFIELD, MIDDX.

Glasses are clinked at a toast because in days gone by they were subsequently thrown and smashed in the fireplace after an important pledge so they would never be used again – to prevent the promise being defiled. In these less flamboyant and more thrifty days, glasses are clinked as a symbolic breakage.   N. J. SHAW, SHEFFORD, BEDS.

This tradition goes back to the ancient Greeks when poisoned chalices were often on the menu for the unwary guest. Many a political or military rival was seen off in this fashion, hence the need for royalty and nobles to employ 'official tasters' before a banquet. It became the tradition of host and guest to pour a little wine from their glasses into each other's to show there was no poison. Over the centuries, this gesture has been abbreviated to the symbolic 'clinking' of glasses harking back to those dark days when your next drink could have been your last.

SHANE SEAGRAVE, WEYMOUTH, DORSET.

80: What determines whether a country is referred to as the motherland or the fatherland?

This issue is related to how well female figures have established themselves in a nation's history and culture. In Britain, we have had a succession of strong female historical characters, for example Boudicca, Elizabeth I and Queen Victoria, all of whom are closely identified with Britain's nationhood and the Britannia of mythology. Britannia's feminine form has come to stand for Britain itself and given us, as well as our motherland, the Mother of Parliaments and the mother tongue. The Russians are in a bit of a dilemma. They have Catherine the Great to admire, but a bear as their national emblem. The French can look back to Joan of Arc. But in both countries even the predominantly male revolutionaries saw the essentially female figure 'Liberty' as their goal. Thus post-revolutionary France and Russia remained motherlands. Germany, by contrast, has a strongly patriarchal military and political system, has never produced a female heroine to compare with the mythical Brunhilde, and has kept its maleness as the fatherland. The Netherlands, and the Boer republics, also without historical female leaders, have also remained in the fatherland club.   TERRY JOHNSTON, NORTH SHIELDS, TYNE & WEAR.

81: Do carrots really help you to see in the dark?

Carrots get their distinctive colour from yellow and orange pigments called carotenoids. These contain components which help make up vitamin A. One form of vitamin A, called retinene, joins with the protein opsin to make the pigment rhodopsin, which is sensitive to light. Rhodopsin is found in the rod-shaped cells of the retina, which are used by the eye to see in the dark. It is not so much a question of carrots helping you to see in the dark, but that failing to eat carrots may lead to a vitamin A deficiency which may cause difficulty in the eye adjusting to the dark, or even night blindness.   STEVEN GARBUTT, SUTTON COLDFIELD.

82: Why does the water always go down the plughole clockwise?

The short answer is that it doesn't: it depends on many variables. Normally, however, water will turn clockwise down a plughole in the northern hemisphere, anti-clockwise in the southern hemisphere and, as Michael Palin discovered on his Pole To Pole trip, may even go straight down at the Equator. The reasons for this are a combination of gravity and the rotation of the Earth in the phenomenon known as the Coriolis Effect, after Gaspard Coriolis who first described it in 1835.

MARGARET ADAMSON, PLYMOUTH, DEVON.

83: Why do we call the police the Old Bill?

There are several explanations for The Bill or Old Bill but the most likely origin of the modern use dates to 1917 when the Metropolitan Police used a cartoon character called Old Bill in its recruiting campaign. Old Bill was a walrus moustached, disillusioned World War I soldier created by artist Bruce Barnsfather and best remembered for his famous line 'If you knows of a better 'ole, go to it' addressed to his grumpy pal, Bert, while sheltering in a muddy crater during an increasing artillery bombardment. This long suffering, honest old grouser – an earlier version of TV's Victor Meldrew character – encapsulated many people's thoughts about 'duty in adversity' at the time, giving the public strong empathy with the character. He was an ideal vehicle for the police to entice people to play their part by joining the force.   MR W. L. ADAMS, NEATH, WEST GLAMORGAN.

84: Why are crossed fingers supposed to bring you luck?

Back in the days when Christians were persecuted and wearing or carrying an image of the holy cross might mean a death sentence, crossed fingers were used to invoke the symbol of Christianity and God's protection. Later, in medieval times, crossed fingers were associated with good luck through the common belief that mystical power and energy was released through the fingertips. It was assumed that good luck could be prevented from escaping by stopping the flow with crossed fingers.

FIONA RODGERS, BASINGSTOKE.

85: As more people are cremated than buried these days, can anyone think of a more appropriate saying than 'turning in his grave'?

A more appropriate saying would be 'grieving in his urn.'

ROGER VINCE, BOURNEMOUTH, DORSET.

Bob Dylan would no doubt say 'Blowing in the Wind.'

MISS F. COPELAND, ISLINGTON, LONDON.

One could say 'his ashes will be smouldering.'

DOLLINA TATE, MORECAMBE, LANCS.

86: Is it true that pigs don't sweat, despite the expression 'sweating like a pig'?

Pigs do sweat but not in the same way as humans. Pigs have no sweat glands except for one on the snout. They have to roll around in mud to keep themselves from overheating. The expression 'sweating like a pig' dates from the worst days of the Indian Raj, when resentment at the Empire was growing. British soldiers were not as adept at keeping cool as the locals and this inability was associated with the pig, considered by the Indians an unclean animal, used to ridicule the British. Hearing about this association, soldiers began to live up to their new-found reputation as animals and whenever one was too hot it became common for them to say they were 'sweating like a pig.'

DAVID ROSE, DARLINGTON.

87: If Nelson's Victory had had the medical facilities of one of the capital ships of today's Navy, might Lord Nelson have survived the Battle of Trafalgar?

Lord Nelson's fatal injury was caused by a single shot from a sniper. A musket ball passed through his left shoulder epaulet into his neck, damaging the spinal cord. Nelson lived for two hours before dying of circulatory shock and blood loss. The area in which his body was damaged, containing a large number of blood vessels, nerves and lung tissue, is known to modern medics as 'tiger country' because of its complexity. Today's warfare medical arrangements are highly advanced. Capital ships have facilities to rival a district hospital and carry 20 or more medical staff. Anyone wounded in action aboard would be treated on the spot, then moved to the sick bay, with its modern operating theatre. A specialist casualty-receiving boat treats the wounded from smaller ships in a battle group, or there may be Red Cross-protected or neutral hospital ships. Lord Nelson's injuries were such that even if he had been shot on the front steps of the world's top hospital, with a full surgery team on hand, his chances of survival would have been very slim.

SURGEON CAPTAIN RICK JOLLY OBE RN, COMMANDER OF FALKLANDS FIELD HOSPITAL AT AJAX BAY IN 1982. NOW SENIOR MEDICAL OFFICER OF THE ROYAL MARINES.

88: How long is a lifetime guarantee?

When a product manufacturer offers a 'lifetime' guarantee it's in your interest to look carefully at the small print to see what's actually meant. Is it the customer's lifetime, the lifetime of ownership, the lifetime in factory tests or even something as absurd as the lifetime of its rival? Most guarantees of this type are just a gimmick by advertisers and marketing departments to lure customers into buying. Some reputable companies which have tried giving lifetime guarantees have quickly given up after finding it an expensive policy when customers take them at their word, or very embarrassing when they refuse to honour their promise. In short, there is no such thing as a lifetime guarantee and if you see one advertised it probably won't mean what you and I mean by lifetime.

KEITH YOULTON, ASHTON UNDER LYNE.

This somewhat jaundiced view is not the whole truth. Pen and mechanical pencil makers A. T. Cross has been giving lifetime guarantees on all its products ever since Alonzo Townsend Cross set up his business in New England in 1846. This company takes literally the Oxford Dictionary definition of a lifetime: 'The duration of a person's life or of a thing's existence.' Trading standards officers have determined that the normal life of a pen is six years but our guarantee is perpetual. We will repair or replace any of our products still in existence, even if inherited from your grandfather. KIERAN CROWLEY, GENERAL MANAGER, A. T. CROSS (UK) LTD.

89: Why do people fill the kettle with cold water when it would save time and energy if they used hot water?

The kitchen sink cold tap is the one most likely in your home to be connected directly to the water mains and therefore the one with the best quality water. Water from the hot tap, especially in older properties, comes via the copper cylinder which, over the years, collects a nasty, soup-like sludge at the bottom. This sludge comes from the domestic header tank which sends water through the cylinder when the hot water supply is turned on. The top of the header tank is invariably open and all sorts of bacteria, insects, vermin etc may have access to it. The slight amount of energy saved by using the hot tap may be at the cost of an upset stomach, or worse, because most modern kettles turn themselves off at boiling point and don't boil water for enough time to make it sterile.

STANLEY WRAITH, PLUMBER, MEERSBROOK, SHEFFIELD.

90: How is caffeine removed from coffee, and what do they do with it once it is removed?

Two different processes are used by the coffee industry to remove caffeine from the coffee bean: the organic solvent method and the natural water method. The first involves soaking the dry, pre-roasted coffee in an organic solvent which dissolves the caffeine until it can be removed. The decaffeinated beans are then dried and residual solvents evaporated. In the second, water is used to dissolve all the nutrients, including caffeine, from the coffee. The water is then mixed with an organic solvent which removes the caffeine and the caffeine-free water is used to return the taste to the coffee bean. A third method, using high pressure carbon dioxide, is rarely used in the production of coffee. The removed caffeine is sold for a variety of medical and scientific purposes or can be used for 'pepping up' some soft drinks.   JAMES CARLTON, KINGS NORTON, WEST MIDLANDS.

91: Since when, and why, has the British monarch been called Defender of the Faith?

The Latin title Fidei Defendor, 'Defender of the Faith', was bestowed by the Pope on King Henry VIII in 1521, when he was still a Roman Catholic, in recognition of the book In Defence Of The Seven Sacraments Henry had written against the works of the 'heretic' Martin Luther. Henry was very proud of the new title and when he quarrelled with the Pope over his refusal to allow him to divorce Catherine of Aragon and marry Anne Boleyn, and made himself Supreme Governor of the Church in England, he clung on to it. Henry's successors have kept the title and the initials F.D. appear on all coins of the realm.
MRS A. WOOD, CARRVILLE, DURHAM.

92: From where does the expression 'by and large' come?

This was a nautical expression, used for reporting the sailing qualities of square rigged ships. Sailing 'by the wind' meant sailing close to the wind and sailing 'large' was to sail with all canvas set for a following wind. When captains were reporting on ships to the Admiralty they often used the phrase 'performed well both by and large' meaning all aspects of sailing performance were satisfactory.
IAIN MACKENZIE, NATIONAL MARITIME MUSEUM, GREENWICH.

93: Did Adam and Eve have navels?

According to Genesis, Adam was created by God in His own image. He must therefore have been created as a perfect specimen of a human as he was the physical image of the perfect God. A navel would have been a redundant, pointless feature, making him less than perfect because God himself couldn't possibly have needed a navel. So, either God created Adam imperfectly, or the rest of us, apart from Eve, are not created exactly in God's image because we have belly buttons. Eve, meanwhile, being created from Adam's rib, would have had no need for a navel either. This dilemma points to the foolishness of taking Bible stories too literally because they are, as my old RI teacher used to say, merely 'stories with a true meaning.'

ADAM SAMUEL, ROATH, CARDIFF.

It's wrong to think of Adam as being made in any physical image of God. God is a spirit and Adam, in so far as he was made in the image of God, was made with free will, a sense of justice and the ability to control his own surroundings, all things which distinguish him from animals. Adam may well not have had a navel because he was not born of a woman and Eve, as she was cloned from Adam's body base, may not have needed one either.

R. G. SAXENA, KETTERING, NORTHANTS.

94: We're told 50,900 immigrants came to Britain in 1992, but how many people emigrated?

The Home Office UK immigration figure for 1992 shows a total of 52,570 people were granted citizenship: 4,630 came from Europe, 7,260 from the Americas, 8,980 from Africa, 2,340 from Australasia, and 25,260 from Asia, with the remainder being mainly refugees. The Census Statistics Office's latest calculations for 1991 show 136,700 people left the country for longer than a year: 46,700 went to EC countries, 54,900 to Commonwealth ones (Australia got 23,600), and 35,100 to others (12,500 to the U.S.). A large proportion are expected to return eventually.

KATEY HOLGATE, HALE, CHESHIRE.

95: William Webb Ellis famously 'picked up the ball and ran with it' and thereby invented rugby: but did he squash the ball, too, or did that come later?

By the 1820s most English schools had their own variations of football. Almost all these games used a leather-bound ball, inflated with a pig's bladder, and generally oval because it was very difficult to make a perfectly round one. William Webb Ellis didn't actually pick up the ball, but caught it, as allowed in the rules at Rugby School, where he played. But then he ran with it instead of kicking it, which was not allowed. At the time he was severely chastised but his action captured the imagination of others and, over the next ten years, running with the ball caught on, developing into today's game of rugby. The ball was never squashed later as the question implies. The first perfectly round balls didn't appear until 1863, when the Football League was formed.

RONALD JONES, CHIPPENHAM, WILTS.

96: Who awarded the medals worn by Prince Charles, and what are they for?

Prince Charles's medals are all commemorative and were bestowed on him to signify his high standing within the Royal Family. Round his neck he wears the Order of the Bath and on his chest he wears, from left to right: the Queen's Service Order (New Zealand) 1983, the Queen Elizabeth II Coronation Medal 1953, the Queen Elizabeth II Silver Jubilee Medal 1977, the Canadian Forces Decoration 1991 and the New Zealand Commemorative Medal 1990. Beneath these he normally wears the breast star of the Order of The Garter. SEAN FLEMING, WARD END, BIRMINGHAM.

97: Why does steam rise from New York pavements?

New York is laced with miles of underground pipes that use excess steam from power generation to heat Manhattan office buildings. Occasionally the steam escapes but sometimes it is deliberately vented into the street for technical reasons by repair staff from Consolidated Edison – the company which provides the steam. It is not evidence of a new Hades. In New York, that's on the surface. JEFFREY BLYTH, MADISON AVENUE, NEW YORK.

98: What replaces the billions of gallons of oil taken from the ground?

Talk of oil 'reservoirs' in connection with the discovery of oil is a common misconception. There are no pure lakes of oil beneath the ground, but quantities of oil held within porous rock. When the oil is removed the rock still remains in place. Nature sometimes finds its own way to replace the oil, when water in the ground gradually filters its way into the area from which oil reserves have been removed. JIM ARNOTT, SHELL UK.

99: Why does the England football team play in red, white, and blue, when the English flag is only red and white?

There's no obligation for any international football team to wear the same colours as its national flag. The Dutch and Australian teams are well-known examples of those who don't. The England team originally wore all white, with just a red rose badge. Versions of the present red, white and blue strip first took the field with the Great Britain team which won the 1908 and 1912 Olympic football events in London and

Stockholm. On occasion, the England team has worn a plain red and white strip, notably while winning the World Cup final in 1966.

DAVID BARBER, FOOTBALL ASSOCIATION.

100: Why are the numbers on a calculator in a different arrangement to those on a push-button telephone?

On old-fashioned dial telephones, dialling the digit '1' sent one pulse down the phone system, while the digit '0' sent ten pulses and was really the equivalent of the number ten. Consequently, the '0' had to be after the '9' to generate one more pulse as the dial turned. When new push-button telephones were being tested by the GPO in the early Sixties, various number configurations were tried, and the most convenient system adopted had the digits going in numerical order from the top to the bottom of the pad, with the zero figure at the base representing ten. On a calculator, the '0' digit represents zero and is also located at the bottom. But because it represents zero, and not the number ten, the figures 1 to 9 start from there in ascending order.

PAUL SHARMA, BRITISH TELECOM.

101: Why was Britain called 'Blighty'?

This is another expression which came to Britain during the days of the British Raj in India. It comes from the Hindi *bilayati* which translates roughly as 'foreign' and stems from the Arab *wilayet,* meaning 'far off', 'removed from where you belong.' Indians used *bilayati* to describe British soldiers, who gradually anglicised the word to 'Blighty' and used it as another word for home. It achieved its greatest popularity during World War I through songs such as Take Me Back To Dear Old Blighty and There's A Ship That's Bound For Blighty. Soldiers in the trenches dreamed of getting a 'Blighty wound' – not bad enough to kill or maim but serious enough to involve being shipped back to Britain for treatment.

HERBERT JACKSON, PORTSMOUTH.

102: Why did Lady Godiva ride naked on a horse?

Lady Godiva, who died in 1067, is said by mediaeval chroniclers to have pleaded with her husband Leofric, Earl of Mercia, to lighten the burden of taxes on the good people of Coventry. He agreed to do this only if Godiva would ride naked through the town, thinking she wouldn't dare. But Lady Godiva had more resolve than her husband assumed and made her famous naked ride through Coventry. Later generations added the refinement that all the townsfolk were ordered to remain indoors during the ride but one man, Peeping Tom, disobeyed and looked at Godiva, causing him to lose his sight.

TIM JUBY, COVENTRY CITY COUNCIL.

103: Why do we call toy bears 'Teddy' bears?

The first teddy bears were made in Germany by Margaret Stieff who ran a successful cottage industry making toy bears for children. Later, her brother Richard travelled to America to manufacture and sell the bears. When President Theodore Roosevelt (1858-1919), commonly known as Teddy, went on a hunting trip he was reported to have refused to shoot a bear cub and his act of compassion inspired cartoonist Clifford Berryman to draw the scene. Instead of drawing a real bear cub, he drew one of the Stieff toy bears. The cartoon increased interest in toy bears and Richard Stieff, identifying a great marketing opportunity, quickly renamed his products 'Teddy bears' in honour of the President. They soon became all the rage. JANET BURHOLT, DORCHESTER, DORSET.

As the mother of a confirmed arctophile (teddy bear lover), I can put the record straight. Cartoonist Clifford Berryman drew not a Stieff toy bear with President Theodore Roosevelt but a sweet little bear cub. New Yorker Morris Mitcham saw the cartoon and had a bear made to put in his window, with a copy of the cartoon, to advertise his photography business. He wrote to 'Teddy' Roosevelt asking for permission to use the name 'Teddy's bear.' At the same time, in Germany, Margaret Stieff's toy factory developed a toy bear, designed by her nephew Richard Stieff, and an American toy agent there sent a large consignment to the USA. They proved very popular and rapidly became known as Teddy Bears, one of the best-loved toys of all time. JAN BARRON, CHORLTON CUM HARDY, MANCHESTER.

104: Why is dogfood never in flavours we know a dog would love – such as cat?

It is generally incorrect to assume dogs would prefer the taste of cat to other food. They much prefer eating rabbit, liver, beef, lamb, etc, which are available in commercial dog foods. In the wild, a dog is a natural scavenger, feeding on the carcasses of animals that have already been killed in preference to hunting its own prey. Dog food manufacturers have been aware of this since the beginnings of their industry. Dogs may chase cats but generally have better taste than to go in for eating them. MARY McKENDRY, SPILLERS FOODS.

105: Why 'cowboy' for shoddy workman?

Long before the term 'cowboy' was used in the cattle industry of the old Wild West, it was applied to members of bands of irregular cavalry who operated in the Eastern United States during the War of Independence. Many of these spent most of their time stealing cattle while diligently avoiding contact with the enemy. 'Cowboy' was such a derogatory word that the original ranch workers tried to style themselves 'cattle drovers' to avoid the connotations of 'cowboy.' The relationship with shoddy workmanship came later when these drovers began the habit of working their way back to the ranch after a cattle drive by taking odd jobs across the country. Because of their general lack of skill they were notorious for their bad workmanship.   D. P. R. ROCHE, EDGWARE, MIDDLESEX.

106: Is it true that members of the Household Cavalry may not be awarded the Victoria Cross?

This curiously common rumour is completely incorrect. The idea that a VC could not be awarded to a member of the Household Cavalry probably stems from the fact that our two regiments, the Lifeguards and Blues and Royals, are so closely associated with the Queen. Our regiment has possession of a VC awarded to Second Lieutenant J. S. Dunville for bravery in Epehy in 1917 when serving with the First Royal Dragoons.
MAJOR A. W. KERSTING, CURATOR, HOUSEHOLD CAVALRY MUSEUM, WINDSOR.

107: Why don't elephants forget?

An elephant's brain is roughly five times the size of a human's and, although it is not as sophisticated or as powerful, puts them in the top ten thinking animals. Elephants do, of course, forget some things but they tend to remember some specific things, such as trainers or keepers who have shown them exceptional kindness or cruelty, very well indeed.
SUE LLEWELLYN, ELEFRIENDS, DORKING, SURREY.

108: Who has the highest number street address in Britain?

The practice of numbering houses began in Paris around the year 1463. The house with the highest street number in the United Kingdom belongs to Mr and Mrs Malcolm Aldridge who, for the past 16 years, have lived at 2679 Stratford Road, Hockley Heath, West Midlands. How do I know? I live down the street from them – about two miles away!
JANE SMITH, HOCKLEY HEATH, WEST MIDLANDS.

109: Why doesn't the longest day of the year have the latest sunset?

Spinning daily round an axis through its poles, the Earth behaves pretty much like a regular gyroscope in space, apart from minute variations, retaining its 24-hour revolutions which we calibrate as 'clocktime.' Meanwhile the Earth swings round the Sun in an elliptical orbit induced by mutual gravitational pull. Each pole inclines alternately towards, or away from, the Sun and this gives us our seasons. Because the Earth's orbit around the Sun is elliptical rather than circular and the Sun is not at the centre of the orbit, the Earth slows as it goes further from the Sun at the far limits of the ellipse, and speeds up as it moves nearer. As a result, the apparent movement of the Sun through our sky varies slightly in speed during the year. When this annual variation is applied to the 24-hour daily rotation of the Earth, the Sun's actual position in the sky at a particular time on any one day is modified so that 'sundial time' is ahead of, or behind, 'clock time.'   COLIN LEWIS, CHELTENHAM, GLOS.

110: Why do people look in the mirror when they clean their teeth?

This is part of British tradition, reinforced at every stage of a person's life. Parents encourage children to look in the mirror to make sure they're doing a good job. For teenagers the mirror is in constant use as we become more concerned about our looks and need reassurance that we haven't left spinach on our teeth or toothpaste round our mouth. And as adults (if we have any teeth left), we fit mirrors over the bathroom basin, making escape from the mirror impossible.   DR ADRIAN WALSH, FINSBURY PARK, LONDON.

111: Are we ever likely to discover new colours?

Different colours of light have different frequencies similar, in a way, to different musical notes. The human eye can sense only a very small segment of these frequencies of electromagnetic radiation, a general term for light, but this is enough to give us millions of variations of colour. With suitable equipment we can discover the whole range. These are, at the lowest frequencies, radio waves, followed by microwaves and infrared. In the middle we have visible light, red through to violet, and at the higher frequencies we have ultraviolet, then X-rays, followed by gamma rays. It's possible that in the future we may discover new colours at the lowest or highest end of the spectrum. Meanwhile, within the colour range of the human eye, we're seeing new colours all the time as every colour we look at is fractionally different from a similar colour we may have seen before.   DR TREVOR BARKER, GUILDFORD, SURREY.

112: Do cows really know when it's going to rain?

Most animals can detect the increased charge in static electricity which goes with the approach of thunder storms. But how far ahead they are able to forecast weather conditions is a completely different matter. A close study of cows in Yorkshire in 1980 came to the conclusion that although they did react to the onset of bad weather by sitting down this was, at most, only two hours before the rain started, a period we at the Met Office can easily beat.   DEREK HARDY, METEOROLOGICAL OFFICE HQ, BRACKNELL, BERKS.

113: What is so wise about wisdom teeth? Why do we have them when all they seem to do is cause problems?

Wisdom teeth are the last group of molars to grow in the mouth. They usually appear when people are aged between 18 and 20, when most of us are presumed to have acquired a certain amount of wisdom. As our species evolves our jaws are becoming smaller and the number of teeth we require is diminishing because we no longer have to tear raw meat off bones. Effectively, wisdom teeth are being phased out by evolution. In some people they do not develop at all. Wisdom teeth can also cause problems when people are unable to clean them properly as they are too far back in the mouth. In most cases they are better taken out, because they are quick to decay.   SALLY-ANN MONTGOMERY, ALVECHURCH, WORCS.

114: Why is the score 'love all' at the start of a tennis match?

This strange appellation is derived from the French *oeuf,* egg. The digit 0, at which each player starts the game, looked like the shape of an egg and when tennis (originally the version now known as Real, or Royal, tennis) was developing in Anglo-French royal circles, the name stuck.
JOSH BAXBY, YORK.

The suggestion that this is derived from *l'oeuf* is often quoted but seems rather fanciful. More likely is the way that 'love' in the sense of 'no score' was used in 18th century gaming circles as a derivative of the phrase 'for love' meaning without stakes, for nothing. An example of this occurs in the common phrase 'neither for love nor money.' In the same way amateur, meaning unpaid, comes from the French and Latin equivalents of 'love.' Medieval games of tennis were often played for money, when winning points were scored, or just for the pleasure of the game itself, without scoring points. This association of money with points and of love with no scoring led to the use of 'love' for nil.   ALAN DUKE, SWINDON, WILTS.

115: Is love really a drug?

When we fall in love we produce a substance called phenylethylamine (PEA), chemically similar to amphetamine. PEA is still a mystery. No one knows where it is produced but it has been identified in the blood of people who describe themselves as in love and appears to plug into receptors in the brain, evoking feelings of comfort and bliss. The best

alternative source of this chemical is cocoa and it is also found in rose-water, which should give heart to all men who like to woo women with chocolate and roses. PEA is addictive and withdrawal symptoms may include cravings and a mild form of depression. Some people say that the agony of ending a love affair can compare with amphetamine withdrawal symptoms. So although love can seem magical, it is firmly rooted in biochemistry.
GLEN BRADBURY, WARRINGTON, CHESHIRE.

116: Who was the last person to do National Service, and where is he now?

This comes down to a choice between two men. The last man called up was 23819209 Private Fred Turner of the Army Catering Corps, at the time attached to 13/18 Hussars. He was discharged on May 7, 1963. The other candidate is 23819144 Lieutenant Richard Vaughan of the Royal Army Pay Corps, who left his unit in Germany on May 17, 1963, and had to travel back to England so was not officially discharged until May 20, 1963. Last man in was Turner, last man out was Vaughan.
R. H. BOND, CHELMSFORD, ESSEX.

I am he; still standing prepared and spending most of my time these days in Chislehurst High Street, Bromley, where I run my own accountancy firm. Thanks for your concern.
RICHARD VAUGHAN, CHISLEHURST, KENT.

I'm sorry to disappoint Fred Turner and Lt Richard Vaughan but it was I who was the last National Serviceman to commence National Service and the last to be demobbed, on May 30, 1963. The last intake of servicemen was supposed to be in November 1960 but, as a reluctant participant, I didn't commence training until January 19, 1961, after being persuaded to do so by two large gentlemen wearing red caps. Two years later the government extended National Service by six months for all those serving in the British Army On the Rhine, including me. The plan caused a public outcry and, as the regular recruitment into the Army increased, it was decided the enlisted men should finish by May 30, 1963. The Army retained me until the last moment and I was presented with an engraved 'last man out' tankard by Regiment 24, Royal Artillery.
GUNNER R. AYLWARD, OXFORD.

117: What are the environmental effects of the barbeque season?

Barbecue charcoal, like newsprint and tissues, is made from trees grown in specially planted forests. These forests are well managed, provide habitats for wildlife and are one of the few instances where commercial gain and environment are in harmony. Burning charcoal releases carbon dioxide (a greenhouse gas) into the atmosphere but no more than the tree took from the air while growing. Unlike fossil fuels, charcoal forests can be sustained indefinitely so the use of charcoal for cooking is actually kinder to the environment than conventional fuels. Some concern has been raised about carcinogens given off during barbecuing by burning fat and juices dropping on the charcoal but this is thought to be negligible.

DAVID WALTER, WOKING, SURREY.

Almost all charcoal is imported, with tropical forests, particularly mangrove, the single largest source. Mangrove is an important habitat which is now under increasing threat. Charcoal can be produced from UK woodland, using low quality wood as a by-product of good woodland management. The revival of UK charcoal production is being supported by the major environmental organisations (WWF, RSPB, and the Countryside Commission) as well as the National Trust and Kew Gardens.

POORAN DESAI, SUTTON, SURREY.

118: Why is most tomato soup an orange colour when most tomatoes are red?

The traditional recipe for tomato soup consists of various ingredients mixed together to create the orangey colour we all know. Our recipe, using all natural ingredients, consists of skimmed milk powder, oil, spices and various other special ingredients which, when added to tomatoes creates the creaminess that changes the colour from red to orange. Red tomato soup could be made but not without added colourings, which most consumers would probably reject.

BRIAN THOMAS, CULINARY CONSULTANT, H. J. HEINZ.

119: Where exactly is the middle of England?

In purely geographical terms, the centre of England is the small village of Meriden, between Birmingham and Coventry, just down the road from the National Exhibition Centre in the West Midlands. Strangely enough, if the centre of the UK is sought, using population instead of geography as the main factor, this village is also within ten miles of the centre.

JOHN PACKWOOD, REDDITCH.

120: Can you get a suntan through normal glass? If not, is there special glass available which would allow tanning?

If you try to sunbathe under normal glass you will not get a tan although you may get hot and go very red. Ordinary glass lets through about 90% of the visible light from the sun but admits less than one or two percent of the ultraviolet light which causes tanning. A special glass which lets through ultraviolet rays is used on the tubes in a sunbed but has a very delicate surface which is easily marked and is therefore not suitable for use in normal windows. 'Tan through' glass will probably not be made available to the public in the next few years, in fact, demand shows people at present are more interested in glass that keeps the sun out.

RAY JENNINGS, PILKINGTON GLASS, ST HELENS, MERSEYSIDE.

121: Is it true that Adolf Hitler once lived in Liverpool?

Though it sems unlikely, this may indeed be true. In 1979, journalist Michael Unger (later editor of the Manchester Evening News) discovered the diaries of Irish born Bridget Hitler, sister-in-law of Adolf Hitler. They suggested that while she was living in Liverpool in 1912 with her husband Alois, his half brother Adolf visited them. He apparently travelled to live with his brother in an attempt to avoid conscription into the Austrian army. The diaries tell how he arrived penniless and stayed for five months, surviving mostly by selling his drawings and living on the generosity of his restaurant waiter brother. Historians have long tried to discover Adolf Hitler's movements during his early years and these diaries claim he spent one segment of his life living on Upper Stanhope Street, Toxteth.

JULIA CAMPBELL, SOUTHPORT.

122: When did 'Britain' become 'Great Britain'?

The term 'Great Britain' is purely geographical. It was first used officially in 1604 when King James I of England and VI of Scotland was proclaimed 'King of Great Britain'. It had been used previously by some writers to distinguish Britain from 'Britannia Minor' – Brittany. Great Britain consists of 'Britannia prima' (England), 'Britannia secunda' (Wales) and 'North Britain' (Scotland), united under one rule.

KEVIN HENEGHAN, ST HELENS, MERSEYSIDE.

123: Which company or individual has made the largest donation to a UK political party?

Far higher sums have been given to political parties than the £440,000 donated by runaway tycoon Asil Nadir, though the donors and recipients of personal gifts are not obliged to publish details. The largest donations come from overseas for the benefit of the Conservative Party and include notables such as the Sultan of Brunei, Chinese billionaire Li Ka Shing and the Kuwaiti and Saudi Royal Families. The largest ever single donation is believed to be £2,000,000 given by Greek shipping and oil tycoon John Latsis in 1991. The highest total income for any political party in a single year is estimated to have been £22,000,000 raised by the

Conservatives in the 1991/92 financial year. Companies which give political donations are required by law to disclose the amounts in company reports.

PAUL TADLEY, NOTTINGHAM.

124: Are complete strangers we see in our dreams people we have made up?

People we see in our dreams are created from images in our subconscious, an amalgam of people we have seen before with our own personality, self-view, fears and aspirations. Some studies claim that when we see a person in a dream we have never met before we are looking at ourselves from a different perspective. A second view, also unproven, is that dreams are prophetic. Masculine and feminine sides of a dreamer's personality (which Jung called *animus* and *anima*) may also be pictured in dreams as significant strangers. A woman dreaming of a weak man, in need of help, may be aware that she is neglecting a practical, 'masculine' side of her nature. Similarly a man who dreams of a friendship with a strange woman may need to develop his compassionate or 'feminine' side.

KATE SHAW, DREAM ANALYST, CAMDEN, LONDON.

125: I hear that England won the World Conker Championships. Is this the only thing England can win or are there other examples?

Of course England are champions at sports other than conkers. Some recent examples of English champions are Mucky Maureen, World Mud Wrestling Champion; Brian Cromble, World One Armed Golfing Champion; Robert Fulford, World Croquet Champion; The England Girls Team, World Junior Squash Champions and Edith Barnes, Ladies' World Clay Pigeon Shooter. England is a proud sporting nation and although some of our representatives get hammered at football, cricket and rugby, this is just a passing phase.

'UNION' JACK JACKSON, ROTHERHITHE, LONDON.

Two girls from Basingstoke won the World Duo title in baton twirling in Marseilles and my two friends Tracey and Dawn Hayman came second in their age group. Britain has had several other world champions in baton twirling, beating the Americans at their own sport.

CHARLOTTE KENNEDY (11), NEWBURY, BERKS.

126: Fifty years ago, it was said that the entire population of the world could stand on the Isle of Wight. Is it true now?

If the world's population tried to stand on the Isle of Wight at the same time it would cause quite a problem. The island is only 381 square kilometres (147 sq miles) while, at the last count there were 5,246 million people on the planet. On the basis that ten people, including children, can fit onto one square metre, that would allow 3,810,000,000 people to stand on the island at any one time, leaving 1,436,000,000 people, the combined populations of China, the US and the UK floundering in the Solent. Fifty years ago, when the world population was only 2,295,000,000 it would have been possible but since then the Isle of Wight has decreased slightly in size, some areas being eroded into the sea, and world population has grown rapidly. It ceased to be true around 1970 and has been about 170,000 people further from the truth every day since then. RODNEY PAXTON, GLASGOW.

127: Has Lord Sutch got a daytime job? And where did he get his title?

'Screaming' Lord Sutch doesn't have a day job. However, he's well known as a rock and roll singer, makes frequent guest appearances, has written his autobiography and is famed as an interviewee. Born David Edward Sutch, he changed his name by deed poll to Lord David Sutch.

KIM PAVEY, WOLVERTON, MILTON KEYNES.

128: Why do males go trainspotting?

Dr Uta Frith of the Medical Research Council's Cognitive Development Unit has suggested that keen trainspotters may be suffering from the incurable Asperger's Syndrome, a mild form of autism, identified by Dr Hans Asperger at the University of Vienna, shortly after World War II. Symptoms include social ineptness, an over-literal and pedantic approach to language (the 'little professor' mentality), a lack of sense of irony or humour and obsessively pursued hobbies, like being able to name 50 varieties of carrot or the serial numbers of lamp-posts. Dogged collectors of railway engine, and even coach and wagon numbers, would appear to fit this bill. ARTHUR HIRST, NEWTON ABBOT, DEVON.

Men who go trainspotting may not know it but they are acting out the last vestiges of the hunting instinct which was so vital to survival in primitive times. Man the hunter had to acquire a detailed understanding of his prey, its movements, numbers, strengths and weaknesses, when it would be around and when it would be difficult to track down. Thus, knowing the timetables of trains, which locomotives are likely to be pulling them and where they can be seen equates to knowing how to bring home the nightly meal for the family. LOGAN McCAE, GLASGOW.

Like many thousands of others – not all male – I was a trainspotter in my youth in the late Fifties, as were men who are now accountants, surgeons, headteachers, industrialists and bishops. Most would no doubt resent the implication that they are somehow mentally deficient. On summer Saturdays, hundreds of spotters congregated at any major railway stations: it was a very well behaved, all-day social gathering. Railway operations provided a spectacle regarded and it was all free. It led to an appreciation of order and classification, of geographic distribution, statistics, engineering and aesthetic design, historic development, literature and classics (from those wonderful engine names) and photography: a sound basis for a lifetime's wider interests.

DR K. A. JAGGERS, CHESHIRE.

Probably for the same reason we females do: it's an interesting, relaxing, sociable, educational, cheap and fun pastime. In the four years since I became a train enthusiast (trainspotter is so demeaning) I've accompanied my husband on many trips around the country as well as to South Africa and India following our interest, and we are sure of a friendly welcome from fellow enthusiasts. Through this interest I've enjoyed an increased understanding of the Industrial Revolution and its effects on the nation and the world. I'm aware of the 'anorak' label attached to what we do but I think it beats sitting by a river waiting for a fish to pop its head out.

MRS JANET BEWDLEY, YORK.

129: Who has the most children in Britain?

The parent with the most children still living with her is Mrs Jessie Campbell of Struan, Isle of Skye, Scotland who gave birth to her 20th child on January 22, 1990. Two other women, Mrs Margaret McNaught, of Birmingham, and Mrs Mabel Constable, of Warwickshire, have given birth to 22 children each but in both cases some of the children have grown up and now have families of their own. Mrs Campbell doesn't live in a shoe and isn't particularly old. She lives in a cottage and is only 47.

DEBBIE CHEVELL, HALE, CHESHIRE.

130: What is the origin of the expression 'at death's door'?

Though often taken to mean literally on the threshold of death, the phrase does have a more prosaic meaning. In the late 18th and early 19th centuries, the publican at the Falcon public house at Clapham Junction in London was also the local hangman. And his name was Robert Death. An etching exists from 1801 of undertakers at Death's Door. They are shown drinking at the pub in Battersea Rise, with the name Robert

Death clearly visible on the pub sign which hangs from the distinctive shape of the gallows. W. S. MARSH, BATTERSEA, SW11.

131: Did cavemen ever share the planet with dinosaurs?

Most scientists agree that dinosaurs died out more than 60 million years before the advent of modern man but certain findings do suggest otherwise. In 1924, the Doheny Expedition found very ancient rock paintings in the Havaspai Canyon near the Grand Canyon, one of which showed men attacking a mammoth, a tyrannosaurus standing on its tail, a stegosaurus and other prehistoric animals. In 1945, near the village of Acambaro in Mexico, clay statuettes were unearthed depicting monkeys, camels, horses, rhinos and dinosaurs of the Mesozoic era (225 million to 65 million years ago). One figure closely resembled a brachiosaur suggesting that the artist had actually seen the creature. Carbon 14 tests on the figures indicated they were from 3,000 to 6,500 years old. Images of stegosaurus have also been found scratched on a rock at Big Sandy River, Oregon.

MARK EWING, ST IVES, CAMBRIDGE.

132: Why do some people salute when they see a magpie?

According to ancient folklore the magpie is the Devil in disguise. Seeing a magpie is supposed to bring bad luck and the old rhyme 'one for sorrow, two for joy, etc' is linked to this belief. Saluting a magpie, or doffing your hat and saying 'Good morrow, magpie,' as practised in some rural areas, is supposed to show the magpie and those around you that you recognise it for the Devil and are countering any bad luck he may bring you.

IAN HARRISON, EASTBOURNE, SUSSEX.

133: What information, if any, is hidden within the three letters and six numbers of a National Insurance number?

National Insurance Numbers were introduced in 1948 when the national insurance scheme started by Lloyd George in 1912 was extended to include the whole working population. The format of the N.I. number has always been two letters (starting at AA), six numbers and suffix letter A, B, C, or D (for the quarter of the year in which you were born). Before 1948 the 'approved societies' which administered the early insurance schemes each had their own registration numbers, made up of six digits. When these were amalgamated into the extended national scheme, the Social Security Ministry translated the societies' numbers into the numbers we see today, with the addition of the two initial letters and the one at the end. The number carries no hidden code; subsequent numbers are issued by computer on a sequential basis covering the one million new registrations every year. SARA RAGAN, CONTRIBUTIONS AGENCY.

134: What's the difference between cottage pie and shepherd's pie?

Both are made in exactly the same way and were originally intended as a way of using leftovers from the Sunday joint. The difference between the two is that, under the potato, shepherd's pie should have minced lamb, whereas cottage pie has minced beef. Clearly a shepherd would have access to sheep meat while cottage dwellers would be closer to the farmyard cattle. FAITH TIPPETT, COLCHESTER, ESSEX.

135: Were there ever any cuddly dinosaurs?

Unfortunately, the potentially friendly, plant-eating dinosaurs were just too large to cuddle, ranging in size from that of a modern elephant to the average house. Smaller dinosaurs were hunters which would probably bite and scratch. However, the newly-hatched babies of the big plants eaters might have been quite small and, perhaps, sweet. IVOR L. CHALLIS, BRIGHTON.

136: Who was the last person beheaded in Britain?

Simon Fraser, 12th Lord Lovat and one of the Jacobite leaders of the 1745 rebellion was beheaded by executioner John Thrift on April 8, 1747. As a Scottish nobleman he petitioned King George II to be allowed to die by the Scottish Maiden, a kind of guillotine, but this was refused. As the sentence was carried out, the axe stuck several inches into the block: both axe and block can still be seen at the Tower of London. Lord Lovat was 80 when he died and 20 spectators at his execution also met their end when a grandstand collapsed. GEOFF ROBINSON, NOTTINGHAM.

Though Simon Lord Lovat was the last person of rank beheaded in Britain, the last executions by axe of commoners on Tower Hill were of two prostitutes and a one-armed soldier for their part in the anti-Catholic Gordon Riots of 1780. The last people to actually lose their heads in the judicial process were the notorious Cato Street conspirators who planned to murder the whole Cabinet. They were first hanged, then decapitated by surgeon's knife at Newgate in 1820. A. J. MATON, WIMBORNE, DORSET.

137: Does an apple a day really keep the doctor away?

Only if used as a missile – an apple's nutritional value is insufficient to provide any special immunity from illness. A raw eating apple is about

83 per cent water, 12% sugars, 0.6% malic acid, 0.3% protein, with various mineral salts and vitamins. Its vitamin C (ascorbic acid) content is very low, only five mgs per 100g of apple, further reduced by cooking. However, apples contain 2% of fibre, mainly pectin, which lowers cholesterol and slows down glucose absorption which may be helpful in preventing heart attacks and preventing diabetes. And the texture of a raw apple is ideal for removing sticky decaying substance from the teeth and promoting increased saliva flow: so perhaps it would be more appropriate to say 'An apple a day keeps the dentist away.'

BARRY BEACHAM, EPSOM DOWNS, SURREY.

138: Can your blood really boil?

Yes. If you were to leave a spaceship without the proper equipment, the low pressure outside your body would allow your blood to heat up to boiling point. This is what was supposed to be happening to Arnold Schwarzenegger in the film Total Recall, when he fell on the open surface of Mars. To be technical, boiling occurs when the vapour pressure of the liquid equals the pressure of the gas above it. Since there is no air pressure in space, the pressure of the water vapour in the blood immediately exceeds it, causing boiling. A similar condition occurs in the divers' nightmare condition, the bends. The blood fizzles as nitrogen comes out of its solution, due to a change in pressure on ascent to the surface. It's rather like opening a bottle of champagne.   GWYN DAVIES, ABERDARE.

Blood will not heat up when the body is exposed to a vacuum in space. In fact, it will cool because the latent heat of vaporisation has to come from somewhere. The term 'boiling' is misleading, as one automatically thinks of 100°C. In fact 'boiling' and 'freezing' occur simultaneously at body temperature in space. Men and animals have frequently been exposed to vacuums in medical tests; and the only sensation is a tingling of the skin, though death by anoxia will occur eventually.

ARTHUR C. CLARKE CBE, SRI LANKA.

139: Which of Britain's major cities receives the most rain in a year?

Surprisingly, the answer isn't Manchester. Though nicknamed 'Rainy City', Manchester receives an average of only 809mm rain a year. The title of rainiest city goes instead to Swansea, in Wales, with a rainfall average of 1,150mm per year – almost twice as wet as London (593mm) and marginally higher than other cities in the wetter, Western side of the country such as Glasgow (1,109mm), Plymouth (950mm) and Belfast

(845mm). Outside our cities, the wettest place is Styhead Pass in the Lake District, with an average 4,306mm rainfall a year.

BARRY PARKER, MET OFFICE, BRACKNELL.

140: What is on the piece of paper that is rolled up and pushed in the railings outside 10 Downing Street?

Contrary to misinformation sometimes given by police officers on Downing Street duty, the paper in the railings is not the Prime Minister's pizza order but just a list of names, titles and expected times of arrival of various people who will be visiting No 10 that day. The paper is pushed in the railings purely for the convenience of the policeman at the door of No 10.

DAVID JORGEN, HAMPSTEAD, LONDON.

141: Why do some war memorials say 1914-1919 for World War I when we know it ended in 1918?

Although the guns fell silent on the Western Front on November 11, 1918, the end of fighting there was only brought about by an Armistice. The war did not officially end until Germany admitted final defeat and signed the Treaty of Versailles on June 28, 1919. In the meantime hundreds of British soldiers died from accident and disease during demobilisation and from continuing engagements in other parts of the world, not least with White Russian forces fighting against the Red Army. Towns and villages which lost men during this period acknowledged the fact by including their names, and the later date, on their memorials.

OLIVER BURNS, SHEFFIELD.

142: As ice takes up more volume than the same amount of water, wouldn't the sea level go down if the North Pole melted through the greenhouse effect, rather than rising, as we are told?

Due to its lesser density but larger volume, ice readily floats in water. According to Archimedes' principle, the floating ice displaces its own weight in water, so upon melting, no change in water level would be observed. However, an increase in global temperature would produce a rise in sea level: while most of the Arctic ice floats in the sea, most of the Antarctic ice is on the land continent and would melt into the sea. And a general temperature rise would cause all the water in the oceans to expand slightly, contributing to raised sea levels.

DARREN HEATON, LEEDS.

143: Where did our ancestors obtain the boiling oil they used to defend their castles?

In Outremer, Palestine, during the crusades and in sieges around the

Mediterranean, olive oil was heated and poured on to attackers. In Britain and Northern Europe hot rendered-down animal fat – dripping – was used. It was effective, as anyone who has spilled chip pan fat on their feet will know. However, the material most commonly poured on the besiegers was hot fine sand. Contemporary accounts relate how painful this was when it penetrated inside armour.   NEVILLE SLACK, LANARK, SCOTLAND.

144: Royalty apart, who has the longest-standing peerage in Britain?

Burke's Peerage gives the following dates for earliest creations of various ranks of peer: Dukedoms: Norfolk, 1483; Marquessates: Winchester, 1551; Earldoms: Shrewsbury, 1442; Viscountcies: Hereford 1550; Baronies: de Ros 1264. However, peerage and pedigree should not be confused. Queen Victoria once remarked that many of the landed families of England had superior pedigrees to those of many German princely families. Nevertheless, in 1859 it was noted that only 50 families in England still retained the lands they held at the time of William the Conqueror, whence they took their names. Examples given were the Ashburnhams of Ashburnham in East Sussex, the Berkeleys of Berkeley, Greenwells of Greenwell in Northumberland, and Lumleys of Lumley in Co. Durham.
L. SCOTT-THOMAS, LONDON.

145: How many tons of food does the average person consume in a lifetime?

The Central Statistical Office says the average Briton eats his or her way through roughly six kilograms of food a week, including fruit juices and milk, etc, but not water. Over an average expected lifespan of 75 years, this amounts to 23,400 kilograms of food or 23.4 tons, equivalent to eating your body weight about 300 times.   DAVID ECKINGTON, DUNDEE.

146: Is it possible to die from seasickness?

Yes. One tragic example was that of Richard Spriggs, 23-year-old sound recordist with the ITV team covering the return of Sir Francis Chichester's successful round-the-world voyage in May 1967. To film Sir Francis out at sea, a team of journalists and technicians hired the yacht Braemar, which was hit by gale force winds and almost foundered. The Scillies lifeboat took off the team and crews, then battled its way back through heavy seas to Penzance. Richard Spriggs, suffering from acute seasickness, was taken to hospital but died shortly afterwards. The ITV team later won an award for its film Home Is The Sailor. The four ITV companies involved decided Richard should be remembered and formed a memorial fund which supplied a TV studio at Loughborough College School where he had been a pupil.   WALTER HIGGINS, GREAT GLEN, LEICS.

During the last War, while serving in the Royal Navy aboard the destroyer HMS Ilex, we once experienced rough seas for at least three days and nights, and several of the ship's company were very sick. One of our seamen died because his constant retching apparently ruptured his stomach muscles. A doctor on board fought desperately to save him but failed. The seaman was just 21 and was buried at sea. When seasick, it is always advisable to try to eat something, even if it's only hard biscuits. Go on deck in the fresh air and look at anything but the motion of the ship or sea.   LES REYNOLDS, GATLEY, CHESHIRE.

Seasickness can occasionally be fatal, normally due not to the illness itself but inhalation of vomit. Fortunately for our Navy, Merchant Navy, and ferry operators this is extremely rare and when it does occur is usually associated with other factors, such as alcohol, general health of the person, and ability to remain calm when vomiting. If it's any comfort, you're more likely to die from falling overboard while trying to be sick than from the illness itself.   DAWN HINCHCLIFFE, PORTSMOUTH.

147: Do fingerprints have any racial, genetic, gender or other characteristics?

Fingerprint experts have found certain racial patterns but these are too insignificant to be useful in the detection of crime. It is possible to trace particular patterns within some families but the differences in 'ridge characteristics' are always more significant than the similarities. Even the prints of identical twins are more different than alike. Women generally have smaller hands but experts ignore this and examine fingerprints on the assumption of 'unknown gender'. The chances of just one distinguishing characteristic of a fingerprint being identical to that of another person are roughly one in ten. Fingerprint bureaux in the UK look for a minimum of 16 characteristics 'in sequence and agreement.' If these match, the chances of two prints coming from different people are 10,000,000,000 million to one. With world population presently five billion, it's impossible for two people to share the same fingerprints.   TIM BROWN, HALIFAX.

148: Why is the Welsh flag not used as part of the Union Jack?

The reason for the omission of the Welsh banner from the flag of Great Britain dates back to 1536 when, under Henry VIII, Wales was incorporated legally and politically into England. When James VI of

Scotland became James I of England in 1603, unifying the two kingdoms, he called himself King of Great Britain. This union produced the first Union Flag, incorporating only the banners of St George and St Andrew. There was much objection to his title and it was declared illegal but it has persisted and was confirmed in 1707. At the union with Ireland in 1801, the banner of St Patrick was added, creating the second and current, Union Flag. When the Irish Free State came into existence in 1922 it was represented by its own tricolour flag; the banner of St Patrick remained in the Union Flag to represent Northern Ireland. The often used term 'Union Jack' is strictly only accurate when the flag is flown on the jackstaff of a warship.

EDDIE NOLL, LONDON.

149: What is the origin of the expression 'hat trick' applied to sporting performances?

The term was first used in the game of cricket. When a bowler took three wickets with three successive balls it became customary to give him a new hat at the expense of the club. The term 'trick' was a common older English word for three, still used in card games. The term has since evolved to mean any three scores or successes in sport of any kind.

PATRICK MALEELY, BASINGSTOKE.

150: Why do escalator handrails travel slightly faster than the staircase?

The answer is they shouldn't. Badly set up, maintained or adjusted escalators may exhibit this problem but it is a fault. The huge imbalance of load imposed on the steps compared with the handrail should be worked out and compensated for when the escalator is set up. From then on it should be maintained so that steps and handrail travel at the same speed. The disparity of speeds allowed by British standards in the synchronisation of steps and handrail is plus or minus two per cent.

KIERAN GHOSH, OTIS ESCALATOR DIVISION, LONDON SW9.

151: If moths are so attracted to light, why don't they come out in the day?

Moths are naturally nocturnal but appear to be attracted to light and to congregate around bright lights. Before man pock-marked the countryside with illuminations, moths navigated at night by the moon. A moth flew away from its home at the start of the night, hunting for food and/or a mate, keeping the light of the moon at a fixed angle to its flight path. To return home it had only to turn around and fly with the moon at the relevant angle behind it. Any changes in direction during flight could be rectified by re-establishing this angle to the moon, while allowing for the moon's shift in position during the night. This works because the moon is so far away that movement does not cause an apparent shift in the position of the light source. With artificial lights, moths become disoriented. Light sources are too close, so as the moth obliquely approaches a street lamp, flying in a straight line, the light appears to the moth to move. The moth interprets this as itself turning away from the light and tries to compensate by turning back towards it. By trying to maintain a constant angle between itself and a nearby light, the moth executes a spiral path into the light.   NIGEL FREESTONE, LONDON.

152: Where did the expression 'I should cocoa' originate?

It has been suggested that this began with fashion designer Coco Chanel but this expression is in fact good old rhyming slang. It started out as 'coffee and cocoa' meaning 'I should say so' and gradually changed to the phrase we know today.   SUSAN DEAMER, CHATHAM, KENT.

153: Why do we sing the hymn Abide With Me at the Cup Final?

Abide With Me was introduced into the communal singing at the Cup Final in 1927 because it was known to be Queen Mary's favourite hymn. That same year the FA Cup left England for the one and only time when Cardiff City beat Arsenal 1-0. It has been sung since then at every Cup Final except in 1959 (when Nottingham Forest beat Luton Town 2-1) when it was omitted because the Football Association changed the pre-match entertainment by introducing a display by the Coventry Ladies Keep Fit Team. So many people contacted the FA afterwards to show their disappointment at not having the hymn included that it was reintroduced the following year. Over the 65 years of its inclusion in the pre-match programme, celebrities who have led the singing have included Ed 'Stewpot' Stewart, Gerry and the Pacemakers and Frankie Vaughan.
DAVID BARBER, FOOTBALL ASSOC, LONDON.

My grandfather Arthur Caiger DCM led the community singing at the Cup Final for 20 years. He sang Abide With Me every year at Wembley from the years following the war until 1962. I never knew him as he died before I was born but I have seen photographs and read the memorabilia that my parents keep. It would be nice for him to be remembered too.
VERITY CAIGER, UXBRIDGE, MIDDX.

154: What is the authentic origin of the phrase 'It's a piece of cake'?

Not the most exciting answer but certainly the most authentic is that it comes from the original saying 'It's as easy as eating a piece of cake' first used in Victorian times, when cake took a larger part in the diet of the average person. It was later shortened to 'It's a piece of cake,' or even 'piece of cake.'

ROGER GRANT, SWINDON.

155: Can anyone complete the Cockney alphabet which begins 'A for 'orses, B for mutton, C for th' Highlanders', etc?

There are many versions of the 'Cockney alferbet' found all over the world. However, the most popular seems to be: A for 'orses, B for mutton, C for th' Highlanders, D for rential, E for brick, F for vescence, G for police, H for retirement, I for Novello, J for orange, K for teria, L for leather, M for size, N for lope, O for the wings of a dove, P for a whistle, Q for a bus, R for Mo, S for Williams, T for two, U for me, V for La France, W for a fiver, X for breakfast, Y for mistress, Z for breezes. Other versions include: C for yourself, C for miles, D for dumb, E for Adam, G for whizz, I for Lutin, I for the engine, K for rancis, N for eggs, O for the garden wall, P for relief, P for a penny, Q for billiards, Q for a song, Q for the pictures, Q for rations, R for crown, S for rantzen, U for got my birthday, U for missum, V for Espana, V for Zapata, V for victory, W for the kitty, X for cougar, Y for husband, Y for not, Y for golf, Y for goodness sake, Z for miles, etc.

DAVID EVANS, ORPINGTON, KENT.

This wasn't so much a Cockney alphabet as a comic one broadcast in the late Thirties by the comedy duo Clapham and Dwyer. I've never forgotten it.

BERT GORDON, WEST DRAYTON, MIDDX.

156: What was the exact wording on the question on the ballot paper in the 1975 Referendum on whether Britain should stay in the EEC?

The only national referendum ever held in the United Kingdom on June 5, 1975, asked 'Do you think that the United Kingdom should stay in the European Community (The Common Market)?' Out of a possible 40.1 million voters, a total of 64% cast their votes. Of these 17.4 million (67%) voted Yes, and 8.5 million (33%) voted No.

PAUL WILDER, ELECTORAL REFORM SOCIETY, LONDON SE1.

157: If I leave a slice of bread and a biscuit out on the worktop overnight, in the morning the bread has gone hard and the biscuit soft. Why?

Most types of bread are baked to retain a fairly high degree of moisture to keep the bread soft and pleasant on the palate. When left on a worktop overnight a certain amount of the moisture evaporates and the bread will begin to go dry and hard. Biscuits are baked to have a very low residual moisture content and, unless kept in an airtight container, absorb moisture from the atmosphere, making them soft.   JOYCE BECK, DUNDEE.

158: Like Patrick McGoohan in The Prisoner, I like to think that 'I am not a number, I am a free man' so why is it that I can receive direct mail from two different companies and yet both use the same code number for me?

This code number is not some evidence of Big Brother but simply a variation on the standard postcode. This variation is used by the Royal Mail for companies and organisations sending very large volumes of post. The system is called 'Mailsort' and the number at the side of the address panel helps the letter travel through the electronic sorting procedure faster than normal.   PRISCILLA TITFORD, DIRECT MAIL SERVICES STANDARDS BOARD.

159: Is it true that half the people who have ever lived are alive today?

Estimates for the world's all-time population vary between 15 and 20 billion people. Five-and-a-half billion of these are alive today and half of these are under the age of 15. So an astonishing one-quarter to one-third of all the people who have ever walked on our planet are actually doing so now. This top-endedness of historical world population (increased from an estimated 9 million at the end of the Neolithic Period) comes about because natural population growth which previously doubled every 700 years, has speeded up. The United Nations estimates that the population of the world will reach a 'half alive, half dead' position by around 2070 when the projected population will be more than 10 billion.
          RICKY YIANNI, NOTTINGHAM.

160: Why are laburnum seeds so poisonous to children but apparently harmless to the birds that eat them?

Laburnum seed can be very poisonous to humans and consuming them is considered potentially fatal though there have been no substantiated deaths in this country for several years. The seeds contain an alkaloid poison called cytisine which is released if they are broken or damaged before swallowing. The poison affects the nervous system causing nausea, vomiting, abdominal pain, drowsiness, headache, increased temperature and, in more severe cases, difficulty in breathing, convulsions or coma. The effect would be very similar in birds but because they tend to swallow seeds whole and their digestive systems, unlike those of humans, do not break the seeds down, they are unlikely to absorb the cytisine into their system in sufficient quantity to be affected.   IAN MORGAN, NATIONAL POISONS UNIT, LONDON.

161: Who, for Pete's sake, is Pete?

There does not appear to be a definitive derivation and the expression could be simply the invocation of St Peter's name. It is generally used as an expression of impatience and it should be recalled that a pete or pete-box was a safe and when it came to cracking open a safe, speed was essential. In the criminal world a safe-blower was known as a 'peterman' and saltpetre is a constituent of gunpowder. Alternatively 'for Pete's sake' could stem from popular 1860s circus clown Pete Jenkins whose stooges, planted in the audience, were said to be working 'for Pete's sake.'

DAVID NEWMAN, PAIGNTON, DEVON.

162: What is the significance of the jerky head movements in the tango?

The tango originated in late 19th century Cuba, from where it passed first to Argentina, then Spain and France. Unlike the flowing, constantly moving dances – the waltz, foxtrot and quickstep – which were popular at the time, the tango introduced a static, stop-start dance form with aggressive, rather than progressive, movements using whole body technique in which the jerky motion, particularly of the head, is reminiscent of a strutting cockerel. The novelty of the tango meant it quickly travelled all over Europe, becoming popular in England at the turn of the century.   FRANK GIBSON, FINNEGANS DANCE ACADEMY, MANCHESTER.

163: Will the 21st century start on January 1st, 2000 or 2001?

In strict mathematical terms the 20th Century will end, and the 21st Century begin, at midnight on December 31, 2000 Anno Domini. Our 'AD' calendar is based on the supposed year of the birth of Jesus, beginning with a 1, not a 0. Jesus is now generally thought by biblical scholars to have been born somewhere between the years we call 8 BC and 4 BC, so Christ's Second Millennium probably occurred sometime around 1996 and the calendar millennium will mark nothing more momentous than a nice round number. Preparations are being made for massive government sponsored celebrations on the night of December 31, 1999/January 1, 2000. Only pedants and killjoys are likely to hold the champagne on ice for another year.   B. H. MARTIN, WATERLOOVILLE, HANTS.

164: How can an electric fan make warm air cool just by moving it around?

It doesn't. Things only appear to be cooler when blown by a fan because they are obeying the laws of fundamental physics; the transfer of heat from one body to its lower-temperature surrounding area. For example, when you blow across the top of a drink to cool it you replace the hot air above the cup with air of a lower temperature. The heat from the drink moves into the cooler air and the drink is cooled. An electric fan supplies a constant flow of cooler surrounding air so whatever the fan is pointing at will feel cooler. In fact, the fan will eventually cause a overall rise in temperature as the heat from its electric motor dissipates into the surrounding air by the same principle.   MIKE LAWTON, PLYMOUTH, DEVON.

165: Why does my cat always come and lie across whatever I am reading on the table?

This is an attention-getting ploy. By lying on top of your reading material, your cat realises you must transfer your attention, even if only to yell at it to get off. The higher-tech equivalent of this problem involves working at a word processor when one's cat will invariably saunter all over the keybocg87649ard.   GRACE MCHATTIE, CAT CONSULTANT, SHOREHAM-BY-SEA, WEST SUSSEX.

166: What is the origin of the term 'Yank' or 'Yankee' applied to an American?

Although outside the U.S. we know all Americans as 'yankees' or 'yanks', in the country itself the word generally applies to New Englanders or somebody from north of the Mason-Dixon line. The word's origins are thought to be from the Indian pronunciation of the French word for the English, *Anglais,* and this was readily adopted by Dutch settlers of New Amsterdam to mean English settlers. The first use of the word yankee in written form appeared in the early 1700s when the Massachusetts farmer Jonathan Hastings, when hiring out horses to Harvard students, called his stock 'Yankee good horses', to signify they were well bred in the local area. During the American Civil War the name was applied by the rebel Confederates to mean specifically northerners. Proud Americans from the Southern states still object to being called 'yankees.'   RODNEY PATEL, MANCHESTER.

The suggestion that 'Yankee' came from indigenous Indians mispronouncing *Anglais* is unnecessarily complicated. The two most common names, even today, in the Netherlands are Jan, pronounced Yan, and Kees, pronounced Kase. Early Dutch settlers in the New York (New Amsterdam) area would have included a fair number of Jan Keeses and their name came to stand for all settlers there.

MRS A. M. GONLAG, BROCKENHURST, HANTS.

167: Why is polling day in this country always on a Thursday?

The fact that every General Election and most Parliamentary by-elections since 1935 have been held on a Thursday has arisen by custom rather than any regulation. Reasons in the more distant past included the fact that Thursday is market day in many rural areas when far-flung farming populations could be expected to be in town to vote. The importance of Thursday being the last day before payday on Friday when working men would have run out of drinking money was not lost on the powerful non-conformist lobby earlier this century. And Thursday was thought to be sufficiently far from Sunday for voters to be safe from the influence of the pulpit on their voting intentions.   PAUL WILDER, ELECTORAL REFORM SOCIETY.

168: Why don't the palms of our hands get tanned?

All humans, regardless of their natural skin colouring, have very few melanocytes in the palms of the hands and on the soles of the feet. Melanocytes are the pigment cells which cause tanning when exposed to sunlight, so we have virtually no facility for tanning on the palms. The lack of melanocytes on palms of hands and soles of feet probably goes back in evolutionary terms to a time when we walked on all fours and had little use for pigmentation in areas that would not get sun.

KATHY WILKINSON, BOOTS BEAUTY AND PERSONAL CARE, NOTTINGHAM.

169: Why are certain cricket games called 'test' matches and in what way are they different from other sorts of matches?

A 'Test' match is a five-day international game, of 30 hours' playing time, arranged between two selected nations by the International Conference. A Test is different from county games and one-day internationals by virtue of its length though the rules are basically the same. The word 'Test' came about around the turn of the century when these games were arranged between countries as matches that 'tested' the skills of the top players from each nation against each other.

CLAIRE FATHERS, TEST AND COUNTY CRICKET BOARD, LONDON.

170: Why do firemen slide down a pole to reach the fire engine? Wouldn't it save time if they were both at the same level?

An increasing number of firefighters are women and they, too, are required to slide down a pole. Firefighters originally lived above their stations and needed quick access to their engines. The pole was found to be the quickest and safest method to get a full team from one floor to another, rather than running down stairs, which caused a number of injuries. Use of a pole (now stainless steel rather than wood) continues in about 90% of the more than 2,000 fire stations in the UK. Stations which house the firecrew on the same level as their engines are unusual because the extra land needed makes them more expensive.

DAVE MATTHEWS, FIRE BRIGADES UNION, KINGSTON-UPON-THAMES.

171: When we smell flowers, do we inhale a gas? If not, how does smell travel?

Relatively small volatile molecules in specialised parts of the flower are released in very small quantities into the air. They are like essential oils used in perfumes and, although in vapour form, they are not a gas. When released from the flower they mix with the atmosphere and are picked up by receptors in the nose which respond to volatiles and through neurons transmit information to the brain which recognises them as a smell.

QUENTIN RYE, ROYAL BOTANIC GARDENS, KEW, SURREY.

172: Who was the last person in Britain to be burned at the stake?

It was an ancestor of mine, Edward Wightman, from Burton on Trent, Staffs, who was burned for heresy on March 9 and April 11, 1612. He was famous for his Anabaptist views, made public at local meetings of the Puritan Divines. In March 1611, he presented a petition to James I at Royston. The king sent him to London to be locked up and examined by Richard Neile, Bishop of Westminster. From April to ·October, Neile talked to him and reported that he became more obstinate and blasphemous by the day. King James sent Wightman to the Consistory Court at Lichfield for trial and he was sentenced on December 14, 1611. When the fire scorched him at his first burning on March 9, he shouted that he wanted to recant. The watching crowd rushed forward and saved him but when he was asked to recant before the Consistory Court he refused and was burned to death on April 11.

SHIRLEY SUTTON, KIDDERMINSTER, WORCS.

According to J. F. Sutton's Annals Of Crime, published in Nottingham in 1859, 30-year-old Phoebe Harris was burnt at the stake in front of Newgate Prison a few days after being sentenced at the Old Bailey on

July 21, 1786, for 'coining false money', which was then classed as high treason. Sutton also notes that two other ladies, Eleanor Elsom and Mary Johnson, met the same fate at Lincoln in 1722 and 1747 respectively, for poisoning their husbands. BARRY HOLLAND, NOTTINGHAM.

173: Could sacked Chancellor Norman Lamont or any Minister of the Crown have sued for unfair dismissal before an industrial tribunal when they're dismissed?

Most employees in the UK can complain of unfair dismissal to an industrial tribunal so, in theory, this included Norman Lamont when he was dismissed as Chancellor, or any other Minister of the Crown who could show continuous employment for more than two years of at least 16 hours of work a week. But Cabinet Ministers, like football managers, however disgruntled or badly-done-by they may feel, are generally persuaded to 'resign' rather than be sacked, leaving them with the far more difficult course of claiming 'constructive dismissal' should they want to make a claim. JULIAN KENDRICK, LONDON W1.

174: What is the most commonly eaten food on the planet?

According to the United Nations Food And Agriculture Organisation the food most commonly grown and harvested is wheat with a production level of 595 million metric tons per year, closely followed by rice (518 million metric tons) and maize (475 metric tons). Other commonly grown foods are potatoes, barley, cassava, sweet potatoes, soy beans and sugar cane. VINCENT BRADY, KINGS NORTON, BIRMINGHAM.

175: What is the origin of the expression 'pushing the boat out'?

In times when most sea voyages lasted several months or even years, the sailor's last night on home ground was an emotional one. The departing seaman, leaving family and friends, had good cause for some serious partying with no expense spared. 'Pushing the boat out' came to mean a celebration which would last in the memory for quite a time. There is no recorded date for the first use of this saying though it has been used for 200 years and may have been coined far earlier. P. J. GIFFARD, PLYMOUTH.

176: Does most traffic in world drive on the left or the right?

Of the 178 countries in the world, only 42 drive on the left and this number has been steadily declining over the past 50 years. Most of the countries in the 'left is best' club are former British colonies which decided (largely for financial reasons) not to change when they gained independence.

The country with the largest number of vehicles driving on the left is Japan, which has roughly twice the number found on UK roads. The largest network for cars that drive on the left is in India, with more than a million miles of road. In future, the number of left-hand nations will probably reduce still further as various African countries change to the right to allow a fully right-hand continent.   FELICITY CHAMBERS, EXETER.

177: What is a TOG, as in the TOG ratings given to duvets and sleeping bags, and how is it measured?

TOG rating was devised as a measure of the ability of quilts or duvets to retain heat. Hence a duvet with a six TOG label will not retain heat as well as a 12 TOG. It will be cooler and perhaps more appropriate for summer use. TOG ratings are measured under laboratory conditions to a British Standard by using simulated beds with thermostatic nodules providing a heat source at normal body temperature. An average TOG value is attributed to the combination of fabric, sewing, and filling used in the duvet. A TOG measure is not a measure of quality but merely an informational figure as to the heat retention qualities of the duvet or sleeping bag.   MIKE DUDLEY-JONES, SLUMBERLAND, OLDHAM, LANCS.

178: Where does the phrase 'on your tod' come from?

'On your tod' – meaning 'on your own' – is rhyming slang for 'on your own' contracted from the name of popular American jockey Tod Sloan (1874-1933), who visited Britain just before the turn of the century and rode here for three seasons. He revolutionised riding by introducing the modern crouch position: previously, jockeys sat upright and employed long stirrups. After some early ridicule by punters, his style of riding began to pay dividends as he won a string of races, including the prestigious 1,000 Guineas at Newmarket.   GREG PARKER, NEWMARKET, SUFFOLK.

179: What is Joanna Southcott's box and why don't the bishops open it?

Joanna Southcott was a religious enthusiast, born in 1750, who founded a sect which is still in existence and is now called the Panacea Society. At the age of 42 she began to hear a 'still small voice'. She recorded every word she heard in 65 publications and many unpublished works. Certain of her writings were divinely ordered to be sealed up and placed in an ark or box, to be opened only in a time of national danger. This ark, kept at Home of Mist, Blockley, Worcestershire, is supposed to be the one mentioned in Revelation, and the 24 bishops who should be on hand to open it are the 'elders' referred to therein. At least four such boxes have already been opened, though not with the required number of bishops, and found to contain nothing of consequence. Thus we can understand their lordships' reluctance to open yet another box.

R. J. CONDON, HORNCHURCH, ESSEX.

180: Why are English ties striped in one direction and American ties in the opposite direction?

This is not always the case, and some exceptions to this rule are the ties of the RAF and Royal Marines, which are cut in the 'American way' in this country. In the United States, a notable exception to their rule was ex-President George Bush, who nearly always wore 'British-style' ties. Stripey ties first appeared in 1880, instigated by university and school clubs. The direction of stripe, high left to low right, in this country came about because the British heraldic tradition suggests that a stripe from high right to low left denotes a bastard line in genealogy. In the U.S. the stripes' direction came about because the tie industry cut cloth in bulk with the pattern face down, resulting in the stripes running from high right to low left.

JAMES WESTON-PHILLIPS, CHELSEA, LONDON.

181: Is there a technical name for someone who collects pens?

The name is stylophile and there are at present about 20,000 serious collectors. It is only since the early Seventies that this pastime has really attracted large numbers of people (and big money), turning it into one of the top 25 hobbies in the UK.

DONNA WARING, THE PEN SHOP, MANCHESTER.

182: How many tube trains are running at any one time during the rush hour on the London Underground system?

The two 'rush hour' peak times in each weekday are 8.50am and 5.30pm, when the London Underground is running at full capacity, carrying about 450,000 passengers. The usual number of trains on the system during these periods is 460, with each train carrying about 1,000 people. The busiest point on the system is Victoria Station, where about 480 people per minute are pouring into the system. As an example, only eight of the 460 trains scheduled to run on July 13, 1993, were cancelled: two for maintenance, two which proved defective in the morning and four which developed problems in service.

STEPHEN MILTON, LONDON UNDERGROUND.

183: Who divided the circle into 360 degrees and why?

Ancient Babylonian mathematicians divided the circle, or one revolution, into 360 equal parts. They believed the solar year was 360 days long and considered this a convenient figure to use. Each of the 360 parts is called a degree. Each degree is split into another 60 parts called minutes and each minute is again divided into 60 parts called seconds.

TIM JONES, CINDERFORD, GLOS.

184: If I had all the equipment necessary, what would be the maximum number of television channels I could receive at any one location in Britain?

There are potentially 200 channels available to people who live in areas serviced by the IBA, BBC, a cable network and the various satellite television services. Satellite and cable provide the vast majority of these channels through cables and satellites such as Astra, Eutelsat, Intersat, Kopernikus, Telecom, Tele-X, Olympus, TVSat, TDF, Hispasat and others centred on Europe. Many channels are encrypted and dedicated for use in certain countries only. These are normally received only by decoder. South-east England is probably the best area for satellite channels because it is closer to their normal orbits. For cable, the city of Bradford is probably the best area: it has up to 40 channels, plus the four normal programmes, as well as satellite. Of the 200 channels available, only about 35 are in the English language.

DERRICK WALKER, CONFEDERATION OF AERIAL INDUSTRIES, LONDON.

185: Why do we put stamps on the top right hand corner of envelopes?

During the reign of Charles II, Colonel Henry Bishop was appointed Postmaster General with the task of reducing the number of complaints about non-arrival and late delivery of mail. His solution was to make sure each letter was embossed with an impression containing the date when it was posted. This gave birth to the franking mark. Improvements on transport by the mid-19th century meant the costs of the increased service were so cumbersome that any meaningful calculations of tariff were impossible to enforce. Postmaster General Rowland Hill revolutionised the system by introducing pre-paid postage stamps, of which the Penny Black was the first and most famous. Col Bishop's block stamp still had to be applied to Rowland Hill's stamps to cancel them from further use and so it became customary to place the stamp in the top right hand corner to facilitate quick and easy cancellation by postmasters, most of whom were righthanded. These days, mechanised cancellation makes it even more important for stamps to be placed in a standard position.

M. MAGOWAN, SUNDERLAND.

186: Why do we call making a mistake 'making a pig's ear'?

This is the opposite of the old saying that you 'can't make a silk purse out of a sow's ear' and dates from a time when killing the pig was an annual occurrence. To achieve the best results in any endeavour, an individual likes to have the right materials and skills. Clearly it is difficult to make a premium item like a silk purse from poor quality materials, like the least-prized part, the ear, of the pig, a peasant's measure of prosperity. Conversely, if someone is given every opportunity to do something really well but still succeeds in making a hash of it, they are said to have 'made a pig's ear' of the situation.   COLIN DIETRICH, WALTHAM ABBEY, ESSEX.

187: We have Mothering Sunday and Fathers' Day, why isn't there a Mother-in-Law Day?

This country has no specific celebration of a mother-in-law's day because most spouses include their partners on greetings to their respective mothers on Mothering Sunday. A mother-in-law's day celebration was once proposed by a radio presenter in Texas but, although it was heavily publicised, with cards being made available in the shops, it ceased after its first occurrence.   KATE O'REILLY, LIVERPOOL.

In our house we celebrate mother-in-law day on October 31: Hallowe'en.
                    MRS M. CLARK, TOWCESTER, NORTHANTS.

188: Why are number plates white at the front, yellow at the back, and other colours abroad?

Regulations introduced in 1973 compel all new vehicle owners to show registration plates with black lettering on a white background at the front and black lettering on a yellow background on the rear of their vehicles. The two colour system was designed to improve road safety by allowing others to see in which direction a vehicle is facing simply by looking at the colour of its registration plate. Yellow and white were chosen by the Department of Transport as the most noticeable colours. Each country makes its own regulations regarding vehicle registration plates; most use a single colour system for front and rear.
                    ALISON LANGLEY, DEPARTMENT OF TRANSPORT.

189: When I lived near Abbey Road in North London, immortalised by The Beatles, I noticed a Quex Road and a Mazenod Avenue lettered in the same black and white tiles as on the eponymous album cover. Is this just a case of the local

council having a few lettered tiles left, as in Scrabble, or do
these names have any meaning?

The whole area was originally part of the estate belonging to the Powell-Cotton family, well known land owners during the 19th century. The family's country seat, called Quex Park, was on the Isle of Thanet so, in 1866 the first section of the new estate built there was called Quex Road. Mazenod Avenue is named after the French Bishop, Eugene de Mazenod who formed a society with a school and church on the site where the houses of the second phase of the development were built. The tiles used in the street nameplates date from the 1920s when they were fashionable. So far, the 'Scrabble factor' hasn't come into play in deciding what to call streets. However, with the cutbacks local councils are facing, this may become the case in future.   CHARLES WRIGHT, CAMDEN COUNCIL.

190: What is the name for a 75th wedding anniversary?

Very few couples actually reach a 75th wedding anniversary and by then they have probably bought each other everything they could possibly need. Perhaps this is why no official name has yet been given. Even the Greeting Card and Calendar Association hasn't allocated a name. The longest marriage in the UK was between James Burgess and his wife Sarah, both from Bermondsey, South London, which lasted 82 years and one day before Sarah's death in 1965. Tradition suggests that in the case of a 75th wedding anniversary we revert back to the name Diamond Wedding (normally used for 60th anniversary). Personally however, I feel it should be an Aluminium Wedding in honour of the material used in the manufacture of zimmer frames.   DIANA GREGORY, DUNDEE.

191: Why does a cockney refer to his home as a 'drum' or his 'gaff'?

The word 'drum' dates from 1846 and comes from *'drumming':* the practice of knocking on the door of a house to see if it was occupied before attempting a robbery. So robbers started to call houses 'drums.' 'Gaff' is much later, from around 1932 and derived from the word 'gaffer', a contraction of 'godfather' – the house that controls everything.
                    DAVID J. NEWMAN, PAIGNTON, DEVON.

192: Who invented the jigsaw puzzle?

As with many inventions two people claim to have been first to come up with the idea. In France they say a man called Dumas began cutting up maps and selling them as an educational toy in 1762. In this country, around the same time, John Spilbury began putting maps of Britain onto a thin layer of mahogany and cutting them up along the county borders. The idea was not a great success and he died a poor man at the age of 29. Jigsaws started to become popular about 25 years later when William Darton, an Englishman, began producing puzzles with portraits of every monarch since William the Conqueror. This time the idea was a success and so began the growth of the jigsaw industry. The name jig-saw comes from the type of saw used to cut up the wooden pieces and has now become synonymous with the puzzle itself.   SUZANNE IRWIN, STOKE ON TRENT.

193: Is there anyone called 'Nat West' working for the National Westminster Bank?

Of the 90,000 or so employees of the National Westminster Bank there are actually 66 people with the surname West but only one of these is referred to as 'Nat' and it's only his nickname. Nat West has worked in one of our London branches for several years but is not particularly keen to disclose information about himself, for obvious reasons. A check with the other high street banks shows no other Nat West working for them, though Lloyds Bank has 88 employees called Lloyd, seven Barclays, two Coutts and 41 Banks.   ANTHONY FROST, NATIONAL WESTMINSTER BANK, LONDON.

194: Why, when somebody dies, has he 'kicked the bucket'?

The two most commonly cited explanations are that the saying comes from either the simple method employed to hang somebody – stand them on a bucket with a noose round their neck and kick the bucket away – or from kicking, or shaking, the bucket used for a whip-round when somebody had died, to make others believe you had given a donation. Neither of these is correct. 'Kick the bucket' actually stems from the now obsolete Old French word *bucket,* the large wooden beam used to suspend pigs for slaughter in an abbatoir. The pig would jerk in its death throes, banging its trotters against the beam, quite literally 'kicking the bucket.'   LORRAINE TANDY, SCARBOROUGH.

195: Why, when we go upstairs, do we arrive on the landing?

In the 17th century, 'to land' could mean 'to arrive at a stopping place on a journey', either the destination or a stage along the way. Use of the word in connection with the top of the stairs can be traced to 1679, when it was written 'landing by the first pair of stairs…' By 1789, 'landing' had found its way permanently into common usage to describe the resting place between flights of stairs.

EDMUND WEINER, OXFORD UNIVERSITY PRESS, OXFORD.

196: Why is May 29 known as Oak Apple Day?

In September 1651, my ancestors, the five Penderel brothers, hid King Charles II from Cromwell's troops in the Royal Oak at Boscobel, Shropshire, after the battle of Worcester. The romantic idea of a king hiding in the most English of trees caught the public's imagination and when Charles II was restored to the throne on his 30th birthday, on May 29, 1660, the day become known as Oak Apple Day and was celebrated as a public holiday until the middle of the 19th century. It is still commemorated at the Royal Hospital, Chelsea, founded by Charles II, and at Groveley, near Salisbury, by the wearing and carrying of oak leaves. We should still celebrate Oak Apple Day because, but for my ancestors' courage, we might be without our constitutional monarchy.

GEOFFREY WHITTINGTON, CROSSMICHAEL, CASTLE DOUGLAS.

Today's oak at Boscobel is thought to be a self-seeded sapling from an acorn of the original tree. BAMBER GASCOIGNE, AUTHOR: ENCYCLOPEDIA OF BRITAIN, LONDON.

A special service was inserted in the Book of Common Prayer to be used on Oak Apple Day and people wore sprigs of oak with gilded oak apples. The service was expunged in 1859. SUE MAYHEW, SWALECLIFFE, KENT.

In my schooldays, those wearing a sprig of oak leaves and oak apple on May 29 were at risk of being stung on the legs with stinging nettles by the school bullies. H. TILL, WOLVERHAMPTON.

197: Would filling my garage with exhaust fumes from my car exterminate the woodworm?

Definitely not – and don't do it. It would be ineffective, illegal and hazardous. From a practical aspect, any fumigation gas would get dispersed around your garage. You might kill a few woodworm but to exterminate them from timber completely you need a precise calculation to ensure the right concentration to do the job. The only legal, cheap and safe way to do it is to buy an approved woodworm killer and follow the instructions on the can. PETER BATEMAN, RENTOKIL.

198: Why is the Royal Navy sometimes referred to as the 'Andrew'?

It's usually accepted that this is due to the zealous activities of a lieutenant Andrew Miller, a press-gang officer. It was said he 'pressed' so many men into the Navy during the Revolutionary and Napoleonic wars that it became known as 'Andrew's navy' – later evolving as 'The Andrew'. When anyone went missing, it was said that 'Andrew's got him'. Press-ganging was allowed under the 1795 Quota Act which required each district to provide a number of men for the Navy because the stream of men achieved by the Vagrancy Act was insufficient to man the ships. Unfortunately, there is no solid evidence that Andrew Miller ever existed in the 'Impress Service' or Royal Navy at all. An alternative story, current during the last century, had it that a West Country woman named Ann Drew had so many sons in the Royal Navy that the Fleet became known as 'The Ann Drew Navy' or 'The Andrew'.   LIEUT E. C. COLEMAN, ROYAL NAVY.

199: Where does the practice of throwing a penny into a wishing well come from?

Throwing a penny or any coin into a wishing well derives from Greek mythology and was thought to help a deceased person's soul by paying their passage to Hades. All souls had to cross the River Styx, the underground river between here and the afterworld, and were supposed to pay the mythological boatman Charon his fee. If they had no cash, they had to hang around in a sort of hinterland before they reached the heavenly 'plains of asphodel'. By throwing money down a well, passers-by could help any penniless souls pay for a safe journey.

BOB MCBRATNEY, MOTHER SHIPTON'S CAVE AND PETRIFYING WELL, KNARESBOROUGH, N. YORKS.

200: If ghosts can supposedly slide through walls and doors, why don't they fall through the floor?

Ghosts, if they exist, are non-material entities not subject to the physical laws of the time and place in which they seem to appear. They are not susceptible to gravity or the density of matter. Whether aware or not of their physical surroundings, they are operating, as it were, on a different frequency and can pass through walls or floors if they so choose just as high frequency waves for radio or TV do. Ghosts seem to exist partly in their own time and partly in another. Many cases are recorded of apparitions passing through brick walls at points where doors existed years before. Ghosts are also said to have been observed crossing rooms but visible only from the knees upwards and it is suggested that the floor-level in their original time was lower than at the time of the sighting.

MICHAEL BARRETT, PITTON, SALISBURY.

201: Why have athletes vastly improved their race times in recent years but track times for horses have largely stood still?

People who believe horses aren't running faster than they did 20 years ago should remember that the two sports occur under different conditions.

Horse racing times haven't stood still; it's more a case of them gradually being improved upon whereas in athletics the improvements are on a more noticeable scale. Athletics has always taken place on a racing surface which, over the years, has been improved and made faster. By contrast, improvements in turf husbandry, watering facilities and techniques have produced not firm, fast courses, but softer and slower 'good' going. When the ground is firm, as at Ascot in 1992, records are often broken. Progress in training and feeding techniques has produced fitter and faster thoroughbreds. If they all raced on uniform surfaces, under identical conditions, most track records would date just from the Nineties.

SIMON CLARE, THE JOCKEY CLUB.

202: Why is it said to be bad luck to first see a new moon through glass?

From ancient times the moon has been believed to hold magic and mystical properties and getting first sight of a new moon was held to be fortunate. This fortune could, however, be recast as ill luck if the sighting was through glass. Early glass had blemishes, cracks, chips and ripples which distorted any significant sighting, negating the moon's positive qualities and making them harmful. Anyone unfortunate enough to catch sight, inadvertently, of the new moon through glass should remedy the effect by going outside and looking at it over their right shoulder.

TOM F. CROCKER, SOUTHPORT, MERSEYSIDE.

203: Did the hamburger originate in Hamburg?

The hamburger appears to have originated in the Baltic region in the 17th century before becoming popular in Hamburg, Germany. The proper name for it is 'Hamburg steak.' When the word 'hamburger' appeared in mid-19th century America it was a derogatory term used by Chicago workers who believed German expatriate co-workers were ruining best beef by mincing it, making it into patties and cooking it. Eventually it became naturalised into American society and is now the most common way to eat meat in the western world.

PHILLIP SOLDING, LISKEARD, CORNWALL.

204: Why is it that, at 72, I can remember my 1939 identity card number but not where I've just left my spectacles?

You learned you identity card number a long time ago and, in repeating it many times, memorised it well. But putting down your spectacles daily over and over again in different circumstances means it is easy to remember you've taken them off but not where you put them.

Remembering that calls on a new and recent memory which is interfered with by every other time you've put your spectacles down. This is episodic memory and forgetting where you've put your spectacles has nothing to do with being elderly. We all forget parts of recent episodic actions but the elderly are more likely to attribute it to age.

DR ELIZABETH STYLES, DEPARTMENT OF EXPERIMENTAL PSYCHOLOGY, OXFORD UNIVERSITY.

205: Would any modern building firm be prepared to take on construction of the Giant Pyramid? How much would it cost?

We would love to take on the job. The original Great Pyramid took 30 years to build by 4,000 people working round the clock. It is approximately 146.5 metres high with a base 230 metres square. Roughly 2 million limestone blocks, weighing about 2.5 tonnes would have to be provided and placed in position. Forget rolling blocks on wood and pushing them up mounds, as the ancient Egyptians did. Using a fleet of specially made trucks and 16 tower cranes, we would employ 390 workers to do the job in about eight years, at a cost of between £600 and £750 million. Electricity and plumbing to comply with modern expectations would cost extra. And the highly particular furnishings are not really our line – you'd probably have to try Fort Knox for those. To put it in context, several of today's construction projects, not least the Channel Tunnel, would dwarf the building of the pyramids.   JOHN HALL, GEORGE WIMPEY PLC, HAMMERSMITH, LONDON.

206: Why do mourners throw a handful of earth on the coffin after a burial service?

This is symbolic of the body returning to the earth. The minister or cemetery superintendent usually scatters a little soil on the coffin as he says the words '…ashes to ashes, dust to dust…' and mourners throw on earth at the end or during the service to take a personal part in the burial. Funeral customs vary around the country but there is a move for families to become more involved in this way.

SIMON TRUELOVE, NATIONAL ASSOC OF FUNERAL DIRECTORS.

207: I have heard that Lenin possessed 12 Rolls-Royces. Is this true and is it a record?

According to our records, the first Soviet leader only ever possessed two Rolls-Royce cars at any one time during his life. At Rolls-Royce, we are keen to maintain the privacy of our client list and we have never released the exact details of our clients, or the number of vehicles they have bought. However, I can inform you that owning 12 Rolls-Royce cars at one time is not a record.   SUE LANGER, ROLLS-ROYCE, CREWE, CHESHIRE.

208: Who was Larry and why was he so happy?

The expression 'Happy as Larry' originated in Australia during the last century and was coined in honour of Australian boxer Larry Foley (1837-1917), known as the 'father of Australian boxing.' He was popular with the punters and undoubtedly a very happy man after he was able to retire undefeated in bare-knuckle contests at the age of 42 with a fortune of £1,000, a considerable sum in those days. JOSH MAUNDERS, KEIGHLEY.

209: What are Ps and Qs and why should I mind them?

They are exactly what they appear, letters of the alphabet. We are asked to 'mind them' because the most common mistake in the early printing industry was confusing a lower case letter 'p' with a lower case 'q' when seeing them in reverse and preparing a passage for print. This may sound trivial but if the mistake wasn't spotted before printing it could cost a printer quite a sum in reprinting. Thus the warning was continually stressed to apprentice printers and joined the language as a saying in its own right. Most people these days think 'Ps and Qs' are a shortened version of 'please' and 'thank you.' DAVID ASHCROFT, PRINTER, FAILSWORTH, LANCS.

210: Who was St Pancras and why did he have a station named after him?

Saint Pancras was the boy martyr Pancratius, beheaded in Rome in AD304 because he refused the Emperor Diocletian's order to give up his Christianity. The original St Pancras church, near the site of the station, was first built in his memory. The small village around the church also adopted the name St Pancras and when this area was chosen for the site of the Midland Railway Line station in 1868 it was decided to keep the same name. There is still a small church by this name behind the station. PIPPA SHAW, BLACKBURN.

211: How many ears of corn go into making a standard loaf of bread?

An average of 200 ears of corn are required to produce enough flour to make a 1lb (450 gram) loaf of bread. Bread is one of our oldest and most important forms of food and, regardless of whether brown or white, the 200 ears of corn we are provided with give us the essential (starchy) carbohydrates, protein, vitamins and minerals necessary to complement a healthy diet. GEORGINA HOLLIDAY, FLOUR ADVISORY BUREAU, LONDON SW1.

212: Why is there no plural in the English language for 'sheep'?

Nouns in Old English formed their plurals in many different ways. One was by adding '-u'. When the singular word consisted of a monosyllable with a long vowel sound, the '-u' ending became weakened and finally disappeared, so that the singular and plural were identical. Many of these words were the names of animals, for example 'horse', 'swine', 'deer' and 'sheep.' Horse later added a regular '-s' for the plural, 'swine' became established as a plural without a singular, except as a term of abuse for a human animal – 'You swine!' Deer and sheep, perhaps because people used these words more often to refer to a number of animals, remained as unchanged plurals.   DELIA TAITT, LONDON SW19.

213: Why is tepid water known as lukewarm?

Luke comes from *lewu*, an Old English variation on the Norse *hleowe*, meaning cold. Warm, meaning the same as it does today, came from Norse *varmr*. When both words are put together it gives a mixture of cold and warm, in other words, a fair description of tepid water.
                    DAVID J. NEWMAN, PAIGNTON, DEVON.

214: The poorer countries of the world are often described as the Third World, so what are the First and Second Worlds?

The term Third World refers to all those countries which are not part of the Old or New Worlds. In the 1820s, British Prime Minister George Canning took the novel step of calling for support from America for his global policies and it was said of him that he 'called the New World (meaning America) into existence to redress the balance of the Old' (meaning Europe). So Third World has nothing to do with countries being richer or poorer, communist or non-communist. It simply means all those countries outside Europe and its immediate sphere and the Americas.   GEOFFREY BULL, LONDON N5.

215: Why 'somersault', which appears to have nothing to do with summer or salt?

Somersault is simply a combination of two Latin words. The first part is derived from *summus* meaning the top, or highest point, as in the English words 'summit', 'sum' and 'summer' (the top beam supporting floor joists). The second part comes from the verb *salio* meaning to jump or leap, as in the English 'salutation' and 'salient'.
                    BRIAN WOODHEAD, BLACKPOOL.

216: Which city or town in Britain gets the most sunshine in a year?

In general the South and South-East of the country have less cloud and higher levels of sunshine, because they have more shelter from the prevailing Atlantic weather systems. A quick check through the records for the past 30 years shows that the town with the most sunshine has been Shanklin, on the Isle of Wight, with an average 1,855 hours of sun per year. This is closely followed by Bognor Regis with 1,847 hours, the sunniest town on mainland Britain. Looking at the whole of the British Isles, the sunniest place is St Helier on the island of Jersey, with 1,944 hours.

MARTIN ALLWRIGHT, MET OFFICE, BRACKNELL, BERKS.

217: What is haywire and why do we go it?

Haywire is the type of wire used by farmers for binding bundles of hay and for making minor repairs to gates and fences. Handled inexpertly, the coils of wire can easily become entangled and unmanageable. Thus anyone who runs riot or behaves uncontrollably is said to go haywire.

KEVIN HENEGHAN, ST HELENS, MERSEYSIDE.

218: Why does sour cream have a sell-by date?

It may sound like a contradiction in terms, yet sour cream is not just cream which is old and sour, but a fresh product. Like yogurt it can go off and has a relatively short shelf-life. To produce it, single cream is soured by the addition of a starter culture of artificially-produced bacteria, which usually comprises strains of lactococci and leuconostocs. These are similar cultures to those used in the manufacture of buttermilk and cheese. The safety of chilled foods depends on good hygiene and maintaining the correct low temperature throughout the manufacturing and distribution chain, otherwise the culture continues to grow, producing acid and making the product unpalatable. For this reason the product is marked with a 'use-by' date to ensure it is sold and eaten while still fresh. Food manufacturers are required by law to give a clear indication of the expiry date on product labels, assuming the product is stored under ideal conditions.

TONI HENSBY, ST IVEL LTD, WOOTTON BASSETT, WILTS.

219: Why, when on the ground, do blackbirds hop and starlings run?

Both blackbirds and starlings actually do both. As a general point most birds use less energy running but it is much easier and convenient for them to hop when in a tree. Birds hop partly for safety as they can make a quick exit, but in a safe environment they may walk or run around. There is no real logic as to why birds occasionally run, and at other times hop, other than it feels right for them at the time. One of the few exceptions is the woodpecker which always hops due to the physical make-up of its feet which make it difficult for it to walk on the ground.

DEREK NIEMANN, ROYAL SOCIETY FOR THE PROTECTION OF BIRDS, SANDY, BEDS.

220: Why do visitors always take grapes to patients in hospital?

Grapes are no easier to digest than any other fruit but they are easier to eat and may tempt patients who have lost their appetite. Along with chocolates and flowers, grapes are traditionally thought of as a special treat. For reasons of food hygiene, many hospitals actually limit edible gifts from visitors to fruit, sweets and squash. So grapes are fine as a gift to patients. However, patients with kidney failure should not be given grapes, as they contain potassium, which dysfunctional kidneys can't excrete.

SUE BOOTH, SENIOR DIETITIAN, ST JAMES'S HOSPITAL, LEEDS.

221: Is it true that British motorists have killed more British citizens than Hitler's armed forces did?

Sadly the answer is Yes. It is difficult to obtain a breakdown of the number killed during the war by Hitler's troops or by the Japanese or Italians etc so the figures are based on the forces killed by all the Axis powers. From 1939 to 1945 enemy action killed 357,116 British citizens, of which 92,673 were civilians and 264,443 were in the armed services. The Department of Transport has been publishing road death figures since 1926 and these show a total of 409,348 deaths since then. These days it's encouraging to note that although the number of cars on our roads is increasing, the number of deaths each year is now declining considerably.

ALISON LANGLEY, DEPARTMENT OF TRANSPORT, LONDON.

222: Do fish drink water?

Yes and no. There is an important difference between marine and freshwater fish in the way they're affected by the water around them. Freshwater fish absorb water through osmosis and so must pass copious amounts of urine to prevent themselves from bursting. In other words, they take on large amounts of water through the skin but don't actually drink in a conventional sense. Marine fish, however, have to cope with the reverse situation. They are constantly losing water through the skin to the stronger concentration of salted seawater outside, so they have to drink large amounts of water to keep body fluids at the correct concentration. This is done through conventional 'drinking.' Fish that live in both sea and fresh water, such as salmon, flounder, and sea trout, have the ability to use both processes.   ARTHUR RUFFELL, UNDERSEA WORLD, BLACKPOOL.

223: How far would a bullet travel if it was fired on the Moon? Could a gunman inadvertently shoot himself in the back?

How far the bullet would travel depends on the direction in which the gun was aimed. As the Moon is one-sixth the size of earth, a projectile has to travel at only one-sixth of the speed needed on earth to escape its gravitational pull and carry on into space. Earth's escape velocity is seven miles per second so the Moon's is 1.166mps. A bullet from a normal gun would achieve this escape velocity and, if aimed at earth, would not burn up until it entered our atmosphere. If it were aimed at deep space, it could travel for several billion light years. To shoot yourself in the back the bullet would have to go into low lunar orbit. In theory this could be achieved with a scaled down charge in the cartridge. Orbital velocity for the Earth is five miles per second so the Moon's is 0.833mps. With accurate lunar charts it might be possible to find a trajectory without landscape features in the way. The rather slow travelling bullet in the back might not dispose of the gunman directly but would certainly puncture his space suit and bring about his demise.

DR DAVID MORTON, DRIFFIELD, EAST YORKS.

The mass of the Earth is approximately 81 times that of the Moon, while the diameter of the Moon is a little over a quarter the diameter of the Earth. The Moon has a surface gravity of approximately a sixth that of the Earth, and escape velocity from the Moon is merely 2.37km per second as against 11.18km per second on Earth. It would be impossible for a lunar gunman to shoot himself in the back as – apart from the two hours it would take for the bullet to return – the differences in mass distribution in the Moon's crust would affect the orbit.

JOHN W. BURLEY, BRITISH INTERPLANETARY SOCIETY, DEVON.

224: Is there any meaning to the word '-royd' at the end of a surname, eg Oldroyd, Ackroyd, Boothroyd and my own maiden name, Murgatroyd?

The word '-royd' at the end of a surname comes originally from Yorkshire, from the same stem as the word road. The name literally means 'dweller by the clearings' and was added to the name of anybody who did just that. Another version of '-royd' is '-rod', as in the surname Ormerod. Speaker of the House of Commons, Betty Boothroyd's surname probably stems from the fact that a person or family called Booth once lived in Yorkshire in a dwelling by a clearing. I bet she wishes she was back there.

CHARLES FARNELL, MANCHESTER AND LANCASHIRE FAMILY HISTORY SOC, MANCHESTER.

225: My RAF number was 756215. Who was number 1 in the Royal Air Force?

The RAF was formed on April 1, 1918, by the merger of the Royal Flying Corps and the Royal Naval Air Service. Royal Flying Corps members already had service numbers, beginning with No.1, and these were carried forward into the new RAF. The man who was number one in the RFC was Mr H. Edwards, who joined the army in 1895 and retired from the RFC on October 16, 1913, so although he was officially No. 1 in the RAF, he never actually served in it. The RAF Muster Roll begins with No. 5, which belonged to W. E. Moore, who enlisted on December 9, 1889, and was Warrant Officer on April 1, 1918.

CLIVE HALLAM, RAF MUSEUM, HENDON, MIDDLESEX.

226: Who was the original Smart Aleck?

No one knows for certain but some authorities suggest it may have been the 16th Century scholar and general know-all Alexander Ross. There is no written record of Smart Aleck until the 1860s when the phrase was first noted in the US. It is widely agreed that, whatever the origin, a Smart Aleck thinks he knows everything.

GRAHAM BAKER, HARTLEPOOL.

227: Why are people 'sent to Coventry'?

The expression 'sent to Coventry' dates back to the English Civil War of 1642 to 1651. Coventry was staunchly Parliamentarian but at the beginning of the war, in August 1642, was surrounded by the armies of Charles I. Coventry invited the King and Prince Rupert into the city for negotiations but demanded he leave his army outside the city walls. Infuriated at such disloyalty, King Charles unleashed a furious assault and his armies attempted to blast their way through the city's walls but the attack was repelled. Coventrians were particularly bitter at having their offer of negotiations met by a hail of cannon balls and the resulting animosity lasted the duration of the war. They refused even to speak to Royalist prisoners housed in St John's church. The resulting fear of the Royalist forces at the prospect of being 'sent to Coventry' can be measured by the revenge exacted by Charles I's son, Charles II, on the restoration of the monarchy. In 1662 he ordered that Coventry's city walls be demolished so that never again could the city bar its gates to the Monarch.

BOB WADE, COVENTRY CITY COUNCIL.

228: Do the French ever call condoms 'English letters'?

It would make a good story if they did but unfortunately it is only half right. The French use the term *capote anglaise,* which translates as 'English hood' or 'English overcoat.' This term originated during World War I when it was considered particularly amusing by British soldiers sitting in the trenches in military greatcoats. Condom is in fact the name of a town in south west France. The official French for a condom is *preservatif,* a little irony in itself.   VIVIAN MARR, COLLINS BILINGUAL DICTIONARIES, GLASGOW.

229: Why are people with the surname Clarke called 'Nobby'? while those called Wilson are known as 'Tugs'?

During the early days of British rule in India, the local name for an office clerk was *nobi.* Under the influence of Army slang this soon became the nickname for any service personnel called Clark and few of us survived Army life without the addition of this title.

KENNETH CLARKE, CHINGFORD, LONDON E4.

A 'nobby' is a protective piece of material, elasticated at the wrist and elbow, with which an office clerk would cover his sleeves to prevent them getting worn and dirty while working with dusty ledgers etc.

M. CLARKE, COVENT GARDEN, LONDON.

'Tugs' Wilson has naval origins. An Admiral Wilson, well known for his sarcastic signals, repeatedly gave an order for a particular ship to enter harbour. The ship had engine trouble and couldn't move so Admiral Wilson sent a signal saying if it didn't comply he would 'give the bloody battleship a tug into harbour.' The name has carried on ever since for anyone in the Royal Navy with the surname Wilson.

BERNARD WILSON, PORTSMOUTH.

230: Why do so many pub names include the word 'arms'? What does it signify?

There are roughly 2,000 pubs in Britain whose names include the word 'arms.' Originally, inns on manorial land supported the local Lord of the Manor and those on Crown land advertised their allegiance to the reigning monarch. Complete royal coats of arms are rare as pub signs but part of the crest of a particular monarch has often been used rather than risking his or her portrait. Good Queen Bess issued fearsome warnings to signwriters not to do so. So we have the White Hart for Richard II, Antelope for Henry V, Greyhound for Henry VII, Rose and Crown for Henry VIII and so on. Some signs refer to a particular noble family, such as the ubiquitous Red Lion, originally the sign of John of Gaunt, while the White Horse stood for the county of Kent.

GORDON WRIGHT, INN SIGN SOCIETY, NOTTINGHAM.

231: Why do we 'lick someone into shape'?

The noted Arab physician Avicenna (979-1037) published in his journals the tale of how bear cubs were physically licked into shape and form by their mothers when first born and this incorrect fact became legend of the time. In Europe, the fact that bear cubs were licked into shape was taken to be true and stayed as such for several hundred years.

KEVIN LALLEY, CAMBRIDGE.

232: What is the origin of the phrase 'to go on a beano'?

This is a corruption of the word 'beanfeast'. A beanfeast was a free annual meal, organised by an employer for his staff. It was called a 'beanfeast' after the migratory bean goose, the food traditionally eaten at such meals.

KATE SHERRINGHAM, MUSTON, YORKSHIRE.

233: Why 'as daft as a brush'?

This expression, meaning 'stupid' was adapted from an earlier northern saying 'as soft as a brush' by comedian Ken Platt while entertaining during World War II. He used the word 'daft' instead of 'soft' to make the meaning clearer to audiences including many southerners who were unfamiliar with the meaning of 'soft' as somebody who was a bit slow. 'Brush' was probably used because it was familiar in every household. The modern version would probably be 'as daft as a Hoover' or, better still 'as daft as a Hoover promotion.'

JAMES DEAKIN, BRADFORD.

As I'm now in my 70s and clearly remember my grandmother and her twin sister using a similar expression, it must cast doubt on the idea that it originated in the last war. The full version used by those ladies was: 'As daft as a brush baht bristles.' 'Baht' means without, as in Ilkley Moor Baht'at, and it meant as useless as a brush without bristles.

BILL HENSMAN, KEIGHLEY, WEST YORKS.

234: Who was Fred Karno and what was his army?

Fred Karno was the stage name of Fred John Westcott, a comedian and stage burlesque producer popular during World War I. His army consisted of him and his troupe of entertainers who, by their eccentric humour, poked gentle fun at the new army being raised by the British Empire to fight in the trenches. Their song went: 'We are Fred Karno's Army/Fred Karno's infantry/We cannot fight, we cannot shoot/So what damn good are we?/But when we get to Berlin/The Kaiser he will say/Hoch, hoch, mein Gott/Vot a bloody fine lot/Fred Karno's infantry.' Incidentally, both Charlie Chaplin and Stan Laurel first went to America with Karno's troupe in 1910.

SIMON WESTCOTT, BIRMINGHAM.

235: Why can I get off 'Scot free' if I 'Welsh' on someone? Why not 'Irish free' if I 'English' on someone?

Scot, in this case, derives not from Scotland but from the Old Norse *skot*. Skots were local taxes paid between the 12th and 18th centuries to bailiffs or landowners. If you avoided paying these you could go 'skot free.' 'Welsh' is more contentious. The English quote the offensive old rhyme 'Taffy was a Welshman, Taffy was a thief, Taffy came to my house and stole a side of beef.' The Welsh believe it comes from the name of a corrupt English bookmaker by the name of Welch who worked the Epsom races. He was renowned for reneging on his debts.   TOBY DEARLING, CANTERBURY, KENT.

For all those worried about the pejorative use of 'to welsh', Collins dictionary says it describes bookmakers who cheat by absconding from a race course without paying out winning bets and comes from the German *welken,* to fade.   MARY BIRCH, CAERNARFON, GWYNEDD.

236: Who was the original Riley who enjoyed 'living the life of Riley'?

The origin is in a comic song called Is That Mister Reilly? written by Irish American musician Pat Rooney and popular in the USA in the 1880s. The song was about what Reilly would do if he became rich and the chorus went as follows: 'Is that Mister Reilly, can anyone tell? Is that Mister Reilly, that owns the hotel? Well, if that's Mister Reilly, they speak of so highly, Upon my soul, Reilly, you're doing quite well.'
                    DAWN HARGREAVES, BERWICK UPON TWEED.

The legendary figure of Riley is older than suggested. He figures in a number of 19th century Liverpool folk sayings apart from 'living the life of Riley.' 'When Riley docks' meant never, and 'one-eyed Riley' was any exasperating character. Sayings and songs always represent him as a seafarer, usually of Irish extraction.   ANTHONY COONEY, LARK LANE, LIVERPOOL.

237: Why are there two different types of 10p coin being minted, one with 'rounded off' edges and one with the full thickness of the coin to the edge?

To date, just over 1.1 billion new ten pence coins have been produced since the first issue on September 30, 1992. When first minted, all new ten pence pieces had a rounded edge but it was discovered that this created problems in the production process, leading to wastage of imperfect coins. So it was then decided these coins would be made with an edge that was slightly more pronounced, hence the squarer edge. Production of the round edged coins ceased after 500 million were produced and we now only produce the squarer edge.   LINDA VINER, THE ROYAL MINT.

238: What name is given to the little metal or plastic tip on the end of a shoelace?

Shoes have been worn since the very earliest days of mankind. Primitive shoes were usually made from the hide of an animal wrapped around the feet and attached with a thong also made of hide. Originally, most peoples made their own shoes though the trade of shoe making came about quite early. Then shoes and boots were made for use with laces or straps. The introduction of shoelaces as we know them probably dates from at least the early 17th century, the tip of the shoelace being knotted to stop it from fraying. From the knot at the end of the shoelace we moved in to the modern shoelace manufacture around the start of the 19th century. The knot was replaced firstly by glue or wax, then by metal and then the plastic most commonly used today. And the name of the metal or plastic tip – the tag.   BRIAN HENSMAN, NORTHAMPTON CENTRAL MUSEUM, BOOT AND SHOE COLLECTION.

The common name is 'tag' but the correct name is 'aglet' or, as there are two on each lace, a pair of aglets. The word is derived from the French *aiguillette* meaning a little needle.   BARRY SAUNDERS, WATFORD.

239: Why is a halo the sign of holiness?

A halo is a ring of light which is depicted because the Church acknowledges that the saints reflect Jesus, the light of the world. The Church honours its saints in this way. They reflect something of the glory of God and the light of Christ. The depiction of a halo in Christian art came around the 4th century and continued right through the middle ages up to the present, although these days it is not so commonly used.
THE VERY REV DAVID FRAYNE, PROVOST OF BLACKBURN.

It may surprise Christians to learn that the halo has non-Christian origins. In many ancient Middle Eastern cultures the halo symbolised the solar disc and was incorporated into representations of sun gods. Christianity incorporated many non-Christian concepts. Constantine, the first Christian Roman emperor, retained the pagan high priest's title 'Pontifex Maximus' and the use of the halo in pictures. Maintaining 'pagan' symbols was important for continuity as the Roman Empire faced social and economic disintegration. Early Christian writers used sun imagery to identify Christ as the light of salvation. As early as the 3rd and 4th centuries Christ is depicted with the 'pagan' halo about his head, incorporated with the cross.
MARTIN JOHN FAULKNER (BA HONS THEOL), NORTHWICH, CHESHIRE.

240: As teflon is a non-stick substance, how do manufacturers stick it to the pans?

The non-stick coating adheres to the pan by a combination of chemical and mechanical adhesion. Chemical adhesion is achieved through specially developed primer systems and the mechanical adhesion is by grit blasting. The primer systems contain some PTFE (polytetrafluoroethylene) so that during curing stratification takes place which binds the primer, intermediate and topcoats.   DAVID D. GALLANT, MEYER (UK) LTD., UPTON, WIRRAL.

241: As archaeologists have to dig for remains, does this mean the circumference of the Earth is getting greater?

Remains are only dug for where they have been deposited, for example by coastal or river material, which can change soil levels by several metres. In many places natural erosion has completely destroyed any archaeological deposits. We have recently seen this in terms of modern buildings such as Holbeck Hall Hotel in Scarborough, a dramatic example of a slower process which is constantly destroying our archaeological record. My colleague Dr C. W. A. Browitt of Global Seismology maintains that there is no scientific evidence to suggest the circumference of the globe is getting greater.

MRS J. ALLSOP, GEOARCHAEOLOGICAL CO-ORDINATOR,
BRITISH GEOLOGICAL SURVEY, NOTTINGHAM.

242: When you wash and wax your car in an automatic car wash, does it wax the windscreen too?

It's inevitable that the 'wax' gets everywhere the water goes in an automatic car wash, including the windscreen. Many car washes use a 'wax' which is not real wax but a cross-linking polymer to protect the car body. This causes water on the windscreen to form droplets. Initially the windscreen wipers wipe better, but then judder and squeak. The 'wax' also attracts road dirt thrown up with spray in wet weather, increasing the problem of obtaining a good wipe. Some products remove the 'wax' from the windscreen so each time you use the car wash with 'wax' you have to clean the windscreen and the wiper blades all over again.

DAVID SNELL, RESEARCH AND DEVELOPMENT MANAGER, TRICO LTD, PONTYPOOL, GWENT.

243: How does a fly land on the ceiling?

A fly has jointed, segmented legs with a pair of claws and suction pads at the end of each. It has one pair of wings and two projections called halteres, which vibrate rapidly in flight and assist balance. When it flies up to the ceiling, it stays upright until the last moment, then does a rapid backward half-somersault and lands with its feet on the ceiling.

JANET BURHOLT, DORCHESTER, DORSET.

244: A talented young footballer these days is often referred to as 'a new George Best.' With whom was George Best compared when his talent was emerging?

In his early days at Old Trafford, George Best was referred to in the press as 'the new Peter Doherty.' Peter was another brilliant footballer who won the FA Cup with Derby County in 1946, one of the finest inside forwards produced by Northern Ireland.

JOHN ROBSON, SOUTHPORT.

During my early years as an emerging footballer I wasn't actually compared with anybody but was accepted on my merits. In my recollection, the first subsequent footballer to be labelled 'the new George Best' was a young Belfast lad called Trevor Anderson who began playing for Manchester United. He was followed by Willie Morgan and a host of others until the present day when the term is applied to Ryan Giggs.

GEORGE BEST, LONDON.

245: Why do we never see an electric kettle in American films and TV movies?

In the USA, as in most countries of the world, good old electric kettles are rare. This is not because kettles are unfashionable or that they prefer to use percolators but is due to the fact that they use a different electrical voltage system to us. The US works on 110volts AC whereas the UK uses the much more powerful 240volts. For a domestic appliance, a kettle is a heavy user of power. Three kilowatts is typical and would draw a current of 27amps in the US but only 12.5 here. It would need a very thick flex and bulky cut-off switch to handle this current and the size of the element in the kettle would need to be considerably larger.

A. B. DAVIS, ST BRELADE, JERSEY.

246: Do people who are blind from birth have dreams which contain images? Do blind people see things in their dreams?

People who are born totally blind do not have dreams which contain images. Instead their dreams consist of events and experiences constructed from their other senses, such as touch or sound, and emotions, such as happiness or fear. However, very few blind people are born totally blind. Most blind people lose their sight gradually as they get older. Four out of five blind people will regain some useful vision. Because of this most blind people have dreams which contain pictures.

BERNARD FLEMING, ROYAL NATIONAL INSTITUTE FOR THE BLIND.

247: Why is Peggy short for Margaret?

Peggy is a variant of Maggie or the obsolete Meggie, both pet forms of the name Margaret, meaning Pearl. The alteration of M- to P- can be ascribed to Celtic influences and also occurs in Molly and Polly, long established pet forms of Mary. DAVID J. NEWMAN, PAIGNTON, DEVON.

248: What is the purpose of the symbol which appears in the top right-hand corner of the TV screen just before the adverts start?

The black and white square known as a 'cue dot' reminds the TV company that the programme is ending and to prepare the commercials or the next programme for transmission. With network programmes this is particularly important for the various regional companies. On ITV and Channel 4 the cue dots appear on the right-hand top corner of the screen, at 60 seconds and disappearing five seconds before the programme finishes. The BBC cue dot appears on the left-hand top corner of the screen at 30 seconds before the end, disappearing 20 seconds later, and reappearing five seconds before the end of the programme. JOHN FOX, LONDON E7.

249: What is it about frogs that gets them into so many of our fairy stories?

One of the most amazing things about frogs is the metamorphosis they go through from spawn to fully grown adults. Children can watch this change and so from a very early age are fascinated by these creatures. Frogs can swim, they can jump, they can sing and croak and they make very versatile and lively characters for fairy tales and children's books. There are also many varieties of frog from the red-eyed tree frog to the pygmy golden frog and the goliath frog which can measure up to 75cm. Not only are they able to capture the imagination of a child, thus aid the learning process, they are also perfect subjects for the illustrators of children's books. ALISON STANLEY, EDITOR, PENGUIN CHILDREN'S BOOKS, LONDON.

The fact that adult frogs are produced by metamorphosis from tadpoles – as if by magic – makes them ideally suited to fairy stories where miraculous changes are common. The frog is often used in mythology as a fertility symbol and its moist skin represents renewal of life. Plato called the frog a rainbringer while Celtic tradition calls it Lord of the Earth and associates it with healing waters. In Christian fable the frog is ambivalent, representing new life and resurrection as well as the dark repulsive aspect of sin. LOUISE CATHCART, DUNDEE.

250: Why are hilly areas, which go up, called 'downs'?

Our word 'down' is derived from *dun,* an old Celtic word meaning hill. This word was borrowed by the Anglo Saxons in whose language the word dune meant 'from the hill', or 'in descending direction.' In Middle English this became *adown.* The first letter was then lost and by Shakespeare's time the word 'down' had acquired its present meaning. This explains the paradox that today 'down' means both 'upland' and 'in a descending direction.'   KENNETH H. SHOESMITH, CROYDON.

251: Why is the day after Christmas Day called Boxing Day?

The day after Christmas is properly known as St Stephen's Day but more often called Boxing Day. St Stephen was the first Christian martyr, a Deacon appointed by Christ's disciples to administer the practical side of the early Church's organisation, including providing for the poor. He was accused of blasphemy by the Jewish authorities and stoned to death. He is remembered in the Christmas carol Good King Wenceslas. Boxing Day got its name from the 'poor box', the tradition of placing boxes in churches to collect casual offerings for the poor all year round. The boxes were opened on Christmas Day and their contents distributed by the priests on St Stephen's Day.   JOHN MEREDITH, DURHAM.

252: Does anyone know what it was Whistler said that made Oscar Wilde say 'I wish I'd said that' to which Whistler replied: 'You will, Oscar, you will'?

This celebrated exchange came about as a result of a remark made by Whistler to Humphry Ward, art critic of The Times. At an exhibition of Whistler's painting, Ward expressed the opinion that one painting was good and another was bad. Whistler told him 'My dear fellow, you must never say this painting is good or that bad. Good and bad are not terms to be used by you. You may say "I like this", or "I don't like that", and you will be within your rights. Now come and have a whisky; you're sure to like that.' It was at this point that Wilde made the famous remark to which Whistler replied so acerbically.   MARY SMITH, FERRYHILL, ABERDEEN.

253: What is the role of the 'best boy' mentioned in film credits?

The 'best boy' is assistant to the chief electrician, known as the 'gaffer.' The terms originated during the heyday of Hollywood in the Twenties when large number of electricians were required to work the complex sets. From among the team the 'best boy' was chosen to be the main person to carry out, and pass on, the orders of the chief electrician.

STEVE JAGGS, PINEWOOD STUDIOS, IVER HEATH, BUCKS.

254: We often hear of MI5 and MI6, but whatever happened to MIs 1 to 4?

The secret services were re-organised shortly before World War I, and given the names Military Intelligence 1, 2, 3, 4 and 5. Each unit represented one of the five continents as areas of operations with Europe being covered by MI5. With the beginning of the war in 1914, these were all merged under MI5 to deal with the immediate threat in Europe. As the Germans began to show success in beating the efforts of MI5, it was obvious that a separate counter-espionage group was needed and this was called MI6. JOHN McINTYRE, BEDFORD.

255: What is the natural lifespan of a garden slug? How many young can it produce in that time?

Most authorities reckon that the average lifespan is about 12 months though certain species that hibernate can live up to 18 months. There are 108 British species of slug, of which only six are real garden pests. Mostly nocturnal, they are killed off when the first frosts appear, unless they find shelter under plant pots, paving slabs or in damp houses. Slugs are hermaphrodite and during their lifespan produce about 25 transparent eggs each. The incubation period is roughly one month and from egg to adult takes about another six months. So in the lifetime of just one slug it is possible that nearly 18,000 other slugs may be born from it and its offspring. This number is reduced drastically by weather, pesticides and natural predators such as birds, toads, hedgehogs and some beetles. The largest slug, *Arion Ater,* can grow to 5ins (14cms) long.

PETER BATEMAN, RENTOKIL, EAST GRINSTEAD, WEST SUSSEX.

256: What is the origin of the symbol for the American dollar?

The dollar sign, first used in the US in 1794, is supposed to be derived from the modification of the number 8, as it appeared on the old Spanish 'pieces of eight' coin, which was roughly the same value as a dollar. The dollar sign can also be seen to incorporate the letters 'S' and 'U', supposedly to stand for United States. The word 'dollar' is of German origin, coming from *thaler,* a coin so called because its silver was mined from a place called Joachimsthal (Joachim's Dale) in the 15th century. The word travelled to England as 'dollar' and was used in colloquial English to mean a Crown – a 5s coin. HELEN TURNBULL, LEICESTER.

257: Why are there so few green cars?

It could be that you just don't notice them. Green cars tend to blend more easily into the background by day or night and this goes a little way to substantiate the myth that green cars are unlucky: other road users are not so aware of their presence. They also become black under sodium street lights. In fact, British Racing Green metallic is the most popular colour in the Rover 800 Series and green has been a standard colour in most manufacturers' ranges for years. KEVIN JONES, ROVER CARS, BIRMINGHAM.

258: What is the origin of the golfing terms birdie, eagle, albatross, bogey, etc?

The term 'birdie', meaning one shot under the par for the hole, is thought to have originated in 1899 in the US from the fact that the first ball shot through the air like a bird. After the term 'birdie' became popular it led naturally to the terms 'eagle' and 'albatross': rarer birds denoting rarer events, an eagle for two under par for the hole and an albatross for three. The term 'bogey' was used in this country in 1890 for a player who had played one shot over the par for the hole. It was referred to as 'bogey' in reference to the mythical 'bogey man', a popular character in a contemporary music hall song. A 'double bogey' means two shots over par for the hole. The warning shout 'Fore!', an elision of 'Forward ball!' was originally voiced as a warning to the 'fore caddy' who travelled ahead to mark the lie of the ball. FIONA GRIEVE, BRITISH GOLF MUSEUM, ST ANDREWS, FIFE.

Derivation of the 'bogey' dates from 1890 when a certain Hugh Rotherham, of Coventry Golf Club, devised a system of counting up so many shots over or under the norm for each hole on a golf course. Describing his system during a match with Thomas Brown, of the Great Yarmouth club, he was accused of being 'a regular bogey man' and the phrase stuck. It is still used on some Scottish courses in its original meaning which would be termed the 'par' for the hole, though in many cases this is one shot more than the expected par these days. As equipment and technique improved, when Americans began arriving in Scotland to play golf in the early years of this century, the achievable standard for each hole was in many cases reduced by one shot. This came to be known by the American term 'par' while the Americans took the comparative term 'bogey' back to the US in the form of 'one over par.' With US domination of the international game in the years that followed, this meaning became general. IAN SIMPSON, INVERNESS.

259: The last decade was the Eighties and this is the Nineties, but what will the next decade be called?

At the start of the 1800s and 1900s the decades were known quite simply as the 'eighteen hundreds' and 'nineteen hundreds.' However, in these supposedly sophisticated days the simple answer is that whoever coins the phrase that captures the imagination of the media and the public will have answered the question. My suggestions of the 'first decade', the 'millennia', or considering we will be following the 'caring nineties,' how about the 'naughty noughties'? JANET HUTTON, LITTLE LEVER, BOLTON.

260: Why does bad weather always depress us?

The depression suffered by some people in winter or any prolonged bout of bad weather is believed to be due to lack of sunlight. There seems to be a link between the amount of light the body receives and the state of the mind. Certain weather conditions, such as the passage of a low pressure system and the cold winds at the rear of the depression, are definitely 'biologically unfavourable' and affect our ability to work efficiently. An increase in the frequency of accidents generally coincides with these periods and physical ailments can be aggravated by it, adding to our misery. Perhaps, in far off times, we were meant to hibernate, like bears and tortoises and sleep the cold dark months away. But humans had to stay awake – so we could complain about the weather. DR G. KINGSTON, LIVERPOOL.

261: There's a band named it and a song by Steely Dan but who or what was 'Deacon Blue'?

The name Deacon Blue appears to be an invention of the song's composers, Walter Becker and Donald Fagen of Steely Dan. Yearning for an alternative to a humdrum nine-to-five existence, the protagonist of the song dreams of an 'after-hours' world populated by gamblers, jazz musicians and enigmatic femme fatales. He pictures himself entering this world and partaking of its imagined pleasures; drinking expensive scotch, paying court to languid beauties and becoming a renowned jazz saxophonist. Deacon Blues is the alias he intends to use once this exciting new lifestyle gets underway, an exotic nickname like Mister Bojangles or Captain Soul. Hence the chorus: 'Call me Deacon Blue.' In choosing this name, Becker and Fagen were probably influenced by the tradition of the picaresque 'Deacon' character who appears frequently in lyrics of blues songs from the Twenties onwards. NICK WAISENFELD, BURTON-ON-TRENT, STAFFS.

The answer may be less exotic than has been thought. Recently returned from North Carolina, I discovered the clue lies in the song line: 'They call Alabama The Crimson Tide; call me Deacon Blue.' This area of the US is a hotbed of rival college basketball teams. The Alabama team is known as The Crimson Tide because of its red shirts. Their great rivals are the Deacons, known as the Deacon Blues. The protagonist of the song is simply swearing allegiance to his old college team.

LEON GREENWOOD, WILMSLOW, CHESHIRE.

262: What makes a rainbow bowshaped and not straight?

The rainbow is part of a circle of light, reflected in raindrops and can be seen only as you look away from the sun. The rainbow seen by one person will be slightly different from that seen by someone standing next to them because this is purely an optical phenomenon. As we only see rainbows only in raindrops then obviously the horizon stops the full circle from forming. When the sun is just setting it is possible to see almost a complete half-circle but when the sun is high in the sky it is only possible to see a shallow arc of the rainbow. It is not possible to see a straight rainbow, though at certain extreme times, such as when the sun is at its highest point a rainbow may seem straighter. This comes from seeing just the top of the rainbow. There are other phenomena caused similarly by reflection and refraction. Most of these are halos which appear around the sun when a layer of high cirrostratus comes across the sun. These can form a variety of shapes, parts of a circle and are usually white though they can give off an iridescent colour.   BARRY PARKER, MET OFFICE, BRACKNELL.

263: Why are clothes labels made out of the scratchiest possible material?

Modern clothes labels have to be colourfast at any temperature and carry the brand name and washing instruction symbols in easy-to-read type. Designer labels are often positioned in seams which will not hang close to the body to prevent irritation and the temptation to cut them off. Some modern labels are made from economical paper fibre and these are obviously not meant to last long.   JANE RENWICK, BRADFORD.

264: How did the expression 'laughing like a drain' originate?

Eric Partridge's Dictionary of Forces Slang, published 1948, says this expression originated among Army and Navy officers who likened loud laughter in the officers' mess to the sound of drainage systems.

AMANDA HOOLEY, ASHTON UNDER LYNE.

265: How on earth do they start to build a lighthouse in the middle of a rough sea?

Building rock lighthouses requires a remarkable amount of skill, courage and determination from engineers and seamen, contending with severe weather and sea conditions. The last rock lighthouse built by Trinity House was Bishop Rock, started in 1857. The site was surrounded by a heavy 'coffer' dam dropped in place while waves swept over the rocks. The sea water was then pumped out so that masons could start work on a dry rock face. The lowest building stones were laid 1ft beneath the low water mark. Granite blocks, weighing one to two tons, were set in position and dovetailed at sides, top, and bottom forming an immovable mass. The lighthouse was completed in 1858. An inspection in 1881 revealed extensive structural damage and heavy granite blocks had to be sunk into the surrounding rock, held in place with heavy bolts. A new masonry casing averaging 3.5ft thick was built around the lighthouse encasing the original structure.   RUSSELL DUNHAM, TRINITY HOUSE LIGHTHOUSE SERVICE, LONDON.

Bishop Rock lighthouse was unlucky not to have been built by my forebear, Robert Stevenson – perhaps then it wouldn't have needed massive repairs just 23 years after its completion. Robert was commissioned to build a lighthouse on Bell Rock, in the North Sea, 12 miles off Scotland, opposite Arbroath. At high tide it was covered to a depth of 12 feet and was only briefly about four feet above the waves at low tide. Work began in 1806, on chipping foundations with pick axes. With each tide, Robert evacuated the men to a ship but this was hazardous and time-consuming so he built a wooden beacon next to the lighthouse into which the men retreated. The blacksmith even had his forge there. A tuck box, containing rations and water, was kept in the beacon and I now have that box. The beacon had rooms for supplies, for mixing cement, a dormitory and Robert's own cabin and office. The lighthouse cost £62,000 and was lit on February 1, 1811. It's still there although, like most offshore stations, it now works automatically.

JOHN POPLOE, CHIPPING NORTON, OXON.

266: Who were the two 'lily white boys' in the song Green Grow The Rushes O?

The ancient folksong Green Grow The Rushes has appeared in many languages over several centuries and in many forms, some going back to the dawn of known culture. Its repeated refrain is associated with the symbolism of the 'tree of life' from pre-Christian times. Christianity took over some of its verses, adding an extra two: '12 for the 12 apostles' and '11 for the 11 who went to heaven' and sticking the 10 Commandments in at number 10. Also recognisably Christian is the 'four for the Gospel writers.' The two 'lily white boys' have been identified as Jesus and John the Baptist. Or they may be the Eternal Twins, the waring factions of character in every person, a regular image in Celtic poetry, like the white dragon and the red.   KEITH FANSHAW, CARLISLE.

267: Why, when a band plays somewhere, is it referred to as a 'gig'?

The origin of the word is obscure but was probably first heard in the 13th century to describe a flighty girl. The word used in connection with entertainment came in the 16th century with a lively French dance known as a 'jig.' The word was adapted to 'gig', meaning to 'entertain with music' by jazz musicians in America's Deep South. The increased popularity of the jazz scene in the Twenties expanded the influence of jazz musicians and their vocabulary and the word eventually came to mean any type of entertainment booking. DAVID J. NEWMAN, PAIGNTON, DEVON.

As a musician, I've always understood the word 'gig' to be a slang abbreviation for 'engagement'. A 'gig' is an engagement or booking. ANGELA CARRINGTON, LONDON.

268: Why are money spiders so called?

In West Country folklore if you take a money spider *(arauna scenica)* by its thread and swing it three times round your head without throwing it off, then put it in your pocket, it is believed it will bring money your way. This supposed financial luck led to the nickname. JILL BAXTER, BRISTOL.

269: After a couple are married, they have a honeymoon. Where does the word come from?

The word 'honeymoon', now in common use as the holiday taken after the wedding, originally meant the period of one month (one moon) after the wedding ceremony, a time when bonding of the two people was at its most important. Old Teutonic custom required newly weds to drink mead at their wedding feast to ensure a sweet and hopefully fertile future life together. The couple were supposed to continue drinking mead, the sweet, honey-based drink, for the specified one-month period. LISA DEAKIN, LINCOLN.

270: What sales figure makes a book a best-seller?

Everything is relative. A best-selling paperback might sell anything from 300,000 to half a million copies but the time over which those sales are made determine whether it gets into the 'charts.' Some books comfortably sell on for years without going out of print or making it into Bookwatch magazine's list of best-sellers. Other titles explode onto the market, swamping the media for a few crucial weeks then, as public interest wanes, are replaced by something else. Then there's the genre factor. A certain gardening title may be acclaimed as the best book of its genre and find a comfy niche in the best-seller ranks. But, as far as the sales figures go, when competing with mega blockbusters such as Delia Smith and Jeffrey Archer, there's simply no comparison. Lists which appear in the Sunday papers and trade press are based on polls rather than sales and tend to be compiled from limited sources, without always reflecting the opinions of the majority. CHARLOTTE TUDOR, VIRGIN PUBLISHING.

271: What do you call a female daddy-longlegs?

Who, on seeing a long-limbed insect fluttering erratically against a sun-warmed window, stops to determine its sex before declaring it a daddy-longlegs? It is merely the popular nickname given to what is, in reality, a Crane Fly. Except for the most fanatical feminists of the species, female crane flies have far more urgent matters to concern themselves with, including the avoidance of rolled-up copies of the Daily Mail. Science, ironically, classifies all crane flies as feminine – *tipula simplex* – from the Tipulidae family. COLIN PARNELL, PLYMOUTH, DEVON.

In Glasgow these creatures, regardless of their sex, are known as 'Jenny Longlegs.' MARY DRUMMOND, MANSFIELD, NOTTS.

272: Why are men sometimes referred to as 'blokes'?

The slang term 'bloke,' meaning 'honourable fellow' comes from Shelta, the ancient and somewhat hybrid patois supposedly passed from generation to generation by Irish Tinkers. The term found its way into general use from the mid 1800s and in 1914 was used as Naval slang for the commander of a ship. From there it passed into more general use until the modern day when the description 'He's a good bloke' is just about the ultimate accolade which can be bestowed on a man in the English tongue. TOM BLACKBURN, KINGS NORTON, BIRMINGHAM.

273: We all know about, or have flown in, Boeings 707, 727, 737, 747, 757, and 767 and now there's a 777 but was there ever a Boeing 717?

Yes and no. In 1952 Boeing invested $16 million in building the prototype of a jet-powered transport plane which carried the designation 367.80. Its outcomes were the 707 civil aircraft and a military craft called the KC-135 Strato Tanker which went into production and was used for refuelling bombers. The KC-135, which first flew on July 15, 1954, was given the designation 717 within the company. It was similar in design and size to the 707 prototype but had a single large cargo door instead of two, and a different internal lay-out. In all, 732 KC-135As were built, plus 88 special purpose aircraft, before production ended in 1986. Many were based at Mildenhall airfield in England and there are quite a few still flying. PETER MIDDLETON, BOEING AND FLYNN COMMUNICATION, LONDON.

274: What is the origin and covert meaning of the French Resistance code poem 'The life that I have is all that I have. And the life that I have is yours'?

Possibly written by Special Operations Executive (S.O.E.) heroine Violette Szabo's husband Etienne, before his death at El Alamein, this poem was given to her by Leo Marks, Head of Codes for the Special Operation Executive, to use as a cipher for secret communication with Britain while working with the French Resistance. The poem is recalled in the film Carve Her Name With Pride which told the magnificent story of Violette Szabo, an S.O.E agent executed at Ravensbruck in 1945 along with Cecily Lefort, Denise Bloch and Lillian Rolfe and the similarly magnificent Odette Hallowes. To the young and war widowed Violette the poem was more a cipher, it was her explanation, and legacy, to her daughter Tania. It goes in full:

The life that I have/Is all that I have/And the life that I have/Is yours. The love that I have/Of the life that I have/Is yours, and yours, and yours. A sleep I shall have/A rest I shall have/Yet death will be but a pause. For the peace of my years/In the long green grass/Will be yours, and yours, and yours.

Lest we forget. RICHARD TARLING, LONDON.

275: What happens to the millions of pins used to attach cheques to application forms for privatisation shares?

Lloyds Bank Registrars manage the BT share register. During the peak fortnight of the third tranche of shares released in BT, we received 45.29 kilos (99.86 lbs) of pins attaching cheques to share application forms. A rough figure would be about 1.7 million pins. These are stored until they can be re-used in the next big share operation.

BRIAN JOHNSON, LLOYDS BANK, LONDON.

276: Who was St Swithin and what is the origin of the belief that it will rain for the next 40 days if it rains on his day?

St Swithin (or Swithun) was Bishop of Winchester and advisor to Egbert of Essex. Before his death in AD 862 he asked to be buried in the cathedral churchyard 'so the sweet rain of heaven might fall upon his grave.' At canonisation in 971, the monks thought to honour the saint by moving his body into the cathedral choir. They chose July 15 for the ceremony but it rained for 40 days, delaying the proceedings. St Swithin's shrine was destroyed during the Reformation but a new one was dedicated in 1962. People who believe the superstition that if it rains on St Swithin's day it will rain for 40 days and 40 nights thereafter are probably unaware that the date is based on the Julian calendar rather than the present Gregorian year. BYRON McGUINNESS, ASHTON-UNDER-LYNE.

277: How far could you travel back in time in England and still be able to hold a conversation with the natives?

The pace of change in the English language is so rapid that going back just ten years may cause a few conversational problems. Fifty years ago many more modern words would have been absent and, although we could manage a decent chat a century ago, the vocabulary might be a problem. Go back 200 years and you would probably notice people sounded a bit odd. Their pronunciation was different and may have sounded more American than English. Conversation may have halted at the first 'Hello' – the greeting wasn't invented until the advent of the telephone. Four hundred years ago it would have been very difficult to understand the accent though most of words we use today were in use then with much the same meanings. With a bit of practice and a good ear you could have a chat with Shakespeare and his fellow Elizabethans. Beyond that, a glance at Chaucer shows us that things would start to become very difficult. Conversation would be severely limited and the accent would become unintelligible to modern ears. Though many words sounded the same, the syntax might have you baffled. Before about 1300 you would certainly need the services of an interpreter.

EDMUND WEINER, DICTIONARY DEPARTMENT, OXFORD UNIVERSITY PRESS.

278: If you stand facing north or south, why do the clouds nearly always travel from west to east?

Wind direction and speed which determine the movement of clouds, depend on atmospheric pressure distribution. Low level winds can be extremely variable but the prevailing winds at higher altitudes are normally from west to east around the world. Winds blow in this direction largely because of the effect of the Coriolis force, whereby moving air turns to the right in the northern hemisphere and to the left in the southern hemisphere. DEREK HARDY, MET OFFICE, BRACKNELL, BERKS.

279: Why are the inhabitants of Holland called Dutch?

According to H. Riemens's book The Netherlands (New York, 1944) the English used the word Dutch to refer indiscriminately to the languages spoken across the North Sea, and the people who spoke them. At an early date the language of the Netherlands occupied an independent position among the Low German dialects spoken along the Baltic and North Sea coasts from Poland to Dunkirk. Historically one can divide the Netherlands language into Oudnederlands (old Netherlands), Middelnederlands (middle-Netherlands – called Diets or Duuts) and Nieuwnederlands (new-netherlands, also called Nederduits). The word 'Dutch' is not found in the Dutch language though our word for German is Duits/Duitse/Duitser etc.   JEANNETTE SEPPEN, ROYAL NETHERLANDS EMBASSY, LONDON.

280: What is the meaning of -stan as in Pakistan, Afghanistan, Turkestan, Kazakhstan, Turkmenistan etc?

'Stan' means 'state' and, in the case of Pakistan, which was set up after partition from India in 1947, the P is supposed to stand for the Punjab, the A for the Afghans of the North-West Frontier, the KI for Kashmir and the S for Sind.   ELIZABETH BAILEY, READING, BERKS.

'Stan' doesn't mean 'state' but equates more to the English 'land' as in England. 'Pak' in Urdu means 'pure' so Pakistan means 'land of the pure.' The name originated among a group of Cambridge students in 1932-33 who formulated the idea of a land for Moslems. Chaudhari Rahmet Ali, who led the group, also characterised the name as coming from the initial letters of Punjab, Afghania, Kashmir and Sind with the '-tan' coming from the final part of Beluchistan. His idea was initially dismissed by the Moslem League but was revived in 1940.   W. EMERSON, SOUTH NORWOOD, LONDON.

281: Why don't professional caddies use golf trolleys?

Simply because it's much easier and quicker for a strong young man or woman to carry a bag rather than pull a trolley. They can stay closer to the golfer throughout play, particularly around the greens and in rough situations, and ensure that they keep up with the player on the fairways and help with club selection quickly and without fuss. In bad weather situations it's also the case that the use of trolleys is often banned so that no damage is caused to the course.   CAROLINE OWEN, PGA EUROPEAN TOUR, WENTWORTH.

282: Why do groups of midges fly endlessly round and round more or less in the same spot?

It is part of their ritual. Each swarm consists of large numbers of males who assemble and fly above a particular object, known as the swarm marker. The marker can be anything from a bush to a human being and the males fly around it trying to stay on the outside of the swarm in readiness for a female's approach. Every now and then a female will be attracted to the swarm and she and the male which gets to her first will drop to the ground to mate. Then the female lays eggs while the male re-joins the swarm. JOHN BRATTON, JOINT NATURE CONSERVATION COMMITTEE, AMBLESIDE, CUMBRIA.

283: Why is the spiral staircase from a London underground station halfway up a rock face in Sri Lanka?

One of Sri Lanka's main tourist attractions is the Sigiriya rock, on top of which is the famous Sigiriya Rock Fortress dating from the 5th century. Close to the main route up to the fortress, in a sheltered gallery high up on the rock face, are 22 frescoes known as the Sigiriya Damsels, the only ones left of a collection that probably numbered about 500. The former British masters of what was then Ceylon decided in the Twenties to erect a convenient route up to the frescoes and obtained a spiral staircase left over from the decommissioning of some of the older tube stations built in London at the turn of the century. No one is certain which station the staircase comes from but it was shipped to the Far East and erected at great expense. JACKIE HOLLAND, YOU MAGAZINE TRAVEL EDITOR, LONDON.

284: The Michael Douglas film Falling Down portrays him as an unlikely killer with glasses but is there any evidence for the idea that people who wear spectacles are less likely to act aggressively?

Many people wear a certain style of spectacle frame to portray a particular image. As an opthalmic optician, I have clients who wish to look more intelligent, older, eccentric, good looking, kinder or, as in this case, less aggressive. Many people, some of whom do not even require glasses, come to me for advice on achieving a certain image just through the use of spectacles. It is in this way that the director of Falling Down has given Douglas the 'unlikely killer' image. Most images of killers are of men without specs. Where this comes from, I am not sure but considering two of my clients are the finest exponents of boxing this country has ever produced I doubt if there is any evidence to support the idea of 'specky wimps.' ANGELA CAMPBELL, RAMSBOTTOM, LANCS.

285: The USS (United Star Ship) Enterprise has a registration number prefixed with 'NCC.' What do these letters stand for?

The letters stand for 'Naval Construction Contract' and are supposed to signify a ship built at an official naval dockyard (in this case, the Starfleet construction yards orbiting Earth) under contract from the designated military authority of the area (the United Federation of Planets Starfleet). The number '1701' that follows these letters is composed of two two-digit codes. The first signifies the ship's class ('17'), the second the individual ship of the Constitution Class, the USS Constitution NCC-1701 being the first.

ANIL HAJI, LONDON E11.

286: Did Benito Mussolini ever say 'I'd rather be a lion for a day than a sheep for a hundred years'?

Various versions of the famous quotation appear in Benito Mussolini's speeches and the inscription on the Italian commemorative 20 lire silver medallion of 1928, depicting Mussolini in helmet with lion and fascia, says: *'Meglio vivere un giorno da leone che cento anni da pecora.'* In English this means: 'It is better to live one day as a lion than a hundred years as a sheep.'

TED KOWALEWSKI, SLOUGH, BERKS.

This phrase was not original to Benito Mussolini. He quoted it in his speeches but it was originally noticed written on a house partly demolished by artillery during World War I. A photograph of this house often appeared in newspapers and books during the Fascist era. Another of Mussolini's favourite phrases was *'Se avanzo, seguitemi; se indietreggio, uccidetemi'* ('If I advance, follow me; if I retreat, kill me') which he cribbed from Garibaldi.

L. DALMAZZEO-AUCKLAND, THURSTON, SUFFOLK.

287: Why don't we have metric time?

During the French Revolution, from 1789 to 1791, the National Assembly called for uniform weights and measures to wipe out confusion and fraud. The Academy of Science established new decimal units for weights and measures and recommended decimal time and currency. The suggested decimal division of time was: one day equalled ten new hours; one new hour equalled 100 new minutes; one new minute equalled 100 new seconds; and one new week equalled ten new days. The existing 86,400-second day would in future consist of 100,000 new seconds. But plans were abandoned in 1795 because they met with so much opposition, although a few decimal clocks and watches are still in existence. The second, minute and hour are recognised as units of The International System of Units (SI), used exclusively throughout the world, and it is inconceivable that they will ever be changed.

BASIL SWINDELLS, TWICKENHAM, LONDON.

288: Are we still paying money to America for helping us out in World War II?

From the entry of the US into World War II on December 1941, until the end of the war in August 1945, all war materials supplied to the UK under Lease-Lend were free. In exchange, Britain paid for the subsistence of US servicemen while in Britain, though this came nowhere near the value of Lease-Lend. Lease-Lend terminated with the end of the war on August 17, 1945. On December 6, 1945, the Labour Government requested a large loan from the US government, related not to fighting World War II but to pay for post-war development in Britain, such as the National Health Service. It had nothing to do with Lease-Lend, which had supplied trillions of dollars-worth of tanks, guns, planes, ships etc to Britain, free of charge, during the fighting.   TIM BROWN, MANCHESTER.

The United Kingdom is still paying money to the United States for assistance given during World War II. On December 6, 1945, a financial agreement was made between the two countries in which Britain took out two loans, the US Line of Credit and a Lend Lease. The total amount outstanding at March 31, 1993, was $1,357,249,068.16. On December 31 each year the British Government makes two payments, one on each loan. Payments made on December 31, 1992, were: US Line of Credit $99,854,122.05 principal, $19,482,127.05 interest, Lend Lease $15,615,609.87 principal, $3,046,489.45 interest.

IRENE CAMPBELL, H.M. TREASURY.

289: What were the last 78rpm records to be produced in the United Kingdom and the United States?

The last 78s in British EMI records were withdrawn from the catalogue on March 31, 1962. They were mainly royal recordings, such as broadcasts of the Coronation, and a long-running series called The History Of Music In Sound. However, these recordings were produced many years previously and were slow but regular sellers. A company called Oriole, now part of Sony Music, was still producing 78s in the UK after EMI. Oriole was recording and issuing music in 78rpm format in late 1961. These were quite old-fashioned music such as Phil Tate and his Orchestra. An interesting exception to the passing of the 78 was the release by EMI in 1992 of a limited edition 12-inch single by Irish tenor Josef Locke of Hear My Song, Violetta. In the U.S. the production of 78s did not end until about 1969, although these were for sound libraries and not for public release.

ALISTAIR BAMFORD, BRITISH LIBRARY NATIONAL SOUND ARCHIVE, LONDON.

290: If she were to abdicate, would the Queen be known as the King Mother? Or, if she abdicated in favour of William, would she be the King Grandmother?

There is no way of knowing what the Queen might choose for a new title and this is a purely hypothetical question. 'Queen Mother' has been used particularly for Queen Elizabeth because she has the same Christian name as the Queen. Previous 'queen mothers' continued to use their titles, such as Queen Mary and Queen Alexandra, so, hypothetically, there would be no need to choose a title other than Queen Elizabeth II or just The Queen. DAVID WILLIAMS, CO-EDITOR OF DEBRETT'S, LONDON.

291: Why are corned beef tins such a frustrating shape to open?

Although we know corned beef was first made in 1899 near the town of Fray Bentos in Uruguay, where there was a plentiful supply of cheap beef, it is not known exactly when the traditional corned beef can was first introduced. One reason put forward was that squarer-shaped cans took up less space than round ones when shipped to Europe. The can is tapered to allow the corned beef to be removed from the can more easily. If the sides were straight a vacuum could form as the corned beef was being removed and there would be greater friction along the sides of the can. Recent Fray Bentos research showed that the majority of consumers preferred to keep the traditional can shape, though 22.8 per cent voted for a round can. JIM HARRINGTON, FRAY BENTOS, KING'S LYNN.

292: Why is the wearing of a copper bracelet supposed to alleviate the pain of rheumatism?

After conducting research with a sample group of 110 patients, I can see no hard clinical evidence to suggest that the use of a copper bracelet prevents the progression of any form of arthritis or rheumatism. But wearing these bracelets does tend to make patients feel more secure. I first heard about the use of copper bracelets about 20 years ago and have since discovered that they were used as far back as the times of Henry VIII, who apparently gave them to his subjects. My advice to anybody who wants to wear these bracelets is simple: if you feel good wearing one, then continue to do so. DR FRANK DUDLEY HART, CONSULTING PHYSICIAN AND RHEUMATOLOGIST, HARLEY STREET, LONDON.

293: Water is H_2O – hydrogen, a highly flammable gas, and oxygen, essential for life and for combustion. Why won't it burn?

A scientific synonym of the word 'burning' is oxidation, the combination of oxygen with another element to form a separate compound often with the generation of heat. Hydrogen combines explosively with oxygen, producing water as a result. Hence, water cannot 'burn' any more.

CHARLES POLAK, BOURNEMOUTH.

294: Do people with red hair really have bad tempers?

Natural red heads do not lose their tempers any more than anyone else. However, in my experience, people descending from the Celts – Scots, Irish, Welsh and Cornish – have very pale porcelain skin giving an angelic, romantic, fairytale appearance so when they do lose their temper it can appear totally out of character. I should also point out that if you come into any of our salons and look at the redheads around you, you would be surprised to learn that about 85% are not wearing their natural hair colouring and therefore could not be expected to conform to any supposed 'redhead' standard of irascibility.

ANNIE HUMPHREYS, VIDAL SASSOON, LONDON W1.

295: Why is a kiss written as a cross?

In Medieval times, kings and queens, even the literate among them, signed documents with an X as a symbol of good faith, an oath that the contents of the document were true. In some cultures X became a compulsory binding oath without which a contract or agreement was considered invalid and not legally binding. To guarantee the sincerity of intentions further, people in the Middle Ages solemnly kissed their signatures, in a gesture similar to putting one's hand on a Bible when taking the oath in court today. The kiss became known as the 'kiss of truth' and because the kiss, as the X finalised and bound many agreements, it spawned another saying that many people think had romantic origins: 'sealed with a kiss.'

DANE KURTH, BUSSWIL, SWITZERLAND.

296: Were our great Gothic cathedrals built to formal plans, and if so, where are those plans now?

Gothic Cathedrals were indeed built to formal plans though in this country only about a dozen drawings survive. Plans are still in existence at Canterbury Cathedral and RIBA keep three designs for a chapel at Winchester Cathedral. The largest collection of drawings in this country is for Ulm Cathedral in Germany, kept at the Victoria and Albert museum. Many more examples can be found on the continent. There are dozens of plans at Strasburg Cathedral and many more in Vienna. Cathedral plans were generally drawn on parchment and many did not survive various fires and floods.

JILL LEVER, ROYAL INSTITUTE OF BRITISH ARCHITECTS, LONDON W1.

297: Why do most older houses have high ceilings in comparison with today's houses?

Today's lower ceilings result from the simple matter of money. Most modern housing is built by private developers, local councils or housing associations, all of which are subject to the need to reduce costs wherever possible. Lower ceilings reduce building costs quite considerably. Older houses had high ceilings for the sake of the grace and status provided by lofty rooms and the more practical reason of having more space above people's heads where the smoke from open fires could gather. While genteel older homes had higher ceilings, the dwellings of the poor were often tiny hovels with ceilings so low they would not now be permitted. Modern building regulations forbid ceilings lower than 8ft and this minimum has been adopted as a standard throughout the building industry.   Bob Kentish, Swindon, Wilts.

The last edition of the Building Regulations to include a minimum ceiling height was in 1976, at which time the minimum requirement was 2.3 metres, that's about 7ft 6½ins. No minimum heights were provided by either the 1985 or the current 1991 editions of the Building Regulations. Ceiling heights reduced for reasons of economy in labour and materials and to conserve energy by reducing the space to be heated.
                                  R. N. Cowling M.B.I.A.T., Spalding, Lincs.

298: Why is steak used to cure a black eye?

This is a bit of an old wives' tale, usually blamed on a Colonel Robinson of Newcastle who, many years ago, suggested laying a thick piece of prime lean beef steak against a black eye would return it to its normal colour. His theory was based on the principle of reverse osmosis. He believed the tissue around the eye would absorb blood from the steak to disguise the blackness. The meat normally came from a cool storage place so its coldness would also reduce the swelling. Doctors now question the validity of this theory. They still recommend cooling a swelling but their preferred cold compress is normally something other than steak.
                          David Lewis, Meat & Livestock Commission, Milton Keynes.

299: In the well known old dish, which is the 'Bubble' and which is the 'Squeak'?

Bubble and Squeak is the name for a dish of boiled potatoes and a mixture of greens with the occasional addition of some meat, normally sausage. It was invented as a way of using up on Monday the remains of Sunday's roast dinner vegetables. There is no 'bubble' or 'squeak' as such:

the name comes from the 'bubbling' and 'squeaking' of the food as it is reheated in semi-solid form in a frying pan or baking tray.

ERIC ANDERSON, STIRLING.

300: Why does the adhesive on the back of a stamp taste so nasty?

The adhesive on the back of stamps is made from PVA and PVA Dextrin. It is a common problem that gum tastes slightly bitter. Unfortunately flavourings are not the answer because research has shown that when applied to thin films they deteriorate rapidly. To help customers who do not like the taste, there are sponges at every Post Office counter so they can avoid too much licking. Experimental self-adhesive stamps are currently being introduced.

ALISON DAVIES, THE POST OFFICE, LONDON.

301: Why are number plates which include the figure 786 cherished by Muslim drivers?

Those Muslims who originate from the Indian sub-continent are often very keen on these number plates because all Arabic letters have corresponding numerical interpretations and the numbers 786 correspond with the expression Bismillah Arrahman Arrahim, which translates 'In the name of God, the compassionate, the merciful.' Muslims who cherish these numbers do so because carrying them is seen as a respectful alternative to carrying the words. Having these numbers on your number plate is similar to a Christian carrying a St Christopher medallion.

GAMAL SOLAIMAN, MUSLIM COLLEGE, EALING.

302: Why does a page from a newspaper make such a good glass cleaner?

Newsprint is paper made from the cheapest forms of pulp without exotic chemical additives. Originally it was about 80% mechanical pulp (ground off the tree with a grindstone) and 20% chemical pulp (chemically digested woodchips). Today this ratio is constantly changing and also includes a high proportion of recycled waste paper. So a sheet of newsprint is easily crumpled up like a duster and highly absorbent to moisture. Both these qualities make it ideal for cleaning glass as it sucks up any dirt or film on the glass without leaving a residue. The ink on the paper doesn't affect its cleaning ability.

PHIL HOWARTH, NATIONAL PAPER MUSEUM, MANCHESTER.

303: In the Old Testament, Moses fed the Israelites in the wilderness with manna. Has anyone ever found out what it was?

The Old Testament describes manna as falling like frost, white and sweet.

It did not keep overnight, did not fall on the Sabbath, could be ground like grain and either boiled or made into cakes which tasted like wafers with honey. In fact, manna appears to be the sweet resinous substance exuded from the tamarisk, and one of two other desert shrubs, when the tree is punctured by the insect *Gossyparia mannipara*. It is edible but appears only in small quantities and has none of the miraculous properties attributed to manna. The name 'manna' is likely to be related to the Egyptian *mennu,* the tamarisk exudation. KEVIN HENEGHAN, ST HELENS, MERESEYSIDE.

304: It used to be said that if you threw a half-crown from the top of St Paul's Cathedral it would penetrate a car roof in the streets below. Given the changes in our coinage and the construction of our cars, would a modern 50p piece still pierce that car roof?

The metal now used in cars is lighter and thinner but stronger than 30 or 40 years ago. Using computers and a calculation known as 'finite element analysis' engineers can work out exactly how much strength any given part of a car needs and thus save material and weight by having the metal only where it needs to be. The roof panel on a modern car carries relatively little load as this is taken by the frame in the A-post at the windscreen, the door pillars and the edge of the roof. The roof panel itself is not much more than a lid. It's unlikely that a 50p coin dropped from the top of St Paul's would reach a speed high enough to penetrate because of its low weight and wind resistance. It might chip the paint and make a little dent but that would be all. SCOTT BROWNLEE, BMW GB, BRACKNELL, BERKS.

305: Why is the Duke of Devonshire not the Duke of Devon? The Dukes of Kent, Somerset, Northumberland, for example, have not had '-shire' tacked on to their titles.

The title of Duke of Devonshire rather than Duke of Devon is used to distinguish it from the title Earl of Devon. In 1618, James I granted the title Earl of Devonshire or Devon to William Cavendish, son of Sir William Cavendish and Bess of Hardwick, believing it was vacant. Their family seat was at Chatsworth, Derbyshire, rather than Devon, but the king had the right to grant any title irrespective of where the holder might live. The fourth Earl of Devonshire was raised to Duke in 1694. Much later it was discovered that the Courtney family of Devon also claimed the title which wasn't vacant after all. So now the Courtney Earls of Devon continue holding their title while the encumbent at Chatsworth is known as the Duke of Devonshire. PETER DAY, KEEPER OF COLLECTIONS, CHATSWORTH HOUSE, DERBYSHIRE.

306: The laws of physics say that water always finds its own level, so why is the water at the Atlantic end of the Panama Canal at a different level from that at the Pacific end?

The Pacific and Atlantic Oceans are at the same level. The questioner is simply confused because ships cannot sail straight through but have to climb and then descend from ocean to ocean. Vessels using the Panama Canal from Atlantic to Pacific Ocean are raised first by means of the Gatun Locks, from which they reach the natural lake of Gatun. They then travel down the Gaillard Cut to the Port Miguel Locks, Miraflores Lake and on to the final Miraflores Locks. Once they have descended these they can sail on at Pacific Ocean level.   MRS H. BOLTON, HALE, CHESHIRE.

In fact, the Pacific and Atlantic Oceans are not at exactly the same level. Mean sea-level on the Pacific coast of Panama is more than one metre higher than on the Atlantic side. The oceans are trying to find their own level all the time but, due to tides, winds, rainfall and earth movement, this level is constantly varying. The infamous Cape Horn cold current is forever trying to top up the Atlantic.   RAMSEY WILSON, FULHAM, LONDON.

307: Whatever happened to the £2 coin?

The £2 coin was last issued in 1989 to commemorate the Bill of Rights and the Scottish Claim of Rights. In all, 4.7 million of these coins were minted but they were never intended for general circulation. They are still legal tender and no doubt are in various family coin collections.
LINDA VINER, ROYAL MINT, LLANTRISANT.

308: Who are the 'six proud walkers' and what are the 'five symbols at your door' in the song Green Grow The Rushes-O?

The 'six proud walkers' are those who had washed their feet in the six water pots used by Jesus when he turned water into wine at the wedding feast: his first miracle. The five symbols were special objects placed on or outside front doors to deter evil spirits from entering. The 'seven stars' of the song are the seven planets known to the medieval astronomers. The eight 'April rainers' are Noah and his family, the 'nine bright shiners' are the nine orders of angels and the 'three rivals' are the Holy Trinity.
ROBERT MURRAY, SWINDON, WILTS.

309: Is it bad for your eyes to watch TV in the dark?

No problem is caused visually with watching TV in the dark for long periods but people may think there is a problem because when they look away from the screen the high contrast from bright to dark causes an after image which may last for up to five minutes. The eye can adapt within seconds to a vast range of brightness levels and this ability allows us to see things on bright sunny days and keep us aware of objects in the darkest of nights. 'Discomfort glare' occurs when a very bright object is present in the line of vision. Examples of this are the need to squint the eyes in very bright sunshine or when looking at car headlights on full beam. It's very rare for the television brightness to cause significant levels of discomfort though occasionally, when the screen changes quickly from dark to light in a dark room, discomfort may occur. No lasting damage to the eye occurs from images given off from a TV screen though looking at very bright objects such as the sun can cause permanent damage to the retina.

DAVID WHITAKER, DEPT OF VISION SCIENCES, ASTON UNIVERSITY, BIRMINGHAM.

310: Why are potatoes called spuds?

Calling a potato a 'spud' is peculiar to England and Scotland. It originally meant a kind of spade or digging fork and, more particularly, the three-broad-pronged fork used to lift potatoes from the ground. The word then transferred to the vegetable itself. The word 'spuddy' was slang for a man who sold bad potatoes. ROS COOPER, POTATO MARKETING BOARD, OXFORD.

311: How would our lives be affected if the moon suddenly disappeared?

The main effect would be on ocean tides. No longer under the influence of the Moon's gravity they would be much calmer and shorelines would be more constant. Everything from global weather to insect mating rituals would be disrupted. Moonlight would be a serious loss in extreme latitudes, like parts of Norway, where it provides the only light for several months. Likely changes in the atmosphere differences would be difficult to calculate though there would be a loss of oxygen through reduction in photosynthesis. Animal and plant life would feel the difference mainly in the complete destruction of tidal/coastal eco-systems, affecting the whole food chain. Night hunting animals and birds would be severely hampered and migratory birds and insects would lose their way. The possibility of the Moon leaving our solar system is remote. It has been our companion for million of years and is, if anything, gradually getting closer to us. On the social side, the effect of losing our Moon would be unbearable. Romance would take a hammering as a walk in the moonlight would be the stuff of fairytales. Wolves and coyotes would have nothing to sing to or would have to use streetlights. There would be no more NASA moon missions and we'd have to change many of our popular songs. The cow would have nothing over which to jump. But, on the good side, we'd be rid of lunatics.   DAVID LUCAS, JODRELL BANK, CHESHIRE.

The major large difference would be to change and destabilise the combined mass of Earth and Moon in their rotation round the Sun, probably altering the Earth's orbit, with untold and probably disastrous consequences for the whole of Earth's ecology.   SIMON WHITTAKER, LONDON N5.

312: Who was the first person to wear spectacles and who prescribed them?

The invention of spectacles preceded a clear understanding of eye optics by several centuries so the first 'correction' of eyesight was very much a matter of trial and error. In the 13th Century, English philosopher and scientist Roger Bacon noted that small spherical bits of glass could magnify letters and figures. He suggested small lenses might be useful 'to old persons and to those with weak sight.' The first person to put lenses into frames in front of the eyes was probably the Italian monk Brother Alexander da Spina, who lived in the late 13th Century.

DAVID ROSE, ZEISS GERMANY, WELWYN GARDEN CITY.

313: Why is it the 'man in the street' but the 'word on the street'?

The difference between a person being in the street and the word being on the street is not so much grammatical as idiomatic. The saying 'the word on the street' originates from the newspaper practice of posting up headlines on street billboards. With a phrase like 'we watched the video on television,' the video is the object and inanimate. Humans, on the other hand, can move, and so the 'in' preposition is more often used, capturing this possibility of movement.   AMANDA ARMSTRONG, WRITERS MONTHLY, LONDON.

314: From what, who or where did Plymouth Argyle Football Club take the Argyle part of their name?

The club may have originated, and got its name, from the Argyle Athletic Club, founded in Argyle Terrace, Mutley, Plymouth, in 1886. Alternatively, the name could have come from the town's long association with the Argyll and Sutherland Highlanders, based at Seaton Barracks, Crownhill, Plymouth, in 1886 when the club was founded and on many occasions since then (though the spelling is different). This association reached a peak in 1941 when Royal Marines, many from Plymouth, who survived the sinking by the Japanese of the Royal Navy ships Prince of Wales and Repulse, joined the Argyll and Sutherland Highlanders in the subsequent fighting through Malaya to Singapore.   PAT HARRINGTON, PLYMOUTH.

315: The British Army honours civilians for outstanding services by offering them a military funeral. This was rendered to kite expert S.F. Cody in 1913 for aviation services to the Royal Engineers and Royal Flying Corps, and six sergeants carried Florence Nightingale's coffin to her grave. Have any other civilians been so honoured?

Crew members of the British airship R101, which crashed at Beauvais, northern France, on its maiden flight in October 1930, were given a full military funeral even though most of them were civilians. Their bodies were allowed to lie in state in Westminster Hall, an honour normally reserved only for royalty, apart from that other well-known civilian recipient of a military funeral, Winston Churchill.   ROY L. OUGHTAN, CAMBRIDGE.

316: How was it that the two very different traditions of football and cricket both finished up with 11 players in a team?

There is no recorded evidence as to why both ended up with 11 players. The rules for the two sports were drawn up independently. When the Football Association was formed in 1863, no provision was made for the number of players each team should have or, indeed, how long a game should last. That was left to the captains of the competing teams to decide. This changed in 1871 with the introduction of the FA Cup competition whose rules stipulated that teams could field a maximum of 11 players. Organised cricket had already flourished for almost 200 years when, in 1884, the revision of the laws confirmed the number of players at 11 per side, unless otherwise agreed. The earliest articles of agreement (for matches between the Duke of Richmond's and Mr Broderick's teams, near Godalming, in 1727) specified '12 gamesters' on each side but it was already customary to play 11-a-side. When the first general Code of Laws was drawn up in 1744 by members of the Star and Garter club in Pall Mall, all 'grand matches' were 11-a-side but those concerned missed the opportunity to enshrine the number in the laws.

DAVID BARBER, FOOTBALL ASSOCIATION; DAVID FRITH, WISDEN CRICKET MONTHLY.

317: When 'Jack fell down and broke his crown' he was treated with 'vinegar and brown paper.' Would this have done any good?

Jack's mother's household remedy for his broken crown was probably quite effective. The vinegar (acetic acid) would have stung for a while but its antiseptic qualities would have cleaned the wound. There would have been a certain amount of evaporation which would have had a cooling effect on the bruise. The vinegar was applied with a brown paper plaster whose absorbent properties should have helped the healing process. We also learn that Jill was given a very different remedy: a good spanking by her mother. This sort of thing cannot be countenanced today but the young lady probably benefited from the short, sharp shock.

B. H. MORLAND, TAVISTOCK, DEVON.

318: Is there any meaning to the words of the song A Whiter Shade of Pale?

The lyrics of A Whiter Shade Of Pale began life as a poem written by Keith Reid. In 1967, he met Gary Brooker who set the poem to music and created the band Procol Harum to record it. The meaning of the lyrics has never been fully explained but in all probability they describe the sub-conscious images experienced by someone under the influence of drugs. The marriage of these 'mysterious' lyrics with a haunting melody, based on Bach's Air On A G-String, made it one of the most distinctive and biggest-selling pop songs of the Sixties.   BEV TILLING, CHESTER.

To anyone in the Lower VIth in 1967, those words were full of the deepest meaning available at the time (short of Leonard Cohen).

'We skipped a light fandango': we're at a dance but not any ordinary dance, it's a new-fangled, exotic one, with shades of sophistication, unlike your local disco. And there are elements of traditional exuberance, with a nod to 'tripping the light fantastic.'

'Turned cartwheels across the floor': now we're showing off; typical adolescent behaviour, energetic but harmless. 'I was feeling kind of seasick': and no wonder; there has clearly been some drinking going on here. 'The crowd called out for more': the self-conscious antics of youth played out on a gilded stage.

'The room was humming harder': familiar to anyone who has had a few too many dances/drinks at any rock venue. 'As the ceiling flew away': okay, so there may be something a bit harder than alcohol going down here but it may just mean we're in a high-ceilinged, posh ballroom rather than some low dive.

'When we called out for another drink': yes, that's it; no hours of queueing at a beer-swamped bar here, there are blokes in white jackets at our beck and call. 'The waiter brought a tray': and, yes, he brings a whole tray which means we've got money and the drinking is going on for a while here tonight.

'And it was later, as the Miller told his tale': in the stretched vowels of the refrain, we are carried through into the quiet aftermath of the dancing.

We're sitting around now amid the weary limbs, empty glasses and full ashtrays, listening to a story. And what a story – the most ribald of Chaucer's Canterbury Tales. Pure third-term Eng Lit A-level stuff.

'That her face, at first just ghostly, turned a whiter shade of pale': and, yes, we're looking across at how the story affects the girls, but this one doesn't snigger. Face it: you're smitten. She's not highly tanned like all the other Carnaby Street hippies. She is pale and enigmatic. And she turns from merely ghostly to 'a whiter shade of pale' – not death but virginity.

We are faced here with the reaction of the adolescent male contemplating a young girl he idolises being confronted with the bawdy antic's of Chaucer's feisty Alisoun.

So let's listen to the girl: 'She said 'There is no reason…'': a common adolescent fallacy and, if it needed reinforcing, we were studying Camus as well as Chaucer. This belief will allow her to behave unpredictably.

'And the truth is plain to see': this belief allows her to expect me to behave as she expects. At 16 or 17, we are all for seeing plain truth. (There was even an odd magazine called it). 'That I wandered through my playing cards': she is accusing me of failing to live up to my expected behaviour, not playing my hand with sufficient determination, in an image from the Bridge Club, where we spent rainy lunchtimes.

'And would not let her be': she's turning me down, but I'm not taking no for an answer. 'One of 16 Vestal virgins': ah! the key phrase, straight out of Latin class (this is a grammar school romance, after all). And yes, it appears I've been asking her to go a bit far in practical biology.

'Who was leaving for the coast': this is the end of the summer term and she's probably going away to distant exotic beaches, where she'll meet other boys. Allegorically, she is approaching the shores of womanhood.

'And although my eyes were open, they might just as well have been closed': perfectly straightforward: I can see all of this but there's nothing I am willing, or able to do about it. Simple – and beautiful.

ANDY SMITH, LONDON N16.

319: If I accidentally drive into a river, will the electric windows on my car still operate underwater?

Should you be unfortunate enough to drive your car into a river (a very rare event) you will be pleased to know that in most cars the electric windows should still operate for long enough for you to escape. Even when the battery short-circuits, most vehicle manufacturers have a safety mechanism which makes the windows open automatically. If you do find yourself and your car in the middle of a river it may well be worth remembering that if you can keep calm and allow the water to fill the inside of the vehicle you can quite simply open the doors and swim to the surface. ARTHUR FAIRLEY, VAUXHALL MOTORS, LUTON.

320: We all know about, or fought against, Hitler's Third Reich, but what were the First and Second Reichs?

The First Reich was the Holy Roman Empire, beginning under the Frankish Emperor Charlemagne in the 9th century. It is generally supposed to have lasted until Napoleon effected the break-up of the various German principalities in 1806. The Second Reich was the German Empire of the 19th and early 20th centuries founded in 1871 under the 'Iron Chancellor' Bismarck, which came to an end in 1918 with the defeat of Germany and the abdication of Kaiser Wilhelm. The phrase 'Third Reich' was first used by the German writer Moller in the Twenties and was taken up by Hitler on his assumption of power in 1933.

K. P. BARNES, ALDERSHOT, HANTS.

321: Why aren't biscuit tins square?

When I started work in the Twenties as a grocer's apprentice, biscuits were always delivered from the wholesalers in 'tins' and 'half tins.' These containers were 'charged returnable' with a deposit of 1s (5p) on each. As the biscuits themselves were 1s per pound, it was important to return the tins. Because of the slightly 'over square' shape of the tins, it was possible to pack two half-tins inside one full-size one, saving a lot of space on the returning vehicle. I expect this is still the case.

JOHN B. HALFORD, BROWNSOVER, RUGBY.

322: Does the mint in mint sauce bear any relation to the mint in a Polo?

Mint sauce is made from the leaves of garden mint, which is spearmint, *mente plicata*. Polos are flavoured with peppermint, an oil distilled from the flowers of *mente piperita*. Pennyroyal, *mente pulegium,* is another mint and they are all related botanically. W. C. SUMMERFIELD, KING'S LYNN, NORFOLK.

323: When I was in the RAF and we had to move an aircraft, the cry would go up: 'Two – six!' and I heard this again during the Tall Ships Race. What does it mean and where does it come from?

Despite suggestions that it originated from the number of a Ministry of War form, an RAF engineering manual or the practice of having three men at each wing and two at the tail when moving an aircraft on the ground, the expression 'Two – six!' or, to give the proper command, 'Two – six, heave!' actually comes from the capital ships of the Royal Navy in the late 18th and early 19th centuries. Gun crew members were numbered and it was the job of numbers two and six to man the hauling tackles (pronounced 'tay-cles') to heave their cannon back into the firing position after its recoil from the previous shot. After reloading, the gun captain would give the order 'Two – six, heave!' ready for the gun to be fired again. This order passed into general use in both the Navy and, later, the RAF, and even in the mines when any tough manual heaving job was required.   DAVID ROBERTSON, EX-RNVR, DARTMOUTH, DEVON.

I believe 'Two – six!' or 'Get a move on!' was once *'Tout de suite!'* French for 'Immediately!' This is one of many foreign phrases which have been cheerfully garbled by servicemen into something completely different.
                                                                        B. CLIFFORD, KEW, SURREY.

324: What is the 'kibosh' and how do we put it on something?

To put the 'kibosh' on something, meaning to dispose of or ruin it, seems to have developed from the Irish *cie bais*, pronounced 'ky bosh', meaning 'cap of death'. Most famous use of the word was in the World War I soldiers' song Belgium Put the Kibosh on The Kaiser.
                                                                    GRAEME TURNER, LUTON, BEDS.

325: Why don't you get spiral escalators?

You do, though they're still very rare because they're very expensive. The first one, built by the Mitsubishi Electric Company, came into operation in a Tokyo shop in 1985. There is also one in a San Francisco department store which cost £2 million to design and build. Its spiral shape serves the store's ten levels in a manner which looks complicated but is in fact quite simple.   BARRY SALTER, LONDON N5.

Spiral escalators simply can't be made to work efficiently and economically. Otis Elevator Company, which manufactures 2,000 escalator systems a year, made a working prototype a few years ago but decided there was insufficient demand to go ahead with full production. Not only would a spiral escalator cost several times more to make than a conventional one, it would also be much more expensive to maintain because of its complicated internal mechanisms.   KIERAN GHOSH, OTIS ELEVATOR COMPANY, LONDON.

The remains of a spiral escalator were recently discovered at Holloway Road Underground station on the Piccadilly Line in north London. It was installed in 1906 by the Reno Electric and Conveyor Company, subsequently taken over by Otis, but was never used. Originally made as a fairground exhibit for display in the US, its mechanical problems were never resolved and a safety certificate never granted. You can see a photograph of it in the London Transport Museum.

PHILLIP CARTER, LONDON UNDERGROUND.

326: By whom, when and where, was Velcro invented?

Velcro was invented by George de Mestrel in 1954. The name Velcro is based on the words *velours crochet* meaning velvet hook. The story goes that de Mestrel was taking a walk in the Alps when he was inspired by the sticky seed pods of burdock burr which stick to clothing. This gave him the idea for his new 'touch and close' fastening for clothing. Nylon hooks and eyes are woven on to strips of fabric and heat treated to temper them. Only a small effort is required to pull it apart directly but when pulled laterally its adhesion is very strong. Velcro has been successful as a strong and quick form of invisible fastening for clothing, as an alternative to zips and buttons and has been particularly useful for quick theatrical changes.

LAURA TAYLOR, THE SCIENCE MUSEUM, SOUTH KENSINGTON, LONDON.

327: Why is the city of New York known as the Big Apple?

This name derives from the Jazz Age, when musicians' slang for an engagement was an 'apple.' New York was the booking everyone wanted, a sign that you had arrived in the business, so it became known as the Big Apple. But, just as Londoners never call their own city 'The Smoke', I have never, in the course of several dozen visits, heard a New Yorker talk about the Big Apple – it's a term used only by people from elsewhere and a sure sign that you're a provincial hick.

STEVEN HOGARTH, ST MARGARETS, TWICKENHAM.

328: How did passengers embark or disembark from those huge airships like the Hindenburg?

There were basically two methods for embarking and disembarking used during the airship era. German airships, like the the Hindenburg, carried a set of steps which could be let down to meet another set of steps pushed towards it from the ground. English airships, such as the R100 and R101, were loaded by means of a mooring mast, a steel structure between 150 and 200 feet high, attached to the nose of the airship while it was at rest. Inside the mooring mast a lift and stairs brought passengers to and from the airship for boarding or disembarking. There was a small waiting room at the top of the mast. A total of four masts were built throughout the Empire, for example in India and Egypt, along the route planned for airships. It was also possible to load the English airships from the ground. DENNIS BURCHMORE, CURATOR, FRIENDS OF CARDINGTON AIRSHIP STATION.

329: Why are people who look down on others called 'toffee-nosed'?

The expression 'toffee-nose' came about when the 'tuft', or gold tassel on the top of the cap worn by Oxford and Cambridge undergraduates kept flopping forward over their faces. The recognised method of stopping this happening was for the undergraduate to slightly tilt back his head. This stance had the effect of making the students look very pompous and arrogant and became known as 'tuft-nose' which evolved to become 'toffee-nosed.' DAWN MELLOR, CARNFORTH.

330: In the TV programme Thunderbirds, what did F.A.B stand for?

'F.A.B,' as used in Thunderbirds has been said to mean 'Firing on All Boosters' or 'Following As Briefed.' In fact, though, F.A.B. has no real meaning at all. The series was made in the mid Sixties when it was fashionable to say such things as 'Hey man,' 'far out' and 'fab [as in fabulous] gear.' The creators of Thunderbirds, Gerry and Sylvia Anderson, shortened Fabulous to F.A.B, more or less because it sounded trendy. PAUL CARRINGTON, VOICE OVER ARTIST FOR GERRY ANDERSON AND DISC JOCKEY FOR SIGNAL RADIO, STOKE.

331: Who was Chad and why is he forever looking over that wall?

Cartoonist George Edward Chatterton, known as 'Chat', created Chad, or Mr Chad, the cartoon of questioning bald head and fingers peering over a wall, around 1938 and Daily Mirror artist Jack Greenall included a similar chap in his Useless Eustace drawings at about the same time. But the popular form, with plus and minus signs for eyes, spread through British Forces from Royal Electrical and Mechanical Engineers (REME) colleges like those at Gainsborough, Lincolnshire, and Sidcup, Kent, from early 1941, until innumerable copies proliferated on every Forces noticeboard, lavatory wall or other available space. Army commanders had realised the need for an elite force of highly trained mechanics to service fighting vehicles in the field and began setting up the REME. Some say an army instructor called Chadwick, known as Chad, drew part of a circuit diagram on a blackboard and either he, or some wag when his back was turned, 'personalised' it into the Chad character asking 'Wot, no electrodes?' 'Wot, no .... ?' became a protest by the grumbling masses against every petty wartime restriction. Chad was such a symbol of the common man's impertinent questioning that some officers tried to ban him. One angry CO threatened 28 days' detention for the next man caught drawing a Chad only to return to his desk to find a face on his blotter asking 'Wot, only 28 days?

ARTHUR MILLER, LONDON E9.

332: What method of test is required to establish the alcohol content of wine by percentage after it has been bottled?

The same test of alcohol content is applied to wine, irrespective of whether it has been bottled or not. If a wine has been bottled, the bottle has to be opened and a small sample taken for testing. Wine contains ethyl alcohol, water, natural flavourings and sugars. To obtain an accurate reading of the alcohol content, the sample has to be distilled to get rid of the elements that would affect the specific gravity and thus distort the results. The sample is heated until a clear liquid containing only the alcohol remains; this is then measured using a hydrometer to determine the true strength of the alcohol.

DAVID CLUTTON, INTERNATIONAL DISTILLERS AND VINTNERS, HARLOW.

333: Who was Parker and why was he so Nosey?

The phrase by which we call somebody who enjoys poking their nose into somebody else's affairs – a 'nosey Parker' – seems to have been applied originally to Matthew Parker, Archbishop of Canterbury from 1559 to 1575, who had a reputation for extremely detailed inquiries concerning ecclesiastical affairs and the conduct of the clergy within his diocese.

GLADYS ROWEN, CONSETT, DURHAM.

334: What were electric storms called before electricity was discovered?

Electricity has been with us since time began and there have always been electrical storms. However, we may have seen the effects, but for thousands of years we didn't understand the workings. The word electricity comes from the Greek *electron,* meaning amber. The philosopher Thales first noted around 600BC that when amber was rubbed with silk it attracted feathers and other light objects. Electron's Latin equivalent is *electricus* and the Oxford Dictionary finds the first written use of the word 'electrick' in 1646. The word electric, or electricity came into common use only after 1752 with the discoveries of Benjamin Franklin. Before that period, such storms were called thunder storms or thunder and lightning, as in Shakespeare's Tempest.

ROGER POPE, ELECTRICITY ASSOC, LONDON.

335: Why is the game of golf played over 18 holes? Why not 20, or 16 perhaps?

When St Andrews became the accepted capital of golf, taking over from Leith, one of the most important outcomes was the adoption of 18 holes as a round. Earlier, there had been no fixed number. The original layout at Leith had five holes, ranging from 414 to 495 yards, on which golfers would play three turns. The course at Blackheath was laid out as an imitation of Leith and extended to seven holes in 1844 when the Leith Course had grown to seven. The adoption of 18 holes at St Andrews was purely accidental. Originally the course had 12 holes, laid out in a strip along the shore running out to the River Eden. The golfers would begin a round from beside the home hole and play 11 holes to the far end of the course, then turn around and play them in reverse order, holing out at the home hole. In 1764, the Royal and Ancient Club passed a resolution that the first four holes should be converted into two, reducing a round from 22 holes to 18.   GRACE DONALD, BRITISH GOLF MUSEUM, ST ANDREWS.

336: Whatever became of the little girl playing noughts and crosses in the BBC2 testcard transmission? Is she an actress?

Carol Hersee first appeared on screen in July 1967 after her engineer father used her picture in his design for a testcard for the coming of colour television on BBC2. She now has a child of her own and works as a freelance theatrical costumer for stage, film and television productions.   ANN MILLS, BBC, LONDON.

337: 'All my eye and Betty Martin': so who was Betty Martin?

This phrase is a corruption of the Portuguese soldiers' prayer, brought back to England by troopers from Wellington's army in the Peninsular Campaign. Before going into action, the Portuguese would pray to the patron saint of their country, St Martin, saying: 'Ora mihi, Beate Martin' ('Pray for me, blessed St Martin'). British soldiers, having a low regard for the valour of their Portuguese allies, corrupted this phrase into a criticism of their ability, calling it 'All my eye and Betty Martin.'   J. L. BENNET HUGHES, WHITECROSS, HEREFORD.

338: Why do burglars in cartoons carry a sack marked 'swag'? How did the word originate?

There doesn't appear to be any certain derivation for the word 'swag', which can be found in English, as slang for a crook's haul, as early as the 18th century. In its early use, it appears to mean a bulky bag or sack and, slightly later, any collection of small valuable items, with the exception of cash. In Australia, until recently, it meant the tools and personal effects of an itinerant workman or tramp. The words swygman and swig-man were in use as early as the 16th century to describe a pedlar who went round with a sack of goods. The dubious reputation of pedlars aroused suspicions about the contents of their bags.   R. POTTER, REDRUTH, CORNWALL.

When articles of a suspicious nature, whose origins were vague, were sold in street markets, second hand shops, pubs, etc, they were 'sold without a guarantee.' Many of these articles were the proceeds of burglaries and so the cartoon burglar carries his booty in a SWAG bag.

JOEL MARCUS, CLACTON-ON-SEA.

Swag may derive from the Norse *swagga,* meaning to sway from side to side, associated with carrying one's possessions in an awkward sack or bundle. Burglars are traditionally supposed to carry their ill-gotten gains in a sack.   PAUL STEWART, LEEDS.

339: When did Members of Parliament start referring to each other as 'honourable'?

The terms Honourable or Right Honourable predate the first reliable verbatim reports of events in Parliament made more than 150 years ago. This style of address within the House is intended to maintain its dignity and make criticism less direct. Within the chamber, MPs are known as 'Honourable' or 'Right Honourable' if they are a member of the Privy Council. MPs refer to a member of their own party as 'My Honourable Friend' or 'My Right Honourable Friend' and to members of another party as 'The Honourable Member for…' or 'The Right Honourable Member for…' followed by the name of the constituency represented by that person. Outside the chamber, 'Honourable' is not applied to an MP but to the sons and daughters of peers if they are not entitled to any other courtesy title. Members of the Privy Council, however, retain the title 'Right Honourable' outside the House.

SARAH PEPIN & DAVID INNS, HOUSE OF COMMONS, LONDON.

340: Why do people nod their heads for 'Yes' and shake their head for 'No'?

Charles Darwin, in his 1873 work The Expression of the Emotions in Man and Animals, put forward the theory that the actions of nodding and shaking the head to suggest 'yes' and 'no' are connected with a baby searching for, or rejecting, the breast. However, the meanings to which Darwin refers are not universal. In Greece and Turkey people toss their heads back for no and dip their heads forward for yes. Bulgarians and Indians toss their heads back for no but roll their heads from side to side to signal yes. There is such a variety of ways of saying yes and no it would seem that the actions are not instinctive but acquired.

DR PETER COLLETT, AUTHOR, FOREIGN BODIES (A GUIDE TO EUROPEAN MANNERISMS).

341: Is there the same amount of 'life' in an ant as in an elephant?

Although an ant and an elephant are very different creatures they both have the same amount of 'life'. In fact every creature on the earth, regardless of size, intelligence, longevity, etc. possesses an equal amount of 'life force'. Ants, despite weighing only a fraction of a gram, are as sophisticated as elephants. Their social structure is extremely complex, designed to maintain and develop the welfare of the colony. A single ant is proportionally far stronger than an elephant, being able to carry up to 50 times its own weight. At London Zoo, leaf-cutting ants in the invertebrate house are every bit as popular with visitors as the elephants.

DAVE CLARKE, SENIOR KEEPER, INVERTEBRATE CONSERVATION CENTRE, LONDON ZOO.

342: Why is the tail end of a bird called the 'parson's nose'?

This term was first used in the 19th century to refer to the tail end or rump of a bird prepared for the table. It followed an earlier, more derogatory, expression, 'The Pope's Nose', believed to have originated with the strong anti-Catholic feelings in the years following the Catholic King James II (1655-88). NIGEL WILCOCKSON, BREWER'S PHRASE AND FABLE, LONDON.

343: Why are numbers on a dartboard so placed?

The numbering system on dartboards is highly ingenious and laid out to encourage the need for accuracy. Low numbers are positioned either side of higher ones (20 has a five and a one on either side, the 19 has a three and a seven, the 18 has a one and a four etc), to make it more difficult to achieve a high score. Statistically the best side of a dartboard for a newcomer to throw at is the left hand side, known as 'the married man's side', where there is a greater chance of getting a better score. Who first devised the numbering system is a mystery, though a strong case has been put forward for a Mr Brian Gamlin of Bury, Lancashire, in 1896.

JIM BOWEN, BULLSEYE, CENTRAL TELEVISION.

344: How are TV viewing figures calculated?

TV viewing figures are produced by the Broadcasters' Audience Research

Board (BARB), set up in 1980. Through two research contractors AGB and RSMB, it collects viewing information from a representative sample of the UK population. More than 43,000 interviews are conducted throughout the year and from this number a representative group of 4,435 homes, known as the audience panel, are selected. TV sets and video recorders in each selected home are fitted with electronic monitoring equipment to record every day whether the TV is turned on, to which channel and who is watching it. All this information is collected in a central computer which sorts the data to produce weekly audience listings, as well as three specialist reports, the Network Report for ITV and Channel 4, the BBC report for the BBC, and the Astra Report for satellite broadcasters.

BILL MEREDITH, DIRECTOR OF AUDIENCE MEASUREMENT, BARB, LONDON.

345: How long will it take before the population of Australia becomes greater than that of its mother country, the UK?

Nobody can predict exactly when this might happen, if ever, but present growth rates for each country do allow limited projections. The population of the UK at the 1991 census stood at 55,486,800, and that of Australia at 16,849,496. Annual population growth rates of the UK is only 0.3% compared with Australia's 1.4%. If these rates remain constant, Australia will reach the present population of the UK around 2077 by which time the UK population would be about 71 million. All things remaining constant, both countries would have the same population of 76 million in the year 2100. Only 10 years later Australia would have nearly 10 million more people than the UK. However, all this is hypothetical and it's unlikely that current birth and immigration rates will remain the same for the next 107 years.   KEITH YARBOROUGH, EXILED AUSTRALIAN, LONDON NW10.

346: Why do bridesmaids in America walk down the aisle in front of the bride, but in Britain they walk behind the bride?

There don't appear to be any rules for the variation. In the UK the reason seems to be based on the practicalities of the wedding. The main role of the bridesmaids is to look after the bride so, for example, if the train of her dress became tangled they would be in the right place to straighten it. Also, in church, where most marriages take place, the bridesmaids might get in the way if they were in front. In America, the bridesmaids walk in front, usually with the shortest going first, with the bride's attendant to the left of the bride. There is a much wider choice of venue in which to get married so the problems of overcrowding wouldn't necessarily apply.   DEBBIE DJORD JEVIC, WEDDING AND HOME MAGAZINE, LONDON.

347: What is the origin of the expression 'happy as a sandboy'?

A sandboy was a boy or man who, in an attempt to make some quick money, would take his donkey through the streets, trying to sell bags of sand which he had usually obtained free from local beaches. Sandboys were held to be 'happy' because they had an uncomplicated life and a reputation for taking their day's earnings to the nearest hostelry.

HELEN MATTHEWS, OLDHAM.

348: Daily Mail colour pages have Y, M, C and K printed in the margin. I can work out yellow, magenta and cyan, but what does K stand for?

The abbreviation K stands for the key, or black plate used in four-colour process printing. Some sources say K is used rather than B for black to avoid confusion with blue even though the abbreviation for printing process blue is C (cyan). Historically, 19th Century colour picture printers would first have printed the core elements of a picture in black to use as a key on top of which other colours would be applied. Without these black key lines, it would have been difficult to tell if lighter colours were being printed in the right place.

NIALL COOK, DEPARTMENT OF TYPOGRAPHY AND
GRAPHIC COMMUNICATION, UNIVERSITY OF READING.

349: Is it true that Manchester City FC once had an amateur goalkeeper called Mitchell, who played in glasses?

My father, James Frederick Mitchell, kept goal for Manchester City in the mid-Twenties. He was an amateur and wore glasses, as well as a bandeau to keep sweat off the lenses. Born in Waddington in 1894, the son of the Amateur Billiards Champion of Great Britain, he first played football for Blackpool and moved to Preston North End in 1921. He was an amateur international for England and a member of the Olympic team. He won a runners-up medal with Preston in the last Cup Final played at Stamford Bridge in 1922. Huddersfield won 1-0 with a disputed penalty awarded in the closing moments of the game. My father jumped up and down on his goal line in an attempt to put the penalty kicker off and his antics resulted in a new law obliging goalkeepers to remain still until the ball had been struck. He played as an amateur in his first game for Manchester City at home to Birmingham City on September 9, 1922. In 1926 he left his teaching job at Arnold House School to become welfare officer for footwear firm Stead and Simpson, where he later became managing director. He turned out alternately for Manchester City and for Stead and Simpson's works 2nd XI.

J. MITCHELL, HARRINGWORTH, NORTHANTS.

In common with another famous amateur goalkeeper of the time, B. Howard Baker of Chelsea, Mitchell was noted for the prodigious length of his goal kicks. I recall watching a game when they were on opposing sides and amused themselves by kicking the ball to each other the full length of the pitch. Manchester City's captain at the time was another amateur, centre-half Max Woosnam, who used to carry a hankerchief in his hand throughout matches and was also a Wimbledon tennis player.

STAN WALLACE, NEWPORT, SALOP.

350: Why is the number 7 considered lucky?

It occurs as a special number in many cultures and traditions. There were seven days of creation, seven days in a week, seven deadly sins and seven virtues. The Lord's Prayer has seven divisions, Rome is built on seven hills, people in a state of enrapture are said to be in the seventh heaven and in the ancient world there were seven wonders. Under Pythagoras's system, one was unity, representing Deity, two was diversity, representing disorder, three was the union of Unity and Diversity, displaying perfect harmony, four (the first square 2x2=4) was perfection. Seven is made up of four and three, numbers which have been regarded as bringers of good luck since early times. Seven also features heavily in the Hebrew belief system. The three great Hebrew feasts lasted for seven days and between the first and second there were seven weeks. To swear in Hebrew is 'to come under the influence of seven things' and every seventh year was Sabbatical, a time according to Mosaic law when the land had to lie fallow. In the old ecclesiastical number system three was the Trinity, four the number of the Evangelists and seven the gifts of the Holy Ghost and the seven times that Christ spoke on the cross.

JEREMY ADELMAN, NEWLACE, MANCHESTER.

351: Whatever happened to the hue and cry?

The 'hue and cry' was a common law requirement on all members of the community to join in the pursuit of a felon by running after him and shouting loudly for the assistance of others. Its name comes from the old French verb *huer*, 'to shout' and the practice dates from the time of King Alfred (AD 849 to 899). Hue and cry was effectively in force until the formation of the first police force, the Metropolitan in 1829. It is still the duty of the public to render assistance to a police constable when requested.

METROPOLITAN POLICE SPOKESMAN, LONDON.

352: Why do people 'scream blue murder' as opposed to any other colour?

In France around 1612 there existed the word *morbleu!*, an exclamation formed from the words *mort,* death, and *bleu.* blue. The *bleu* was a euphemism for *dieu,* meaning God, so the full expression was not so different from the English 'God's death!' of about the same period. The better known *sacre bleu!* contains the same euphemism. The expression is now virtually redundant in the French language but by the mid 17th Century it had travelled to this country where it was translated into the now familiar 'blue murder.'   JOAN COOK, CHEADLE HULME, CHESHIRE.

353: Why does the brush in a nail polish bottle never reach the bottom?

The type of blown-glass bottles used for nail polish do not have an exact inner size: every bottle is unique. The brush has a minimum standard length but under certain conditions the plastic stem can react with the polish and expand. As the fibres of the brush must never be bent (which would cause problems in applying nail polish) this expansion must be allowed for so that the brush will never reach the bottom of the bottle.
                                    KATHY WILKINSON, BOOTS COMPANY, NOTTINGHAM.

354: If a golf ball and a ten-kilo steel ball were dropped together from an aircraft flying at 20,000ft, which would hit the ground first?

If both bodies were smooth-bodied and falling in a vacuum, despite having different masses they would thud into the ground at the same moment. But the problem here is one of air resistance. A golf ball has a dimpled surface to achieve a laminar flow effect, making it more aerodynamic and less affected by air friction. The 10-kilo steel ball has much greater mass but no aerodynamic advantages and would be subject to greater drag than the golf ball. The question doesn't state the forward speed of the aircraft which would make a difference to the distance these objects with different drag characteristics would travel. The golf ball would retain more of its forward motion for longer than the steel ball and would have further to travel before it ran into the ground, but it will be travelling faster and would be more affected by wind speed. As a scientific problem, we need more data input. As the basis for a practical experiment, I suspect the only way to find the answer is to get out in the field with an open mind, a hefty research grant and some pretty sophisticated tracking equipment.   J. KIM SIDDORN, HEADLEY PARK, BRISTOL.

Both objects will achieve their terminal (maximum) velocities on the way down. This velocity is governed by the drag of each object, a function of their mass (weight) divided by their frontal area. The steel ball will have a frontal area of about 142sq in, compared with the golf ball's 2.2sq in, at a weight of 47 grams. This means the steel ball has a weight to frontal area factor of 70 and the golf ball only 21. Clearly the steel ball will arrive on earth long before the golf ball. No amount of dimpling on the golf ball can reduce its drag factor sufficiently to overcome a disadvantage of more than three to one.   MICHAEL DUNCOMBE, MAIDENHEAD, BERKS.

355: What is the longest book ever published in a single volume?

The longest publication was the Yongle Dadian, or the Great Thesaurus of the Yongle Reign, written by 2,000 Chinese scholars in 1403-08 but its 22,937 manuscript chapters were arranged in 11,095 volumes. The longest work in this country was British Parliamentary Papers published in 1968-72 by the Irish University Press, weighing 3.3 tonnes and costing £50,000. It would take six years to read at a rate of ten hours a day but it was in 1,112 volume. A definitive longest book published in a single volume has yet to be established.

CAROLE JONES, GUINNESS PUBLISHING, ENFIELD, MIDDLESEX.

356: Where does the expression 'to boot', meaning 'as well', come from?

The expression used today comes from the Old English *bot*, which meant advantage or benefit. The saying has become much broader in interpretation to mean 'as well', and although still applicable to advantageous benefits or extras of an action it now also applies to the negative ones.   KEITH DANIELS, STONE, STAFFORDSHIRE.

357: Who was 'the man they could not hang'?

The 'man they could not hang' was John 'Babbacombe' Lee, born at Abbotskerswell, near Newton Abbot, Devon. He worked as a footman at the home of Miss Emma Keyes, The Glen, in Babbacombe, after being invalided out of the Navy. On the night of November 14, 1884, Miss Keyes was found murdered at her home. Lee was prime suspect, although he always maintained his innocence, and after a three-day trial, he was sentenced to death by hanging. On the morning of February 23, 1885, Lee felt reassured after being told in a dream that he would not die. He was put on the scaffold at Exeter jail three times but on each occasion the trap refused to drop, although each time Lee was removed, it worked perfectly. The sentence was commuted to a lifetime of penal servitude. Lee was released from prison 22 years later and emigrated to the US where he died in 1933. In 1971 the folk/pop group Fairport

Convention released an album called Babbacombe Lee, based on the incident. The Glen in Babbacombe no longer exists but there's still a prison in Exeter.   JULIE HANCOCKS, PAIGNTON, DEVON.

No one knows for sure why the Exeter scaffold trap door failed to work three times but the most often believed explanation is that the other prisoners who were obliged to help erect it – a temporary structure in the prison coach shed – fixed a warped plank at the point where the chaplain would stand to jam the trap shut when any weight was applied to it. The chaplain was not on his normal spot when the successful tests were carried out.   I. REES, BRIDGEND, GLAMORGAN.

Another 'man they could not hang' was a man called Clempert who toured the music halls with my father in the Twenties with an act in which he defied the normal laws of nature by using his prodigious neck to escape dying when 'hanged'. The man who escaped hanging at Exeter when the trap failed to work three times should rightly be regarded as 'the man they did not hang', since any other prison could have done the job in a trice.   JACK THOMPSON, SCARBOROUGH, YORKS.

I believe my father, escapologist John Clempert, was in a different league to more famous Houdini, who in fact copied parts of his act. Houdini claimed to have invented the milk churn escape, and several others, all regularly performed by Clempert before anyone had heard of Houdini. Houdini played only to Europe and America whereas my father toured the world, earning up to £5,000 a week. Houdini was a showman who capitalised on Clempert's fame. When challenged by Clempert to perform head-to-head, Houdini declined.   MAURICE CLEMPERT, CASTLE DOUGLAS.

358: What is the RPM (revolutions per minute) of a compact disc?

Unlike a conventional record player, the laser in a CD machine 'reads' the tracks from the inside out and the rotation speed varies from 500 to 200 revolutions per minute as the disc spins. The sound is encoded as digital data in the form of tiny pits – one 50th the width of a human hair stamped on the disc in a continuous spiral.   SIMON TURNER, THE PHILIPS COMPANY.

359: What are the 10 different ways of getting out at cricket?

They are: bowled, caught, stumped, leg before wicket, run out, handling the ball (as then England Captain Graham Gooch was reminded to his cost in the 1993 season), obstructing the field, hit wicket, hit the ball twice (unless in defence of the wicket) and, most commonly forgotten, timed out – an incoming batsman is timed out, on appeal, if he 'wilfully takes more than two minutes to come in' – two minutes from when a wicket falls until he steps onto the field of play.

BELINDA BLACKMAN, TEST AND COUNTY CRICKET BOARD, LONDON.

There is in fact an 11th way which can be entered against a batsman's name. The official textbook of cricket umpires and scorers, recognised by the MCC, states in Law 2: 'When a batsman has left the field or retired and is unable to return owing to illness, injury or other unavoidable cause, his innings is to be recorded 'Retired Not Out'. Otherwise it is to be recorded 'Retired Out'. There's nothing in the laws to prevent a captain whose side is chasing quick runs 'calling in' a batsman at the wicket whom he considers is scoring too slowly, in which case that batsman is 'Retired Out.'

E. JOHNSTON, RUISLIP, MIDDX.

360: Why do we use the name Jack Robinson in the saying 'Quicker than you can say Jack Robinson'?

There are several sources for this saying, which means 'immediately'. It may be connected with Sir John Robinson, officer commanding the Tower of London from 1660 to 1679, referring to the speed of execution with an axe.

Another popular theory connects it with an 18th Century gentleman of that name who paid flying visits to his friends but then changed his mind and went to visit somebody else.

Linguist Eric Partridge says the name was a made-up one, using common first and last names. Playwright and theatre manager Richard Brinsley Sheridan, an MP from 1780, used the phrase in the Commons when attacking the government on bribery charges. It was, and still is, the custom in the House to avoid using a member's name. In response to demands of 'Name, name!' Sheridan looked straight at Secretary of the Treasury John Robinson and said: 'Yes, I could name him as soon as I could say Jack Robinson.'

JACK ROBINSON, LINCOLN.

361: What is the origin and meaning of the expression 'touch wood'?

According to an ancient pagan superstition, touching wood was believed to avert bad luck. Certain trees such as oak, hazel, willow and hawthorn were sacred and believed to have strong protective powers. The expression came much later as a verbal echo of this practice, by now showing itself through the Christian faith as the unofficial ritual of touching any relic believed to be associated with Jesus Christ, the wooden cross, or the Saints.

JAGDISH PATEL, OSWESTRY.

362: What is the difference between a cathedral and a minster?

The answer lies at the end of the 6th century when Pope Gregory the Great sent a Christian mission to the pagan Anglo-Saxons. The clergy who came to Britain to preach the Gospel set up churches as centres of worship and places from which the teaching of Christianity might be carried to the surrounding countryside. In Latin they were *monasterium* which, in time, turned into the Old English *mynster* from which the modern term minster is derived. Some 'mynsters' were incorporated into abbeys or monasteries and some later became parish churches. Others, like York, moved up the ecclesiastical scale and became cathedrals, the seats of bishops, whose name is derived from the Greek/Latin *cathedra*, a seat or throne, though they retained the name minster, showing their early origins.

DOROTHY LEE, YORK MINSTER.

363: Why do corns hurt when rain is threatening?

A corn is an accelerated growth of the surface layer of skin or epithelium. Corns on toes develop as a result of excessive pressure, usually caused by ill fitting shoes. Their hard points press inwards, touching the nerve endings and making the toe sensitive to even the lightest pressure. Patients say even the weight of a sheet can cause them pain and increases in atmospheric pressure just before it rains can also produce discomfort.

JONATHAN BUTCHER, THE CHIROPODY SURGERY, STOCKPORT, CHESHIRE.

364: Why do we have a large number of people with the surnames Brown, Green, Black and White, but no one named Yellow, Red or Blue?

Most ordinary British surnames originated in the Middle Ages when a man was often distinguished from his neighbours by appearance, occupation or residence. Some colours as names arose obviously from distinctive complexions or hair colouring. The name Green comes from a placename. Red survives as Reed, gold as Goulden, blue as Blewit and so on. Yellow seems to have virtually died out.

DR COLIN ROGERS, AUTHOR, FAMILY TREE DETECTIVE, TINTWISTLE, CHESHIRE.

Yellow may have 'virtually died out as a surname' but my sister and I, both named Yellow, are very much alive and residing in Newcastle. We were both teachers, so many people in this area must know our name. Our father was born in Stockton-on-Tees so the family may come from that area. We are proud to have a very uncommon surname.

SHEILA AND DOREEN YELLOW, NEWCASTLE UPON TYNE.

Sheila and Doreen Yellow, who identified their name as coming from

Stockton-on-Tees, may like to know that the captain of Stockton cricket team from 1940 to 1950 was Mark Yellow. I played in that team.

JACK CONNORS, NORTHANTS.

I, too, was born in Stockton and my name was also Yellow.

MRS A. SQUIRES (NEE YELLOW), STOCKTON-ON-TEES.

The name Red is common in Scotland and Northern Ireland, though people are misled by its use in the Scots dialect form 'Reid' – just as 'head' in Scots is pronounced 'heid.' Reid can refer to someone's bloody actions but comes mostly from ancestors with red hair and weather-beaten faces. Both sources are appropriate in Scotland with its bloody history, bleak weather and wealth of redheads.

D. R. REID, SYDENHAM, KENT.

365: Whatever happened to Junction 6 on the M27?

Motorways are built in sections with junctions in numerical order. There were plans for a Junction 6 on the M27, leading towards Allington Lane, but the plans were changed and the junction scrapped after the sections either side, including junctions 5 and 7, had been completed and numbered.

ROGER GOODE, DEPARTMENT OF TRANSPORT, LONDON.

366: When a signpost shows so many miles to London, to what area of London does it refer?

This depends on which part of the country you are coming from. Approaching London from the north, it's Marble Arch; from the south or west, it's Charing Cross (traditionally the Eleanor Cross outside the station), from the east it's the boundary of the City of London. These variations are traditional, based on where the original roads into London would have terminated.

ALISON LANGLEY, DEPARTMENT OF TRANSPORT, LONDON.

My 1950 AA book says there are seven traditional markers from which stagecoach routes were marked in different directions: Whitechapel Church, Shoreditch Church, the site of Hick's Hall in St John's Street, Tyburn Turnpike at Marble Arch, Hyde Park Corner and the southern ends of London and Westminster Bridges.

PETER EMBREY, LONDON.

367: How did our present alphabet obtain its sequence of letters?

The sequence has evolved over almost 4,000 years. The word alphabet is derived from the first two letters of the Greek alphabet, alpha and beta. The earliest known version is the North Semitic, developed between 1700 and 1500BC in and around Palestine and Syria. Hebrew, Arabic and Phoenician alphabets were based on this. From the 11th century

BC, Phoenician traders travelled through the Mediterranean, setting up colonies and taking with them a version of the alphabet, containing 22 consonant letters, written from right to left. The Greeks adapted the Phoenician model in about 1000-900BC, adding the vowel sounds central to Greek word formation. The principle of writing left to right appears gradually at this time. In about 800 BC the Etrusians of northern Italy had a version of the Greek alphabet which was modified by their neighbours, the Romans. The original Latin alphabet had 23 letters, but the germs of the future J and U were contained in the letters I and V. The final letter to enter our alphabet was W which came with the doubling of U and V in the Middle Ages. When the Romans invaded Britain, their alphabet replaced the old runic forms.

MARGOT CHARLTON, OXFORD UNIVERSITY PRESS, OXFORD.

Anglo-Saxon Britain used an old script known as 'futhork', developed from the Germanic 'futhark', so named because of the initial sequence of its letters, as in our alphabet. It appeared in Britain with the arrival here of the Anglo-Saxons in the early 5th century. When the Anglo-Saxons eventually became Christian in the 7th century, they adopted the 'insular', ie Irish, form of the Roman script. A trace of the old Futhork alphabet is found in the phrase 'Ye Olde...', where the letter 'thorn' is written, for convenience, like a Y.   REV JOHN G. LOVEJOY, SUTTON, SURREY.

368: Who invented the term 'Ms'?

The abbreviation 'Ms', used to replace Miss or Mrs in a female title, has its origin in the Women's Liberation Movement in America in the early Fifties. As with most movements and the terms they use, no one person has been accredited with coining the title. It took roughly 20 years before it gained prominence in the women's movement as a whole, suggesting that it may have been re-invented several times.

MRS (PREVIOUSLY MS) JO WARHURST, SUTTON, SURREY.

Though adopted by Sixties feminists and popularised when the American Women's Liberation Movement launched Ms magazine in 1972, many now believe 'Ms' wasn't invented as a great liberating leap forward for women but first used by the American mail order industry simply as a way of indicating a person's gender in two convenient letters, without bothering about their marital status.   MARIA MANLEY, ORPINGTON, KENT.

369: Why is thousand island dressing so called?

The Thousand Islands are to be found in the St Lawrence River, Ontario, one of which was at one time owned by George Boldt, proprietor of the Waldorf-Astoria in New York. Boldt's steward devised a salad dressing which so pleased Boldt that he gave it the name by which it is now so well known. The steward later became the famous Oscar of the Waldorf.

NORMAN S. ASTON, ABBEYDALE, GLOUCS.

370: Who was Springheeled Jack?

Exactly who or what Springheeled Jack was has never been established. First reports of the phenomenon came from people crossing Barnes Common, London, in 1837, who reported seeing an alarming figure, wearing a white costume and helmet, flying through the air in great leaps. For the next 67 years he was regularly sighted all over England and blamed for a series of vicious attacks, particularly on young women as they walked alone. Some reported that he spat fire in their faces. On one occasion he is said to have called to a young lady at a country house: 'Hurry, bring a light, for we have caught Springheeled Jack in the lane.' She hurriedly got a candle and went outside where he pounced on her, clawing at her face and neck. Soldiers refused to go on night duty, claiming Jack would slap their faces and jump on their sentry boxes. There were rumours at the time that he was the Marquis of Waterford, but the Marquis, though mad, was never vicious. Jack was last reported in 1904 in Everton where he was seen leaping from the street onto rooftops. A group of people cornered him there but he just smiled and disappeared and has not been seen since.

SUZANNAH TIPPETT, EGHAM, SURREY.

371: In Lancashire, anyone guilty of a minor misdemeanour is warned: 'You'll find yourself in Dickie's meadow.' Who was Dickie and what was his meadow?

Having spent much of my youth in Lancashire, I take great delight in using expressions like this to my southern friends. It originated from Richard III, the Yorkist king, who came to a sticky end in battle at Bosworth Field, on August 22, 1485. Hence, anyone in trouble is said to be 'in Dickie's meadow.'

DANIEL J. EGAN, SUNBURY-ON-THAMES, MIDDX.

References to Richard III and Bosworth Field may be too elevated an explanation for this down-to-earth expression. The 1811 Dictionary Of The Vulgar Tongue says 'dickie' was a slang word for a donkey, so if you were in Dickie's meadow you were generally in the mire.

COLIN PARTIS, GRIMSBY, SOUTH HUMBERSIDE.

372: Where do the expressions 'high jinks' and 'put a jinx on it' originate?

These are two different words with different meanings. A 'jink' as in high jinks, is probably 17th Century Scottish, meaning a frolic at a drinking party. Such a frolic would maybe lead later to you avoiding the lady you took to the party for another. Hence the U.S. Air Force used the expression 'to jink' as a way of changing altitude and direction simultaneously to avoid enemy fire. *Jinx* with an x is medieval Latin for hoodoo or bad luck. *Jynges* in primitive Latin and *Iunx* in Greek both relate to the casting of spells. Rev W. Jinks, who asked the question, can rest assured his name is not bad luck or a reason to avoid him: it's probably a shortened version of Jenkins. DAVID NEWMAN, PAIGNTON, DEVON.

High jinks was a dice game in which the loser had to assume some fictitious character or repeat a number of scurrilous verses in a particular order. Failure demanded that he take a hearty drink, so the result was often a high-spirited and noisy party. The term was also applied to a gambler who tried to make his opponent drunk. 'Put a jinx on it' is American in origin and comes from the use of wrynecks (*Jynx torquilla*, sometimes known as the Snake Bird, or *Jynx ruficollis*) in witchcraft. These birds belong to the woodpecker family and twist their necks when surprised. KEVIN HENEGHAN, ST HELENS, MERSEYSIDE.

373: Mutton was common in the past; why do we never see it today?

Mutton is any sheep meat, castrated male or female no longer required for breeding, over the age of 12 months and is still available in some traditional butchers' shops. Consumer demand for convenience cooking has changed farming systems towards younger, leaner and tenderer lambs. Stronger tasting, but slower cooking mutton has declined in popularity and farmers can now realise their assets sooner instead of keeping lambs into their second year. A small amount of mutton is still produced in upland areas of the UK, where hill breeds of sheep mature more slowly and there is a need for older, stronger sheep to assist the whole flock. These mature animals would then be eaten at festive times or when neighbours gathered to help with shearing or harvesting. Herdwick mutton was served at the Queen's coronation.
CHRIS LLOYD, NATIONAL SHEEP ASSOC, MALVERN, WORCS.

374: If we are still paying the Americans for Lend Lease, how much are the French, Dutch, Belgians, Norwegians, Danes, Italians, etc. paying us for liberating their countries from the Germans?

Unfortunately for the British Chancellor of the Exchequer, the UK is paid nothing. No agreement was made for reparation of costs incurred by the UK in liberating those countries from the Germans. It is a point of contention as to whether the costs to the UK of winning the war, particularly those incurred when we were fighting alone before the U.S. entered the conflict in 1942, inhibited our ability to compete economically in the post-war world so far as actually to outweigh the benefits of victory. A reparations agreement was made with the defeated German nation, which authorised the UK to take the Volkswagen factory. Expert representatives who went to assess the value of Volkswagen decided the Beetle car had little future and turned down the factory as a bad financial proposition. The Gulf War, by contrast, was much more businesslike. The Kuwaitis agreed to make a contribution to the costs incurred by the Allies and the final part of our payment was received in 1992.   D. M. HOLBROOK, TADCASTER, N. YORKS.

When occupied by the Germans in 1940, Norway successfully shipped out her gold, some of which is still in Fort Knox, and paid for its own Free Forces throughout World War II. Norway had at that time the third largest merchant shipping fleet in the world and, when news of the invasion was received, every ship put into an Allied port and then played a full part throughout the rest of the war.   B. K. OVSTEDAL, ROMSDAL, NORWAY.

By contrast to the behaviour of others, there is some evidence that we British were more prompt than others in paying up for the cost of World War II. The book The Wooden Wonder, on the pinpoint bombing raids by the RAF's Mosquito aircraft, says the attack on the Gestapo's Copenhagen HQ went wrong when the leading aicraft crashed into a school. Some aircraft mistook this scene of destruction for the target and bombed the school, killing many Danish children. On August 17, 1945, Air Chief Marshal Sir William Sholto Douglas presented a cheque for £20,000 to the Crown Prince of Denmark as a contribution from the RAF to aid Danes injured in raids on the Copenhagen and other Gestapo buildings.   MR G. INGLEBY, LONDON E17.

375: Had Jesus not been born, what would be the date today?

Before our modern system of dating years as Anno Domini, since the generally supposed birthdate of Christ, years were commonly dated by the length of reign of a particular monarch. The ancient Roman world dated its years by the reigns of its emperors as well as from the founding of Rome by Romulus and Remus; and this system was common in Britain on legal documents until the last century. Clearly now we would be in the 46th year of the reign of our monarch Elizabeth II.

DAVID STAINES, HOLLOWAY, NORTH LONDON.

376: In the saying 'It gets my goat', why goat? Why doesn't it get my sheep, horse, cow or anything else?

The goat has long been associated with the devil and sin in many civilisations. In early English history, the Devil was believed to have created the goat and is often shown in goat-like form. The uniquely destructive nature of the goat is generally held to have produced this association with sinfulness. 'It gets my goat', meaning to make one annoyed or angry, originated in America and suggests the subject complained of really brings out the goat-like qualities (devilishness or sinfulness) in the person complaining. TANYA MATHERS, BIRKENHEAD.

377: When a budgie looks in a mirror it thinks it sees another budgie. But cats and dogs are generally indifferent to their reflection. Why is this?

Budgerigars in their natural habitat in Australia go around in flocks that can number thousands. They are very sociable birds, totally reliant in the wild on constant interaction and can become upset if left without company. Most pet budgies, when confronted with a mirror, see another budgie and automatically attempt to communicate with it by tapping on its beak. In the eyes of the budgie it sees the other bird in the mirror move towards it and make contact with its beak. The fact that the beak of the budgie hits something hard, added to its strong desire for company, reinforces the belief that another bird is actually in front of it. Dogs and cats generally sense the presence of another animal by smells and sounds before they confirm the impression by sight. When looking in a mirror they are normally aware that another animal is not actually present because they cannot smell or hear it.

GWYN EVANS, BUDGERIGAR WORLD MAGAZINE, BALA, GWYNEDD.

378: Why do US gallons have one pint fewer than British ones?

One US gallon is equivalent to only 0.833 of the British Imperial Gallon, which is more than a pint short. Since the days of King John, British monarchs have continuously adjusted weights and measures in the attempt to establish uniform standards for accuracy throughout the land and stamp out cheating. The US Gallon is the equivalent of the Wine Gallon, established under Queen Anne in 1707. While Americans stuck to the Queen Anne Gallon, weights and measures in Britain continued to be redefined, their today's British Gallon being finally established by Act of Parliament in 1824.

INGRID MAXAM, AVERY BERKEL, WALSALL, WEST MIDLANDS.

379: Did Noah include woodworm on his passenger list?

It would seem that Noah did take the risk of allowing woodworm and termites aboard the Ark but as the voyage lasted only 40 days and 40 nights they were unlikely to sink it. Both would certainly have been around; termites evolved about 50 million years ago and woodboring beetles belong to an order that now has a quarter of a million species. The Bible, of course, assures that Noah took the precaution of treating the Ark within and without with pitch which was the most effective wood preservative available. It certainly survived a nasty case of rising damp.

PETER L. G. BATEMAN, RENTOKIL, EAST GRINSTEAD, WEST SUSSEX.

The previous answer saying woodworm would not have been much of a threat to the Ark as its voyage only lasted 40 days and nights is incorrect. The rain lasted for 40 days. Noah had to remain in the Ark for more than a year (see Genesis 8 v13-15 and 13 v5-7).

S. FROGGETT, WAKEFIELD, WEST YORKS.

380: Why do animals which lay eggs have ears on the inside of their heads and those which have babies have ears on the outsides of their heads?

All hearing organs are in fact inside the head, the distinction being that some animals have external lobes to channel the sound into the head. There are exceptions to the rule that only animals with ears produce live offspring, such as whales, dolphins etc. The primitive mammalian echidna has ears but lays eggs. Some snakes and lizards bear live young, though technically these develop from eggs held internally. Giving birth to live young is a speciality of the placental mammals, considered to be the group most advanced in the evolutionary process. Special appendages outside the head to trap and funnel incoming sounds towards the hearing organs might also be considered an advance in evolutionary complexity. Giving birth to well-developed live young can generally only be achieved by the more advanced forms of life.

A. KNOWLES, COLCHESTER, ESSEX.

Egg-laying animals such as reptiles and birds do have ears but as hearing isn't such an important sense to them, they haven't evolved visible flaps of skin around them – the 'ears' of long-eared owls are just tufts of feathers used for display. Most reptiles and birds have to move their heads to locate sounds, though many owls, which rely on hearing their prey, have one ear higher than another to achieve 'bi-focal' hearing.

CHRIS HARBARD, RSPB, SANDY, BEDFORDSHIRE.

381: If Edward VIII had not abdicated in 1936, but ruled to his death in 1972, without having had children, who would have succeeded him then and who would be monarch now?

If Edward VIII had reigned childless until his death in 1972, the throne would have passed to his rightful heir and niece, Princess Elizabeth, the same Princess Elizabeth crowned as Queen in 1953, and still reigning. Elizabeth would have taken precedence over her uncle, Prince Henry, Duke of Gloucester, in the same way that Queen Victoria succeeded to the throne in 1836 on the death of her uncle, William IV, taking precedence over his younger brothers, the Dukes of Cumberland, Sussex and Cambridge. Victoria's father, the Duke of Kent, died in 1820, soon after his daughter's birth.   DAVID WILLIAMSON, CO-EDITOR, DEBRETT'S PEERAGE, LONDON.

382: Is it true that the greeting 'hello' was invented for answering the telephone?

'Hello' as an exclamation to call attention is listed in the Oxford English Dictionary from 1854 with its various predecessors, halloa, halloo, hollo etc going back hundreds of years. The telephone was developed later so the strict answer to the question must be no. In 1854 the speaking tube was in common use in large offices and department stores and the standard method of 'calling up' the person at the other end was with a sharp whistle or hearty cry of 'halloo!' The translation of this greeting to the telephone was natural. 'Ahoy, ahoy!' was the call-up used when the world's first public exchange, which served 21 subscribers in New Haven, Connecticut, opened in January 1878. When the first public exchange in the British Empire opened in Ontario six months later, operators there employed 'Well?' and 'Are you there?' In his book The Birth and Babyhood of the Telephone, published in 1913, Alexander Graham Bell's assistant Thomas Watson notes 'Ahoy!' was the first telephone shout used during experiments, superseded by 'Hello!' when the telephone got into practical use.   ROBERT DUNNETT, BRITISH TELECOM.

383: Sod's Law and Murphy's Law dictate that bad events will happen, but is there a law for good things happening?

Someone who expects good things to happen is known as a 'Pollyanna' after the constantly cheerful and optimistic heroine of the children's books by Eleanor Hodgman Porter (1868-1920). Such a person, who always looks on the bright side of things and is only aware of good things happening to them is subject to the 'Laws of Pollyanna.'

LESLIE BLACK, SWINDON.

Horace Walpole coined the word 'serendipity' to denote the faculty for making lucky and unexpected finds by accident. This was based on the fairy story The Three Princes Of Serendip (the ancient name for Sri Lanka), who were 'always making discoveries, by accidents and sagacity, of things they were not in quest of'. Serendipity has long been one of my favourite words and deserves a wider circulation.

RICHARD BURROWS, TUNBRIDGE WELLS, KENT.

384: An aircraft flies because the flow of air over its upper wing surface produces lift. How, then, can it fly inverted?

An aircraft achieves lift partly through lower air pressure over the upper surface of the wing, by virtue of the airfoil shape, and partly by means of the 'angle of attack', the angle between the wing and the relative airflow, forcing it upwards. Lift achieved in this latter manner breaks away, causing the wing to stall at about 16 degrees. To fly inverted, an aircraft must reverse the roles of the upper and lower wing surfaces. To produce the correct angle of attack and maintain flight while upside down, most aircraft adopt a nose-high configuration. With carburettor piston engines, this produces fuel starvation and inverted flight cannot be sustained for long periods.

PATRICK TULL, TAUNTON, SOMERSET.

385: If Bogart never said 'Play it again, Sam' and Garbo never said 'I want to be alone', did Captain Kirk ever say 'Beam me up, Scotty'?

Captain Kirk did not once utter the immortal words throughout the whole 78 episodes of the original Star Trek series. However, the voice of Captain Kirk, actor William Shatner, does say 'Beam me up, Scotty' in several of the 22 animated versions of Star Trek. Live long and prosper.

KEVIN BLACKMORE, STAR TREK MEMORABILIA DEALER, PAGHAM, WEST SUSSEX.

386: Are oranges called oranges because they are orange, or was the colour named after the fruit?

The orange was brought to Europe from south-east Asia by Arab traders around the 9th century. It was known by the Arabic name *naranj*, apparently after the colour of the desert sands. Arriving first in Italy, then Spain, it acquired the names *narancia* and *naranja* respectively. Oranges first arrived in Britain from Spain so we adopted their name, changing it slightly to 'norange.' Over the years the letter 'n' was dropped from the beginning of the name. It appears then that the fruit was originally named after the colour but that in this country we named the colour after the fruit.

TONY GADSON, OXFORD.

387: Why do daughters seem to be more attached to their fathers?

The first love of every child is its mother. Boys can carry on quite happily in this way, but girls, when only a few weeks old, start to respond differently to their fathers. Young children have strong powers of imitation. A baby girl instinctively mimics her mother and, seeing her attachment to her father, soon starts to regard him as important and rival her mother for his attention. This tendency in daughters to please daddy is reinforced by the responses of fathers, who tend to treat girl babies in a specially protective way, so it's not surprising if daughters grow up into daddy's girls.   STELLA ACQUARONE, THE PARENT INFANT CLINIC, LONDON.

388: Where did the word butterfly come from?

The most likely answer is that in England the first butterfly to be seen each year is the Brimstone. It is a bright yellow species, which may have given rise to the name 'butter-coloured-fly'. Another, more fanciful, possibility is that in years long gone, when people were more superstitious, it was commonly believed that butterflies were fairies wearing a disguise. Fairies were accused of stealing butter and milk, so the name could have come from that.

JOHN STILL, BUTTERFLY CENTRE, EASTBOURNE, SUSSEX.

389: Why are white people called 'gringos' by South and Central Americans?

The saying 'Gringo' comes from the Spanish word *Griego,* meaning Greek. The word is used in reference to something foreign, much in the same way that we in Britain say 'It's all Greek to me' when we don't understand something. Its application to white Americans comes from the fact that during the Mexican War, American soldiers made popular a variation on a familiar song by Burns whose first lines went: 'Green grow the Rashes O, The happiest hours that ere I spent, Were among the lasses O.' Mexican soldiers, who heard this song being sung without understanding its words, noted the way the soldiers apparently used the word 'foreign' when they started to sing. So the combination of the word *Griego* with the opening two words of the song 'Green grow' became the nickname for the Americans and was quickly reduced to the now common 'Gringo', made so famous by the likes of Clint Eastwood and Lee Van Cleef.   JOSH SILVERTON, AMERICAN IN EXILE FOR 18 YEARS, LONDON, W1.

390: What is the origin of Punch and Judy? Are they named after anybody in particular?

Some believed Punch was named after Pontius Pilate and Judy after Judas Iscariot, but Punch and Judy have their origins in Italy, where the comic theatre *commedia dell'arte* sprang up in the 16th century. Using clowns and characters borrowed from folk culture, this influential public entertainment employed improvisation as its most important characteristic. Stories and characters were used to mock well-known rulers or typical peasants and this method travelled right through Europe, bringing with it other characters we know today such as Harlequin, Columbine, Pantaloon, Scaramouche and Pierrot. Arriving in England at the end of the 17th century, it sowed the seeds of today's pantomimes as well as puppet shows. Pulcinella, also known as Punchinello (and in French, Polichinelle), was one of the characters of the *commedia dell'arte* created by Italian comedian Silvio Fiorillo around 1600 and renamed Mr Punch in England. Traditionally he kills his child in a fit of jealousy, defends himself against his wife's attacks, eventually killing her too, is then arrested, only to kill or outwit everyone (including the Devil) who gets in his way. Mr Punch was originally married to Joan but this changed to Judy during the 19th century.   JACOB WRIGHT, EDINBURGH.

In his 90s, my grandfather, born in Somerset in the 1850s, remembered a story told to him as a boy by his grandparents. They knew old people in their village who had known a man named Carcass Staddon who came from Italy and brought the Punch and Judy show with him. My grandfather's name was Staddon as, apparently, were three quarters of the folk in the village there.   BETTY HILTON (NEE STADDON), WALLASEY, MERSEYSIDE.

391: Why is Portsmouth nicknamed Pompey?

There are several theories, ranging from the similarity made by Portuguese sailors between Bombay, which they pronounced Bom Bahia, and our own port; a reference to the Roman influence; or the idea that the Portsmouth Football Club created the nickname. Then again, the job of lining a march-past, a demeaning task, being given to the Royal Artillery, meant they were compared by other soldiers to 'Pompiers' after the Paris Fire Brigade. My favourite theory is that the name stems from the Spithead Mutiny of 1797, in which the captured French vessel the Pompee played a key role, being used by delegates as a meeting place while in Portsmouth. Sailors all round the country referred to Portsmouth as Pompee, because everything was going on there.

DIANE CLARKE, PORTSMOUTH CITY COUNCIL.

A lady temperance reformer (possibly Agnes Weston who founded the homes for sailors) was addressing a large crowd in the town and warning Portsmouth that if it did not mend its ways it might be buried under a volcanic eruption like the Roman town Pompeii. At this, a drunken sailor cried out 'Good old Pompeii!' and the cry was taken up all round the meeting and eventually used by the townsfolk.

OWEN ROBINSON, CHEPSTOW, GWENT.

In 1781, Portsmouth-based sailors scaled Pompey's Pillar near Alexandria and toasted their ascent in punch, 98ft up above Egypt. This feat earned them the Fleet's tribute as the 'Pompey Boys'.   GAVIN LONG, GOSPORT, HANTS.

392: What makes voices instantly recognisable? How can there be so many permutations to the timbre of the human voice?

Everyone is built differently; no two people have precisely the same shape of flesh or bone, and so there are endless permutations among the many body parts which help produce the human voice: skull, throat, mouth, teeth, tongue, jaw, diaphragm, lungs, spine, ears and so on. Just as some people can mould themselves physically to look like other people, so some can train themselves to imitate different voices. We can also pick up speech patterns by close association with others, just as we may pick up a way of walking or dressing; but the natural timbre of a human voice remains unique.   L. HOLBROOK, MUSIC TEACHER, HALIFAX.

393: Why do women rarely whistle?

There is no physiological barrier to women whistling except that, as with the spoken voice, a woman's whistle is usually of a higher pitch. In the Middle Ages whistling was thought to be 'the devil's music' and superstitious sailors believed a storm could be raised by too much whistling. A well-whistled tune was also thought to carry seductive powers, so was considered an unsuitable sound to issue from the lips of a woman. It is reported, however, that wolf-whistling is becoming more common among females as a result of the Chippendale culture.

LINDA ASKWITH, HULL.

There's certainly no physiological reason why they shouldn't. I've whistled since I was about five years old and I am now in my 80s. I was always told: 'A whistling woman, a crowing hen, is fit for neither God nor men.' My mother whistled as far back as I can remember and two of my three daughters have whistled for most of their lives. My youngest can put two fingers in her mouth and be heard 100 yards away.

E. G. COLLEDGE, MARKFIELD, LEICESTER.

In the Royal Navy signals were given by using the bosun's pipe (or whistle) and whistling on board was strictly forbidden as it may have been mistakenly interpreted as an order from the bosun's pipe, with confusing or even tragic consequences.   H. SOULSBY, BIRTLEY, CO DURHAM.

For many years I kept a newspaper cutting which reads: 'From the age of eight I was an avid whistler and my grandfather often repeated the "whistling woman" rhyme to me until one day my grandmother replied: "Ah, but a whistling woman and a hen that crows, get on in the world wherever she goes."' My grandmother, born in 1895, was a great whistler with a repertoire drawn mainly from Gilbert and Sullivan operas. My mother was a good whistler too and I am a whistler who was nearly turned out of an exam once because, without knowing it, I whistled while I worked.   BARBARA DALZELL, BEXHILL ON SEA, SUSSEX.

394: What is the origin of the saying 'sold a pup'?

In days gone by it was common practice to sell small animals in sacks for transportation purposes. Piglets were sold thus for convenience or because of the secrecy surrounding the sale of pork in areas of southern Europe. Some of these areas had been invaded by Muslims during the 8th century who, of course, had banned its pork, believing it to be unclean meat. The actual saying itself comes from the sharp practice, common in country fairs throughout the Middle Ages, of a person buying a sack said to contain a piglet only to find it had been swapped for a cat or a puppy. The expression to 'let the cat out of the bag' has similar origins.

JANET CARLTON, BARNSLEY.

395: How did the practice begin of launching a ship by breaking a bottle against its hull?

The earliest mariners put to sea in flimsy craft with no communications and only the simplest navigational aids. In nearly all cultures, sailors sought some form of spiritual protection. Boatbuilders in ancient Greece invoked the protection of the gods by sprinkling holy water or wine over the craft. Over the centuries, other valuable liquids, alcoholic spirits or perfume have also been used to 'inoculate' a boat against danger. The tradition has come down to the modern day with virtually the same purpose. Champagne is normally used now.

GILL HAYNES, P & O PRINCESS CRUISES, LONDON.

396: Why were spies, during the war, known as fifth columnists? What were the first, second, third, and fourth columns?

The idea of 'Fifth Columnists', traitors within a country, community or army working in key roles with the aim of helping the enemy, is not new though the term 'fifth column' only came about this century. During the Spanish Civil War of 1936-39, when Franco's forces were attempting to take the capital city Madrid from government forces, General Emilio Mola, who was leading the siege, claimed he had 'four army columns encircling the city and a fifth column within the city which was working on his behalf.' The fact that it was a civil war led to a situation where almost anybody could be working for 'the other side' and General Mola's statement added to the distrust within the government forces in Madrid and many innocent people were killed as suspected 'fifth columnists.'

JOHN DARREN, SOUTHAMPTON.

397: Have we any way of knowing who was our least popular ruler before opinion polls started?

Examination of the English Civil War, the proceedings that led up to it, and its results will all point to our most unpopular ruler before the advent of the opinion poll being Charles I. Born in Dunfermline in 1600 and King of Great Britain and Ireland after 1625, the evidence for Charles I's unpopularity comes from two facts: first that so many men and women supported the Parliamentary cause against their 'natural king', many dying in battle to get their opinions heard, and second, the massive crowds who converged on a snowy Whitehall on February 7, 1649, to see him executed.

KEITH GARFIELD, NEWCASTLE.

398: Why are things said to be 'as right as rain' when rain is generally a dreadful nuisance?

Most people actually see rain not as a 'dreadful nuisance' but as a bringer of one of the most important elements in our lives: water. The saying has its roots in the days before we could just go to the tap for a quick drink, for washing and cleaning, for sprinkling water on gardens etc. In those days, lack of water could spell death and any new rainfall was accepted as a good thing and not, as now, just an inconvenience to sun worshippers.

JOAN DEVLIN, MAIDSTONE.

399: Are the medals worn by athletes made of real gold, silver, and bronze?

The metal used is often determined by the nature of the event. Virtually all medals for amateur sports events are made from base metal, gilding metal which is gold coloured, cupro-nickel which has a silver colour, and bronze which is also used at all other levels. More prestigious events may feature gold plated and silver plated base metals for first and second prizes. Occasionally, a first prize will be a gold medal and a second prize will be in sterling silver. The third prize will still be in bronze.

GEORGE FELTRUP, IMI BIRMINGHAM MINT LTD, BIRMINGHAM.

400: Why was a sixpence called a 'tanner', a shilling a 'bob', ten shillings 'half a nicker', and £1 a 'quid'?

First minted in 1551, the six penny piece acquired its nickname 'tanner' in the mid 18th century in honour of Royal Mint engraver John Sigismund Tanner. It existed as part of our currency for 429 years until being withdrawn as the 2½p piece in 1980. The nickname 'bob' for a shilling (5p piece) began in the early 1800s when the word 'bob' also meant 'whole' of 'well in health,' possibly suggesting the nickname meant 'the whole shilling.' 'Half a nicker' for ten shillings (50p) comes from the Cockney word for £1, nicker, which may be related to the clay marble known as a nicker or knicker which was about the same size as a sovereign. 'Quid' was first used in the late 17th century in reference to a guinea, then a sovereign and later the £1 note. Its suggested derivation from the Latin quid pro quo – 'something for something' was reinforced when currency notes started to carry the words: 'I promise to pay the bearer...'

HUGH RESTON-MAINE, SHREWSBURY.

401: An old saying around Peterborough whenever black clouds develop is 'it looks bad over Will's mother'. Who was Will's mother?

This saying is used to mean 'over yonder', meaning not here, but not far away. 'Will' is likely to have been someone from the next village or valley who had married into a family. The name varies with areas and family groups. My husband's family always say '...over Bill's mother' because they had a Bill in the family. My relatives say '...over our Jack's mother' because there's a Jack in their family.

MRS M. A. TURNER, SUTTON-IN-ASHFIELD, NOTTS.

402: Do the babies who appear in TV serials and soaps get a fee for their acting?

Yes, they are paid a fee, sometimes quite a handsome one too. The money is normally paid by cheque directly to the baby rather than to a parent or guardian to ensure the children are not taken advantage of. A baby is only allowed on set for a limited number of hours and its feeding and sleeping patterns must not be affected. Very young children are chaperoned at all times, normally by their mother, who are also paid. Such famous names as Michael Portillo, Patsy Kensit, Jonathan Ross and Martyn Lewis were once child models or TV babies.

JENNY HEYES, TUESDAY'S CHILD MODEL AGENCY, MACCLESFIELD, CHESHIRE.

403: Why is a dishonest transaction known as a fiddle?

The word 'fiddle' comes from either the Latin *vitula,* or Saxon *fithele,* both of which are musical instruments. It was first used in connection with some form of dishonesty around 1604 when it was employed by Puritans as a criticism of fun and games. The fiddle represented 'good fun' which, to Puritans was associated with the Devil. The victim of a swindle was said to have been 'fiddled out of their money' as if they had been intoxicated by the music of the fiddle and taken leave of their senses. The term was revived by the London underworld around 1840 but had to wait another 100 years before first becoming popular in the context we now know it during World War II. JEAN HARVEY, DURHAM.

In 1986 divers recovered some artefacts from HMS Invincible, a ship which went down in 1758 during the Seven Years War. Among these was the square board on which sailors were served their meal, which gives rise to our modern expression a 'square meal'. There was a line around the edge of the board, called the fiddle, and any sailor whose meal went over the limit drawn by the line was liable to be thrashed. Hence the expression 'on the fiddle'. DESMOND CAMPBELL, CRICKLEWOOD, LONDON.

404: How do hospitals work out the price of an operation?

The estimated cost of an operation is based on the cost involved in the average patient undergoing that type of surgery. It takes into account such factors as time spent in the operating theatre, and recovery time; staff costs for that time (calculated by type and grade of consultants, registrars and nurses); the cost of materials used in the operation; and the cost of diagnostic tests undertaken in the theatre.

BERNARD CHALK, ASSISTANT DIRECTOR OF FINANCE, ST JAMES' HOSPITAL, LEEDS.

405: Why do we say 'right as ninepence'?

From ancient times the number nine has held special significance because it represents thrice three, a trinity of trinities, regarded as the perfect plural in both Christian and Arabic societies. So the number often forms part of folklore and popular sayings. The expression 'right as ninepence', meaning in perfect condition or in fine form, has its roots in the popular silver ninepenny pieces, common until 1696, which were pliable enough to be bent into different shapes and were traditionally used as love tokens. KERRI DEYES, WIMBLEDON.

406: Why is £25 known as a pony?

There is a strong link between the nickname 'pony' for a sum of money and the Old German word *poniren*, to pay. Use of 'pony' as we know it today began at the start of the 19th century when it referred to any small sum at a time when a pony was something smaller than a horse. The amount of money involved later became fixed, probably due to its frequency, as a nickname for £25. JEREMY KEMP, COLCHESTER.

Not just £25 but anything that involves the number 25 can be known as a pony. Stockbrokers call 25 £1,000 stocks 'a pony' and some people refer to a Silver Wedding as a pony. Most authorities on slang terms say this arose during the early 19th century from sayings such as: 'There's no touching her, even for a poney' supposedly referring to a widow by the name of Mrs Robinson, the suggestion being that she wanted a full size horse. KATHRYN MAXWELL, LUTON.

407: Why is it rude to poke your tongue out?

Linked with 'cocking a snook', this dates from the 19th century. The cocked snook had different meanings according to how it was performed. One hand held up to the nose with spread fingers meant 'go to hell', two hands, 'go to hell and stay there' while both hands, vibrating fingers and protruding tongue, meant 'go to hell, stay there and consort with the devil.' The poking of the tongue has passed the tests of time and is still with us, although nowadays it is used as a playful, if somewhat aggressive gesture, mostly employed by children as an act of defiance. To show how different our own culture is in comparison with others it may well be worth pointing out (no pun intended) that in some parts of Tibet people poke out their tongues as a form of greeting. GRAHAM WESTON-GRANVILLE, EASTBOURNE.

408: Is it true that most warm-blooded creatures, including humans, have approximately the same number of heartbeats in a lifetime?

This is true for most mammals. Whether you are an elephant or a mouse, your heart beats an incredible 800 million times in a lifetime. All mammals, whatever their size, breathe once for every four heartbeats, that's 200 million breaths per life. The heart acts like a pump. If you have a small heart like a mouse it has to pump much faster than an elephant's to get enough blood around the body to keep up with oxygen demands.

Hence the mouse lives fast and dies young; the elephant lives at a noble pace. But before the sceptics start counting their pulses, humans live three times as long as our pulse tells us we should, so we need three times as many breaths to keep up. Why we should be graced with such longevity we can only guess but Man is an unusual mammal in many ways.

PENNY SMITH, BBC NATURAL HISTORY UNIT, BRISTOL.

409: I have a silver plate with a picture of soldiers or sailors, inscribed: 'Commemorating the Gaspee Incident.' What was this?

Just before the American War of Independence, Rhode Island colonists were prevented from smuggling goods without paying taxes by several armed cruisers sailing up and down their coast, under the command of Admiral Montagu, a man passionately despised by the local population. On the evening of June 9, 1772, one of these cruisers, the schooner HMS Gaspee, commanded by Lt William Duddingston, while pursuing a smuggling ship, went aground at Namquit Point, close to the town of Providence. News of the grounding travelled quickly and by midnight a crowd of 100 men and boys, led by merchant John Brown, were set to take revenge on the helpless vessel. They rowed eight small boats out to the schooner and, after a short fight in which Lt Duddingston was injured by musket fire, took over the vessel. The crew were bound and taken ashore and the ship set alight. The perpetrators were rounded up in the following days but, after some bitter wrangling as to where they should be tried, the whole incident was pushed under the carpet and the men released. The incident was a source of embarrassment for the British and was used by the revolutionaries to promote further incidents of resistance in the knowledge that they could be successful.

JANE DERLING, OXFORD.

410: Is it true that on a hot summer's day a cup of hot tea is more refreshing than a glass of cold orange squash?

Yes. In hot weather, especially when exercising, the body brings into effect a mechanism which protects the organs and deep tissues from rising temperature. The core temperature of the body is monitored by part of the brain known as the hypothalamus which switches on perspiration and opens up blood vessels in the skin, allowing the skin to cool and carry away heat more effectively. The skin may feel hotter, but it is cooling us down. Drinking a cold drink briefly cools the blood running from the heart to the brain. The hypothalamus senses this cooled blood and responds by switching off the cooling mechanism, making you feel less comfortable as a result. A warm drink warms the blood running to the brain from the heart making the hypothalamus increase its efforts to cool the body, leaving you feeling more refreshed. However, both these feelings are only transient.

DR R. D. E. RUMSEY, DEPARTMENT OF BIOMEDICAL SCIENCE, SHEFFIELD UNIVERSITY.

411: Who is Bob and why is he your uncle?

Two very similar sources give rise to 'Bob's your uncle', now used to mean 'that's that' but previously meaning 'everything will be all right.' The first comes from Sir Robert Walpole (1676-1745) regarded as a prime minister who, through the power of his position, leaned towards helping out his closest friends and relatives in any way he could. The saying 'got an Uncle Bob' came to be directed at anybody who had done anything without apparently having to work for it. About 150 years later, another prime minister, Robert Gascoyne Cecil, 3rd Marquis of Salisbury (1830-1903), relaunched the phrase after blatantly appointing his nephew, Arthur Balfour, to high posts including Chief Secretary for Ireland, First Lord of the Treasury and Leader of the Commons. This nepotism helped propel 'Bob's your uncle' permanently into our language.

HARVEY STEADMAN, LONDON.

412: As a war-time wireless operator, using Morse code, I have often wondered how pictographic languages such as Japanese were rendered in wireless code.

The Japanese have several phonetic versions of their language, the most used being the Katakana Syllabary, consisting of 51 characters and 23 modifications, each of which has a Morse equivalent. In English Morse no letter is represented by more than four elements (dots and dashes), with five for some figures. Japanese Morse is extended to five elements. As a Naval telegraphist I had to learn Japanese Morse towards the end of the war. It wasn't as difficult as it sounds, though Japanese operators used to send messages very fast, at about 30 words a minute, by hand, not automatically, and tended to run modified letters together.

ANTHONY HARRIS, PLYMOUTH, DEVON.

I served in the Royal Navy intercepting enemy Morse coded messages and receiving Japanese was the hardest of the lot. Those who mastered it got 6d a day extra.

H. JACKSON, NORBURY, LONDON SW16.

As well as the standard International Morse code, used world-wide by English-speaking operators, special symbols are allotted to the accented letters of French and other European languages. Languages with totally different characters have Morse codes of their own. Japanese Morse uses the katakana alphabet and there are Morse codes of Arabic, Greek, Hebrew and Russian languages.

GEOFF ARNOLD, EDITOR: MORSUM MAGNIFAT, BROADSTONE, DORSET.

413: What is 'the gift of the gab'?

The original 'gab' probably derived from the identical Gaelic word for mouth, developed as a colloquial word related to our 'gabble', indicating too much talking or idle chatter with the suggestion of indiscretion. 'The gift of the gab' carries the more positive meaning of having a natural flair for using words.

RICHARD PATEFIELD, PRESTON.

414: If the House of Stuart had not been replaced by the House of Hanover, is there anyone alive today who could nominally have claimed the throne?

The direct Stuart line died out with the death of Bonny Prince Charlie. The man regarded as the senior representative and 'heir general' of all British royal houses – Stuart, Tudor, Bruce, Plantagenet, Cedric, etc. – and therefore the Jacobite claimant to the throne, is HRH Prince Albrecht, Duke of Bavaria. His grandmother Maria Theresa, wife of the last Bavarian King, was a direct descendant of King Charles I via his daughter Henrietta. Prince Albrecht himself is referred to as King Albert I by those who consider him to be our rightful king. His son Franz is next in line for his titles. The duke has never expressed any desire to press his claim to the throne but neither does he deny it. He is, however, on excellent terms with his distant cousins in the House of Windsor.

DALE A. HEADINGTON, CRICKHOWELL, POWYS.

415: One often hears of servants and employees referring to the boss as 'his nibs': what is the origin of this?

This expression goes back to *nebb*, the Anglo-Saxon word for a bird's beak, which developed into our word 'nib', as used with a pen, because the writing tool was similar to a bird's beak. Fresher students at Cambridge University in the 19th century were known as 'nibs' or 'his nibs' (as opposed to the 'nobs', the senior students) and from there the expression came to signify someone who thinks himself important but has a lot to learn. To 'nebb' was also an Anglo-Saxon word, describing the action of a beak and has connections with our words 'snip' and 'snap'.

C. TOMKISS, LIVERPOOL.

416: Why do people who use lipsalve feel a compulsion to keep using it? Is it addictive?

Lipsalve is not addictive and there is no such thing as lipsalve abuse. Because salve prevents the lips from drying, a user can become accustomed to a certain degree of lip suppleness. Exceptionally frequent reapplication of lipsalve may be viewed by some non-users as anti-social behaviour but the user is simply reacting to the change in lip suppleness as the salve wears away, a process sometimes accelerated by speaking or drinking. The lips are sensitive areas so the change in suppleness is quickly noticed.   KATE WILLIAMSON, NOTTINGHAM.

417: How did my name, Jack, come to be used in so many contexts like lumberjack, Union Jack, bowls jack, car jack, and Jack of all trades?

Jack, a diminutive of the common name John, is so common that it developed into a general term for the ordinary man and now crops up in numerous affectionate expressions such as Jack Frost, jack-in-the-box and Jack Tar. The name Jack is also given to objects which take the place of working men: the jackknife, jack plane, smoke-jack, bootjacks and car jack. In bowls the jack is the little fellow that takes all the pressure. The Union Jack is the name for the union flag when flown on the small upright at the bow of the ship, known as the jack. Jack also crops up in the names of certain wild plants, particularly in the US, with Jack-by-the-hedge for garlic mustard and Jack-go-to-bed-at-noon for goat's beard. In the animal kingdom, too, a male may be a jack, as in jackass, jack-snipe and jack-rabbit. Chaucer referred to fish as Jakke of Dover in the Cook's Prologue. In Australia Jack has taken on some slightly different connotations; it's a slang word for a policeman and is often used by schoolchildren to denote a student who is an expert in his field, as in 'a jack at games.' The Jack system is an Australian phrase alluding to the pursuit of self-interest at the expense of others.   MICHAEL WOOD, CARLISLE.

418: Why do children in Walthamstow, East London, make grottos from shells?

Grotto Day was an old London custom observed by children until as late as the mid-Fifties but which now seems to have died out. Originally it was part of the celebration of St James's Day on July 25. The most popular pilgrimage destination in medieval Europe was Santiago de Compostela in north-west Spain and pilgrims who went there wore the saint's emblem of a scallop shell to advertise their mission. Devotees of the saint who could not make the journey travelled instead to makeshift alternative shrines, built by enterprising people at home. This practice gradually declined until only children continued it, making a cave-like grotto of shells, lit with a candle inside and decorated with whatever came to hand. They asked passers-by to 'remember the grotto' and for 'a penny for the grotto.' The tradition received a boost with the change to the Gregorian Calendar in 1752, which involved dates leaping forward by 11 days. This landed St James's Day on August 5, the first day in the year when oysters were sold from London's Billingsgate Market. Children set up their grottos close to the street stalls which sold oysters to make use of the discarded shells.   ARTHUR PENNY, ISLINGTON, LONDON.

419: I have read that the galaxy Andromeda is about 2,120,000 light years away from us. This means we see it as it was many millions of years ago, so where is it now?

Andromeda is the closest major galaxy to our own Milky Way and a member of our 'local group of galaxies'. It is twice the size of our own galaxy and contains some 300,000 million stars. Under the Big Bang theory, most galaxies are rushing away from us, but Andromeda is approaching at a rate of 310 kilometres per second. Light travels at about 300,000 kilometres per second, so for every kilometre moved by Andromeda, the light from it has moved 1,000. So, over a period of 2.2 million years, the light reaches us and the galaxy has moved 3.3 x 10 to the 14 kilometres. This huge distance represents only 0.0015 per cent of the distance separating Andromeda from the Milky Way, so its motion is imperceptible in galactic terms.   JIM ALLEN, SOUTHAMPTON, HANTS.

420: Why do visiting football fans chant 'Who hung the monkey?' at Hartlepool fans?

During the Napoleonic Wars, a French ship was wrecked off the coast of Northumberland and the only survivor was a dressed-up pet monkey, captured on the beach at Hartlepool. Whether ignorantly mistaking the animal for a Frenchman, or indulging in patriotic satire against the nation's enemies, the citizens of Hartlepool put the monkey on trial, found it guilty of being a French aggressor and hanged it. 'Who hung the monkey?' has been the mocking charge regularly levelled at Hartlepoolers ever since.   MIKE KANE, FENSTANTON, CAMBS.

My forebears were personally involved in the case of a monkey tried for being a French spy and hanged from a gibbet on the shore at Hartlepool during the Napoleonic wars. My father, grandfather and early relatives back to my great-, great-, great-grandfather, and myself, were all local fishermen and lifeboat crew. My ancestor, old Tom Moore, was both judge and hangman in the trial of the monkey. When I was a youngster, anyone who asked 'Who hung the monkey?' in Hartlepool was stoned out of town.   BOBBY MOORE, BROADSTAIRS, KENT.

The 'simple fisher folk' of Hartlepool may not have been so stupid in hanging the monkey from the wreck of the French ship. Salvage rights do not permit rescuers to benefit from a ship while any living soul is still aboard. Taking the monkey ashore and trying it for spying left the ship free to be claimed for salvage.   PAUL DUNN, SOUTH WINGFIELD, DERBYS.

421: Is it true that it is an offence in some parts of the US to put out male and female underwear on the same washing line? If this is so, why?

There is no law saying male and female underwear cannot share the same washing line but there are several laws governing the hanging out of female underwear. In Nappanee, Indiana, a local ordinance (equivalent of a bylaw) forbids the use of washing lines longer than 50 inches for female underwear hanging in view of the general public. In Scranton, Pennsylvania, it is an offence to hang out women's lingerie without a fence high enough to screen the items from public view. Los Angeles prohibits its citizens from hanging out women's lingerie in winter. I imagine these rules exist because they once had a purpose but the passage of time has made them seem ridiculous. Slow procedures in most elected bodies mean it is often better to keep irrelevant laws than use up legislative time repealing them.   CHRISTY MARR, PROVO, UTAH, USA.

422: What happened to the Marie Celeste, the ship which was found mysteriously abandoned? Was she ever sailed again?

The brig Mary Celeste – wrongly named the Marie Celeste in Sir Arthur Conan Doyle's first short story, J. Habakuk Jephson's Statement – had a chequered career even before the famous drama. She started life as The Amazon but suffered deaths, collisions, fires and bankruptcies by various owners before her name was changed to Mary Celeste to try to bury her reputation as a jinxed ship. The captain of the brigantine Dei Gratia, which found her abandoned in mid-Atlantic, could afford only three men to sail her to Gibraltar where she arrived on December 13, 1872. The British authorities there suspected the Dei Gratia crew were responsible for the Mary Celeste's plight and awarded them only one fifth the prize money instead of the traditional half. After that sailors refused to serve on her and she changed hands 17 times in 11 years. Finally a Boston consortium over-insured her and sent her to Haiti where her captain deliberately grounded her. This attempted fraud was detected and the master and owner prosecuted while the 'ghost ship' was left to rot away on a remote Caribbean reef.

THOMAS A. LEWINGTON, POPLAR, LONDON.

423: Who were Tom and John Collins after whom the drinks are named?

There was no Tom Collins as such but John Collins was a popular servant at Limmer's Hotel, London, in the early 19th century. An item of contemporary doggerel records: 'My name is John Collins, head waiter at Limmer's/Corner of Conduit Street, Hanover Square. My chief occupation is filling the brimmers/For all the young gentlemen frequenters there.' His 'brimmers' were probably akin to a modern Gin Sour. A modern John Collins consists of dry gin, sugar and lemon juice, poured over ice cubes and topped with soda water. Dry gin was evolved in about 1860. Before that pungent 'Old Tom' gin was used, and 'Tom' was frequently substituted for 'John' in naming the drink.

JOHN DOXAT, AUTHOR OF THE GIN BOOK, CAMBERLEY, SURREY.

424: What are those poles capped with a bright yellow/orange roof we often see on the edges of fields?

They are part of an aerial identification process set up by our gas and oil industries to mark the routes of pipelines. RICHARD DYMOND, BRITISH GAS.

I remember all too well when I was a boy seeing diggers and earth movers cut a wide scar through the lovely countryside near my home town of Tamworth, Staffordshire. To me, at that time, it seemed absolutely catastrophic that all the wild birds and animals, fields, hedges and woodland I knew so well should be disturbed and uprooted in such a callous way, a sort of Watership Down drama in the making. My father said it was for the North Sea gas pipeline and would go the entire length of Britain. Now, two decades or so later, nature and farming have erased this great blemish and all that denotes the route of the pipeline are the posts with the little fluorescent orange roofs, coloured so that they can be seen from the air. DAVID HASTILOW, HAYLE, CORNWALL.

425: Why does my car's engine appear to run better in muggy, wet weather?

Because the atmosphere contains a higher proportion of water which is instantly converted to steam during the combustion cycle of the engine's pistons, giving an extra thrust to the camshaft. During the early Seventies fuel crisis, a 'Zeep' device, produced by Mangoletsi, pumped a water 'mist' into the carburettor. But little has been done to develop it.

WARNER WILLIAMS, BIRKENHEAD, MERSEYSIDE.

The zeep device of the early Seventies wasn't the first time water injection was used to produce better performance in an engine. During World

War II, the Corsair, an American naval fighter used extensively by the British Fleet Air Arm in the Pacific, had two small tanks of water under the engine cowling. In an emergency the pilot could flick a switch to activate a system to blow atomised water in at the carburation stage. It had the effect of speeding up the atomisation of the petrol/air mixture and the result was dramatic as the aircraft leapt forward with an immediate increase in speed of 35 to 40 knots. Why this idea was not taken up and developed after the war, I know not.

S. M. COLLINS, CASTLETOWN, SUNDERLAND.

426: Why are citizens of the Irish Republic allowed to vote in British elections?

The reasons are historical. Until 1922 the Republic of Ireland was part of the UK. When the Irish Free State was formed it remained part of the Commonwealth until withdrawing in 1949. No British government has seen fit to remove voting rights from Irish citizens resident in the UK in the period since. Following a referendum in 1984, the government of Ireland returned the compliment and extended the right to vote in parliamentary and presidential elections to British citizens resident in the Irish Republic. Meanwhile, citizens of any Commonwealth country resident in Britain can register to vote, even though some – Canada and Australia, for example, have removed the right of British citizens resident in their countries to vote in their general elections.

PAUL WILDER, ELECTORAL REFORM SOCIETY, LONDON, SE1.

427: Why 'all shipshape and Bristol fashion'? Why Bristol rather than any other port?

The phrase comes from Bristol's long history and fame as a shipbuilding and trading centre. In past times Bristol's docks were subject to extreme tidal conditions and ships trading there had to be particularly well made to withstand resting on the bottom for long periods. Bristol's strong ships sailed worldwide and carried their reputation with them.

ADRIAN BROWN, BRISTOL CITY COUNCIL.

It was not the strength of the ships' hulls in response to the extreme range of the tide at Bristol which produced this phrase but the fact that square rigged sailing ships, moored alongside warehouses in the docks, had to have their yards hauled into a fore-and-aft configuration to prevent fouling the warehouses or dockside machinery at low water. Consequently, throughout the world, a ship with its yards swung fore-and-aft, and all ropes and sheets neatly coiled, was 'all shipshape and Bristol fashion.'

PETER ROOLE, YORK.

428: Who were the D-Day dodgers?

'We are the D-Day Dodgers, out in Italy/Always at the vino, always on the spree, Eighth Army skivers and the Yanks, who live in Rome and dodge the tanks/We're the D-Day Dodgers, out in Italy.' This was sung to the tune of Lily Marlene by the men who had fought their way across Africa, through Sicily and up Italy because they weren't taking part in the Normandy landings. In fact they carried out three D-Days before Normandy, in Sicily, Salerno and Anzio. Tory MP Lady Astor christened us 'D-Day dodgers' and it still rankles with those who survived the terrible winters of 1943 and 1944. British troops in that theatre served for 4 years without home leave. And don't forget the last verse of the song, which goes: 'Up in the mountains, in the snow and rain/You'll find some battered crosses, some which bear no name, Heartbreaks, toil and soldiering done, the lads beneath them slumber on: The D-Day Dodgers who are still in Italy.'   J. A. Beal, ex-Royal Signals, 8th Army and 5th American Army.

Lady Astor may have been wrongly blamed for this expression. It seems that an officer in a crack infantry regiment, a friend of the Astors, wrote to her from Italy and signed his letter, in jest, 'D-Day Dodger.' Nancy Astor replied, addressing her letter 'Dear D-Day Dodger...' Sadly, the officer was killed in action before the letter arrived and it was opened and the contents became public. Hence the myth. Our Monte Cassino Veterans Organisation always leaves out any reference to Lady Astor when we sing the D-Day Dodgers' song, as we have for nearly 50 years. Men of the 5th and 8th Armies felt bitter because they perceived that their sole purpose was to draw the cream of the German army away from the Second Front in Normandy. Men were sent from Italy to reinforce the Second Front while infantry units in Italy were at half strength, using naval and airforce reserves to make up losses. No new equipment was available, our artillery used clapped-out guns and ammunition was rationed, while we were fighting the cream of the German Army.

John Clarke, Monte Cassino Veterans, Manchester.

British troops in Italy who, quite logically, took no part in the D-Day landings in Normandy on June 6, 1944, were officially the Central Mediterranean Forces (CMF) but were often referred to jokingly as Churchill's Missing Forces.   Arthur F. Kirk, Alderney, Channel Islands.

429: What was the first product advertised on British television?

It was Gibbs SR (solium ricenoleate) toothpaste. I was head of sound for Associated Rediffusion when the first commercial was transmitted at 8.12pm on the opening night of ITV, Thursday, September 22, 1955, with an urgent voice proclaiming: 'It's fresh, it's tingling fresh, it's fresh as ice … it's Gibbs SR toothpaste' as the screen showed a picture of a tube of Gibbs SR and a toothbrush, embedded in a block of ice.

JOHN P. HAMILTON, LONDON W2.

This minute-long advert would probably seem naive by today's sophisticated standards of communicating product value but it helped increase the brand's market share and made the iceblock symbol synonymous with Gibbs SR. And it went out live – something unthinkable today.   LOUISE HAYTHORNTHWAITE, ELIDA GIBBS, LONDON.

An advertisement for the Eugene Permanent Wave was transmitted over closed circuit TV, using pictures produced by the Baird system, to the Hairdressing Fair of Fashion at Olympia on November 5, 1930.

GRAEME WORMALD, BEWDLEY, WORCS.

The first TV commercial in Britain was an advertisement for the Daily Mail, shown at a demonstration by John Logie Baird at the National Radio Exhibition at Olympia on September 26, 1928. It was screened on a dozen sets and viewed by an audience of 50.

ALAN BECKEN, MELTON MOWBRAY, LEICS.

430: My name is William but I am called 'Bill.' Where does the B come from?

The name Bill or Billy as a diminutive for William began as a pet name with its origins in the language of baby talk. William is easily reduced to Will, which changes easily to Bill in the mouths of children. The name William, meaning 'resolute', has been popular in Britain ever since the Norman invasion by William the Conqueror in 1066. It remained common until about the 1940s when it began to fade from popularity but, since the birth of Prince William in 1982, has started to make a strong comeback.   JOYCE FAIRCLOUGH, BEDFORD.

431: A visit to St Vitus Cathedral in Prague set me wondering: Who was Saint Vitus and why is 'St Vitus's Dance' so called?

St Vitus, also known as St Guy, was a noble Sicilian youth, converted to Christianity by his nurse Crescentia and her husband Modestus. They fled from his father's wrath to Italy and were martyred at Lucania, in the Diocletian persecution of AD 303. A peculiar form of madness, accompanied by strange twitching, spread through central Europe in the 15th century. This condition, now known as Sydenham's chorea (from the Greek *khoros*, meaning dance) is a disorder of the central nervous system, characterised by uncontrollable, jerky movements. A chapel at

Ulm, dedicated to St Vitus, became a place of pilgrimage for sufferers from this condition. St Vitus is also regarded as the patron saint of comedians.

OWEN PAIGE, SUNDERLAND.

Boswell's Life of Johnson gives an alternative derivation. Johnson suffered from St Vitus's Dance and a footnote in the book suggests that 'from some misunderstanding or inaccuracy of manuscript, *chorea invita,* meaning involuntary dance, the original and genuine name of the disease called St Vitus's Dance, was read and copied *"chorea St Viti."*'

S. P. BRIDGE, BARNES, LONDON.

432: Why is drinking red wine, rather than white, supposed to be good for the cholesterol level?

The differences between red wine and white wine and their effect on cholesterol are the subject of a research project funded by the British Heart Foundation. Current information suggests red wine contains chemical substances which act as 'antioxidants', and may prevent harmful cholesterol being deposited in the arteries. Other forms of alcohol are known to be 'cardioprotective'. Moderate drinkers (14 units a week for women and 21 units for men) tend to have a lower incidence of heart disease than non-drinkers. Alcohol may act favourably by diminishing the clotting tendency of the blood as well as its antioxidant properties. Overindulgence, however, is associated with the serious disease cardiomyopathy. DR I. MCLEAN BAIRD MD FRCP, BRITISH HEART FOUNDATION, LONDON.

433: Why do we put our hands together when we pray?

This wasn't always the common method. Ancient pictures show early Christians praying standing up, with their hands extended. Somewhere between AD 800 and 1000 a change took place and people began to kneel and put their hands together. Symbolically, when we stand to pray we approach God as children but when we kneel there is a greater sense of humility. The last 40 years has seen a revival of the idea of standing to pray and in charismatic circles people once again extend their arms during prayer. CANON BRIAN BRADLEY, PASTORAL SECRETARY OF THE CHICHESTER DIOCESE.

434: Has anybody ever windsurfed across the Atlantic?

There have been several crossings of the Atlantic on craft which could loosely be called sailboards. The first was in 1986 when Frenchman Stephan Peyron and a friend made the crossing on a 26ft craft with two windsurfer sails on the deck. Peyron made a solo crossing in 1987. But there is some debate as to whether such craft are sailboards because they bear little resemblance to the size of craft sailed by thousands the world over. Long distance trips on traditional windsurfers have included Tim Batstone's 1984 voyage around the British mainland in eight weeks, supported by a yacht for accommodation.

TONY DALLIMORE, ROYAL YACHTING ASSOC, EASTLEIGH, HANTS.

435: Who was 'Sweet Fanny Adams'? Was she murdered?

Eight-year-old Fanny Adams was lured away from her sister Lizzie and friend Minnie by a man they had met at Flood Meadow, 400 yards from her home in Alton, Hampshire, on August 24, 1867. Her horribly mutilated body was found by a farm labourer later that evening. Following national outrage at the crime, Frederick Baker, who worked for a firm of solicitors, was arrested for the murder, found guilty and hanged on Christmas Eve 1867. At about this time, sailors in the Royal Navy were issued with an unpopular kind of tinned mutton in their rations and christened it 'Sweet Fanny Adams.' The expression, often shortened to 'Sweet F.A.' came to mean 'nothing.'

ANN-MARIE COOPER, SOUTHAMPTON.

My paternal grandmother, Minnie Warner, was one of the two little girls playing with Fanny when she was lured away and brutally murdered by Frederick Baker.

HILDA WRIGHT, SOUTHSEA, HANTS.

436: What is the most frequently used cash point machine in the United Kingdom?

NatWest's most popular ATM (Automated Teller Machine) sites are at Waterloo Station and our Victoria Branch, in London. Each averages 25,000 cash withdrawals a week. In 1992 NatWest's Servicetills dispensed an average £3 million each. NatWest has the largest number of cash machines and we are still adding to the network. Many are now located at petrol stations, supermarkets and airports – we've even got one at Alton Towers.

K. M. FERGUSON, NATIONAL WESTMINSTER BANK, LONDON.

The NatWest bank lays claim to the most popular 'hole in the wall' site but could only have achieved the figures quoted by having more than one machine at the site. We believe the busiest individual cash point is the Barclays Bank machine at Camden Town, North London, which deals with nearly 4,500 transactions a week, serving roughly 18,000 people a month.

CHRIS TUCKER, BARCLAYS BANK, LONDON.

437: Has anyone ever been born on an aeroplane? If so, what is their country of origin?

The Civil Aviation Authority keeps records of births on board aircraft registered in the UK wherever in the world the plane is flying at the time. The owner or captain of the aircraft is responsible for reporting the birth and the CAA passes details on to the Registrar General. Some births have occurred on short flights from Scottish islands to mainland hospitals but in recent years they have also been reported in British aircraft over Rangoon, Delhi and Algeria. The number of these births is small, only ten in the past five years. The births are assumed to be on British territory and normal nationality rules apply as on British soil.

TONY DOYLE, LIBRARY AND REGISTERS, CIVIL AVIATION AUTHORITY, GATWICK.

Births on board Loganair island-hopping planes carrying ladies with difficult birth problems from the Western Isles, Orkneys and Shetlands to mainland hospitals are a weekly occurrence. Here, of course, nationality is no problem. NEVILLE SLACK, LANARK.

438: We have Irish Guards, Scots Guards and Welsh Guards: why no English Guards?

Although not designated English Guards, the regiment now known as the First, or Grenadier Regiment of Foot Guards, can claim the title. His Majesty's Royal Regiment of Guards, commanded by Lord Wentworth, was formed in Bruges, Flanders, from staunch Royalists who flocked to the exiled King's Standard when it was raised in 1656. In 1665 this regiment was amalgamated with the King's other Royal Regiment of Guards, raised in England under Colonel John Russell after the Restoration. The Coldstream Guards is also an English Regiment of Guards although its place of origin, Coldstream, is close to the Scottish border. This regiment was formed from two Parliamentary regiments under the command of General Monck, made part of the English regimental establishment after the Restoration. The regiment paraded on Tower Hill on St Valentine's Day 1661 and symbolically laid down its arms as a unit of Cromwell's New Model Army and was immediately ordered to take them up again as an Extraordinary Guard to His Royal Person. Later known as The Lord General's Regiment of Guards, it became The Coldstream Guards with seniority immediately after Lord Wentworth's and Colonel John Russell's.

CAPT DAVID HORN, THE GUARDS MUSEUM, LONDON SW1.

439: Is it true Dave Dee, of Dozy, Beaky, Mick and Titch fame, was the policeman who attended the crash outside Chippenham in 1960 which killed Eddie Cochran and injured Gene Vincent?

My grandfather was in the Wiltshire Police and remembers the young Dave Dee, then known by his real name, David Harman. Harman did indeed attend the accident when the taxi being driven back from Bristol after a show at the Hippodrome, the last date of a UK tour, left the road and smashed into a lamppost. Chippenham Sea Cadets took the lamppost from the scene and made it their flagpole, which it remains to this day.

WILL HODGSON, CHIPPENHAM, WILTS.

Yes, I did attend the crash, although I was at the time a young police cadet. On that particular night, as cadet David Harman, I was in the local police station with fellow cadet Dave Sawyer and we were called to assist the regular police officers. After leaving the force to follow my career in music, I re-met two of those who survived, Eddie's girlfriend, Sharon Sheeley, and Gene Vincent. In fact we became good friends. Ironically, I was with Gene Vincent four days before he died in 1971.

DAVE DEE, LONDON.

440: Is pneumonoultramicroscopicsilicovolcanoconiosis the longest word in the English language?

The word pneumonoultramicroscopicsilicovolcanoconiosis, containing 45 letters, is a favourite with many of our contestants and, according to Chambers Dictionary, is indeed the longest word in English. It's a form of lung disease, caused by very fine silicate or quartz dust.

ALISON CHRISTISON, LESLIE MITCHELL ASSOCIATES, PRODUCERS OF BBC2's CATCHWORD.

Although pneumonoultramicroscopicsilicovolcanoconiosis appears in the Oxford Dictionary, with a definition similar to the Chambers, its editors describe the word as 'factitious', as are the 52-letter aequeosalinocalcalinoceracsoaluminosocupreovitriolic, used by D. Edward Strother (1675-1737) to describe the spa waters at Bristol, and the 51-letter osseocarnisanguineoviscericartilaginonervomedullary, used by Thomas Love Peacock (1785-1866) to describe the human physic.

TIM MICKLEBURGH, GRIMSBY, LINCS.

The word cheimacheimatohionochioneinetochionokeraunoebiommio (51-letters) means an allergy to the weather, cold, wind, rain and snow, derived from the medical names of the four allergies. Iron Chancellor Bismarck is supposed to have coined the German word Gesundheit swiederherstellungsmittelzusammenmischungserhaltnisskundiger (60 letters) for 'apothecary.'

EDDIE NOLL, LONDON.

The Book Of Lists says the second longest word in the English language is lopadotemachiselachogaleokranioleipsanodrimhypotrimmatosilphiop-aramelitokatakechymenokichlepikossyphophattoperisteralektryonoptek ephalliokigklopeleiolaoiosiraiobaphetranganopterygon, which has 182 letters, the English translation of a Greek word which occurs in Aristophanes's play The Ecclesiazusae. The word is identified as hash.

However, by far the longest word is that which names a chemical describing bovine Nadp-specific glutamate dehydrogenase, which contains 500 amino acids. The word has 3,600 letters and is very boring.

NICK COOK, ORPINGTON, KENT.

441: Where or what is the Cloud Nine we're supposed to be on when we're in Seventh Heaven?

Generally attributed to the US Weather Bureau in the Fifties, Cloud Nine is said to be a nickname for the cumulonimbus cloud formations found at 30,000 to 40,000 feet. Apart from the obvious associations between sky, heaven and feelings of euphoria, this is not as mystical a notion as Seventh Heaven which originated in both Jewish and Muslim religions which hold that there are seven degrees of heaven, the seventh being the place of greatest divinity.

JEREMY MACHIN, BRIGHTON.

442: Since Britain joined the EC, have we given more money to the Community than we have received?

From 1973 (the year we joined the Common Market) until 1990, the UK paid £41.5 billion directly into the coffers of the EC. From this, we received back £12.5 billion as part of the Fontainebleu Abatement, the refund agreement obtained by Mrs Thatcher in 1984. So the total amount paid in for the period 1973-1990 was £29 billion. Of this we have received about one third back in various grants for things like agriculture, road projects, industrial redevelopment, research and development, education and training, environmental projects, etc. Thus, we have actually paid in £20 billion more than we have received, or about £350 each for every man, woman and child in the country. And we are still paying out at a rate of about £2.7 billion a year. Before these bald figures get the Eurosceptics seething, account must be taken of the 'invisible' advantages of EC membership flowing from access to 340 million consumers on equal terms, increasing our trading and employment opportunities, companies profits and government revenue. Social and cultural advantages alone are worth the estimated £47 EC membership costs each of us each year. We are not the highest contributor: that honour goes to Germany.

JOHN HOUSTON-CARLYLE, NORWICH.

443: What is the origin of 'Anyone for tennis'?

It has often been suggested that the cliche used in numerous theatrical productions up and down the country during the Twenties was the first line uttered by Humphrey Bogart at the start of his acting career – a suggestion he fervently denied when his career in macho roles took off. The line was probably first used in 1911 in George Bernard Shaw's Misalliance and went on to be a favourite in what became known as 'teacup' theatre plays, which used sets of sitting rooms full of 'nice chaps and gels' who all spoke Oxbridge English.   DEBBY HOLGATE, HALE, CHESHIRE.

444: Why does champagne retain its bubbly nature for up to three days in an open bottle if a teaspoon is placed in the top?

In December 1983 a series of tests was conducted by the CIVC (Le Comite Interprofessionel du Vin de Champagne), the body which represents champagne producers, to try to verify the legendary notion that an open champagne bottle would keep its pressure if a spoon was put in its open top. Six bottles of champagne were refrigerated for four hours and then opened. The equivalent of two glasses of champagne were poured out from each and the pressure of each bottle was registered. Two bottles were closed with hermetic stoppers, two were left open with a spoon in their tops, and two were simply left open. All six bottles were put back in the fridge for 24 hours and then re-tested for pressure. Contrary to popular belief, the tests showed that the use of a spoon did not retain a significant amount of the champagne's bubbly nature, though it did prove more effective than if the bottle had been left on its own.

FRANCOISE PERETTI, CHAMPAGNE INFORMATION BUREAU, LONDON.

445: In athletics, why is a steeplechase so called?

The name is inherited from horse racing. In 1850 members of Exeter College, Oxford, were discussing a 'steeplechase' horse race between two villages, over fences and obstacles, in which they had competed. Competitor Halifax Wyatt said he 'would prefer to go over the two-mile course on foot rather than mount that camel again.' His undergraduate friends took these words as a challenge and the debate led to what is believed to be the earliest athletics steeplechase contest of the modern era at Binsey, near Oxford, later that year. It was run over a two-mile course including 24 jumps. Original horse races were between steeples, easily visible markers in neighbouring villages, hence steeplechase.

DAVE SUNDERLAND, NATIONAL EVENT STEEPLECHASE COACH, RUGELEY, STAFFS.

446: Why can't we buy horse meat in Britain?

There is no legal reason to prevent horse meat being sold in Britain. However, for cultural reasons, there is little demand for the product, which has resulted in limited supplies. The 1955 Food and Drugs Act required retailers selling horse meat to display this fact prominently. The

1990 Act, which superseded the 1955 Act, no longer has such a requirement. AMBROSE LANDON, MEAT & LIVESTOCK COMMISSION, MILTON KEYNES.

447: Why does James Bond insist on having his drinks 'shaken, not stirred'? What are the comparative merits of each procedure?

Cocktails are mostly divided into those that are stirred in a mixing glass and then poured into a cocktail glass, and those that are shaken in a special shaker, then poured into the cocktail glass. Stirred cocktails are usually clear, while fruit juices, eggs or cream are added to cocktails that are shaken to ensure a good blend. Shaking a drink with ice produces a better chilling effect and the ice is held back when pouring by using a Hawthorne strainer. Bond is wrong to ask for his martini shaken. Shaking a martini with a gin base would 'bruise' the gin, turning it cloudy. The same would happen with a vodka-based martini. Why Bond has a Martini made with vodka, only he knows. Dean Martin has the right idea about a martini: 'Two fingers of gin and show the cork of a Vermouth bottle to it.' CHRIS SAMUEL, ABERYSTWYTH, DYFED.

Reference to the Bond novels establishes that the film producers stood this saying on its head. The original line was 'stirred, not shaken' because, Bond maintained, 'shaking bruised the spirit.' DEREK B. ARNOLD, NORWICH, NORFOLK.

448: Is there a standard route taken by cyclists or walkers from John O'Groats to Land's End?

There isn't a prescribed standard route as such for cyclists and walkers but several routes are favoured. People such as Ian Botham, looking for maximum publicity for his charity effort, travel on main roads, while those who are walking for pleasure prefer to use long-distance footpaths. Beginning at Land's End, the most popular route takes walkers along the Cornwall/Devon coastline by way of the South-West Coastal Path as far as Minehead; it then crosses the Mendip Hills to Bath and joins the Cotswold Way to Chipping Campden. The next stage goes through the delightful countryside of the Heart of England Way to Cannock Chase, picking up the Staffordshire Way, then on to the Pennine Way, which goes all the way to the Scottish Borders. Scotland has fewer recognised long-distance footpaths than England. Most people prefer to cross the border by the Drovers' Roads and pick up the West Highland Way from Glasgow to Fort William via Glencoe. From there, they tend to take the Great Glen Cycle Way, leading up to Inverness, via Loch Ness. The final part, to John O'Groats, is normally on tracks and local roads. The journey of about 900 miles usually takes five or six weeks.

ANDREW MCLOY, AUTHOR: THE LAND'S END TO JOHN O'GROATS WALK, RAMBLERS' ASSOC, LONDON.

The route taken by top cyclists in record attempts, alone and unpaced, goes roughly: A30 to Exeter, Taunton, A38, Bristol, Gloucester, Tewkesbury, Worcester, Warrington, Preston, A6 Shap Fell, Carlisle, A7 Edinburgh, Forth Bridge, Perth, A9 Inverness, Helmsdale, Wick, John O'Groats. The distance is just short of 900 miles and the record, set in 1990, is held by Andy Wilkinson at 45hr 2min 18sec. The two-day margin was beaten for the first time in 1965 by Dick Poole. Most people go from South to North because the prevailing wind is south-westerly.

KEN BRITAIN, GLOSSOP VELO CYCLING CLUB, DERBYSHIRE.

449: Why was the sea referred to in the Royal Navy as 'the oggin'?

The normal dictionary definition is that 'the oggin' is a corruption of the slang word 'hogwash', which itself came into being as a land-based reference to any liquid (especially liquor) that was undrinkable – the reference being to water that had been used to clean pigs or other livestock. Another body of opinion suggests that 'oggin' is a corruption or mispronunciation of the word 'ocean'. In any closed community, such as a ship's crew, you will always find invented language like 'floggin' the oggin' (sailing the seas), initially applicable only to the people in that community, but later moving out to the rest of society.

IAIN MACKENZIE, NATIONAL MARITIME MUSEUM, GREENWICH.

450: I know it refers to the Royal East Kent Regiment, but who first said 'Steady the Buffs' and why?

A popular expression used by people with no connection to the old Royal East Kent Regiment, it is mistakenly thought to have been initiated as an order or battle cry during the Peninsular Campaign battle of Albuhera in 1811. The truth is less exciting. In 1857 a 2nd battalion was raised in Limerick and moved in 1858 to Malta where it shared the Florian Barracks with the Royal Scots Fusiliers. The adjutant of these '2nd Buffs', as they were nicknamed, had previously been a sergeant-major in the Royal Scots Fusiliers and, as part of his drill parade, was noted for continually saying 'Steady the Buffs, the Fusiliers are watching you', as a way of letting his recruits feel they should try to attain the standard of their barracks' neighbours. This amused the Fusiliers who repeated it whenever possible.

REGIMENTAL SECRETARY OF THE QUEEN'S OWN BUFFS, HOWE BARRACKS, CANTERBURY, KENT.

451: If every employable person in Britain were to earn exactly the same salary, what annual wage would our economy support?

Taking into account income only from wages and salaries, data from the

UK National Accounts Blue Book shows that for 1997 total wages and salaries amounted to £427,042 million. Dividing this by a total workforce of 28,868,000 would give each person an annual wage of £14,792 or £1,232.74 per month. Taking into account all income (including investments, etc.) the annual salary totals £677,574 million which, divided again between the country's 28,868,000 workforce, would yield £23,471.46 per person per year, or £1,955.95 a month. The 1997 average British salary was £367.60 a week or £19,115.20 a year.

ALISON WRIGHT, OFFICE OF NATIONAL STATISTICS, LONDON.

452: The Germans say vierundzwanzig (24) etc, there were four and twenty blackbirds baked in a pie and some older people say five and twenty minutes past or to the hour. Was it ever common practice to say numbers this way round in Britain?

The 'four and twenty' construction is an older form than our current twenty-four and can be traced back to Old English spoken before 1066. It survives into the present century among older speakers and is the commonest form in 16th- and 17th-century literature. In about 1300, mainly in Scotland and the North, a form 'twenty and four' arose and this could still be found as late as the end of the 17th century in parts of England. The 'and' was dropped, originally in Scotland in about 1560, making the common expression 'twenty-four'. This spread southwards until it appeared in most parts of England by about 1611. All this applies not just to twenty-four but to all combinations of tens and units.

EDMUND WEINER, OXFORD UNIVERSITY PRESS, OXFORD.

453: Does a dust mite have animal rights? If not, where do we draw the line?

The RSPCA believes all animals should be spared unnecessary pain and suffering. We have issued guidelines for the humane killing of lobsters, livestock, fowl, etc. All pet vertebrates are protected by the law and experiments are strictly controlled. The RSPCA has a practical approach to the rights of animals, a good example of this being that we believe pets should be regularly deloused, as pests can cause horrible skin conditions. My own view is that any unnecessary cruelty to animals is wrong and all life should be respected.

TANYA MICHELLE, RSPCA, HORSHAM, WEST SUSSEX.

454: What exactly is the 'American Dream'?

It's a set of ideas and values about the meritocratic nature of American society, and rests on the notion of America as a 'land of opportunity' for all, on the value of independence and individualism, hard work in one's chosen vocation, and on worldly success. The 'dream' is that regardless of social rank, birth, or creed anyone can 'make it' in America if they take the opportunities US society offers. Earthly success – ie the acquisition of valued goods and services – is essential, through individual effort. This is linked with religious (Calvinist) notions of being 'saved'. There are obvious flaws in this version of US society, especially with regard to the position of slaves and native Americans, but when the USA first came into being, its freedom from the Old World gave rise to a great deal of truth about the American dream.

INDERJEET PARMAR, DEPARTMENT OF AMERICAN STUDIES, MANCHESTER UNIVERSITY.

Money: what else?   MRS MARGARET DALE, BURTON OVERY, LEICS.

455: Why are people called toe-rags?

A toe-rag was a cloth wrapped around the feet of people who couldn't afford shoes or weren't allowed to wear them. In the Victorian era, these included the poor, the mentally or physically disabled and the majority of prisoners, whose shoes were taken by warders. The word came into use in the mid-19th century and by the start of the 20th century was used as an insult in Britain, Australia and New Zealand. It fell from general use in the late Sixties, but was revived in the Seventies in such TV programmes as The Sweeney and Till Death Us Do Part.

PATRIZIA GARGIULO, WOLVERHAMPTON.

Contrary to previous suggestions, use of the insult 'toe-rag' may have had something to do with the nomadic Sahara tribe called the Tuaregs, mentioned in a television advertisement for a credit card. As with all nomadic peoples, the Tuaregs had to live off their wits, using hard-bargaining, trading and general wheeler-dealing. They were regarded by the majority of the static population with suspicion. In the bazaars of North Africa their name would be uttered under the breath, to invoke the idea of someone not quite above board at best and a treacherous cut-throat at worst. This utterance was picked up by early visitors from this country and on their return became corrupted by word-of-mouth to the present 'toe-rag', which is now used to mean someone of low regard.

MR R. L. REECE, PITSEA, ESSEX.

This expression should be spelt not 'toe' but 'tow,' after the coarse broken part of hemp or flax after spinning. This waste produce, the tow, was used in the 19th and early 20th centuries to wipe down steam engines and the like. The tow became contaminated with oil, grease and dirt. Thus, to call someone a tow-rag meant they were a dirty or slippery customer. Since the 1960s, hemp, with its drug connotations, has been replaced by old rags used for the same purpose and the insult has changed to 'oily rag'.   MARK BAILEY, WALTHAM ABBEY, ESSEX.

I would suggest that this expression was originally 'tow-rag'. Until narrow boats on the canal system acquired engines, they were propelled by horses tramping along tow-paths. The crews handled the tow-ropes, which were invariably filthy and would otherwise burn hands by friction, with 'tow-rags'.   D. J. BRETT, HERNE HILL, LONDON SE24.

456: Why do several very short stretches of the M3 motorway have lighting right in the depths of the country?

Very short stretches of lights appear not just on the M3 but on the whole motorway network. There are several reasons for them including improved visibility in areas deemed 'accident blackspots' or prone to fog; presence of other passing roads needing illumination; cross-over places or opportunities for diversions during roadworks or attention to accidents.
                          ALISON LANGLEY, DEPT OF TRANSPORT.

457: If the postman drops a letter through my letter box with my address but a different name on it, do I have the right to open it, read it or destroy it?

The Royal Mail's responsibility ends when a letter is delivered to the correct address. In extreme cases the sender, or correct addressee, could prosecute someone who opened their post for theft, criminal damage or contravention of Section 56 of the Post Office Act (1953) but they would have to prove that person had the necessary 'mental intent' to wrong them. The Royal Mail spends millions of pounds a year opening and returning 23 million letters which cannot be delivered for some reason, such as an incorrect address. A return address on the back of the envelope would ensure it was returned unopened. The average person receives 293 letters a year. The Royal Mail has launched a new computerised re-direction service to ensure customers still receive their post after moving home. This costs just £6 for one month, £13 for three months or £30 for a year and can be arranged by telephone.
                          JOHN TEW, ROYAL MAIL, LONDON.

458: Who is the little girl always hidden in the background in the Mac cartoons in the Daily Mail?

My lips are sealed on the true identity of the 'little blonde', and must always remain so, but I can tell you that if I leave her out one morning I run the risk of getting no breakfast. Her inclusion began as a little joke but she is such a regular feature of the Daily Mail now that if she doesn't appear I get loads of letters of complaint. Some people tell me they often spend so much time looking for the 'little blonde' in my drawings that they completely miss the point of the cartoon.   MAC, DAILY MAIL.

459: There are often yew trees in our churchyards. Is there any connection between the trees and religion?

The prehistoric tradition of the yew tree as a symbol of mourning was continued by the Greeks and Romans. In Greek mythology, a beautiful youth called Crocus was turned into a flower because of his impatient love for the nymph Smilax. She, in her grief at losing him, was changed into a yew tree, the symbol of sorrow. Both Greeks and Romans used yew wood for funeral pyres and it was probably from the Romans that the Britons learned to attach funereal significance to the yew tree. With time it came to be planted in churchyards, along with cypress, which was regarded as a symbol of death and mourning. Centuries ago it was thought the yew could absorb poisonous vapours: another reason for planting it in churchyards. The branches were sometimes carried in procession and placed under the bodies of the departed. As an evergreen which can live for 1,000 years, the yew was also regarded as a symbol of immortality. However, its status as a symbol of death was enhanced by the fact that its branches were used to make bows and arrows. It has poisonous leaves and berries and it was considered very unlucky to bring yew branches into the house.   WENDY PAGE, HORSHAM, SUSSEX.

Yews may well have been planted in churchyards to prevent sheep and cattle from desecrating the graves. No farmer would so neglect his fences as to allow his livestock access to these deadly poisonous trees. I have bitter experience of the disastrous consequences on my farm when some youths who were building a 5 November bonfire dragged some yew branches across a meadow where cattle were grazing.
                    DAVID CRUDGE, CHIPPING NORTON, OXON.

In pagan times the yew was worshipped as a sacred tree, representing the winter solstice (22 December) in the Druid calendar. As Christianity was established churches were often built on the site of pagan burial mounds which retained ancient yew trees in conspicuous positions. Some of the largest and oldest specimens of yews are found in churchyards all over Britain.   PETER DAVENPORT, GLOSSOP, DERBYSHIRE.

In the indigenous religion of the Germanic peoples, including the English, the yew was associated with the World Tree, Yggdrasil, which has its roots in Hel, its bole in Middle Earth and its branches in Asgarth.

For this reason, yews were popular sites of worship. When Christian missionaries arrived in our land, the conversion to Christianity did not come about overnight; there was a considerable period during which both faiths existed alongside each other. Many of the ancient heathen shrines eventually became churchyards, sacred yews and all. Because of the yew's longevity (up to 2,000 years), the original trees often survived until quite recent years. The ancient association of connections between this world and netherworlds made the yew especially suitable even in the new religion of Christianity, as a guardian tree for graveyards. It is also said that no evil magic can prevail in the presence of a yew.

C. A. SMITH, NOTTINGHAM.

460: What would be the scrap metal value of the Eiffel Tower?

The Eiffel Tower, often described as an oversized electricity pylon with a café on top, is constructed of 7,340 tonnes of wrought iron which has a current scrap metal value of £25 per tonne. So the materials from Paris's most famous landmark would fetch £183,500 from a scrap metal dealer. Dismantling costs, however, would be triple the amount gained from selling the metal, so the French authorities would have to pay to have the Tower scrapped. In 1889 the tower cost 7.8 million French francs and took 26 months to build. If attempted today, it would be possible to put the tower up for about the same price, discounting inflation, in less than half the time because a similar structure would be made of steel, which is cheaper, easier to produce and stronger.   JOHN HALL, GEORGE WIMPEY PLC, LONDON.

461: In which month of the year are most babies born in Britain?

There is only a small variation in the number of births each month, but in most years the summer months of June, July, August and September generally have the highest birth rates. Taking 1991 as an average year and looking purely at England and Wales (Scotland and Northern Ireland have similar trends), the total figure for live births is 699,200: around 1,916 births per day. July has the highest birth rate with 62,000: about 2,000 per day, and September is second at 1,980 a day. August has the second highest total at 60,400, but these are spread over 31 days, giving an average of 1,948 a day. In all cases December has the lowest number of births.   RICHARD BROADWELL, STOKE-ON-TRENT.

462: Why is a match between two teams from the same town referred to as a 'local derby'?

The 18th century saw the origins of the traditional and infamous Shrove

Tuesday football games between neighbouring towns and villages. One of the most famous and anarchic of these games took place annually in Derby, where the young men of All Saints' parish played those of St Peter's. The games were notoriously violent affairs and in 1731 the mayor attempted, unsuccessfully, to stop the event going ahead. Despite the efforts of the authorities, the games continued until 1848 when the mayor of Derby read the Riot Act and called out the troops to put a stop to it. The fame of this event meant the term 'derby' was used thereafter to refer to any local football match at which emotions ran high.

ANDREW ROBINSON, BIRMINGHAM.

463: In the war I often came across Kilroy who always left the same message: 'Kilroy was here'. Who was Kilroy?

The slogan 'Kilroy was here' first appeared in Europe during World War II with the arrival of American servicemen. There is no conclusive proof as to who Kilroy was but the origin is generally associated with one James J. Kilroy, a shipyard inspector in Quincy, Massachusetts, who used the expression to signify those items he had personally inspected. Kilroy Was Here was also the title of a 1947 film starring Jackie Coogan and Jackie Cooper.

MR R. G. BRUCE, READING, BERKS.

Research by Captain H. Eaton (rtd) of the Light Infantry Association presents a strong case for the original Kilroy having been an Irishman serving in the British Army during the 1812-14 war with the United States. On 24 August 1814, a British army entered and burnt the American capital, Washington, including the presidential palace, now known as the White House. When the Americans re-occupied the city they found the inscription 'McKilroy was here' scratched by a bayonet. This was probably Private Michael McKilroy of Captain Charles Grey's company of the 85th Bucks Volunteers Light Infantry. As far as is known, Pte McKilroy survived the war and returned to his native County Down. The 85th later amalgamated with the 53rd Shropshires and became the King's Shropshire Light Infantry, now the 3rd Light Infantry.

RON LARBY, NEASDEN.

464: Why is the law an ass?

This expression has its origin in Charles Dickens's Oliver Twist. Mr Bumble's wife is accused of committing fraud and Bumble denies all responsibility, whereupon Mr Brownlow informs him that 'the law supposes that your wife acted under your direction'. To this Bumble declares: 'If the law supposes that, the law is a ass – a idiot.' Using 'a', rather than 'an', before a word beginning with a vowel was then the norm. Bumble added that the law was obviously a bachelor with no experience in such matters and badly in need of having its eyes opened.

CHRIS DALY, HATCH END, MIDDX.

465: Why has every No 1 hit of the Sixties appeared on compilation CDs except Mike Sarne's and Wendy Richard's 1962 hit Come Outside?

Unlike Mike Sarne's other hits, Come Outside doesn't appear very often (perhaps Wendy Richard doesn't want her early career revisited) but it has been re-issued. I have it on a budget priced CD entitled British Comedy Classics Vol 1 (Adroit Records ACD704) along with Tommy Cooper's Don't Jump Off The Roof, Dad and Benny Hill's Gather In The Mushrooms. But I've never managed to find Vol 2 of the Adroit collection.

ALWYN W. TURNER, LONDON NW5.

466: Where does the name Clarence come from, as in the Duke of Clarence, Clarence House, etc?

Used both as a surname and as a Christian name, Clarence means 'shines brightly'. Though not a popular name these days, it has been in existence for just over 600 years, stemming originally from the Norman de Clare family who, after settling in England during the Conquest, gave their name to the Suffolk town of Clare. The name Clarence in its noble form came from the Latin for Clare Clarentia, and was first used in 1362 by the first Duke of Clarence. The title Earl of Clarence was one of two titles suspended in 1919 after World War I when it was deemed the then Earl had 'adhered to the King's enemies'. The title is now extinct but may re-emerge.

NIGEL MORRISON-HEALEY, CAMBRIDGE.

467: Is there any practical use in the saying 'Feed a cold, starve a fever'?

This expression, as it is commonly used today, is ambiguous. It was originally meant more as a warning than an instruction and should be: 'If you feed a cold, you'll have to starve a fever.' The reasoning was that when fighting off a cold the body's immune system will use all its resources. An already overworked defence mechanism will struggle further if energy is then diverted to digesting heavy meals. This will slow down recovery and increase the likelihood of the cold developing into something more serious.

GRAHAM WU, LIVERPOOL.

468: Who invented the umbrella?

The invention of the modern day 'brolly' is generally attributed to the

18th-century philanthropist and traveller, Jonas Hanway (1712-86). He came across the idea of the umbrella during a trip to Persia where he decided that parasols carried by the locals for protection against the sun might have a better use in Britain as a protector against rain, if they were made of waterproof materials. On his return to London he constructed an umbrella and by the late 1750s could be seen walking the streets, much to the amusement and ridicule of Londoners, with an unfolded umbrella protecting him from the inclement weather. Umbrellas were treated with mistrust by the British public, influenced by the clergy of the time who claimed they prevented God's rain from doing its natural duty. But Jonas Hanway was a determined man and persisted in his efforts until the idea was accepted about 20 years later, transforming us from a nation who despised the umbrella to a nation regarded by foreigners as being its foremost users. The original parasol seems to have been an invention by the Chinese more than 3,000 years ago.

DAVID NASMITH, LAWTEX UMBRELLAS, OLDHAM.

There is another suggestion I learned as a child:

'Under a toadstool crept a wee elf,
Out of the rain to shelter himself.
Under the toadstool fast asleep
Sat a large dormouse all in a heap.
The wee elf trembled, frightened and yet
Fearing to fly away, lest he get wet
To the next shelter may be a mile;
Then the wee elf smiled a wee smile,
Tugged till the toadstool toppled in two;
Holding it over him gaily he flew.
Soon he was safe home, dry as can be.
Soon woke the dormouse: "Good gracious me,
Where is my toadstool?" loud he lamented
And that's how umbrellas first were invented.'

MRS K. P. SIMKINS, HENLOW, BEDFORDSHIRE.

469: What is the origin of the mildly insulting but evocative phrase 'big girl's blouse'?

Regarded as a very weak insult in the sophisticated Nineties, this expression is now on the wane. It came into common use in the north of England in the mid Sixties where it was levelled at men thought to be weak or ineffectual, intended to be more cajoling than offensive. The phrase achieved popular recognition nationally in around 1968-69 through northern based TV programmes such as Granada TV's Nearest and Dearest, starring Jimmy Jewel and Thora Hird.

JEFF THOMPSON, CARLISLE.

470: Why was the standard gauge of our railway system set at 4ft 8½ins?

George Stephenson chose the gauge of 4ft 8ins for the Stockton and Darlington railway, which opened in 1825. This gauge had been used for many years by the horse-drawn wagonways of the colliers of north-east England and may have developed from the normal cart tracks which date back to Roman times. In 1814, Stephenson had designed a steam locomotive, the Blucher, to run on the same gauge on the Killingworth colliery line. The Liverpool and Manchester Railway, opened in 1830, was surveyed by John and George Rennie, who suggested a gauge of 5ft. But Stephenson was appointed engineer and built the line to 4ft 8ins between the rails. An extra half inch was added about three years later to give the rolling stock extra freedom. The standard gauge was finally set at 4ft 8⅜ins (1432mm) after a small adjustment to prevent the tendency of bogies to 'hunt' or vibrate laterally at high speeds. Isambard Kingdom Brunel built the Great Western Railway to a broad gauge of 7ft 0¼in and it remained that size for almost 60 years until changed to match the other railways. Nearly 5,000 men converted the whole GWR track in two days in 1892. D. BITTEN, HALIFAX, YORKS.

471: Is it true that in one American city all citizens are required by law to carry a weapon?

A by-law in the city of Kennesaw, Georgia (population 10,000), compels householders to own a gun, though not to carry one. The 1982 ordinance was passed as a protest against an ordinance in the city of Morton Grove, Illinois, which banned the ownership of firearms, something Kennesaw thought unconstitutional. It is worded: 'Every head of household residing in the city limits of the City of Kennesaw is required to maintain a firearm together with ammunition therefore. Exempt from the effect of said ordinance are those heads of household who suffer a physical disability which would prohibit them from using such a firearm. Further exempt from the effect of said ordinance are those heads of household who conscientiously oppose firearms as a result of religious doctrine or belief, or persons convicted of a felony.' JACK DERIZARIO, LONDON.

472: Did Karl Marx say or write 'Give me 26 lead soldiers and I will conquer the world'? If so, what did he mean?

The exact quotation is: 'Give me 26 soldiers of lead and I will conquer the world.' This refers to the influence of the 26 letters of the alphabet in moveable lead type. It may be wrong to attribute it to Karl Marx; as far as I am aware, it is of unknown origin. ERIC E. GREEN, ISLEWORTH, MIDDX.

473: What inspired the design of the black and white flag used in motor-racing and how long has it been in use?

The traditional chequered flag was originally a naval flag signifying the end of a message. In naval circles it now represents the letter 'N', meaning 'abandonment' among racing yachts or boats. It has been known worldwide since the turn of the century as the flag that indicates that a race is over. Before the use of lights on the racing circuits, a race was always started with the national flag of the host country and finished with the chequered flag. The chequered flag was originally blue and white but has evolved into the more familiar black and white. The design was chosen to be instantly distinguishable and completely unlike any other flags used on racing circuits. STUART SCOTT, BRANDS HATCH RACING CIRCUITS.

474: When deaf people meet other deaf people from around the world, can they communicate in sign language?

British Sign Language (BSL) is the first language for 50,000 deaf people in the UK. It is not a visual interpretation of spoken English but a rich and varied vocabulary with its own rules of grammar and a different syntax. British Sign Language is different from American Sign Language, Irish Sign Language, etc. In fact 'dialects' exist in the deaf communities around Britain, so that, for example, some signs in Manchester are different from some in London. There is also an international sign language, used at international deaf conferences.

PAUL RICHARDSON, ROYAL NATIONAL INSTITUTE FOR DEAF PEOPLE, LONDON.

475: More than 200 years ago the naturalist Gilbert White pondered on why cats, which have a natural aversion to water, should have developed such a taste for fish. Have we yet discovered the answer?

Generally speaking cats do not prefer fish; given the choice, most would choose meat rather than fish. The reason for the assumption that they like fish may well be rooted in the fact that, as a maritime nation, fish was historically the cheaper source of protein. This meant that it was traditionally used to feed pet cats, which were not so highly regarded as dogs. Individual cats will, in due course, develop a preference for a particular food, which could be fish. Cats habitually fed on fish may never accept any alternatives. EVELYN TRUNDLE, SPILLERS FOODS, NEW MALDEN, SURREY.

476: Where did the expression 'bury the hatchet', meaning let bygones be bygones, come from?

North American Indians believed 'The Great Spirit' commanded that when they were smoking their peace-pipes they had to bury their hatchets, scalping knives and war clubs so all thought of hostility might be put out of sight. In 'The Song Of Hiawatha', the poet Longfellow wrote: 'Buried was the bloody hatchet, Buried was the dreadful war club, Buried were all warlike weapons and the war-cry was forgotten, There was peace among the nations.' Thus 'bury the hatchet' became associated with calming a situation down and forgiving and forgetting.

DAVID EASTMAN, COLCHESTER, ESSEX.

477: Why can a sailor have a beard but not just a moustache, while a Royal Marine can have a moustache but not a beard?

A sailor must follow Admiralty Instructions, introduced in 1869 and giving permission to Naval personnel to wear beards. They stipulate full beard and moustache or no facial hair at all. By contrast the Marine follows the Army rule which allows moustaches only. During the 18th Century most officers and men of the Royal Navy were clean-shaven, in civilian fashion. Around 1796, however, some Army officers began to wear moustaches but the Navy never adopted this style. Then in the bitter weather of the Crimea, beards and moustaches were grown by officers and men ashore. The habit persisted but was forbidden under Admiralty Instructions. These did not mention whiskers and in the 1860s officers grew them to such a size and length as to resemble beards. Finally, in 1869, beards and moustaches were permitted but Queen Victoria was adamant that the Navy must not wear moustaches alone as she considered them too soldier-like.

PATRICIA BLACKETT BARBER, NATIONAL MARITIME MUSEUM, LONDON.

478: Why are things said to 'peg out' when they die?

The expression can be traced to the game of cribbage. In this, the game is scored using pegs on a board with holes. When the contest ends, the winner's pegs are in the board's last holes; this is known as 'pegging out'.

ARNOLD KNIGHT, MACCLESFIELD, CHESHIRE.

I believe the expression to 'peg out' arises from the pegs and cord used by grave diggers to outline and guide the required excavation of a grave.

J. R. HALL, BATH.

479: Did one V2 rocket bomb land in London before the attack by V1 (Doodlebug) flying bombs began in World War II?

This story may arise from the fact that two days before the main V1 attack started on a Thursday, something fell and did considerable damage to the railway bridge carrying the Liverpool Street line at Burdett Road, in East London. On the Wednesday morning, the Air Ministry announced that 'one aircraft has been shot down in flames over East London'. The flames from the V1 engine must have been mistaken for a conventional aircraft on fire. After the incident, a rumour spread that the crew members had not been found. Teams scoured the area for them and I, proud in my Army Cadet Force uniform, joined the search of nearby Victoria Park. No doubt the Germans sent over just one V1 as a ranging shot against London on that night and the Air Ministry announcement told them they had hit the bullseye. We had a quiet night on the Wednesday but on Thursday all hell was let loose with V1s coming over thick and fast.

ALEX DIAMENT, LEICESTER.

The first V1 flying bomb fell near Bethnal Green on 13 June 1944, almost three months before my personal experience of the arrival of the first V2 rocket on 8 September. We were having tea when the house was rocked by a huge double explosion. My father and I cycled towards it, finding the crater in Burlington Lane, Chiswick. A Whitehall car arrived, bearing Home Secretary Herbert Morrison. After peering down the hole, wishing to avoid causing alarm, he said to his colleagues: 'Pass the word – exploded gas main.'

DESMOND SEAMAN, BUSHEY, HERTS.

The first V1 appeared on 13 June 1944, three months before the first V2 impacted on Chiswick on 8 September. A significant proportion of flying bombs and rockets landed in areas around London as well as those which hit the city itself. A total of 1,444 were reported in Kent and 886 in Sussex. V1s and V2s were used together until the attacks ended, the last V2 falling on 27 March 1945, and the final V1 two days later. During this time the flying bombs killed 6,184 people and the rockets 2,784.

JAMES TAYLOR, IMPERIAL WAR MUSEUM, LONDON.

480: Why is the card game Bridge so called?

Bridge is a corruption of 'Birtich', a card game played on the French Riviera in the 1870s, but the origin of the game is a mystery. No one knows how old it is or who invented it. What is known is that it was introduced into Europe in the latter half of the last century by an English colonel who learnt to play an earlier form in the trenches at Plebna, while fighting alongside the Turks against the Russians. It was taken up by gentlemen playing cards in the London coffee houses and quickly spread to North America. The number of people who play the game today is believed to exceed 100 million.

DOUGLAS AIKMAN, ENGLISH BRIDGE, OFFICIAL MAGAZINE OF THE ENGLISH BRIDGE UNION, GUILDFORD, SURREY.

481: It's difficult enough for the RAF, so how do birds avoid crashing into each other when flying in formation?

Most birds, being small, have very rapid reflexes and can respond to a movement near them with what seems to be astonishing speed. Birds also have a wider field of view, with eyes on either side of their heads. This means that they can see the movements of birds in the flock very easily: the movement of one bird causes a wave of movement through the flock. Individual birds can anticipate when to move because they see a distant bird moving rather than the one next to them. So their seeming ability to move as one is due to 'sleight of wing' or speed of reaction which the human eye cannot distinguish.   CHRIS HARBARD, RSPB, SANDY, BEDS.

482: When someone or something goes missing we say 'gone for a Burton'. Who was Burton?

This expression was used widely by the services in World War II about someone missing or lost but its derivation is much earlier. In 1878 a Dr Burton stood for election to Birmingham Council and this extract appeared in the Birmingham Post: '…during the whole of polling day men were seen coming from Dr Burton's committee room and parading Steward Street with jugs of beer on which were painted papers "Vote for Burton"'. This gave rise to the expression 'He's gone for a Burton' when inquiring of someone's whereabouts.   MRS J. WILKINSON, LEICESTER.

No 48 Squadron – whose badge is a petrel's head superimposed on a red triangle like the Bass label was based at RAF Down Ampney during the war. This coastal command squadron had chosen the petrel, the far-ranging sea bird, as its symbol while based at Gibraltar and flying Hudsons on long-range missions. It adopted the red triangle because every time a plane went missing, they stuck a Bass label on the ops board meaning 'gone for a Burton'. Bass once sponsored the manufacture of a kneeler in my local church, in memory of 48 Squadron members killed in action.
ALAN HARTLEY, COVENTRY.

Several suggestions have been made as to the origin of the expression 'gone for a Burton', used by RAF personnel, which initially meant someone had disappeared and became a euphemism to indicate they had been killed. These ideas include a radio telegraph training room situated above a Montague Burton's clothes shop in Blackpool and a 19th-century Birmingham election campaign in which slips of paper advising 'Vote for Burton' were given out with jugs of beer. The most likely explanation relates to Burton's Ale, popular in many pubs near airfields in the east of England. The idea that someone had nipped out for a beer was a less traumatic way of describing the tragic and all-too-regular loss of a comrade.
BENJAMIN GRAY, NORWICH.

No one will convince me that the roots of this expression lie anywhere other than in the RAF Basic Signals Training School I attended in Blackpool in 1941. Our Morse training was carried out in a room above Montague Burton's tailor's shop on the seafront which, like the top floor of many Burton's shops, had been a billiards hall. Any recruit who didn't come up to scratch in the tough fortnightly test had to return to Burton's at night for a final assessment. If he still didn't pass the test he disappeared from the unit the following day and was said to have 'gone for a Burton'.

G. H. DREDGE, LEICESTER.

This expression was not instigated by RAF men; I remember it was commonly used of any death long before the war. My own theory is that it refers simply to Burton's the tailors where one bought the black suits which every man wore at a funeral.

C. A. TURNER, LOUGHTON, ESSEX.

Sir Richard Burton (1821-90), the explorer who translated the Arabian Nights and travelled to Mecca disguised as a Moslem pilgrim, disappeared in Africa for many months. His absence was noted in the Press, which viewed explorers akin to pop stars and 'gone for a Burton' became widely used.

MIKE MURPHY, SELSDON, SURREY.

'Gone for a Burton' was Cockney rhyming slang, in use long before the war. It stood for Gone for a Burton-on-Trent = went.

FRED G. MOSSMAN, LONDON WC2.

An old soldier told me the saying meant 'he's gone to be fitted for a wooden overcoat' – a coffin. Burton's was the high street tailor most men visited for a suit or overcoat at the time.

EVE CHALAYE, BOROUGH GREEN, KENT.

A 'burton' is a 'Spanish Burton': a two-block-and-hook set carried, though rarely used, on sailing ships since the 19th century. It was stowed in a locker with other tackle and generally covered and tangled up with other gear. When men were working in groups and one was absent, visiting the heads, having a smoke or wetting the tea, if the man in charge noticed his absence he would more often than not be told: 'He's gone for a Burton', a good excuse to be absent for a while.

THOMAS CAVELL, KENT.

Most of the explanations offered for this phrase are unsatisfactory because they don't imply the sense of doom carried by the expression. The only dictionary reference to rhyming slang using 'Burton-on-Trent' is a late 19th-century use to rhyme with 'rent'. In 1992, however, RAF News published a letter from a German correspondent whose father claimed to have known a similar expression in the 1914-18 war. Bodies of prisoners who died at the PoW camp at Reichtersried, near Ulm, were taken to the nearby village of Burtenbach to be buried there in the Friedhof Burten. Inmates of the camp used to say their dead companions were 'going to Burten'.

ERNEST BROOK, WESTON-SUPER-MARE, SOMERSET.

Earlier answers may have erred on the side of delicacy for the origin of this expression, which was in use long before World War I. The explanation given to my grandfather by a Hoxton resident was that if a person was absent from their place of work, the most plausible excuse offered was that they had gone to attend a call of nature. In an all-male workforce it was not unusual for a more down-to-earth phrase to be used. Sanitised by Cockney rhyming slang, in the era when Montague Burton was the most popular high street men's outfitters, this became 'Gone to Burton for a fit' shortened to 'Gone for a Burton'. Rhyming slang was often used to render acceptable expressions that would otherwise have been very rude. R. P. EDWARDS, RUISLIP MANOR, MIDDX.

483: Who gets the most 999 emergency calls – the fire, police or ambulance services?

The Emergency Services receive on average 22 million calls every year, all of which are dealt with initially by BT's emergency operator service. Only about 12 million are passed on to the emergency services, the rest being hoax callers, misdialled numbers, changes of heart, end of emergency, etc. Of the 12 million calls BT passes on, about 68% go to the police. The fire and ambulance services receive roughly the same amount at 15% each. The other emergency services (not the AA), the Coastguard, and Cave and Mountain Rescue receive the rest.

PETER KINSELLA, BT, LONDON.

484: My telephone number contains the number 1703 but I cannot find any famous event which occurred in 1703. Was that year devoid of historical significance?

Several important events happened in 1703: one of the most famous Englishmen, Samuel Pepys, Admiralty officer and diarist, died. The Scottish Parliament rebelled against the proposed union with England. John Wesley was born, and the Duke of Marlborough seized Cologne. A £50 reward was offered for the arrest of the writer Daniel Defoe for publication of a satirical pamphlet suggesting the execution of all dissenters (his irony escaped the government of the day and Defoe was put in the stocks for three days). There was also a storm which demolished the Eddystone lighthouse, and killed thousands of people (including the Bishop of Bath and Wells). RICHARD HILLMAN, GLOUCESTER.

485: What happened to Fosbury who initiated the Fosbury flop, now used by most high jumpers?

After setting a new Olympic record in Mexico City in 1968, I returned to my studies, which had obviously taken a back seat during my preparation for the Games. I studied philosophy and religion and then moved on to civil engineering, in which I obtained my degree. I now run a civil engineering and lands survey company in Ketchum, Idaho, a town of 3,300 people, where I live with Karen, my wife, Erich, our 11-year-old son, Cammie and Bliff, our two dogs, George, our cat and a boa constrictor called Bo. I am happy with my life and achievements to date and must thank readers of the Daily Mail for asking after my welfare. It's nice to know I'm still remembered.   DICK FOSBURY, KETCHUM, IDAHO.

Dick Fosbury pioneered the 'backwards flop' technique in the 1986 Olympic Games and it is now used by most high jumpers but research shows that a similar method was devised by a German high jumper in the Thirties. I was an RAF corporal physical training instructor at RAF Wilmslow, Cheshire, in 1942 when my sergeant, Ken Alloport, showed me a small book he had got free with a packet of Kellogg's cornflakes before the war. This book clearly described a backward high jump, saying it was used only by one German high jumper who was forced to abandon the style because landing in the then customary sand pit was injuring his back.
                              A. W. CARD, NEWTON AYCLIFFE, CO DURHAM.

486: Is it true that during World War II, all but three of the men aboard HMS Hood died from a single German shot?

There were only three survivors when HMS Hood sank but the destruction was caused by more than one shot. HMS Hood came to grief on May 24, 1941. The official Board of Enquiry reported that the ship was hit by both the third and fifth salvoes fired from the Bismarck. A shell from the fifth salvo is believed to have caused the four-inch, high-angle magazines to explode, leading to the detonation of the aft 15-inch magazines, the sinking of the vessel and the death of the majority of the crew. The three survivors were Midshipman W. J. Dundas, R. A. Tilburn and A. E. Briggs.   IAIN MACKENZIE, NATIONAL MARITIME MUSEUM, LONDON.

A booklet I have, published shortly after the disaster to raise money for dependants of the dead, confirms that only three survived but the battle was far from one-sided. It includes this account: 'The pursuit of the Bismarck, believed by some naval officers to have been the biggest and most powerful battleship in the world, some say nearer 50,000 tons than her specified 35,000, was begun on Friday evening of May 23, 1941.

HMS Hood, accompanied by HMS Prince of Wales, our newest battleship, took up the chase.

'They had to face blinding snowstorms, which for hours hid everything, and visibility was reduced to a matter of yards. They expected to make contact with Bismarck about 0200 but at the last moment the enemy altered course and the two ships steamed on for another four hours. Then there was a sudden abatement of the snow, and visibility became clear. Thus two specks were spotted on the horizon, which proved to be the Bismarck and her cruiser escort.

'The two British ships then put on full speed so as to shorten the range. The enemy also turned, and there was the spectacle of the biggest warships in the world racing towards each other...

'Then came the order to open fire. Immediately, the Hood's forward guns thundered forth. Within a few seconds smoke was seen belching from the Bismarck. She had replied. The Hood at this time was racing forward. Within two or three hundred yards, fountains of water shot up in her wake. Then all of a sudden she was hit. The shell or shells appeared to fall forward of her aft 15-inch gun turrets. A great fire broke out and thick black smoke poured forth. The Hood, however, continued to race forward, guns still firing. 'Then there was a colossal explosion, and the great battleship was completely enveloped in flame and smoke. Masts, funnels and other parts of the ship were hurled hundreds of feet into the air. These crashed back onto the sea and were lost to sight. The bows of the Hood tilted vertically, and within three or four minutes all that remained on the surface, apart from the strewn wreckage, was flame and smoke.

'A destroyer was detailed to pick up any survivors, but alas, there were only three – a Midshipman, a Signalman and an Able Seaman. So ended a noble career of one of the finest ships that ever sailed the Seven Seas. She had, however, done her work well, for she damaged the Bismarck, thereby reducing her speed and leading to the latter's destruction two days later. 'All those who held the ship and her crew dear will never forget that tragic moment at 2100 on May 24, 1941, when the BBC announcer uttered the fatal news that HMS Hood had been sunk, and when it was realised that there was little hope of survivors, the blow was a staggering one...'

JOHN YOUDE (EX RN), LITTLE HAYWOOD, STAFFORD.

I was a radio operator on the battleship HMS Prince of Wales and our ship was fitted with guns designed to outrange the two biggest German menaces, Bismarck and Tirpitz. Our Captain was confidently expecting to be asked to open fire at extreme range, to try to damage the Bismarck without exposing the British ships to return fire. To his horrified amazement the Admiral, in his far older and less versatile vessel HMS Hood, had both ships rush in to suicidal range, while his frantic requests for permission to open fire were refused. The Admiral was either unaware of the gunnery advantage under his command or determined, in fine old naval tradition, to have first crack at the blighter. The angle of our approach meant we forfeited the use of our aft turrets. The culminating horror, when the shooting started, was the realisation that the Hood had concentrated her fire on the wrong ship, the cruiser consort Prinz Eugen, and had ordered us to do likewise. Fortunately, using Nelson's blind eye technique, we shifted our attention to the big one, Bismarck, effectively holing its hull, causing a great loss of fuel oil. But by then the Hood's vulnerable magazine, which should have been properly armoured during the Baldwin years, had been hit, with tragic consequences.

BERNARD CAMPION, PLYMOUTH, DEVON.

HMS Hood was struck by at least one 8in shell from Bismarck's escort, Prinz Eugen, and a few minutes afterwards by Bismarck's fifth salvo, which produced one, possibly two, hits. An explosion occurred, breaking her apart, and the two halves rapidly sank. Hood was extremely unlucky as German shells of the period were notoriously unreliable – only two of the seven hits on Prince Of Wales performed as they should.

CLIVE JACOBS, DINNINGTON, SOUTH YORKSHIRE.

It's quite possible for HMS Hood to have been destroyed by a single hit. Her keel was laid down on the morning of May 31, 1916, just a few hours before the beginning of the Battle of Jutland in which HMSs Queen Mary, Indefatigable and Invincible were destroyed by sustained enemy shell penetration of their gun turrets. This resulted in flashover right down to their magazines, which were linked directly to the turrets. At least five turrets on the German battleships Derfflinger and Seydlitz were pierced by 15in shells in the same battle but their two-stage ammunition hoists saved them from instant destruction. Many modifications were made to the Hood after lessons learned at Jutland but did radical re-design of her ammunition handling system avoid a direct link between turret and magazine?

JOHN BAKER, CHESTERFIELD, DERBYSHIRE.

487: How long is a donkey's year? What is the meaning of the expression: 'Not for donkeys' years'?

This expression, means that something is taking (or lasting) a long time is a misrepresentation of the words 'donkey's ears.' The original makes more sense as donkeys' ears are long, measuring six to eight inches.

DAVID HATHERSAGE, SHEFFIELD.

488: Why are cats referred to as 'moggies'?

The proper term for non-pedigree cats and dogs is mongrel, though very few people use it for cats. Use of the word 'moggie' as an affectionate term for a cat seems to stem from a variation of maggie, once in common use as a name for a scruffy, old woman. In some parts of the country the word was also applied to scarecrows. By the start of the 20th century, maggie was used to describe cats too, likening wild and scruffy city cats to unkempt old women. Between the wars the word was abbreviated to 'mog', with dogs and cats being known as 'tikes' and 'mogs.' After World War II, the word moggie was reinstated as an endearing term for the domestic cat and now the difference between a moggie and a maggie is quite distinct. 'Puss', another popular word for a cat, comes from Pasht, one of the names of the Egyptian cat goddess. PETER EMBLING, CATS MAGAZINE, MANCHESTER.

489: Is it true that a white sports car can be seen in the big chariot race scene in the film Ben Hur?

When working on a documentary on the 1959 version of Ben Hur, I was intrigued by this question. I have seen rushes of the film time after time but have never seen a sports car or, for that matter, anything else that would make the film lose its classical Roman context. I have spoken to several people about this claim and although one other person claims to have heard the rumour before, I doubt very much if it has any factual basis, although I did hear another rumour that it is possible to see a smoking cigarette stub during the race scene.

ADAIR KAISER, TURNER HOME ENTERTAINMENT, ATLANTA, GEORGIA, USA.

I don't know about Ben Hur, but in the epic El Cid, I recall seeing a jet plane trail in the medieval sky and in the shot of cheering crowds waving food at El Cid entering the city whose starvation and seige he has relieved, the camera pans across all the correctly dressed citizens to show a man in modern dungarees, half-heartedly waving a cabbage. HARRY THOMAS, BRISTOL.

490: Who were Darby and Joan?

John Darby and his wife Joan were characters named in a ballad by Henry Woodfall, published in 1735 in the Gentleman's Magazine, and are believed to be the original devoted husband and wife team who inspired the use of 'Darby and Joan' to signify an old-fashioned, loyal and loving, inseparable couple. John Darby, once Henry Woodfall's employer, died in 1730. His wife is described in Woodfall's ballad: 'As chaste as a picture cut in alabaster. You might sooner move a Scythian rock than shoot fire into her bosom.' R DEAN, EXETER.

491: How many people are in flight in aeroplanes at any one time?

Based on the International Civil Aviation Organisation's statistics it would be fair to suggest that there are around 10,000 aircraft in the air at any one moment, of which about 4,500 are commercial aircraft, ranging from small business planes carrying five or six people to huge jumbo jets.

Each year, about 1,250 million passengers make an average trip of about 1,000 miles (1,650kms) on a commercial aircraft, which takes an average of about 2¾ hours. To achieve an average of one passenger in the air all the time would take 3,200 people a year by air (the number of hours in a year divided by 2¾). With 1,250 million passengers there will be about 390,000 such passengers (1,250,000 divided by 3,200) in the air at any one time on commercial aircraft. If we add to that an average of 20 people a day flying in a general aviation craft, we can assume a total of 500,000 (390,000 + 110,000) people in the air at any one moment. Unfortunately we have no information on military aircraft.

HUTTON ARCHER, INTERNATIONAL CIVIL AVIATION ORGANISATION, MONTREAL, CANADA.

492: What was in London's Trafalgar Square, before Trafalgar Square?

Trafalgar Square did not receive its name until 1835. Previously, the site had many uses. 13th Century records show that in the reign of Edward I, the King's Mews were there and so they appear to have remained until 1534. Then Queen Elizabeth 1 had them re-built as stables. Later, the Stuart monarchs housed court officials in the buildings. During the Civil War, Oliver Cromwell turned them into barracks which were later to receive Royalist prisoners. There was more re-building after the Restoration, and in later years there was a menagerie and a store for public records. In 1830 the whole area underwent major demolition to accommodate Nash's plans for his Charing Cross Improvement Scheme. The site sloped and by the time it was levelled, in 1840, Nash had died, and the architect Barry took over the works. All that remains of the original scheme are Nelson's Column and the statues of Charles I and George IV. Fountains and basins were added, and they are said to have been originally fed by springs that ran under what is now the National Gallery. Everything else has been added or remodelled over the years, with the notable involvement of Lutyens in the 1930s. The Square has long been a place for political meeting, and the Chartists started their march there in 1848.

A. E. BAILEY, DOVER, KENT.

493: Why is the mark darts players stand on called the 'ochie'?

The correct spelling is actually 'Oche', and the word derives from the same Norse word for a groove or mark originally etched on the deck of a ship. The mark was a dividing line, normally towards the upper section of the vessel, over which only the captain and his senior men could cross. The word was later used in Old English to mean a groove dug out of the ground from which an archer could take his shot. This later meaning was the natural choice of word to be chosen when applied to the world of darts.

TONY GREEN, VOICE OF DARTS COMMENTATOR FOR BBC SPORT AND TV'S BULLSEYE, LONDON.

494: Who was the 'infant stockbroker'?

If there has ever been an 'infant stockbroker', the junior fatcat in question did not live in Britain as no mention of him can be traced by several economic and financial historians I have spoken to. The 'infant stockbroker' probably refers to what was known as the Little Stockbroker, a penny slot machine found in amusement arcades in the late Twenties. The Little Stockbroker was an early one-arm bandit which fell foul of the law and was made illegal.

BERNARD WOOD, BEXHILL, EAST SUSSEX.

495: How is a ballet written down for future performances?

Ballet, and other forms of dance, are written down using a system of notation called choreology. The person responsible for this is the choreologist, and all the major dance companies will have their own. The two systems used resemble written music, in that it is written on a stave and divided up into bars so that it can then be used in conjunction with the music. It is, however, more complex than written music as there are an infinite number of body movements and many different body parts to be written down. It is worth pointing out that in the main the individual dancer is responsible for remembering their own steps, and quite often also for passing on this knowledge to future dancers, whereas the notation allows for a more permanent record to be kept.

GRETA DAWSON, NORTHERN BALLET THEATRE, HALIFAX.

496: Who or what were the Angels of Mons which supposedly appeared in front of the advancing German troops in World War I, allowing the British Expeditionary Force to escape?

Much fiction was written at the time and since about the Angel at Mons, and it is therefore understandable that the question submitted by J. Harmington indicates a multitude of angels when there was one, and the rescue of the BEF by these immortal beings when there was none. The following account was related to me by ex-Sergeant Daniel Ruffell, of the Grenadier Guards, whom I am quite certain witnessed the event. The basis of my belief is that Sgt Ruffell suffered partial brain damage as a result of his wartime injuries, leaving him with a stable but limited intellect. He had only rare moments of lucidity, but was incapable of fabrication. It was on one of these moments of lucidity that he told me, without prompting, that he had seen the Angel at Mons, with the sudden recollection of something extraordinary that had happened 50 years before.

He said: 'We was moving up the line at night with an ammo column drawn by horses. Suddenly the horses alongside us wouldn't go on. The driver tried to shift 'em with his whip, but they just stood with their heads back looking up, and eyes big as saucers. I thought perhaps they had been frightened by a starshell, but couldn't see anything in front of us.

'I was giving the driver a hand, trying to push his wagon and force the horses forward, when our officer shouts out: "Look up for God's sake, look up there all of you." Then I looked up and see it, plain as I see you, an angel in the sky!

'It was like them statues you sees, with a long white dress and a thing like a crown of thorns on her head. And what looked like wings folded behind her. She was laid out like she were on a slab, with her arms folded across, like she was dead.'

I asked how long she remained there, but he didn't seem to be sure, but thought it could have been five or ten minutes. Then I asked if he could remember which way she faced, and this time he seemed certain that her feet pointed towards the German lines. Then I put what I suppose was the burning question to him: 'What do you think was the reason this angel appeared to you men, including the German soldiers?'

He shrugged, grinned and said with embarrassment: 'I dunno, perhaps it was because of all them blokes what had died.'

'Is that what you and your mates thought afterwards?'

'Well some of them, but some of them wouldn't talk about it, they seemed frightened.'

Danny died in a nursing home five or six years later.

D. E. WILKES, HAREFIELD, MIDDLESEX.

My uncle, Oliver Swann, witnessed the 'Angels of Mons' incident during the Great War. Like ex-Sergeant Ruffell he was in the Grenadier Guards: he died in 1964. His account of the 'angels' was not as emotional as Sgt Ruffell's but it was an event he never forgot. He and his colleagues saw that smoke from gun-fire had formed into the image of a huge angel, just over a hill. There appeared to be one large 'angel' and the trailing smoke also made an impressive background, which somehow looked like a group of other 'angels' surrounding it. Although they were quite sure it was just gun-smoke, they found it an interesting and unforgettable experience and liked to think at the time that it was a sign of forthcoming peace. MRS SUSAN SWANN, BIRMINGHAM.

The Angels of Mons are a legend which began with author Arthur Machen's fantasy story The Bowmen, published in Lord Northcliffe's Evening News on September 29, 1914, shortly after the Allied retreat from Mons. Machen's story imagined St George and the archers of Agincourt aiding the outnumbered British troops and dispatching the enemy hordes. Perhaps because the story appeared in a newspaper, many readers assumed it was a report of an actual event. Occult magazines seized on the tale, declaring that a miracle had occurred on the battlefield, and by the summer of 1915 rumours of divine intervention by 'The Angels of Mons' had people enthralled. A war-weary nation was assured that heaven was on its side. Machen said: 'In the popular view, shining and benevolent supernatural beings are angels and so, I believe, the Bowmen of my story have become The Angels of Mons.' When Machen attempted to explain how the myth had arisen, he was condemned as arrogant by advocates for the 'angels'. The Bowmen appeared as a book in 1915 and the controversy ensured it was a bestseller. Machen died in 1947 aged 84. A Machen Society, formed in his home town of Caerleon, Gwent, in 1986, has a worldwide membership. ROGER DOBSON, OXFORD.

Although Arthur Machen thought his book The Bowmen created the Angels of Mons, Harold Begbie's 1915 book On The Side Of The Angels set out to prove that British soldiers believed they had seen angels before The Bowmen was printed. Some of his proof came from Mr Machen's own postbag. To quote Mr Begbie: 'Whether we choose to believe these testimonies that angels have appeared, each must decide for himself. But beyond the reach of dis-proof, beyond the widest circumference of equivocation, is the now definite fact that some of our soldiers, officers as well as men, believed they saw visions in France long before Mr Machen had published his story.' P. RELF, GRAVESEND, KENT.

497: Now we know what happened to the Mary Celeste in the end, what is the best theory for what happened to her on the fateful voyage?

There are actually two mysteries; why the crew left a ship that was in no danger of sinking and why no trace of them was ever found. The Mary Celeste was carrying barrels of highly inflammable alcohol from New York to Genoa when found on December 4, 1872. She had obviously been deliberately abandoned in a hurry. A section of rail had been removed to launch the ship's boat. One sail was incompletely lowered, two others were still set. All the ship's papers were missing but the captain's navigational instruments were still on board. The fore hatch was displaced on deck and the galley stove was out of place. Some of the rigging had been removed and the broken end of one of the halyards was trailing in the water. And there were strange scars in the wood of the bows above the waterline. Expert fire insurance assessor, Sir William Charles Crocker, noticed the crucially important small hole in the galley floor, draining into the hold. A build-up of alcohol vapour must have exploded there with a shattering bang, doing little harm apart from knocking over the stove, practically invisible and leaving no traces of soot. The crew must have feared that a barrel had ignited below decks and the cargo was about to go up. Captain Benjamin Briggs, with his wife and child aboard, gave the order to abandon ship. The crew had to manhandle the 20ft launch off the main hatch and improvise a way of getting it into the water, using some of the missing rigging. They tied the boat to the end of the long mooring rope and drifted astern, awaiting events. In a light wind but heavy swell, the improvised hawser suddenly parted. In my opinion the crew now caught up with the abandoned ship and tried to get a man on board by way of the bowsprit rigging. But under the influence of an unpredictable swell, the ship's bows suddenly came down on the boat with shattering force, sending it to the bottom with all hands: a perfect example of the ill-luck which always seemed to attend the Mary Celeste.   P. S. CRAWLEY, EBBW VALE, GWENT.

By far the best theory was immortalised on television in the 1965 Doctor Who serial, The Chase. The good Doctor and his friends were being chased across time and space by the Daleks. Trying to elude them, the Doctor lands on the Mary Celeste. Alas, the Daleks landed shortly afterwards. The crew were so terrified they all jumped into the sea. One of the most plausible theories, methinks!   AL DUPRES, TV PRESENTER, HULL.

498: If Prince Andrew were to have a son, would he inherit the title of Duke of York, or is this title reserved for Prince Harry?

According to tradition, Royal and aristocratic titles are always passed down through the male line. So, if Prince Andrew had a son, he would inherit the title of Duke of York, even though that title is normally saved for the second son of the monarch.   DAVID WILLIAMSON, DEBRETT'S PEERAGE LTD, LONDON.

499: 'It's a Catch 22 situation', but does anyone know what Catches 1 to 21 were?

Catch 22, coined in the novel Catch 22 by Joseph Heller in 1955, was supposedly from the United States Army Bombing Squadron's Rule 22. This rule stated that if a flyer wanted to stop going on flying missions because of the onset of insanity, all he had to do was ask and he would be immediately grounded. However, the fact that he had stated he was insane meant he couldn't be because to be insane meant that you wouldn't know you were and therefore wouldn't ask to be grounded. So you would have to continue flying missions. Heller has been quoted as saying he was originally going to call the book Catch 18 but changed his mind at the last minute. NORMAN BLACK, MANCHESTER.

500: Who decides whether a church has a vicar or a rector?

History has decided this for us. Until recently the incumbent of a church was paid by tithes and rents from local lands. If the incumbent himself received the rents, he was known as a rector. But sometimes a squire or landowner collected the rents and paid the incumbent, who was then known as a vicar. Now all vicars and rectors are paid the same amount, most of which comes from donations by members of the church, but the titles of rector or vicar have been retained. In the past 20 years, the General Synod has created various teams of clergy, linked by a Measure of the Synod, whose leader – first among equals – is known as Team Rector, while the rest of the team are called Team Vicars. It is therefore possible that a rector might become a vicar and a vicar might become a rector. REVD DR ALAN SOWERBUTTS, PRIEST-IN-CHARGE, BRINDLE, CHORLEY, LANCS.

501: Why do we kiss under the mistletoe at Christmas? Whose idea was it in the first place?

Mistletoe, a parasitic shrub which grows on other trees, was held in great respect by the Druids, especially if it grew on oak, because they believed it formed when lightning struck the tree. They thought the berries contained the seminal fluid of the tree and they used them as a charm to induce fertility: hence the origin of kissing under the mistletoe. The kissing tradition dates from the early 17th Century. The man should remove a berry each time he kisses a girl under the mistletoe and when there are no more berries left the kissing should stop. WENDY PAGE, HORSHAM, SUSSEX.

502: How were ancient Greek and Roman pillars made so perfectly round and tapered when manufacturing similar ones today would require advanced machining techniques?

The perfection of the columns in ancient architecture is the end result of centuries of practice. By the time the Parthenon was built in the mid-5th century BC, the colonnaded building had been a feature of Greek architecture for more than 200 years. In some of the early examples, the columns are much cruder in shape and construction. It is also possible to see that the workmanship on buildings away from the main cultural centres was sometimes less than competent. Mathematics, algebra and geometry were all developed in the ancient world, and the builders of the Parthenon understood optical distortion well enough to correct it by giving columns a slight backward angle, a technique called entasis. All the work was done by hand – rough cutting by slave labour and finishing by master masons. Mistakes could be corrected if and when they occurred. Mechanical means cannot reproduce this 'fine tuning', which is what gives ancient architecture its refinement.

MAGGIE KNIGHT, EDUCATION DEPARTMENT, VICTORIA AND ALBERT MUSEUM.

503: Could the Black Death, which hit Britain in 1348, ever recur? If it did, what would be the cure?

The Black Death, carried by the flea of the black rat, is still endemic in Asia and South America, but it is very unlikely to recur as a major epidemic. Humans infected by the bacterium Yersinia Pestis from a rat flea bite may also develop and spread it as pneumonic plague, but modern antibiotics can cure the illness. Plague was reported on ships in every year from 1896 to 1935, but most ships are now efficiently de-ratted, although rats occasionally join the jet set aboard aircraft. In 1990 a research worker from Bolivia fell ill before flying to Washington DC, where she was diagnosed as having bubonic plague. A previous case imported into the U.S. was a soldier returning from Vietnam. The less contagious sylvatic plague is present in ground squirrels and other rodents in the western U.S.

PETER L. G. BATEMAN, DIRECTOR, RENTOKIL, EAST GRINSTEAD.

504: Where does the word 'doolally' for someone slightly barmy originate?

Like a lot of our slang, the word 'doolally' was brought back to us from abroad by the armed forces. Up until the end of the 19th century, time-expired soldiers returning from India embarked via Deolali, a camp near Bombay. Depending on when their period of service was completed they could catch a troopship home. This enforced idleness often made soldiers act very strangely and men with exemplary records often got into serious trouble, serving terms of imprisonment before they were sent home. The expression 'he's got the Doolally tap', later 'he's gone Doolally' was applied to anyone who behaved unusually.　　R. C. BYWATERS, EPSOM, SURREY.

505: What is a 'smithereen', as in smashed to?

It is simply the Anglicised form of the Irish *smiderini,* meaning 'little pieces'.
R. McDONALD, HUYTON, LIVERPOOL.

506: How do the members of massed bands turn over the music sheets, read the music, play it and still manage to march in formation?

The simple and straightforward answer is that they don't, because they don't need to. When bands march, all their music is printed on cards which are then held in the lyre on the instrument. All the music for a single march is printed on one side of the card; as the pieces tend to contain a large number of repeats, the music will not take up much space. At the end of each march, the musician will take a new card from the clip and place it at the front.　　BOB BENNETT, MUSICIANS' UNION, BIRMINGHAM.

We teach our players one trick at a time, beginning with the easiest. When young musicians join us, most have some instrumental ability and are soon able to play most of the easier marches in the Parade band repertoire. The drill instructor teaches them to stand up straight, march smartly at 116 paces a minute, take a 30in pace and stay two paces behind the man in front. Experienced players have no trouble carrying out complex marching displays on sight, knowing the music by heart. Our displays for the Royal Tournament, with more than 200 players on the march, are rehearsed in two and a half days. Our worst problems are ruts in the arena surface and the constantly changing lighting – but that's showbiz.
CAPTAIN W.J.P. RIDER LRAM ATCL RM, BAND OF HM ROYAL MARINES.

There is rather more to this than is being suggested. When playing on the march, musicians must maintain military posture, holding their instruments at the correct angle, they must constantly check their 'covering' and 'dressing', that is, march squarely behind the man in front and maintain straight ranks. They are also obliged to listen to the bass drummer who sets the tempo of the band and gives signal instructions like 'cut off music', 'halt' etc. Out in front is the Drum Major whose mace signals must also be obeyed. They inform the Time Beater who passes the information to the band. All this is accomplished only after much training, practice and concentration.
BILL QUINN (FORMER GRENADIER GUARDS BAND SERGEANT MAJOR), MAIDENHEAD, BERKS.

507: Was there ever a real life 'Winslow boy' and, if so, what became of him and that five-shilling postal order?

The real life Winslow boy, on whom Sir Terence Rattigan's play was based, was George Archer-Shee. The case centred around the dismissal in 1908 of the naval cadet for allegedly stealing a five-shilling postal order. George was dismissed mainly on the evidence of the postmistress, who claimed that the stolen postal order was cashed by a cadet, who at the same time bought a postal order for 15 shillings. After the trial, in which George was cleared, he went to school at Stoneyhurst and then on to the U.S. to study banking. At the outbreak of World War I, George returned to England and volunteered for the Army. As a lieutenant in the 3rd Battalion South Staffordshire Regiment, he was killed at Ypres on October 31, 1914, having been at the front for only 26 days. He has no known grave but is commemorated by a plaque on the Menin Gate. Both the postal orders, along with all the other correspondence relating to the Post Office's involvement in this matter, can be viewed at the Post Office Archives and Records Centre in London.

KEVIN SQUELCH, ARCHIVIST, THE POST OFFICE, LONDON.

Apart from his name being on the Menin Gate, 'Winslow boy' George Archer-Shee is also commemorated on the bronze 1914-18 War Memorial tablet on the outside wall of St Martin's-on-the-Quay Jesuit Church in Bristol city centre. George was the son of Martin Archer-Shee, manager of the Bank of England in Clare Street, Bristol.

MARY BRAIN, KNOWLE, BRISTOL.

508: Is there a female equivalent of brethren?

Sistren was once upon a time the female equivalent of brethren and it fell out of usage in about 1550. Brethren and sistren were simply older forms of brother and sister, but the word 'brethren' became used for both genders in connection with fellow membership of a guild, order or Christian society.

RICHARD PATEFIELD, PRESTON.

509: Why is the Isle of Dogs so called?

The first reference to the Isle of Dogs was in 1593 by the writer Robert Greene, the spelling at the time being 'Isle of Doges Ferm'. The area enclosed within the loop of the River Thames is not actually a natural island, although it would regularly flood across the 'top of the loop' which would create an island. Earliest references to the area called it Stepney Marsh. During Henry VIII's reign, a palace was built at Greenwich, opposite the Isle of Dogs. Hunting kennels were a feature of the palace and the sound of the animals was very evident to anyone on Stepney Marsh, giving it the now familiar name of Isle of Dogs.

STEPHEN BECKETT, ISLE OF DOGS NEIGHBOURHOOD OFFICE.

An alternative derivation comes from the 17th century, when Dutch engineers brought their skills to bear on the area's drainage problems, constructing dykes or dijks to control the flooding. It is thought that a simple corruption of the sound turned this into 'dogs.'

C. M. ROGERS, EDGWARE, MIDDLESEX.

510: Who was the first cricket Test batsman to wear a safety helmet?

During the 1933 MCC v West Indies match at Lord's, Patsy Hendren of Middlesex protected himself against a form of bodyline bowling by wearing a cap with three peaks – his wife sewed on the additional peaks – the whole thing looking like a deerstalker with the flaps down. During the 1977 England v Australia Test series, England captain Mike Brearley wore a plastic device like a skull-cap under his normal cap. But the first player to wear a full-face helmet with visor was Australia's Graham Yallop, in the second Test of the 1977-78 series against the West Indies at Bridgetown on March 17 and 18, 1978.

STEPHEN LYNCH, WISDEN CRICKET MONTHLY, GUILDFORD, SURREY.

511: Why is a car's dashboard so-called?

The dashboard, or 'dasher' as it was originally called, was found on horse-drawn carriages predating the motor vehicle. It was an iron-framed device, usually covered with leather, the purpose of which was to stop the driver of the carriage and his passengers being splattered with mud thrown up (or 'dashed-up') by the horses' hooves. As it was that part of the vehicle which separated the carriage from the horses, it seems natural enough that the name has been retained by the part of the motor vehicle which separates the modern traveller from the car engine.

MARIE TIECHE, NATIONAL MOTOR MUSEUM, BEAULIEU, BROCKENHURST, HANTS.

512: When I was put on defaulters' parade in the Army, it was known as doing 'jankers'. What is the origin and meaning of jankers?

To be on jankers means to be confined to camp. Jankers is a pure Army term which rarely shows up in normal slang dictionaries. It comes from a corruption of the Urdu word *jangla,* meaning to fence in. As a third of the British Army served in India before World War II, this is just another example of the many Indian words that have entered our language from the days of the Empire. JANE HAINSWORTH, NATIONAL ARMY MUSEUM, CHELSEA, LONDON.

The term 'jankers', familiar to the thousands of British Army, Navy and RAF personnel as a military punishment or punishment detail, was particularly popular during the Fifties in the heyday of National Service. The origins of the term are obscure, with the first references to its use dating from the late 1910s and early 1920s. Consensus of opinion suggests the word may be related to 'jangle' which, in earlier times, meant 'to grumble', hence a 'jangler' or 'janglers' being a person complaining about his punishment. The term later being applied to the punishment itself.
GRAEME COBB, SALTCOATS, AYRSHIRE.

513: What, if any, songs have actually rhymed the words Moon and June?

Does no one else recall the timeless lyrics sung by that sentimental Frenchman Maurice Chevalier, in the song I Remember It Well? 'The dazzling April moon. There was none that night. And the month was June. That's right, that's right. It warms my heart to know that you, Remember still the way you do. Oh yes, I remember it well.' How could anyone forget? REBECCA ARTHUR, ST AUSTELL, CORNWALL.

The Vanessa Williams hit Save The Best For Last, which made the Top Ten in 1992, starts: 'Sometimes the snow falls down in June, Sometimes the Sun goes round the Moon, I see the passion in your eyes, Sometimes it's all a big surprise.' LIZ FROST, CAMBERLEY, SURREY.

What about: 'I lost my heart in Budapest, On a night in the middle of June, When the gipsy bands were at their best, And the Danube looked up to the Moon.' E. M. CULL, GLOUCESTER.

514: Why the $64,000 question?

The original saying stems from the US television quizgame The $64,000 Question, first shown on June 7, 1955, hosted by Hal March. The programme itself was based on a popular radio show of the time called Take It Or Leave It, a show in which the contestant could continually double his or her money starting from the sum of $1. As a TV quizgame in the US, The $64,000 Question really did have a top prize of $64,000. To reach this sum the contestant started with $1,000, which could be doubled to $2,000 if a question was answered correctly; the $2,000 could double to $4,000, the $4,000 to $8,000 and so on until finally, if the contestant had the nerve, this could reach $64,000, with the question at this level of the game normally very difficult. Thus the

$64,000 question as a common phrase means a very difficult question. The British version of the game has recently been a popular programme hosted by Bob Monkhouse. Unfortunately, due to the IBA code of conduct, we were unable to go to £64,000. However we were allowed to go to £6,400, the highest cash sum yet allowed on British television.

RICHARD HOLLOWAY, CONTROLLER OF ENTERTAINMENT, CENTRAL TELEVISION, MAKERS OF THE $64,000 QUESTION, NOTTINGHAM.

515: Where did the expression 'you're pulling my leg' originate?

To pull someone's leg, meaning to tease or make fun of them, is thought to have originated in Scotland. The saying comes from the physical movement of pulling a person's leg away from them, placing them in a foolish position.

JAMES RAMSEY, BRIGHTON.

516: Does the Paris Metro have a vending machine dispensing pairs of jeans?

There was a vending machine selling jeans on the Paris Metro but it is no longer in place. Travellers using or passing through Auber station in the 8th arrondissement in central Paris in 1989 could buy jeans from it but after four months we decided to remove it and it has not been replaced.

VALERIE BOFELL, PROMOMETRO, (COMPANY RESPONSIBLE FOR METRO MERCHANDISING), PARIS.

517: Who was Sixteen-String Jack?

Sixteen-string Jack was an 18th-century highwayman, whose real name was John Rann. His nickname 'Sixteen-String Jack' refers to his dandified manner of dress, including sixteen silk strings (tags) on his buckskin breeches. Rann was arrested seven times during his career as a highwayman, the last time being in 1774 when he was finally hanged at Tyburn.

MRS PAT HORTON, BOURNEMOUTH, DORSET.

R. S. Surtees's book Mr Sponge's Sporting Tour has a character called Sir Harry Scattercash, described as follows: 'He was a harum scarum fellow, all string and tapes...While his untied waist coat strings protruded. The knee strings were also generally loose, the web straps of his boots were seldom in, and what with one set of strings and another, he had acquired the name of Sixteen-String Jack.'

C. C. KEATING, SWINDON, WILTS.

518: If 'spend' is to part with your money, and 'thrift' is to save it, how do we get 'spendthrift'?

At first inspection the familiar term 'spendthrift' appears self-contradictory but before the word 'thrift' meant being careful to save money it meant simply wealth and substance. So 'spendthrift' means one who squanders wealth, fritters away an inheritance or the family estate. The word 'scattergood', rarely heard today, had the same meaning.

ERNEST GRAINGER, WAKEFIELD, WEST YORKSHIRE.

519: Does the Secretary of State for Scotland have to be Scottish, and the Welsh Secretary Welsh etc? If so, why isn't the Fisheries Minister a fisherman?

The various Ministers and Secretaries for the home countries do not have to be from those particular regions and, while the Secretary for Scotland is generally Scottish there is no fixed tradition for the Secretary of State for Wales to be Welsh. The tradition of having a Scottish Secretary of State for Scotland has been current for more than 100 years but past holders have been non-Scots, the last, according to my information, being the Right Honourable George Trevelyan, born in Leicestershire, who held the post in 1886.

JAREK KLAYA, WALSALL.

520: Why does the addition of salt to food make it tastier?

Reflecting our marine origin, animals, including humans, require salt to maintain the right balance of body fluids. Perhaps because of this need, salt developed into one of the four primary tastes – the others being sweet, sour and bitter. It is probably the most satisfying of flavour ingredients and can give interest to foods which would otherwise have little taste.

KAY MONAGHAN, SALT UNION LTD, RUNCORN, CHESHIRE.

521: Which celebrity has the world's largest fan club?

According to the American Book Of Associations, the largest fan club in the world which publishes its membership figures is for a country/blues band called Alabama, which had an active membership of more than 300,000 in 1992. Other stars organise their fan clubs through large record or marketing companies and these are more like merchandise catalogues than genuine clubs. Figures are seldom given out and clubs tend to be short-lived associations. I was amazed at how low some membership figures were: Laurel and Hardy Sons Of The Desert Fan Club only 8,000; The Beatles Fan Club, 36,000; Phil Collins, 50,000; The Sinatra Society, 4,000; Star Trek, 50,000; Marilyn Monroe International Fan Club, 2,000; Buddy Holly, 5,500; David Copperfield, 75,000. The Guinness Book Of Records has no largest fan club listing though I believe it may soon include a section. Then perhaps we will find out whether Madonna, Michael Jackson, Take That or the Spice Girls, for example, are really as well-followed as people as they are for their music or talent. Donny Osmond still has an active fan club, presently running at 2,000. The king of rock 'n' roll, Elvis Presley, has 425 members alone in the association of Elvis Presley Fan Clubs, the largest being in Britain. If the members from each of these are added together they give a total nearing 400,000 fans.   MORAG BROWN, ABERDEEN.

522: Why are slices of bacon known as rashers?

Rasher is a 16th-century word for slice which, according to the Oxford English Dictionary, is of obscure origin but may derive from a verb 'to rash', meaning to cut or slash. Another source may be the idea of a hurried action, as with the current use of 'rash' as an adjective. A dictionary published in 1627 defined a rasher as 'a piece of meat rashly or hastily roasted' and this could explain why the word 'rasher' rather than 'slice' has stuck with bacon and not with other meats, as bacon tends to be cooked quickly.   TONY PIKE, BUTCHER & PROCESSOR, CASTLE CAMPS, CAMBS.

523: Why are Conservatives called Tories? Is it derogatory in any way?

This term came into common use between 1678 and 1680 when those who backed the right of James II to succeed Charles II were called 'Tories' by their enemies. The word was a sectarian term of abuse for Irish Catholic rebels, stemming originally from the Irish word *toiridhe*, a pursuer. The Tories replied by calling their enemies Whigs, after the cry 'Whiggam!' which the extreme Protestant covenantors or whiggamores of Scotland were accustomed to use to gee up their horses.

PERCY LEVY, PRESS OFFICER, CONSERVATIVE CENTRAL OFFICE, LONDON.

524: Why is the polo ground at Windsor called Smith's Lawn?

By popular legend it has always been thought that Smith's Lawn takes its name from Barnard Smith, a stud groom employed by the Ranger of Windsor Great Park, William Augustus, Duke of Cumberland, second son of King George II. However, it is more likely that Smith's Lawn took its name from a keeper at the time of the Restoration.

CHARLES STISTED, GUARDS POLO CLUB, WINDSOR GREAT PARK, SURREY.

525: Approximately how many words are spoken by the average person in a lifetime, and do women use more words than men?

As no research has yet been carried out on this subject, the only way to answer is to come up with rough guesstimates. The average English speaker in the UK manages about 145 words a minute, just over two words a second. Taking in everybody, from pensioners living on their own and not engaging in too many lengthy conversations, through to telesales workers who are continually talking to potential clients, it would be safe to say that the average person talks for about four hours a day, every day of the year. As we begin to talk around the age of two to three years and are expected to live until the age of 75, we can therefore say that we will speak for about 72 years. This leads to a figure of 914,544,000 words spoken by the average person in his or her lifetime. As for who talks the most, the answer, contrary to public belief, is in fact the male of the species. Scientific research has also shown that men interrupt women far more frequently than women interrupt them.

ISAAC MARKMAN, CAMBRIDGE.

526: Why do I always weigh 2lbs more last thing at night than I do first thing in the morning?

During sleep the body requires less oxygen that in the daytime. Thus, when we wake up, the lungs hold a smaller volume of air than at the end of the day. We lose approximately half a pint of body fluid through perspiration during the night, also making the body weigh less. The previous day's food is digested through the night to make energy. Finally the body's muscles are 'empty' of fluids. These fill up throughout the day, adding to your weight. All the above will naturally differ from one person to the next but is generally in the range of half-a-pound to five-and-a-half-pounds.

R. O'KEEFE, DOCTOR OF DIETING AND ANOREXIA, WIRRAL, MERSEYSIDE.

527: What does the word 'Mizpah' mean on a gravestone?

'Mizpah' comes from Hebrew and means 'The Lord watch between you and I while we are absent from one another.' If you look to your Bible you will find mizpah in Genesis 31 v49. As well as being seen on gravestones, the inscription was once very popular on rings given to loved ones.

MRS HELEN DAVIDSON, LYTHAM ST ANNES, LANCS.

528: Who is, or was, the female equivalent of Casanova?

Synonymous these days with affairs of a romantic nature, there was more than one string to Giovanni Giacomo Casanova's bow. Born the son of an actor in Venice in 1725, Casanova was an accomplished writer, violinist, diplomat and soldier/adventurer who ended his days as librarian for Count von Waldstein. A number of candidates could be put forward as the 'female Casanova' but one of the most likely must be

Catherine II of Russia – Catherine The Great. She was still taking a healthy interest in much younger men until she died at 67 and took at least three lovers while her husband, Peter III, was alive. She even hinted that he was not the father of any of their three children. But Catherine, like Casanova, was very accomplished in other areas too. Under her reign Russia became a major power in Europe. She also had very enlightened views on the emancipation of the serfs and was a keen reader of Jean-Jacques Rousseau, Montesquieu and other liberal philosophers. In this respect we can see the parallel between Catherine and Casanova as two multifaceted personalities now better remembered for their sexual exploits.

JOHN MELLOR, LINCOLN.

529: What is the correct way to hang a lucky horseshoe and why is it lucky?

According to legend, the Devil arrived one day at the smithy of St Dunstan, a noted blacksmith, and asked to have a hoof shod. St Dunstan, recognising his customer as the Devil, chained him to the wall and set to work so vigorously that the Devil screamed for mercy. 'Never again,' vowed the Devil, 'will I enter where I see a horseshoe displayed.' So it is considered good luck to display a horseshoe on your house. The correct way to hang it is with the points facing upwards 'to prevent the good luck from running out of the ends.'   DANIEL MORGAN FAIREST, SHEFFIELD.

530: With the break-up of the Soviet Union, is Canada now the largest country in the world?

The old Soviet Union measured an enormous 22,402,200 square kilometres (8,649,540 square miles) making it by far the largest country in the world. When, in 1990/91, the Union broke up into its component parts, the largest, the Russian Federation, stretching from Eastern Europe across Northern Asia to the Pacific Ocean, still had 17,075,400 square kilometres (6,592,800 square miles). Canada is the second largest country in the world with an area of 9,970,610 square kilometres (3,849,674 square miles) and China is a close third with 9,571,300 square kilometres (3,695,500 square miles) and could move up to second if the unsettled province of Quebec leaves Canada to become an independent state, reducing Canada to 8,429,930 square kilometres (3,254,814 square miles). This would promote the USA, currently fourth biggest with 9,372,614 square kilometres (3,618,770 square miles) and Brazil, currently fifth with 8,511,965 square kilometres (3,286,488 square miles).

BRIAN TALBOT, LEIGH, LANCS.

531: Is it still possible to buy the book Mein Kampf? If so, who receives the royalties?

Royalties from Mein Kampf are directed by way of an agent to a charity which helps the victims of Nazi oppression and their descendants. To protect the client's anonymity, the agent does not wish to be named.
WILL SULKIN, PUBLISHING DIRECTOR, PIMLICO BOOKS, LONDON.

532: Alexander The Great's mummified body, apparently wonderfully preserved, lay for many years in a coloured glass coffin in Alexandria, Egypt. What became of it?

When Alexander The Great died in Babylon in 323BC, his Empire was divided out among his generals. One of them, Ptolemy, became king of Egypt, took Alexander's gold and crystal coffin and enshrined it in a mausoleum, building the great city of Alexandria around it. The mausoleum was later extended and became the famous library of Alexandria, in which a huge quantity of ancient manuscripts and art objects were stored. Ptolemy's successors continued to acquire and store manuscripts and artifacts until eventually the library became the greatest storehouse of knowledge in the known world. However, in AD391, the Roman Emperor Theodosius, a religious zealot, aided by the patriarch of Alexandria, a religious vandal, condemned as paganism any teachings about any knowledge other than the principles of Christianity. They masterminded the destruction of the contents of the library, with the exception of some Biblical and church writings. Alexander's coffin perished in the great fire along with many writings of the early Greek philosophers, fabulous works of art, etc.   W. M. CHRISTIE, EALING, LONDON.

533: While visiting a museum in New England, we were asked if the practice of building old shoes into the walls of early colonial houses was based on old English tradition or superstition. Is it?

This practice goes back to the 13th century and continued until the 19th century from when about 45% of known concealments date. Apart from Britain and America, shoes have been found hidden in buildings in Belgium, Spain, Scandinavia, Turkey and Switzerland. It appears to be some form of a good luck gesture. The shoe moulds itself to the wearer's shape and until relatively recently was the most expensive item of clothing a person would own. Shoes were felt to take on something of the wearer's identity and a lot of folklore surrounded them. Shoes may have been buried in house walls to ward off evil spirits. Many concealments

have been found near doorways, windows, and chimneys – all potential openings for 'the evil.' Shoes have been built into walls along with other items, often animal bones, suggesting that they formed part of a sacrifice to the building.   BRIAN HENSMAN, THE BOOT & SHOE COLLECTION,
                                   NORTHAMPTON CENTRAL MUSEUM, NORTHAMPTON.

I owned two cottages in Boscastle, Cornwall, built in the 12th century, mostly from old shipwrecks. One had two 'clombe' ovens and when I removed the closed one, I found a shoe inside. It had a leather upper and a metal ring known as a 'patten' on the bottom. It was usual in olden days to enclose an article, frequently a shoe, in an old oven before building a new one.   K. GARBETT, PLYMOUTH, DEVON.

Although I have no experience of old shoes being built into walls, I had heard that an old pair of boots or shoes might be left behind by a workman in a completed house as a symbol of good luck and prosperity for the new owner. Few people know of this custom now, but it happened to me in 1951. A nice estate was being built and I bought a semi which was bright, clean and bare when we moved in. Under the stairs was the gas meter and a pair of strong red-brown shoes, left intentionally, perhaps by the plasterer. Now, 42 years later, they are still there and will remain so, for I am superstitious enough to believe bad luck will come into my house if they go out.   JOHN YOUNG, CLONTARF, DUBLIN.

534: Why does my remote control affect my car alarm through human flesh, brick and wood, but my other remote control will not affect my video or TV without a clear view?

Most, though not all, car alarm remote controls use radio waves whereas remote controls for TV sets, videos and hi-fi use infra-red light. Radio waves can, within limits, travel through most solid matter so the car alarm can be activated from within a house. Infra-red transmission requires a line of sight from the transmitter to the receiver and anything blocking its path will scatter the signal. As part of the electromagnetic spectrum, infra-red rays can be reflected off surfaces so it's not always necessary to point the remote control directly at the receiver to achieve the desired effect.   NEIL BARKER, SUTTON COLDFIELD.

535: Honor Blackman is usually said to have been the first female Avenger, but I recall Venus Smith. Who played the role and what happened to her?

Night club singer Venus Smith was played by actress Julie Stevens. Along with Honor Blackman, she was one of two Avengers girls in the second series after Ian Hendry, who played Steed's partner Dr David Keel, quit the series. He was originally replaced by Jon Rollason but when this didn't work the producers decided to use women as main characters. Julie Stevens joined the series in the third programme and then alternated with Honor Blackman as the main female role throughout the second series after which Venus Smith was never seen again. Julie, from Prestwich, Manchester, was a nurse who became a well-known face on several Sixties programmes and films including the sitcom Girls About Town, the quiz programme For Love Or Money, and Carry On Cleo after winning an ABC talent contest. She is best remembered as presenter on BBC's Play School for 13 years. Now 56, she does voice-over work for educational programmes and lives in Rasteau, France, with her husband, actor-director Michael Hucks, and has two children, Daniel (33), and Rachel (31) and two grandchildren, Joshua and Matilda. How do I know? I am the actress in question.   JULIE STEVENS, RASTEAU, FRANCE.

536: Is everything we experience stored unconsciously in our memories?

We have two separate memories in our brains, the Short Term Store (STS) or temporary working memory and the Long Term Store (LTS) or permanent memory store. The STS can hold only about seven articles at any one time for only a limited period. The LTS holds the more permanent memories – childhood experiences, our names, even our phone number. As we sleep each night the brain files through all the STS experiences of the day and categorises them appropriately before sending them into the LTS (which may account for the process of dreaming). But it would appear that only a select few memories are stored permanently. In recent years, under a process known as 'regression', subjects have been known to recall early childhood memories.

JULIAN S. ARNOLD, UNIVERSITY COLLEGE, SCARBOROUGH, YORKS.

There is some evidence to suggest that memory does not exist inside the brain at all but that everything which has ever existed, or is to exist, is 'out there' all the time and our brains act like radio sets in 'picking up' parts of it. The details we 'call to mind' depend on the 'tuning' of our brain. This description has been used to explain déjà vu experiences, telepathy, 'race memory', 'regression' (in which a person appears to remember events from a previous life), all kinds of apparent coincidences, experiences shared by twins etc. To think of it more clearly it is only necessary to appreciate that, viewed from the star Castor, one of our nearer neighbours in space, events on Earth have reached about the year 1948, while an observer with a very big telescope, watching us from our nearest star,

Proxima Centauri, would be seeing the events of about August 1989 unfold. Given the co-existence of everything, divided only by our conventional limitation of 'time', which seeks to put things into order so that one thing comes after another, memory doesn't have to conform to the old-fashioned idea of a card index or filing cabinet or even the newer version of an electronic retrieval system, but is better described as a highly selective radio scanner. DR ALAN SACHS, NEWPORT, RHODE ISLAND.

537: Who was the first woman to cast her vote in Britain, following the success of the Suffragettes' campaign?

My great grandmother, Dinah Connelly, claimed to have been the first woman to cast her vote in an election and her claim has never been bettered. In 1918 she lived in Penn Street, in the West Ward of Halifax, where a local election called on November 13, 1918, is thought to have been the first election in the country using the new roll which included women over 30 years old for the first time after the historic Commons vote in February. Dinah Connelly had been a suffragette and in 1907 spent two weeks, including her 28th birthday, in Holloway Prison after being arrested at a demonstration outside the Commons.
HELEN MAWSON, ILFORD, ESSEX.

538: Everyone knows about giant pandas, but what about normal size pandas? Do, or did, they exist?

There are are two distinct types of panda, the 'giant' and the 'lesser', both of which come from Szechuan province, China, where they share much of the same habitat. The familiar black and white or giant panda is the *ailuropoda melanoleuca*. It is thought there are only about 1,000 of these left alive, in the wild and in captivity. There are about 14 pandas in Western zoos out of a total of 100 kept in captivity worldwide. The other panda *ailurus fulgens* is known as the lesser, or red, panda. It has a long tail, is much smaller than the giant panda and outwardly does not resemble it at all, though the two pandas have more in common internally than they do with other animals. Though much less well-known than the giant panda, the red panda is in much the same trouble in terms of numbers. LINDA DAVOLLS, LONDON ZOO.

539: The first Transatlantic telegraph cable was laid in the 19th century. Are such cables still used for any communications, or have they now been superseded by satellite links?

The first transatlantic cable was laid in 1858 but it failed and it was not until 1866 that a cable which worked efficiently was laid. Following this success, many other cables were laid under the oceans creating a world-wide network. They were designed to carry telegraph messages in Morse code. With the advent of international telephone cable technology and the laying of the first transatlantic telephone cable in 1956, the old cables became obsolete. Telstar, the first communications satellite, was launched in 1962, and satellites soon became the commonest way of connecting international telephone calls. However, in the Eighties, undersea cables were used when fibre optic technology enabled them to carry huge volumes of voice and data, and new cables began to replace satellite links on many of the busiest routes. Modern companies use a combination of satellites and fibre optic cables to provide efficient international communications links. PETER EUSTACE, CABLE & WIRELESS, LONDON.

540: Is it true that the average height of British soldiers in World War I was only 5ft 3ins? How does this compare with the average height of the British male today?

Five feet three inches was not the average but the minimum height required for men in the armed services during World War I, though the average height may not have been much greater. There were, however, some exceptions. Two divisions of men under 5ft 3ins in height were recruited in 1915. Called the 'bantam' divisions, the idea was to make use of types like the 'wiry Welsh miner', because it was anticipated that there were some men shorter than the minimum requirement but more physically capable of fighting than their taller colleagues. In reality this did not prove true. Latest figures from a survey carried out by the Office of Population Censuses and Surveys in 1987 shows the average British male measuring 5ft 8½ins in height. ROBERT GRAHAM, GATESHEAD.

As the son of a 'Bantam' soldier, I must point out that it is wrong to disparage their fighting qualities. Sidney Allinson tells the true story in his book The Bantams. He was wounded three times, and gassed, but he kept going back to the Front and volunteered for the Home Guard in World War II. The Leeds Bantams won one VC, one DSO, three MCs and more than 20 MMs and DCMs and other Bantam regiments can boast similar lists of awards. This sort of record doesn't warrant being written off in history as a total failure or recruiting gimmick. NORMAN BROOKE, DOVERCOURT, ESSEX.

541: Where would you be if you were 24 hours from Tulsa, as in the Gene Pitney song?

Tulsa is a city in Oklahoma State, US, and the lyrics show the singer was travelling by road when he 'saw a welcoming light' and 'stopped to stay for the night.' In a standard US automobile, sticking to a constant speed of 60 mph (speed limits in the US vary between 55 and 65 mph), he could have been 1,440 miles away in Yonkers, a northern suburb of New York City, or in Hollywood, California, if approaching from the other direction. However, in those pre-oil crisis days, he could easily have been travelling at up to 100 mph and singing his heart out 2,400 miles away in Alaska.   KATHRYN McLINTOCK, NEWCASTLE.

542: I remember my father taking me in the Thirties to see the Rev Davidson in a lion's cage at Skegness. What was he doing there?

Rev Harold Francis Davidson, father of five children and Rector of Stiffkey (pronounced 'Stookey'), in Norfolk, was the centre of a major scandal in 1932 after sexual harassment complaints from Lyons Coffee House waitresses reached the Bishop of Norwich. A five-month investigation by a consistory court in the Great Hall of Church House, Westminster, revealed details of the Rector's regular trips to London to visit prostitutes, trips to the Folies Bergere in Paris, and a penchant for kissing waitresses. Mr Davidson was a flamboyant character, who claimed in his defence to be 'the Prostitutes' Padre,' whose role it was to 'save girls from themselves.' He claimed that God 'did not mind sins of the body, only sins of the soul', and freely admitted his liaisons with 'scarlet women'. The Press and public loved every minute of it. Not a day went by without the case receiving coverage on yet another element of scandal. However, the central question, 'Did he . . . or didn't he . .?', was never answered. He was eventually found guilty of disreputable association with women and appealed against the decision, but was defrocked on October 21, 1932. He still relished his celebrity status and made frequent profitable trips to seaside towns, standing in a barrel to tell his story to the public. By 1937 his popularity had waned and he decided to re-inject some interest into his act by placing himself in a lion's cage at Skegness. On July 28, 1937, in front of a large crowd, Davidson met the fate of a Christian martyr – he was mauled by the lion and died of his injuries two days later.   DAVID CRANE, CHRONICLE OF THE TWENTIETH CENTURY, FARNBOROUGH, HAMPSHIRE.

My late father, Jack Boothroyd, was a showman who first exhibited Mr Davidson on Blackpool's Golden Mile and later at Skegness. Despite his notoriety, people would pay to shake the former rector's hand. He was exhibited in a barrel and later in a lion's cage. My father had other acts shown in barrels, including a bride and groom in separate barrels on their wedding day and someone fasting in a barrel. My father later

abandoned this dubious method of making a living and opened a
restaurant in Harrogate.   MRS JOAN GREGG, LEIGH, LANCASHIRE.

When my mother and I visited Stiffkey in the Thirties we found the
church neglected and covered with bird lime. We were told Mr Davidson
was rarely there, arriving at the church just in time to take Sunday
services. He cared more for London life. My husband's first cousin,
Edward Lee, was Town Clerk of Blackpool when Mr Davidson lived in
a barrel on one of the beaches there. The council eventually managed to
remove him from his barrel by declaring it 'unfit for human habitation.'
                            MRS EDWARD LEE JUDSON, BRAINTREE, ESSEX.

543: What is the world's best-selling pop instrumental record? Who composed it, and who recorded it?

The legendary Telstar, by the Tornados, has sold seven million copies to
date, easily outstripping its nearest rival. Maverick Sixties producer Joe
Meek, operating from his independent studio at 304 Holloway Road,
North London, was way ahead of his time in his composition, released
on October 30, 1962, rocketing Telstar, named after the famous
communications satellite, to six weeks at the top of the British hit
parade. A few months later it became the first British single to top the
US charts and was No 1 in 17 other countries worldwide. The tune has
since been recorded by more than 100 other artists, including a vocal
version, called Magic Star, by Kenny Hollywood, which failed to make
an impression on the charts. Of the original Tornados, organist Roger La
Verne, lead guitarist Alan Caddy, bass guitas Heinz Burt, rhythm guitar
George Bellamy and drummer Clem Cattini, only Clem is still playing
with the current line-up of the band.

                    TIM HANLON, TORNADOS FAN CLUB, BLANDFORD FORUM, DORSET.

I'm afraid Joe Meek's Telstar has a little ground to cover before catching
up with the 40 million Anton Karas's The Third Man sold, though that
was recorded in Austria, which means Telstar remains Britain's top-
selling instrumental, with a realistic figure of about six million. As for the
claim that Telstar was the first British single to top the US charts, Dame
Vera Lynn might have something to say about that. Her Auf Wiedersehen
pipped Telstar by 10 years.   JOHN REPSCH, JOE MEEK APPRECIATION SOC, LONDON.

544: After spending a few days on the Norfolk Broads, can anyone explain why, after three days at home, I still feel the sway of the boat?

This phenomenon can affect a minority of travellers even when their trip has been in very quiet water. In some people, the canals of the middle ear, which control balance, become sensitised to the slight motion felt while on the water. These semi-circular canals make an adjustment to accommodate the movement of the deck beneath your feet and this may take a little time to wear off after the sailor or cruise passenger returns to dry land.

GILL HAYNES, P&O PRINCESS CRUISES, LONDON.

545: What is the origin of the expressions 'bull' and 'bear' applied to share markets?

In stock market parlance a 'bull market' is a rising market and a 'bull' is an optimist who buys shares expecting the price to rise so that he can sell at a profit. The origin of 'bull' used in this way is obscure. It may date from the reign of Henry VIII when Obadiah Bull, an Irish lawyer living in London, became renowned for his roistering business ways. Or it could stem from Middle English where 'to bull' meant 'to befool' or cheat. In Old French the word *bole* meant fraud or trickery. 'Bear', meaning a falling or depressed market, appears to relate to what was known as 'selling a bear-skin.' This involves finding a buyer for the bear-skin, then going out to kill the bear. The bear operator in the financial world is someone who makes a fixed-price contract to sell shares he doesn't actually own, anticipating the price falling by the time he actually has to pay for them.

LEONARD D BRENTON, WISBECH, CAMBS.

I believe 'bull' and 'bear', as applied to share markets, originated in the American version of Mexican bullfighting. A large bear was chained in sitting position for a struggle with a standing bull. If the bear pulled the bull down, the bear won. If the bull tossed the bear up on his horns, the bull won. Hence a rising market is a 'bull' and a falling market is a 'bear.'

HAROLD LAMBSHIRE, BROMLEY, KENT.

When I first started work as a dealing box clerk, one of the senior dealers bought me a book explaining all the Stock Exchange terms so I could understand a little of what was going on. This book said the reason for 'bull' and 'bear' was that a bull always raised its victims up on its horns whereas a bear always rises up on its haunches and pulls its victims down.

ANITA BUTLER, LONDON.

546: Why are cigarettes and public school juniors called 'fags'?

The term 'fag' or 'fag-end' has long been synonymous with the last piece of work or worst part of something. In the 19th century it denoted the cheapest, lowest quality cigarettes, before being used as slang for all cigarettes. In old Devonshire dialect, 'vag' is a slang term for burning and the association between cigarettes and 'fag' may owe something to this. Public school fags were not just junior boys but those who ran around performing any number of menial duties for their seniors. It is suggested that this use of the word 'fag' may have been derived from the word 'flag' meaning droop and there is a Middle English word *fagge* meaning 'to droop', suggesting that the young junior pupil was drooping under the weight of his efforts.   EDWARD NICHOLSON, LITTLEHAMPTON.

547: Who was Madam La Zonga?

Six Lessons From Madam La Zonga was a popular song of 1940, by lyricist Charles Newman and composer/pianist Jimmy Monaco. In 1941 the song title was used by Universal Pictures and the part of Madam La Zonga, star attraction at a night club of that name, was played by Lupe Velez.
ERIC THOMAS, PURLEY, SURREY.

I well remember Madam La Zonga because she was responsible for my 'finest hour.' Not long after the declaration of war, the sirens went and my whole school was marched to the air raid shelters in Grosvenor Park, Chester. To stave off a general panic, one of our teachers asked if anyone would sing a song. Fearlessly I volunteered and sang the song which was current at the time, Six Lessons From Madam La Zonga, from start to finish. I can still remember most of the words which began: 'Six Lessons From Madam La Zonga and you will Rumba and do the new La Conga. Six lessons at Madam's cabana and you will imagine that you are down in Havana. Her four Latin daughters will give you a start. While learning the rhythms you might lose your heart...'
MRS D. SWALES, MIDDLESBROUGH, CLEVELAND.

548: Where does the word 'juke', as in jukebox, come from?

'Juke' comes from the Elizabethan word *jouk* meaning to dodge or move quickly. The word was first used in America in connection with music in the prohibition era, when 'juke' was used to mean a dance, which took place at a 'juke joint' or illicit club. With the introduction in the early Thirties of the 'automatic phonograph' the term 'jukebox' was coined.
JOHN D'ARCY AND GEORGE HARDAKER, JUKEBOX RESTORERS AND SPECIALISTS, LIVERPOOL.

When I was a lad in Angus, in Scotland, during and after World War I, the word habitually used to describe the act of ducking and dodging was 'jeuk' or 'jouk.'   G. REID-ANDERSON, WORCESTER PARK, SURREY.

The word can be traced back to the West African *dzug*, used as slang by blacks in the southern US, meaning 'to lead a disorderly life.' During the Twenties, white audiences started frequenting black venues and using black slang so low-life bars became 'juke joints' and their music machines 'jukeboxes.' Manufacturers refrained from using the term until the mid-Forties when Wurlitzer first used it to advertise its new machines, because of its down-market image.   PAUL BOOTH, HARLESDEN, LONDON.

Eric Partridge's etymological dictionary Origins says 'jazz' and 'juke' are both American negro words, traceable to West Africa. Both refer to sexual excitement and activity, hence exciting music. 'Juke house' was a term used by blacks on the South Carolina coast for a brothel.
                                    M. S. GORDON, WORCESTER PARK, SURREY.

549: Is it true that convicted criminals get their mortgage interest paid by the taxpayer while they are in prison?

A person convicted of a crime and sent to prison is not eligible to claim benefits in his own right. But if the criminal has a spouse or partner who would normally be dependent on them, the partner can claim support. If the partner was claiming income support, they could probably get help with their mortgage interest payments.   DAVID TAHERI, HARPENDEN, HERTS.

550: We are told that flies spread disease, but are they in any way beneficial to mankind?

Flies evolved before humans so it's more likely that they benefit from us. They have adapted to our lifestyle, using us as a main source of nourishment, eating food and faeces and contaminating what we eat if they come into contact with it. While I was working in Africa I came across cases of maggots burying themselves in the wounds of patients. On these occasions the maggots were helpful to the patient because they ate all the infected tissue but this is not a treatment I would recommend.
            DR BEHRENS, HOSPITAL OF TROPICAL DISEASES TRAVEL CLINIC, LONDON.

Maggots which clear rotting flesh from wounds are not housefly maggots, but green or bluebottle maggots. As a prisoner under the Japanese, on the Burma Railway, I can confirm that greenbottle maggots were used for the purpose of clearing rotten flesh from gangrenous rodent ulcers. In one case, however, it was found that maggots placed on a man's wounds travelled into his body, right into his chest, causing much more trouble. The grey housefly does not seem to benefit anyone but itself, except perhaps as food for spiders. These flies caused the deaths of thousands of men by carrying the germs of fatal diseases and depositing them on food and eating utensils. We tried to combat this by dipping mess tins and eating utensils in boiling water when possible, but we could not do this when cold rice was issued. We also used to get into the river to let small fish clear pus from our sores.   R. W. WILKINS, RAYLEIGH, ESSEX.

Shortly after World War II, I was treated in a military hospital as a paraplegic, the result of a gunshot wound to the spine. I had extensive pressure sores and was intrigued (to say the least) to find a number of very active white maggots doing a tour around my anatomy. This threw the ward sister not one bit: 'You have some little friends who will clean up your sore spots far more efficiently than I ever could,' was her reaction. They did too, and to this day I feel grateful to the little blighters and any subsequent generations I may have helped create.   PIP MEGRAH, RYDE, IOW.

A friend who worked in a pathology laboratory during the war told me it was standard practice to put maggots inside the plaster casts of airmen who had severe wounds, burns and broken bones. The breaks set normally and the maggots disposed of the dead flesh.   L. COOPER, SHEFFIELD.

551: Why is the Devil associated with the violin?

Guiseppe Tartini (1692-1770) wrote a violin sonata in 1714 which was said to have come from a dream in which he bargained with the Devil for his soul in return for inspiration. The Devil played the sonata to him in his dream. On waking he is said to have immediately written down what he had heard but said the music, as written, fell far short of the Devil's dream performance. The sonata was given the name Trillo del Diavolo (Devil's Trill). Stanislav Falchi (1851-1922) wrote an opera based on the story, also called Trillo del Diavolo.

   EILEEN PRITCHARD, NEW ELTHAM, LONDON.

552: Who was the youngest person serving in British forces in the Falklands conflict?

As a Royal Marine, I was aged 17 years and 7 months when I landed with my unit at Ajax Bay, East Falkland, in May 1982. It seems strange now to reflect upon the fact that had I been killed in action, I would never legally have had the opportunity to buy a drink in a pub or, for that matter, to have voted for the Government that sent me. Minors can fight in a war, just as hard and determinedly as the next man.

   STEVEN JONES, CHIPPENHAM, WILTSHIRE.

553: Why does no jockey ever wear a moustache? Surely not because of the extra weight?

Rumour has it that there used to be a Jockey Club rule, originating in the 19th century, which forbade jockeys wearing moustaches. However, going through the records this appears not to have been the case, though it could possibly have been one of the unwritten laws used by gentlemen of that period. No contemporary jockey who sports a moustache, or indeed a beard, springs to mind though there is no practical reason for this, as a moustache would have no effect on the streamlining of horse or rider and most certainly would have no effect on the jockey's weight.

SIMON CLARE, BRITISH HORSE RACING BOARD, LONDON.

554: What is the origin of our British military salute?

Saluting evolved as a mixture of raising the hat and showing an open palm. The raising of the hat dates from the time when knights in armour would open their visors to each other to be recognised. The open palm is a sign that one has friendly intentions and is not carrying a weapon. This is also the origin of our present-day handshake. The first order enshrining the salute comes from 1762, when the Royal Scots were ordered to raise the backs of their hands to their hats rather than raising their hats, because continual manipulation of the hats was wearing them out. The British military salute is due to all officers, directed not to the individual but to their commission, presented by Her Majesty the Queen. It acknowledges Her Majesty as Head of State. The salute returned by the officer is essential, as it is given on behalf of the Queen.

MICHAEL WRIGHT, CAMBERLEY, SURREY.

As a member of the ATS in the Forties, I was told by an irate major that we had to salute to ensure we were not concealing a weapon. I had not seen him sitting in the passenger seat of a vehicle driven by a friend of mine, and had given my friend a cheery wave.

MARY SAWYER, HORSHAM, SUSSEX.

In Windsor Castle there is an Order Book of the 12th Foot (later The Suffolk Regiment, now part of the Royal Anglian Regiment) in which the following appears for June 11, 1761: 'The soldiers for the future are not to take off their hats to their officers or any other person but put their right hands up to the side of their hats.' The 12th Foot were serving in Germany at the time.

ERIC LUMMIS, CAMBERLEY, SURREY.

555: What is the origin of the word skivvy?

It was originally a specifically female word, used to denote a maid-servant, but is now more widely used as a term of derision for anyone doing a menial task. It is thought that word has only been in the English language since the 19th century, and that it probably evolved from the word 'slavey' which meant 'maid of all work'. In Elmore Leonard's 1878 novel The Switch, 'skivvies' is used as a reference to men's underwear.

MARTIN ROGERS, BASILDON, ESSEX.

556: Is there any significance in the four suits in a pack of playing cards?

Playing cards originated in China and India and were not known in Europe until comparatively late in the Middle Ages. It is said that Odette de Champdivers, mistress of Charles VI, the mad King of France, introduced them at the French Court among her efforts to amuse her royal lover during his recurring fits of insanity. In 1392 a painter was commissioned to make three packs for the King's own use. Modern playing cards are derived from medieval Tarot Cards which consisted of two packs, the Major Arcana and Minor Arcana. The 56 cards of the Minor Arcana were divided into staffs or cudgels, the weapon of the peasant, representing agriculture; cups or sacred vessels, representing the clergy; swords or wands, representing the warrior aristocracy; and pentacles or coins, representing money and merchants. Each suit consisted of a king, queen, knave and knight plus ace, deuce and so on up to 10. The change from swords to spades, cups to hearts, pentacles to diamonds and staffs to clubs occurred in the 16th century. The seniority of the suits reflects the medieval class system. The knight was omitted from each suit in the 19th century, reducing the pack to 52 cards.

NICHOLAS PLISKAR, HOVE, EAST SUSSEX.

557: During World War II, did German forces make an unsuccessful landing on Chesil Beach, Dorset, resulting in heavy losses to the Germans?

There were many rumours of attempted German invasions during World War II but none had any substance. This particular story may have been caused by an incident in 1944 when Americans training in landing craft for the Normandy invasion were torpedoed by Germans off the Dorset coast. There were many U.S. casualties and the incident was hushed up, giving rise to spurious stories. Another invasion rumour spread in Norfolk, following a sea skirmish, when the charred remains of a number of German soldiers were washed ashore near The Wash. It was rumoured that an attempted German invasion had been repelled by igniting floated petrol.

GAVIN McLOUD, INVERNESS.

My father was stationed at Portland, Dorset, during World War II when there was a scare about a German landing on Chesil Beach. One searchlight was sited on the edge of the cliff overlooking the Beach and another was positioned in the Bridport area, so that the beams met somewhere in West Bay to illuminate any invasion force. To my father's knowledge, no attempt to land was made by German forces.

MRS P. A. SAMUEL, SHREWSBURY.

When I was a plane-spotter with 577 Heavy Ack Ack Battery on the cliffs at Weymouth from 1942 to 1944, two unusual events occurred. We had a 'stand to' fairly late one night and fired out to sea with our guns level with the cliffs, instead of pointing to the sky. My captain said we were firing at E-boats. On another night 'stand to' I noticed a small glow out to sea which quickly spread, so that even the sky was aglow. We did not fire that night, though I heard there were E-boats in the bay which had set the sea ablaze. It was said that Americans on night operations were trying out small boats, ready for D-Day, when they were caught by German E-boats. Many died that night, mostly from burns. Perhaps the Germans were attempting something at Chesil Beach but the Americans chose the same night for their operation, hence the clash.

OLIVE TAPP, HEATHFIELD, SUSSEX.

558: Before World War II, I and thousands of others used to spend eight hours a day typing, usually on heavy, manual machines. Why did we never suffer from repetitive strain injury?

A proportion of the cases we treat of people suffering from what the Health and Safety Executive calls 'work-related upper limb disorders' did originate from working with manual machines. As far back as 1885, Professor Poore at University College Hospital reported several cases among typists, though most of the cases he saw were pianists. Work-related upper limb disorders are increasing among keyboard workers for various reasons. Many more people use keyboards for all sorts of data entry, as well as for typing letters. The very rapid and brief travel of the keys on modern keyboards allows even faster speeds than those achieved by skilled users of mechanical typewriters. There were other jobs to be done on older typewriters in addition to pressing the keys: winding on and aligning paper and carbons; spooling and changing the ribbon; and pushing the lever to bring up the next line. The task of a word processor operator is less varied: he or she can sit down and just type for hours at a time, leaving the printing to the end. Work-related upper limb disorders can be serious. However, there are several ways in which they can be prevented, including taking regular breaks to stretch (five minutes every half-hour), getting good ergonomic advice about the layout of the work station, a height-adjustable chair with back support, a copyholder at screen height and varying intensive hand use.

DR RICHARD M. PEARSON, HAROLD WOOD HOSPITAL, ESSEX, AND ST BARTHOLOMEW'S HOSPITAL, LONDON.

A few years ago my hands were operated on for carpal tunnel syndrome, which my surgeon said was caused by too many years typing. I too had toiled for more than eight hours daily on heavy machines – with breaks as my hands flew over a shorthand notebook at about 120 words per minute. SUE SWAN, EDGBASTON, BIRMINGHAM.

In my days as a secretary/personal assistant there existed a condition called Tendosynovitis, caused by repetitive movement and designated an industrial disease. I got this in the Sixties after using a heavy typewriter and pushing the weighty carriage along with my left hand thousands of times a day. This affected my left wrist and after much hassle I was eventually granted £400 by the DHSS. Following several treatments, a change to a lighter typewriter and the permanent use of a leather wrist strap, I was able to continue 'bashing it out.' I take it that today my condition would have been called RSI. GWEN STONIER, EARLSDON, COVENTRY.

Even eight hours a day of typing didn't constitute 'repetitive' stress. At the end of every page we took out the paper, removed carbons, re-inserted them between two or more sheets of paper, positioned them in the machine, and started again. We must have moved several muscles, frequently and in various different ways, even without leaving the chair. Most of us combined typing with other office jobs which varied our posture. We got eyestrain, backache and frustration, but not repetitive strain injury. MRS I. HOWLETT, SHEFFIELD.

559: What is the feminine equivalent of 'avuncular'?

As 'avuncular' comes from the Latin word for uncle, the nearest we can find to a feminine equivalent would be 'materteral', itself the Latin word for a maternal aunt. It is also possible to use the word 'auntly'. If 'materteral' is used, you may like to know that the OED description of the word calls it 'humorously pedantic.'
EDMUND WEINER, OXFORD ENGLISH DICTIONARY, OXFORD.

How about 'tarauntular'? A. KILVERT, STOCKPORT, CHESHIRE.

After the Oxford English Dictionary reply to this question, I found that my inherited Latin-English dictionary, printed in 1746, gives separate words for uncles and aunts on the paternal or maternal sides. *Avunculus* relates to the maternal side, the paternal equivalent being *patruus,* but the adjective 'avuncular' entered the English language coverering both, while 'patrual' never materialised. *Matertera* was a maternal aunt, from which the adjective would be 'materteral', though whether this ever really entered the English language seems open to doubt. The paternal aunt was an *amita,* which would give the much more practical English adjective 'amital.' 'Aunt' is derived from *amita,* firstly from the Old French *ante,* then the current *tante.* Uncle appears to have followed the same course. Perhaps we should use 'amital' as the feminine equivalent of avuncular.   J. W. B. HEANE, LONDON.

560: Why do soldiers like the Hussars wear their coats hanging off one shoulder?

It's not so much a coat as a fur-lined cloak called a pelisse. The original Hussars were marauding light horsemen in Hungary who wore a wolf skin over one shoulder after killing wolves which attacked their flocks and herds. Wearing a wolf skin thus as a small cloak became a Hungarian style of dress in the 17th century. When Britain converted its light-dragoon regiments into Hussar regiments during the 18th and 19th centuries, it adopted a version of the Hussar style of dress, and from 1805 the pelisse became part of the tradition of the British Hussars. The name Hussar has been retained as the British Army has always tended to honour the tradition of its regiments, even though the work carried out by today's army is very different to the duties of the first Hussar regiments.

JENNY LEAKE, NATIONAL ARMY MUSEUM, LONDON.

561: Who wrote Happy Birthday To You, and is the song sung everywhere?

The words to Happy Birthday To You, now the most frequently sung song in the English language, were written in 1893 by Kentucky Sunday School teacher Patty Smith Hill, and her colleague Mildred Hill wrote the music. It actually started life as Good Morning To All, with the words 'happy birthday to you' in the second stanza. It was included in a short book called Song Stories For The Kindergarten, but became a song in its own right in 1935 when a separate copyright was taken out due to its popularity. Although most people think the song is public property, that copyright runs until 2010, and strictly speaking anybody using the tune should pay a small fee. The song is used in most countries in the world, normally with English words, and went 'universal' when it was sung in space aboard Apollo IX in March 1969.   JULIA BLACK, BLACKLEY, MANCHESTER.

562: When a company goes into receivership or liquidation, we say it is being 'wound up'. Why?

Before it became synonymous with liquidation proceedings, 'wound up' had a much more tangible meaning – all documentation relating to a defunct company's accounts, important articles and documents were bound together and stored. The evolution of English means we now also hear 'wound down' being used in a similar context.

LORRAINE JOHNSON-DAVIES, DROYLSDEN, MANCHESTER.

563: Why does peeling onions make you cry?

The onion contains a compound called isothiocyanates and the enzyme alliinase which react when they come into contact with each other. This happens when an onion is peeled or crushed. The combination of the two produces a sulphur-based vapour which irritates the eyes. The horseradish and mustard plants contain similar products.

DR GORDON ROBERTS, FOOD & CONSUMER TECHNOLOGY DEPT,
MANCHESTER METROPOLITAN UNIVERSITY.

As a footnote, here are the three best ways of preventing chopping-board tears: place a teaspoon in your mouth when peeling or chew a piece of bread – odd but effective. Alternatively, peel your onions under running water or under water in a sink or bowl.   LOUISE HAYCOCK, WHITCHURCH, SALOP.

564: If Britain decided to exploit its usable reserves of coal, gas and oil, how long would each fuel last at today's rate of consumption?

The potential duration of coal, oil and gas reserves are not easy to ascertain. Depletion rates, mining techniques, production costs, energy demands and prices of competing fuels are very difficult to forecast even a few years ahead. After a question by the Commons Trade & Industry Committee, British Coal said that we have enough coal currently economically viable reserves at continuing mines for between 20 and 40 years. Oil reserves depend on future exploration. Present reserves would last for just over 20 years at 1991 levels of production. The addition of estimated potential additional reserves would increase this to 27 years. If undiscovered, but predicted, reserves are included, the duration is almost 60 years. Discovered gas reserves are expected to last for just over 30 years at the 1991 level of consumption. The addition of the estimated potential additional reserves would increase this to 35 years, and if undiscovered, but expected, reserves are included the estimated duration exceeds 50 years. For the last 12 years running, the increase in known reserves has exceeded production.   IVAN BAILEY, DEPT OF TRADE & INDUSTRY, LONDON.

The Department of Trade and Industry answer claiming: coal, up to 40 years; gas, up to 50 years and oil up to 60 years is seriously misleading because the amounts are not calculated on the same basis. As well as known existing reserves, the oil and gas figures include potential additional reserves in already discovered fields plus expected reserves in oil and gas fields yet to be discovered. By contrast, the coal reserves figure is based only on coal accessible from existing collieries which it would be profitable to mine at current prices. If UK coal reserves were assessed on the same basis as the oil and gas figures given, the answer would not be

40 years but 400 years. Also, remaining UK gas reserves were calculated by dividing resources by 1991's consumption. In 1991, the 'dash for gas' in electricity generation hadn't happened and none of the present, or planned, gas fired power stations was operating. So the figure for gas was totally false.   J. D. MEADS, BRITISH ASSOC OF COLLIERY MANAGEMENT, NOTTINGHAM.

565: What is the origin of the expression: 'I'll go to the top of our stairs'?

Nobody seems to know who coined this immortal expression but it is generally accepted as being of Northern origin to indicate ironic surprise. It is used to express shock and unrest of an order that inspires the highly undramatic action of walking around the house or going to bed and forgetting all about it. It sometimes appears as: 'I'll go to the foot of our stairs.' My stepfather would say, 'Well, I'll go to the foot of our stairs' when, for example, he was dealt a particularly bad hand in a card game. I always assumed it meant he felt it was time to stop playing and go to bed.
                    WALLACE K. KING, SAXMUNDHAM, SUFFOLK.

566: Why is Father Christmas called 'Father'?

Pre-Christian northern Europe celebrated a solstice festival which resembled the Roman festival 'saturnalia' in which the priest would invoke the restart of the Sun after its apparent standstill. During yule the priests acted on behalf of the god Woden (also called Odin, or Wotan). As the father of all the gods, he was often known just as 'old father.' In Wales, the Celts believed that during winter the god of time was asleep on an island off their coast. Both 'old father time' and 'old father' were part of this celebration of solar renewal. After Christianity was established in Britain, the name of the yule festival changed and the figure of 'old father' became known as 'old Father Christmas.' St Nicholas is an 'Identikit' saint concocted by the Church to oust the heathen deity from public consciousness.
        CHRIS HALL, FORMER RESEARCH STUDENT, CENTRE FOR SHAMANIC STUDIES, TENBY, DYFED.

567: What difference would a Saxon victory at the Battle of Hastings in 1066 have made to history?

To world history, the defeat of the Anglo-Saxons had little impact, but it changed Western European history and culture practically overnight and brought England in line with the rest of Europe's development. When Harold was defeated it secured William as the true King of England and Normandy, and made him the most powerful and wealthy king in

Western Europe. Should Harold have won, little change would have occurred in England and Harold – who was unpopular in England – might have been overthrown by his enemies. King William was very religious and immediately began building castles, cathedrals and churches. He enjoyed hunting, planted and enlarged existing forests and developed the feudal system. He also introduced taxation via the Domesday Book and strengthened links to the papacy. Should he have been defeated, the world would have had no Bayeux tapestry or the Tower of London.   KEVIN HOLDAWAY, BURHAM, KENT.

568: Why is the nine of diamonds known as the Curse of Scotland?

While there is no conclusive proof, there are a few likely explanations. One points to Mary, Queen of Scots, who was responsible for introducing the card game 'comette', in which the winning card was the nine of diamonds. Possibly the expression refers to the 1st Earl of Stair, who was held largely to blame for the Glencoe massacre in 1692. On the earl's coat of arms were nine 'lozenges', which could have been nicknamed diamonds. Another theory is that it may refer to the Duke of Cumberland who became known as the 'Bloody Butcher' after his ruthless suppression of the Highlanders after the Battle of Culloden in 1746. Story has it that the Duke's orders were written on the nine of diamonds from a deck of cards.   ANGELA FROST, BLACKBURN, LANCS.

569: Who invented snooker?

One explanation accepted by many is that Colonel Sir Neville Chamberlain, serving with the Devonshire Regiment in India, developed the game around 1875. Billiards was especially popular with the military, along with two additional games: 'pyramids' (similar to modern snooker as it had a triangle of red balls to be potted) and 'life pool', which involved a number of different coloured balls. Chamberlain is said to have combined the two games and developed a new one, introduced into Britain through officers' clubs by returning servicemen. The term 'snooker' was a piece of contemporary military slang which referred to a first-year military cadet, and was meant to indicate a person's lowly status. The term was used light-heartedly around Chamberlain's snooker table – to imply that someone was playing poorly, and also used as a term of derision by a player who was left unable to hit the target ball by his opponent. At the turn of the century, when the Billiards Association introduced a formal series of rules, the game began to develop more structure. But even in 1926 clubs were following differing rules. This began to change after the first World Snooker Championships in 1927 – organised by Joe Davis, who went on to win the tournament for the next 20 years. ROGER LEE, GAMES MEMORABILIA HISTORIAN, SHERINGHAM, NORFOLK.

570: Why do we get poisonous fumes from a gas fire, but not from a gas cooker?

All fossil-fuel burning appliances need air to burn safely. Badly fitted or poorly ventilated appliances can allow poisonous carbon monoxide gas to enter the home. This will apply to cookers as well as fires, water heaters, central heating boilers or warm-air heaters. It is a relatively rare occurrence in a cooker as they have smaller burners, are usually installed in well-ventilated rooms, and are in use for shorter periods. We always recommend that gas fires and central heating boilers be checked once a year by a registered installer and that anyone with any concerns about gas safety should contact a gas showroom for advice.

RICHARD DYMOND, BRITISH GAS, LONDON.

571: My son was recently rushed to hospital with appendicitis. What is the purpose of this apparently unimportant organ?

The appendix (or vermiform appendix, to give it its full name) no longer plays a part in the human digestive process. However, millions of years ago, our evolutionary ancestors had a use for it. Their mainly herbivore diet contained a high level of plants and grasses, which have large amounts of cellulose. There is no enzyme in the human digestive system which can break down cellulose and the appendix handled the cellulose intake. Plant-eating animals such as rabbits still use it for the prolonged digestion of cellulose. The appendix also contains a high number of lymph cells, and is believed by some to help the immune system detect and fight off infection. GEOFFREY DANIELS, HORSHAM. WEST SUSSEX.

572: Are there any similarities between the assassinations of John F Kennedy and Abraham Lincoln?

Both Lincoln and Kennedy were shot on a Friday in the presence of their wives; both were shot in the head from behind. Lincoln became President in 1860 and Kennedy in 1960. Both their wives lost children through death while at the White House. Their successors, both named Johnson, were both southern Democrats and both in the Senate. Andrew Johnson was born in 1808 and Lyndon Johnson in 1908. Both assassins were Southerners and both were killed before they came to trial. Lincoln's killer, John Wilkes Booth, was born in 1839 and Lee Harvey

Oswald, Kennedy's killer, in 1939. Lincoln's secretary, whose name was Kennedy, advised him against going to the theatre in which he was killed. Kennedy's secretary, whose name was Lincoln, advised him not to go to Dallas, where he was killed. Booth shot Lincoln in the theatre and ran away into a warehouse. Oswald shot Kennedy from a warehouse and ran away into a theatre. MIKE LEADBEATER, KINGSWINFORD, WEST MIDLANDS.

573: Is the Mohican hairstyle, sported by some teenagers, in fact a Seminole hairstyle?

The 'Mohican' hairstyle, as we know it, wasn't worn by either Mohican or Seminole Indians. Mohicans, living in what is now New York state, sported their hair long but became associated with the 'crested' hairstyle through James Fenimore Cooper's 1826 novel The Last Of The Mohicans. After this a large number of very inaccurate stories about Native Americans were published, many showing eye-catching illustrations of Indians with 'Mohican'-style hair. The hairstyle we now know as the Mohican probably originated among plains Indians, such as the Sioux, who did many elaborate things with their hair, shaving it in places or adorning it with ornamental pieces. JONATHAN KING, MUSEUM OF MANKIND, LONDON.

The Mohicans were a fictitious tribe made up by Fenimore Cooper for his novel The Last Of The Mohicans. He derived the name from the Mohegan or Mahigan, Algonquian tribes who wore long hair like the Mohican in the book and the movie. The Seminole and Creek Indians, of the south-eastern woodlands of what is now Florida, wore long hair under a cloth turban, usually surmounted by one or two feathers. The so called Mohican Roached hairstyle, with added animal hair and fur, should be called the Mohawk style and was worn by nearly all the Iroquoian tribes in the north-eastern woods, including the Huron, Petun, Erie, Mingo, Neutrals and the Iroquoi proper, ie the Mohawk, Onandaga, Oneida, Cayuga, Seneca and the Tuscarora, plus a few Algonquian tribes like the Sauk and Fox. The seven tribes of the Sioux Nation always wore long hair, in common with the other Plains Indians such as the Cheyanne, Arapaho, Crow, Blackfoot, Comanche etc, even before they were driven from their homes in Minnesota and Wisconsin by the Ojibwa and the French in the late 1600s. One of the few Plains tribes to wear the Roached hairstyle was the Lawnee, who came originally from an area which is now in Texas.

KENNETH A. PHILLIPS, MILTON KEYNES, BUCKS.

574: What was the longest court case in this country?

June 1997 saw the breaking of a record which had stood for 125 years when the 'McLibel' trial in which the huge McDonald's hamburger chain sued for libel David Morris and Helen Steel who criticised their operation, concluded after a total of 314 days in court, involving 180 witnesses and 40,000 pages of documents. McDonald's won a hollow victory, being awarded by the judge £60,000 in damages against the couple but saw its reputation tarnished in the ruling and faced a £10 million legal bill for the proceedings. Morris and Steel refused to pay any damages and said they hadn't got the money anyway.

Britain's longest trial before that related to the Tichborne personation case, when Arthur Orton (alias Thomas Castro) claimed to be Roger Charles Tichborne, elder brother of Sir Alfred Joseph Doughty-Tichborne (1839-66). The civil trial went on 103 days, collapsing on March 6, 1872. It was followed by a criminal trial which lasted for 188 days, ending on February 28, 1872, when the jury were out for just 30 minutes. Orton was found guilty of perjury and sentenced to two consecutive terms of seven years imprisonment, with hard labour. The whole court case spanned 1,025 days. The impeachment of Warren Hastings lasted from 1788 to 1795 but the trial itself went on just 149 days.

TIM MICKLEBURGH, GRIMSBY, LINCS.

575: Why does Durham, alone among English counties, have the prefix County, like the Irish counties?

In Anglo-Saxon days a 'shire' was a division of the country for administrative purposes. Durham was never a 'shire', but was known as the Bishopric of Durham or Palatinate of Durham. In 1072 William the Conqueror gave the bishops of Durham extraordinary rights and privileges, and they were known as Prince Bishops, a position which came to an end only in 1836. The word 'county' doesn't appear in connection with Durham until the mid-19th century. It seems likely the word was added to avoid confusion between the county and city of Durham.

KATHRYN BARROW, DURHAM COUNTY COUNCIL.

576: If all the wealth in every country of the world were put together and distributed evenly to every person, would we all be quite well off?

Dividing the total gross national product of every country by the population of the world — £13,163,820,000,000 divided by 5,423,000,000 — produces a figure of about £2,427 each per year. This may not sound too good for the UK where the GNP is about £9,027 per person, but would cheer up people in countries like Uganda where the present GNP is only £194. Wealth includes assets as well as income, and if our GNP were thus cut by three-quarters, all money in this country would instantly drop in value and our whole economic structure would collapse along with those of other countries. In the short term, we would all be very much less than well off, even our 'momentarily rich' friends in Uganda.

HUGH LATHAM, LIVERPOOL.

577: How did the expression 'spick and span' come about?

Spick and span comes from Old Norse *span* meaning 'new' and the later *spick*, meaning 'nail'. The original phrase was 'spick and span new', meaning as bright and new as an unused nail. The expression was later reduced to 'spick and span.'

JOHN HUTTON, BISHOP'S STORTFORD, HERTS.

578: Does burning a 150 watt light bulb at half power, by using a dimmer switch, cost more or less to run than a 75 watt bulb?

Running a 150 watt bulb at half power with a dimmer switch costs more than using a 75 watt bulb. Dimming a 150 watt bulb to half power produces less light than using a 75 watt bulb. Reducing the voltage by ten per cent can result in a 30-40 per cent reduction in light output. A 150 watt bulb dimmed to half power might only produce 25 per cent of the light of a 75 watt bulb. So four dimmed 150 watt bulbs would be required to produce the same light output as a single 75 watt bulb at full power, and the cost of an equivalent amount of light from the dimmed bulb is 405.3 per cent more expensive than running the 75 watt bulb. However the price may be worth it, considering the susceptibility of young ladies to soft lighting.

R. P. SUTTON, DARTFORD, KENT.

579: Opposite the London Hospital is a public house called The Grave Maurice. The sign depicts the head of a man wearing an Elizabethan ruff. Who was he?

The word Grave is an English corruption of the German Graf, meaning prince. Graf Maurice of the Rhine was born in 1620. At 22 he fought as a general for King Charles against the Roundheads. After the surrender at Oxford in 1646 both he and his brother Prince Rupert were banished from England. Two years later Prince Maurice became a pirate in the English Channel then sailed with his brother to Portugal and the Gambia where he captured an English ship, the Friendship. On a later voyage to the West Indies his ship foundered and he was drowned, aged 32. The pub bearing his name was built in 1882, in Whitechapel Road. Its name is thought to arise from the Truman's brewery's close links with the royal family at the time. It is the only pub so named. Another, near London's Blackwall Tunnel, has since closed down. KRISTYNA ADAMS, MANAGERESS, THE GRAVE MAURICE.

580: The Suzie B was a rejected U.S. dollar coin. Why 'Suzie B' and why was the coin unacceptable?

The Susan B. Anthony dollar, or 'Suzie B', was a $1 coin first issued in 1980, to replace the paper dollar bill but the American public was steadfast in its refusal to accept the coin and it was withdrawn, though it is still legal tender. The coin was named after Susan Brownell Anthony, an American social reformer and women's suffrage leader, born in Adams, Massachusetts in 1820, who campaigned tirelessly on behalf of the anti-slavery and temperance movements. R. J. CUBITT, LONDON.

The Susan B. Anthony dollar coin, first issued in January 1979, proved unpopular because it is small, only slightly larger than our new 10p coin. It is almost exactly the same size as the Quarter which has caused much confusion. It has not, however, been withdrawn; many automatic ticket machines, including those of New Jersey Transit at Penn Station, New York, still dispense Suzie Bs in change. The previous correspondent clearly had in mind the large, heavy dollar coin which preceded the Susan B. Anthony. It was one and half inches in diameter, weighed nearly one ounce and was in circulation from 1971 to 1977.
ROB BARROW, STATEN ISLAND, NEW YORK, USA.

American feminist Susan B. Anthony was commemorated elsewhere apart from the dollar coin. I was serving on the destroyer HMS Mendip during the D-Day landings when we went alongside the U.S. troop transport Susan B. Anthony to take off wounded and survivors when she was sinking after hitting a mine on her way to a berth in the Mulberry Harbour off the beachhead. I have often thought about one of the casualties whom I helped carry to the sick bay with terrible head wounds. I wonder if he recovered. F. FEATHERSTONE, GRAVESEND, KENT.

581: If today's animals have evolved over millions of years, how will they change in the future, or has evolution stopped?

There is much scientific debate on this question. Many people believe the majority of evolutionary pressures have been removed from most of the higher vertebrates and that evolution as we knew it has stopped, because of man's impact on the world ecosystem. Evolutionary changes occur very gradually. Man has made vast changes to the planet in a very short period. One anticipated change is a rapid increase in global temperatures over the next ten years, lifting the average by between one and two degrees Celsius. In parts of the planet the change will be far greater. Big changes in environment in a short time don't allow animals time to adapt. No animal could be expected to evolve to take account of the current pace of forest clearance. Invertebrates and some of the smaller mammals will cope with these changes but for all too many species the pressure to change has driven them to the edge of extinction: evolution is no longer an option. It is estimated that throughout the world there are between 2,000 and 6,000 species of animal needing to be managed in captivity to prevent them becoming extinct.

DOUG RICHARDSON, ANIMAL COLLECTION MANAGER, LONDON ZOO.

All the evidence for evolution is circumstantial: it can never be proved. There is, however, much scientific evidence indicating that it could not have occurred. Dr W. Libbey found that the amount of radioactive carbon in the atmosphere was increasing at a rate which would indicate the atmosphere was only tens of thousands of years old. Life would have been impossible before then. Measurements of helium released into the atmosphere by decay of naturally occurring isotopes gives a similar age. The 'evolutionary pressures' referred to by Doug Richardson simply don't exist. If an animal encounters a harsh environment it does not have to survive, it becomes extinct.

H. L. BRYDON, LONDON WC1.

Evolution is still happening. Bacteria which cause disease develop immunity to medicines and recent disasters have occurred because of this problem. The peppered moth, which was white and speckled before the industrial revolution, changed colour to black in countries where industry produced large amounts of soot and pollution made the trees black. This is evolution within a limited timescale, but it can be applied across billions of years. Evolution now is helped by humans, especially in agriculture, where artificial selection is used to breed cows to produce more milk or better beef.

CHRIS WATTS, STONE, STAFFORDSHIRE.

Evidence suggests quite substantial evolutionary changes have taken place in the human animal. Due, presumably, to dramatic improvements in medicine, nutrition and environmental health over 100 years, there has been quite a significant lowering of the average age at which the female of the species can become pregnant. And a look at a 100-year-old bed shows how much we have grown in physical stature in that time. Unfortunately, advances in physical maturity have not been matched by similar developments in emotional maturity – young girls and boys are now capable of becoming parents long before they are emotionally capable.

JEREMY CABORN, GORLESTON, NORFOLK.

Despite the suggestion that the atmosphere is only tens of thousands of years old and that life would have been impossible before then, the first air-breathing creatures emerged during the Devonian Period, 350 million years ago. W. F. Libby's method of radio carbon dating is relevant only up to about 70,000 years ago. Potassium-argon dating confirms the man-like creature *Homo habilis* (tool maker) was around as far back as 1,780,000 years ago and Java Man is 500,000 years older.

HUMPHREY DANIELS, CHARD, SOMERSET.

582: Which film was the biggest box office flop of all time?

Measured in total budget against box office receipts, the biggest flop to date is the 1991 Bruce Willis Bond-style spoof, Hudson Hawk. It cost £45 million to make, but returned only £5.5 million in the United States and Canada, making virtually nothing elsewhere. The 1980 film Heaven's Gate cost £25 million, compared with the £5.2 million originally budgeted for it, and took very much less in receipts. The biggest loser in percentage terms was Orphans, made in 1987 and starring Albert Finney. It cost £10.4 million and only took £69,444 in receipts. However, it is worth noting that a film can go on generating revenue as a video release long after it has left the cinema circuit. DAVID JARCEY, CAMDEN, LONDON.

The earlier answer didn't even come close. In 1981 the Moonies leader Rev Sun Myung Moon sponsored the film Inchon! about UN landings in Inchon Bay during the Korean War. There was no pre-organised budget and the film eventually cost $102 million. It was so awful that Warner Bothers had to be paid an amount rumoured to have been a further $20 million from Moon's own pocket to give it just a limited release in south-west America. It was taken off after just four days, having earned less than $5,000, and has never been released in the UK or anywhere outside California. There was no video release and no hope of further receipts. Amazingly, it starred Laurence Olivier in the role of General MacArthur. SAL HOSSER, BLOOMSBURY, LONDON.

583: I have heard that a country issued a banknote about 20 years ago featuring a palm tree design in which the branches of the trees were inadvertently positioned to spell out the word 'sex.' Is it true?

In 1972, while working as an air steward for BOAC, I spent a couple of days in the Seychelles. During our evening meal word spread that the government were withdrawing all 50-rupee notes, because the word 'sex' appeared next to the Queen's head. I carefully examined the 50-rupee note I had just been given in my change (then worth about £3.85) and by turning it on its side the leaves of the palm trees clearly spelled the word 'sex'. The notes, now highly sought after, were in circulation for many years before the offending word was noticed. Despite customs officials' attempts to prevent any notes leaving the country, mine still holds pride of place on my office wall. STEPHEN J. FRAMPTON, WATERLOOVILLE, HAMPSHIRE.

The design and manufacture of the 1970s Seychelles 50-rupee bank note featuring palm trees which spelled the word sex, was carried out by Bradbury Wilkinson & Co, of New Malden, Surrey, which is no longer in existence. My husband was part of the 80-strong reproduction team at the time and he assures me that there was considerable union unrest at that time over various aspects of wages, holidays, working conditions etc, and the employees, machine printers, engravers and artists had a very particular sense of humour. A note designed for Vietnam at around the same time featured the dome of a temple which, when turned on its side, bore a more than passing resemblance to a shapely breast.

MRS JUNE H., WORCESTER PARK, SURREY.

584: Did the two-finger V-sign salute originate from the Battle of Agincourt?

Yes, it was used by England's bowmen, whose archery skill was legendary throughout Europe, to taunt the French, before and during the battle. Whenever an English bowman was captured by French troops, they did not kill him, but cut off the first two fingers of his right hand, making him useless as a bowman. They then set him free again, since bowmen were considered otherwise to be pretty useless as fighters. So, at the beginning of the Battle of Agincourt our bowmen raised their two fingers in the V sign to tell the French: 'Look, matey, I've still got my two fingers, so watch it.'

CHRISTOPHER R. DAVIS, LONDON E1.

The long-bow was used at the Battle of Agincourt with devastating effect. If their own arrow supplies ran short, bowmen would recycle the enemy arrows that had fallen in their midst. At Agincourt, the English used what would be regarded today as a 'secret weapon.' They had perfected a thinner string to the bow and, as a consequence, a much smaller V was cut in the shaft of the arrow. The English were therefore able to fire back the French arrows but the French bowstrings were too thick to fit the English arrows. After their defeat, French prisoners and wounded soldiers were herded into compounds by the English bowmen who raised two fingers in the derisory fashion. The sign was used to show the defeated soldiers which fingers had been used by the victors to discharge the unreturnable arrows.

L. A. TURNER, HORSELL, SURREY.

Henry V's bowmen, who executed 'V signs' at the French, were not English but Welshmen in the service of the English King. Welsh bowmen used their superior skills to turn the tide of battle at Agincourt and again at Crécy. Welshmen were able to shoot 12 to 15 arrows a minute with devastating accuracy and force. The 10,000 Welsh bowmen, whose arrows could pierce a knight's armour and go through thigh, saddle and horse, or kill the horse from under the knight, had a terrible effect on the mounted French cavalry. JOHN CHAMBERLAIN, BANGOR, GWYNEDD.

The V sign gesture was known long before the Hundred Years War and even before the invention of the longbow, which is drawn with three fingers, not two. The sign has long been linked with the occult, being used pointing downwards 'to block the Devil's horns' and stop him rising up to create havoc on earth. Conversely, the sign was used conventionally to wish the Devil on one's enemies. Sexual connotations didn't emerge until medieval times when the V sign merged with a two-fingered gesture created with the index and little fingers to represent the horns of the cuckold. This gesture is still popular on the Continent today. Back in the Hundred Years War, any Englishman falling into the hands of the French would have suffered injuries far greater than the mere amputation of a couple of fingers. M. G. TAYLOR, GROUVILLE, JERSEY.

585: Do animals, other than humans, consciously plan ahead, and if so by how long a period?

It is virtually impossible to say whether behaviour is consciously planned or instinctive. But we can observe the way animals behave and arrive at a number of conclusions. In laboratory tests, rats have shown the ability to find their way through a maze to the place where they will find food – they work to a 'plan.' As winter draws on, birds feed to excess and then fly south, bears find themselves a cave to hibernate in, and beavers build dams to regulate changes in water flow throughout the year. But it would be wrong to suppose that animals plan in the same way that humans do – their behaviour in the wild changes according to the seasons. Some species of wasp exhibit a high degree of advance planning by capturing maggots of other insects and planting their own eggs in them so that when the wasp grub hatches it gets its first meal, courtesy of its host. This behaviour is for the wellbeing of future generations, but there is nothing to indicate that wasps are capable of the complex thought processes needed to plan this consciously.

DR GORDON REID, CHIEF CURATOR, CHESTER ZOO.

586: What was Hopalong Cassidy's horse called?

William Boyd (1895-1972), famous for his portrayal of Hopalong Cassidy, probably had many mounts during the years between 1934 and 1948 during which time he made more than 60 films, but the one which springs to mind as his outstanding partner was a horse called Topper. In his time, Hopalong Cassidy was an international folk hero, who survived the decline of film-making and went on to star in more than 50 episodes of his television show. Hoppy normally rode with two sidekicks, Lucky Jenkins and California Carlson, played by Rand Brooks and Andy Clyde, who seemed to cause him no end of trouble along the way, but always turned up in the nick of time to help him out of a tight corner.

BRIAN BRINDLE, ACCRINGTON, LANCASHIRE.

Just moseying in with a recap about the Clarence E. Mulford Western hero played on screen by Willian Boyd with his horse Topper. Boyd's first film was in 1935 with James Ellison and George Gabby Hayes as his sidekicks Johnny Nelson and Windy Halliday. Ellison went on to the big time playing Buffalo Bill opposite Gary Cooper's Wild Bill Hickok in the then longest-ever western, The Plainsman, in 1936. Gabby Hayes, despite having only just enough strength to write his killer's name in the dust towards the end of the first Hopalong, was in fine fettle a-spittin' and a-cussin' in the second and 20 more tales because in sneak previews, Paramount found that audiences loved the bewhiskered Gabby.

JOHN WRIGHT, SOUTHEND-ON-SEA, ESSEX.

587: Why do we 'make no bones about it'?

This saying, meaning to say or do something without hesitation, is the opposite of a 15th-century phrase 'to find bones in' something, which meant to find a difficulty, connected with finding bones in food, making it awkward to cut or eat. Over a period of time the saying has evolved to a point where the 'bones' are no longer held to matter.

AMANDA PARRY, WEYMOUTH.

588: Of the 286 footballers involved in the Premiership at a weekend, roughly what percentage are English and eligible to play for England?

While it's easy to compile a list of players and their birth-places, it's almost impossible to know if they are eligible to play for England without knowing all their family trees. Ray Houghton of Aston Villa was born in Glasgow and plays for the Republic of Ireland. Andy Townsend, who also plays for the Republic, was born in Maidstone. Both these players must have an ancestor who was born in Ireland. Taking ten Premiership teams on a typical weekend as a sample, numbers given denote players in those teams who were born in England, although any one might have had a great-great-grandfather born in Australia, allowing them to play for the Aussies: Newcastle United 11, Blackburn Rovers 10, Arsenal 9, Coventry City 9, Manchester City 9, Swindon Town 9, Sheffield Wednesday 9, Ipswich Town 9, Leeds United 7, Manchester United 5. Of the 110 players in this sample 87 were born in England and could be assumed to be eligible to play for England. Given there is nothing remarkable about the distribution of English and non-English players within Premiership clubs, 79 per cent of players are English by birth, and could play for England.

RAY SPILLER, SECRETARY OF THE ASSOCIATION OF FOOTBALL STATISTICIANS,

589: Is it true that a fly once broke the telescope at the Royal Greenwich observatory?

One of the telescopes used by the old Royal Greenwich Observatory at Herstmonceux used a delicate illuminated cross-wire to allow a star image to be accurately centred and the telescope to be kept pointing at the required star field. This cross-wire was made of two very thin strands of spider's web which, despite modern artificial alternatives, is still the finest material available. One night in 1987 the observer was starting his work when he found the cross-wires broken. The culprit was a dead fly which had fallen down the telescope tube. These facts were reported in the observatory's in-house magazine and thereafter appeared in the world's press. The telescope was out of action for only a short time.

DR P. J. ANDREWS, ROYAL GREENWICH OBSERVATORY, CAMBRIDGE.

590: What is the translation of the All Black 'Haka'?

The Haka goes as follows: 'Ka Mate Ka Mate, Ka Ora Ka Mate Ka Mate, Ka Ora Tenie Te Tengata, Puhuru Huru Nana E Piki Mai, Whaka Whiti Te Ra Hupanei, Hupanei, Hupanei Kaupanei Whiti Te Ra.' The full English translation is: 'There is going to be a fight between us. May it mean death to you and life to us. We will fight on, or until our side is vanquished. So long as the daylight lasts. We are here to continue the battle. To be either killed or to be victorious.'

MICHAEL CALLAGHAN, ST HELENS RUGBY LEAGUE FOOTBALL CLUB, MERSEYSIDE.

591: There's Never On Sunday, I Don't Like Mondays, Ruby Tuesday, Friday On My Mind and Saturday Night's Alright For Fighting, but are there any songs with Wednesday or Thursday in them?

Try these: Wednesday by The Grateful Dead; Wednesday Night Hope, Andy Kirk; Wednesday Night, Elton John; Wednesday Night Prayer Meeting, Charles Mingus; Wednesday Morning 3am, Simon And Garfunkel; Wednesday's Child, Matt Monro; Wednesday Like A River, Sheila E; Any Wednesday, Charlie Byrd; Wednesday Week, Elvis Costello; Wednesday 19.45, Crazy Pink Revolvers and The Wednesday Race, James Morrison. Thursday, by Count Basie; Thursdays, Joyce

Grenfell; Sweet Thursday, Icicle Works; Thursday Morning, Giles, Giles And Fripp; Thursday Afternoon, Brian Eno; Every Thursday Night, Gregory Isaacs; Thursday 12th, Bank Statement; Thursday's Child, Eartha Kitt and Thursday Girl by Northern Sky.   ERIC THOMAS, PURLEY, SURREY.

My listeners and I like this week-long list: Sunday, Bloody Sunday by U2. Monday, Monday: the Adventures. Tuesday Afternoon: Moody Blues. Wednesday Week: The Undertones. Thursday: Jim Croce. Friday I'm In Love: The Cure. Saturday In The Park: Chicago. Eight Days A Week: The Beatles.   GRAHAM DENE, VIRGIN RADIO, LONDON.

592: What is the method of using a wristwatch as a compass? I was taught it in the services years ago but have forgotten it.

In the northern hemisphere, the formula is to point the hour hand at the sun, then half way between that and 12 o'clock is due south. This applies during Greenwich Mean Time. One must adjust the formula to take account of the extra hour during summer time, bisecting the angle to one o'clock when the clocks are one hour forward.

MISS G. M. FRENCH, HOUNSLOW, MIDDLESEX.

This extract is taken from Notes On Map Reading published by HM Stationery Office for the War Office in 1929: 'True North by Watch and Sun: lay the watch flat with the hour hand pointing to the sun. In the northern hemisphere the direction of true south is then midway between the hour hand and XII. In the southern hemisphere point XII to the sun; then true north lies midway between XII and the hour hand. Thus, in northern hemisphere, time 1500hrs. With watch set as described, south lies in the direction midway between figures 1 and 2 and north in the opposite direction. This method is very rough. It is of no use in the tropics. The farther from the equator the more accurate it becomes. Replacing the watch by a 24 hour dial drawn on a sketch does not make for much greater accuracy in the absence of a special device. If summer time is in force correct the watch before taking the observation.'

KEN BEAUMONT, SCHOOL OF SURVEYING AND ENGINEERING TECHNOLOGY, OAKLANDS COLLEGE, BOREHAMWOOD, HERTS.

This method can still found in some Boy Scout and old military manuals and repeated in an earlier answer, is an unreliable and potentially hazardous method of direction finding. It sounds marvellously simple, and there are times and places when it is reasonably correct, but serious errors of as much as 24 degrees can occur. Between latitudes 40 to 60 degrees, north or south of the Equator, it is sometimes close to the truth, though necessary corrections make the method too complicated for practical field use. The only times when no corrections are necessary is at sunrise and sunset on March 21 and September 23 and at noon on a day where the sun is directly north or south. Better methods of direction-finding use the sun with simplified azimuth technique, or the stars by night. The Pole star, Polaris, gives true North to an accuracy of a fraction of one degree using the eye alone.

PETER LANCASTER-BROWN, AUTHOR OF SKYWATCH, ALDEBURGH, SUFFOLK.

593: Each year Richard Baker appears as compere of the Festival of Remembrance wearing a row of medals. What do these commemorate?

Richard Baker's medals are: OBE (awarded to him in 1976), 1939/45 Star, Atlantic Star, Defence Medal, World War II War Medal, Auxiliary Volunteer Efficiency Medal, for 12 years in the Royal Naval Volunteer Reserve, and Queen Elizabeth II Jubilee Medal 1977. He may not remember me, though our paths crossed in 1938/39, my first year at Kilburn Grammar School, when the school performed Antony And Cleopatra, and my mother, a Shakespeare fanatic, said: 'That boy who played Enobarbus really knows his Shakespeare. Keep your eye on him. I believe he is destined for greatness.' That boy was Richard Baker.

ALAN MEADY, READING, BERKSHIRE.

594: When my holly bush has a good crop of berries is it a sign of a hard winter? How does the holly bush know?

A holly bush can no more predict winter conditions than some of our weather forecasters can put together long-range forecasts. A good crop of berries is no indication of weather to come but a result of weather which preceded it. I have grown holly bushes for many years but still don't know what conditions produce a good crop of berries. A holly grower can tell whether he might get a good crop when he examines his bushes in April or May but even then he may be disappointed. Berries were almost as plentiful in the winter of 1993/4 as they were about 20 years ago, when we had our mildest winter since the war. If we do get a cold winter, don't blame your holly.

G. F. BARKER, ORTON.

595: Which is the oldest, still occupied, city in the world?

It is Jericho on the Israeli West bank, which today has a population of 15,000. Radiocarbon dating has given an earliest date of inhabitation of around 7,800BC. The world's oldest capital city is believed to be Damascus in Syria, which is thought to have been inhabited since around 2500 BC.

THOMAS CAMPBELL, DUNDEE.

596: Did the Gordon Highlanders once shoot some cheese?

The story goes that during World War I a member of the Gordons, on night sentry duty, heard something and challenged: 'Who goes there?' Getting no reply, he opened fire only to find that it was a cheese which had rolled off a supply wagon. Whether this is true or not matters less than the fact that The 5th Black Watch heard about it and every time they passed the Gordons on the way to the Front called out: 'Who shot the cheese?'

D. J. PLATT, EX-LT. A COY, 1ST GORDONS, 153 BRIGADE, 51ST HIGHLAND DIV, WIRRAL, MERSEYSIDE.

This incident took place on the Somme, shortly after the capture of Beaumont-Hamel by the Royal Naval Division and 51st Highland Division in November 1916. The 6th Gordons were in reserve, in shelters at Courcelette/Ovillers. A railway embankment, from which the rails had long since gone, and a sunken road ran beside each other to the ration dump at Cruficex corner, Albert. The Royal Engineers had constructed a track on the railway embankment and one night, on this track, an English ration party was proceeding to its reserve position with rations loaded on a hand cart, including an enormous round of cheese. A party of 7th Gordons was moving up the sunken road with its rations when the cheese fell off the cart and rolled down the embankment towards the Gordons accompanied by a terrible shindy of yells and curses from the bereaved English ration party.

CPTN COLIN HARRISON, REGIMENTAL HQ, THE GORDON HIGHLANDERS, ABERDEEN.

597: Where is the car in which John F. Kennedy was riding when he was assassinated in Dallas?

After the assassination, the modified 1961 Lincoln Continental convertible was flown back to the White House on a C-130 cargo plane, briefly examined by the SS and FBI, then flown within a few days to Ford-Lincoln HQ in Detroit. It was then refitted for future Presidential motorcades, in the process destroying any forensic value it may have had for future investigations. It was rebuilt with new upholstery, a souped-up engine, two and half tons of steel plating, three-inch layered glass and bullet-proof tyres, all ready for the new President. Understandably, Johnson rarely used it. It is now in the Henry Ford Museum in Dearborn, Michigan.

PAUL BELL, SOUTHPORT, MERSEYSIDE.

598: During the reign of our current Queen we are known as Elizabethans. What will we be called when Prince Charles becomes monarch?

Those who live under King Charles can expect to be called Caroleans.

When King James was on the throne, the adjective Jacobean was appropriate. However, a worse prospect looms when our monarch is called William. Can anyone suggest a less cumbersome word than Guillemean?

BEN MORLAND, TAVISTOCK, DEVON.

My parents were Victorians and I have been an Edwardian, a Georgian twice over and now an Elizabethan. Should Prince Charles accede to the throne, I shall doubtless be a Right Charlie.

ELSIE POTTLE, MALVERN, WORCESTERSHIRE.

As former pupils of the only school in the kingdom given its name in 1637 by his late Majesty King Charles I, we are happy with the title of Carolians. On the touchline this abbreviates, conveniently, to Carols.

L. H. WILLIAMS, OLD CAROLIANS ASSOC, KIDDERMINSTER.

599: Why are backless slippers called 'mules'?

The word 'mule' for backless slippers comes from the ancient Sumerian civilisation, situated between the rivers Tigris and Euphrates, in what is now Iraq. This style of shoe, called a mulu, was worn at home there in the same way as modern slippers.

BRIAN HENSMAN, BOOT & SHOE COLLECTION, NORTHAMPTON CENTRAL MUSEUM.

600: On the 11th hour of the 11th day of the 11th month 75 years ago, was France one hour in front of England?

French and British times were the same on Armistice Day, 1918. Both nations then observed what is known to us, though not to the French, as Greenwich Mean Time (GMT). The Germans used Central European Time (CET), one hour ahead of GMT, and one of their first acts in the occupied parts of France was to advance public clocks by one hour. The idea of Daylight Saving in the summer months was first suggested in the UK by William Willett in 1907 but a Private Member's Bill to introduce it failed in 1908. It was introduced in Germany to assist munitions production in 1915 and in the UK, in great haste, on Sunday, May 21, 1916, after which it was also used by the British Army in France. The French, however, did not adopt it until many years later, after they had moved to CET.

M. H. SCOTT, CAMBRIDGE.

601: Are there any regulations about the type of coin tossed at official sporting occasions?

Any coin can be used to start official sports matches. Many football referees have their own preferences or favourite coins. Some always use the same coin: the one they used to start their first professional match, a commemorative coin or one with a personal meaning for them. With the increase in 'mascots', boys or girls who lead the team onto the pitch wearing their club's strip, some referees have acquired the habit of giving the coin to the home mascot after the call has been made by the captains.

Chris Hull, Football League, Lytham St Annes.

602: With all the freshwater rivers emptying into it all over the world, why is the sea still salty?

Most of the world's salt, about 4.5 million cubic miles – 50 per cent more than the volume of land above sea level in North America – is in solution in the oceans. It originates from volcanic activity, from magmas released in the sea beds from within the Earth's crust. The average salt content of sea water is 3.5 per cent; this figure can vary due to inflowing freshwater rivers, but the average remains the same, because the water cycle is a closed loop. Water evaporates from the sea to form clouds, which pass over land and drop their water as rain. The surface waters collect in streams and rivers and return to the sea. On the way, rivers pick up small amounts of salt and minerals from the rocks, but this is minute in comparison with the salt solution in the sea.

Ian Bradley, Salt Union, Runcorn, Cheshire.

603: What is the origin of the political expressions Right-wing and Left-wing? Have they the same meaning in other countries?

They originated in late 18th-century France when Louis XVI's reign started badly, with his coffers empty. Although he enjoyed brief popularity, confrontations with parliament escalated until the Revolution caused the fall of the monarchy. A crisis was reached in August 1788, when the treasury was advised to cease all payments other than those to the military. A National Assembly of the estates of the kingdom met in May 1789 and to this body can be traced the notions of 'left' and 'right' wings. The nobility, most of whom stood for reaction and repression, sat to the right of the king's seat, while the bourgeoisie and commoners, who wanted democracy or revolution, sat on the left.

Isabelle Daniels, Bishop Auckland, Co. Durham.

604: Why do we say 'Oops a daisy' when someone falls over? What has it got to do with daisies?

This expression began life in the early 18th century as a piece of baby talk. 'Oops', sometimes recorded as 'ups', either means 'whoops', often used after a slight accident, or 'up you get.' The 'daisy' part is straight baby talk, though it might just be connected with the word 'lackadaisy' (from 'lackaday', an expression of dismay). Various forms of the expression are recorded, including 'upsey-daisy', 'up-a-daisa' and 'up-a-dazy.'

NIGEL WILCOCKSON, BREWER'S DICTIONARY OF PHRASE & FABLE, LONDON.

It's not 'Oops a daisy' but 'Ups a Daisy' and it comes from the lovely Worzel Gummidge scarecrow stories. In these, whimsical Worzel's wife Daisy often finds her pipe-cleaner legs folding up under her, causing her to fall down. When she is picked up she says, 'Ups a Daisy.' I remember these stories from Children's Hour on the wireless in the Forties.

MISS M. SMITH, GLASGOW.

I remember as a child going on a train journey with my older sister. When we got to our destination, a porter lifted me out of the carriage, saying: 'Ups a daisy.' My sister called out: 'Hey, they call me Daisy. She's Violet.' That must have been 80 years ago.   MISS V. CRISP, CLEETHORPES.

605: How do seedless grapes propagate?

Seedless fruits such as some grape varieties are parthenocarpic, that is they are able to form fruits without pollination or fertilisation having taken place. In the wild, of course, they would not be able to propagate themselves. However, in cultivation, they are propagated by vegetative methods such as cutting and grafting. In fact, all grape varieties are propagated commercially by these methods, the most common being by hardwood cuttings. The propagation of grapes by seed is done only during breeding programmes to produce new types.

DR R. A. DUTTON, HORTICULTURAL CONSULTANT, MERSEYSIDE.

606: I read many years ago that estimated social security fraud cost the taxpayer an extra 1p on his income tax while estimated tax fraud cost an extra 10p. Do these figures still hold today?

Nobody knows the full extent of fraud in either social security claims or tax payments. Government 'guesstimates' are based on departmental experience. The Social Services Department currently estimates around £5 billion a year is lost to fraudulent claims, equivalent to just under 2p in the £ on income tax. The Inland Revenue doesn't have an official estimate but is believed to be losing in the region of £15 billion a year, equivalent to 5p in the £. Both departments are making concerted attempts to combat fraud at all levels. In 1992/3 £560 million in attempted frauds was recovered by the DSS – and £4.6 billion by the Inland Revenue.   SEAN FLEMING, WASHWOOD HEATH, BIRMINGHAM.

607: Prince Philip escorts the Queen to the opening of Parliament sporting a chest full of medals. What do they represent?

Prince Philip's medals, worn at the Opening of Parliament are: medal bar on chest: Queen's Service Order New Zealand; 1939-45 Star; Atlantic Star; Africa Star; Burma Star with Pacific Clasp; Italy Star; 1939-45 War Medal with Mention in Dispatches oakleaf; King George VI Coronation Medal 1937; Queen Elizabeth II Coronation Medal 1953; Queen Elizabeth II Silver Jubilee Medal 1977; Canadian Forces Decoration with two bars; New Zealand Centenary Medal; 1940-45 Greek War Cross and 1939-45 French Croix de Guerre with palme. Additionally, he wears the neck decoration of the Order of Merit, the Grand Cross Stars of The Most Noble Order of the Garter and The Most Noble Order of the Thistle. He is also a Knight Grand Cross of the Most Excellent Order of the British Empire, and has at least 25 foreign awards. In total he has: three Orders of Chivalry; one Service Order; six Campaign Medals and two Foreign War Crosses for war service; four Commemorative Medals; and one Forces Long Service Medal.

JOHN CROSBY JP, ORDERS AND MEDALS RESEARCH SOCIETY,
RIBBON BRANCH, NORTH WEALD, ESSEX.

608: 'All part of life's rich...' Does the saying conclude 'tapestry' or 'pageant', and what is its origin?

'...rich tapestry' is the true ending of the original phrase, as this has been used in a literary and figurative sense back to the late 16th century. The idea of life being a tapestry with a wrong side and right side goes back many years. A piece of literary criticism by Thomas Carlisle in 1831 reads: 'In looking at the fair tapestry of human life... he dwells not on the obverse alone, but here chiefly in the reverse; and, indeed, turns out the rough seams, tatters, and manifold thrums of that unsightly wrong side with... indifference.' The expression 'pageant of life' can be traced back only as far as the late 19th century.

RUTH KILLICK, OXFORD ENGLISH DICTIONARIES AND REFERENCE BOOKS.

609: What is the most popular date to get married?

No figures are kept which indicate an actual day which is most popular for weddings in this country, though the information is collected for each month and 'June brides' are not the most numerous. Of the total 3,766,828 marriages between 1981 and 1991, 492,829 couples, 13 per cent, married in August. At the other end of the scale is January, when only 126,805 couples, 3 per cent, chose to marry. June, in fact, comes 4th, with 416,772 marriages, 11 per cent of the total. Marriages are very seasonal with the months of August, September, July and June, when people expect favourable weather, accounting for the vast majority. Tax advantages, which used to dictate the most popular months to marry, no longer apply. PATRICIA McGLONE, GLASGOW.

610: Where did the word 'scam' come from?

The word 'scam', meaning fraud, deception, swindle or 'confidence trick', is an Americanism which became widespread in England only from the late Seventies. It is a popular word in business circles where its near-criminal undertones give it an appealing and glamorous air. A similar word was in use in England in the 18th century, pre-dating the Americanism. The word 'scampery' used to describe highway robbery, and is almost certainly the fore-runner of 'scam'. DAVID WATSON, LEEDS.

Sgam is an old Welsh word which means dodge or a scheme. Perhaps the word has returned to us via America. W. L. KEMBLE, CARDIFF, SOUTH GLAMORGAN.

611: Why is the oval-shaped loaf with a ridge cut on top called a 'bloomer'?

A good loaf is judged by its 'bloom', the colour of its crust after baking. The 'bloomer' is a baton-shaped loaf with the maximum amount of crust on top effected by the diagonal cuts which expose more of the 'bloom.' The oven-bottom baked bloomer, first produced by London bakers and known originally as a 'London Bloomer', was at its most popular between the two World Wars. CHAS DOWNES, RETIRED CRAFTSMAN BAKER, GOUDHURST, KENT.

612: What exactly is a person entitled to when given the freedom of a city?

The award shouldn't be taken too literally. These days people become 'Honorary Freeman', mainly as a recognition of personal achievement or services rendered to a city. It conveys no real practical privileges, other than the honour of its bestowal, though some rights – such as allowing an army regiment to parade through the streets with band playing and bayonets fixed, or being allowed to drive a herd of sheep across London Bridge – have survived from earlier eras. The title of honorary freeman is not transferable. Before the reform of local government in the Sixties there was an office of Hereditary Freeman, which could be passed from father to son and this title can still be granted in towns which have a tradition going back before 1835. JONATHAN PARDOE, DURHAM.

There are some practical advantages: a person given the Freedom of the City of London cannot be arrested on the street for being drunk.

THE HON C. T. WILSON, CUMBRIA.

613: When was the last day that there were absolutely NO road works on the M6?

Motorway maintenance work is split into major maintenance – which involves closing carriageways, creating large-scale diversions etc, when the whole road surface needs to be changed – and minor maintenance which occurs when safety barriers need to be repaired, lights need attention or parts of the carriageway have to be patched-up. The 341km-long M6 is one of the country's busiest motorways and in need of constant attention to ensure it remains practical and safe, so the strict answer to the question is never.

ALISON LANGLEY, DEPARTMENT OF TRANSPORT, LONDON.

The earlier answer was too pessimistic. On November 18, 1988 a reunion dinner was held for those involved in the design, building and maintenance of the M6, to mark the 25th anniversary of its opening through Cheshire. The now sadly departed Brian Redhead, founder of Friends Of The M6, accepted an invitation. As it was also Children in Need day, the county surveyor arranged with agent authorities from Staffordshire to Cumbria for every traffic cone to be removed from the M6 on that day. With Mr Redhead's publicity, this enabled a considerable sum to be collected for the appeal at all service areas.

D. R. ELLIOTT, PRESCOT, MERSEYSIDE.

614: Is it true that gin and tonic was originally popularised as a prophylactic against malaria? And is there any 'tonic' value in drinking 'Indian Tonic Water'?

The benefits of quinine, made from the bark of the cinchona tree, were known by South American Indians for centuries before it was used against malaria during the days of the British Empire. As quinine's use became more widespread it was made more palatable by turning it into a medicinal draught – the forerunner of today's Indian Tonic Water. It was made still more attractive to British taste by being mixed with gin, combining social drinking with medicinal virtues. A minimal amount of quinine is added to tonic water today and its effects are hardly noticeable. If drunk with gin, the diuretic qualities of the juniper in the gin are probably better for the body than any sugary tonic.

JOHN DOXAT, AUTHOR OF THE GIN BOOK, CAMBERLEY, SURREY.

615: Are airlines doing anything to combat some people's problem of acute pain in the ears when flying, which sometimes lasts for days afterwards? The normally suggested remedy, sucking sweets, does little to help.

The human body was designed only for altitudes that most healthy people could climb to: about 10,000ft. The middle ear (space behind the eardrum) can normally cope with the slow pressure change of climbing a mountain but aeroplanes ascend fast to 40,000ft so manufacturers make the cabin strong enough to be pressurised to a point where we can be comfortable: equivalent to about 7,000ft. As the aircraft climbs, air in the ears expands and escapes via the Eustachian tubes, tiny tubes running from behind the eardrum to the throat: this rarely causes more than a passing twinge. As the plane descends, however, pressure increases and pushes the eardrums in, causing discomfort. The connecting tubes are soft and collapse unless the throat muscles move to open them which is why sweets may help if they promote saliva and swallowing. Some people with sinus and nose problems cannot clear their Eustachian tubes. The eardrums then get sucked in, causing pain. If this lasts more than a few days it is important to see a doctor. To prevent this, eardrums can be perforated to allow immediate equalisation of pressure. Some dive bomber pilots had this done during the last war. Maintaining sea level pressure in the cabin would mean stronger, heavier and more expensive aeroplanes, which would use more fuel. Dr R. A. Pearson, Civil Aviation Authority.

I always had this problem and felt giddy and faint when arriving at my destination airport and sucking sweets didn't help me either. My doctor told me to pinch both nostrils at the bottom with a hankerchief and blow as if blowing into the hankerchief without releasing the nostrils. This makes the ear wax move and, although it can be painful, gets it all over in one blow as the pressure is released from the ear. I find I need to do this two or three times as the plane descends. Mrs M. J. P. Bisset, Romford, Essex.

My wife suffered great pain in the ears for years until a fellow passenger recommended inhaling the fumes of a Karvol capsule half an hour before landing. Our stewardess provided the capsule and hot water and my wife found rapid relief. E. D. H. Hall, St Albans, Herts.

616: Why a 'feather in his hat'?

This stems from the well-documented custom among native Americans of wearing a feather in their hat, hair or headpiece to show they had killed one of their enemies. A similar practice was reported by a Dr Wolff in 1854 among the Kaffr Seeyah Poosh (infidels in black clothing) who lived in the Himalayas. Dr Wolff said: 'They are great enemies of the Muhamadens and for each Muhamaden they kill, they wear a feather in their head.' He went on to say that a similar thing was done by the Abyssinians and the Turcomans. His colleague Alfred Gatty pointed out the similarity with the American Indians and wondered if the eagle's feather in the bonnet of a Scottish Highlander had a similar significance.

DR T. HEALEY, BARNSLEY, SOUTH YORKSHIRE.

617: Is it possible to score an 'own goal' in rugby union?

As far as I know, it's impossible to score an 'own try.' If a player touches down after his side has carried the ball over their own goal-line, the referee awards a scrum, five metres out, to the opposition. If the ball is touched down after being kicked over the line by the opposition, a drop-out is taken from the 22-metre line. The nearest I have seen to what could be termed an 'own goal' came while playing for my old club, Harrow. The action was within a few feet of our goal-line and a maul was set up in which one of our forwards decided an opponent was where he shouldn't have been and pulled him out to behind our line. Unfortunately the other player also had the ball – and the result was a try to them.

T. JONES, ABBOTS LANGLEY, HERTS.

Different scoring systems were tested in the 1870s. Touching the ball down behind your own try line counted against you and if you did it three times it was deemed the equivalent of a try.

JOHN GRIFFITH, ROTHMANS RUGBY YEARBOOK, WATFORD, HERTS.

618: Does anyone know the origins or meaning of the name Kylassa, carved in the stonework above the doorway of a turn-of-the-century house?

The fashion in the late 19th century was to christen houses with a name connected with their builder or developer. The name Kylassa doesn't seem to exist in any form, past or present. It isn't a word in any other known language, or a place name listed in any atlas. It is possible that it is formed from a combination of the names of the builders or an anagram of their name. The best anagram seems A. S. Lasky, of which there are 17 families in the nation's phone books.

DAVID MOORE, BOURNEMOUTH.

'Kylassa' is a Finnish word meaning 'in the village', signifying that the owner has become an established member of the community.

STEPHEN HART, SHELFORD, CAMBRIDGESHIRE.

The house may be named after the 8th century Temple of Kailasa, the largest feature of the Caves of Ellora, between Bombay and Hyderabad, in India. This series of caves are Hindu, Buddhist and Jain holy places, the greatest being the Hindu Temple of Kailasa, which means paradise. The elaborately carved and structured Ellora Caves were one of the greatest sights I had ever seen when I visited them in 1935.

VALENTINE ffRENCH BLAKE, READING, BERKS.

In ancient Hindi texts there is a reference to Mount Kailasa, said to be the abode of the god Shiva, one of the trinity of gods in the Hindu pantheon, in the Himalayan mountains. It is not unusual on the Indian sub-continent to find this name over house doorways.

S. RAMAKRISHNAYYA, LONDON.

619: What do the residents of Coronation Street watch on ITV at 7.30pm on Mondays, Wednesdays and Fridays?

Most of them lead such traumatic lives that tuning in to TV drama is understandably low on their list of priorities, particularly as crises invariably reach boiling point on Monday, Wednesday and Friday evenings. But what is being transmitted on those evenings may be a long-running folk opera, produced by Granada, called Florizel Street. This would seem appropriate as it was the original working title for Coronation Street.

C. W. BLUBBERHOUSE, SALISBURY, WILTS.

620: After urging my children to hurry to catch a bus, they both had a 'stitch' in their sides. Now they want to know what it is.

The exact causes of the 'stitch' remain unknown, though there are several possible reasons for its occurrence. It could be a spasm of the diaphragm, the membrane separating the chest and abdominal cavities; or it may be air trapped in the bowel. It could also arise from blood being diverted away from the bowel to the working muscles during intense exercise, or it may be due to part of the bowel slapping against the abdominal wall. In any cases the pain eases rapidly as soon as the exercise stops. If pain persists, see a doctor.   DR PHILIP BELL, SPECIALIST IN SPORTS MEDICINE, LONDON BRIDGE CLINIC.

Use of 'stitch' to describe pain in the body pre-dates its use in sewing and was first noted in the 11th century. It stems from the original meaning of 'stitch.' The word didn't appear in connection with sewing until the 13th century.   EDMUND WEINER, OXFORD ENGLISH DICTIONARY.

A 'stitch' is caused by a build-up of lactic acid. This forms in muscles as a by-product of anaerobic respiration, where the exercising muscles' demand for oxygen exceeds supply. As a person gets fitter and more agile, their susceptibility to a stitch decreases as their cardiovascular system gets stronger and more efficient. It becomes more able to cope with the increased demand for oxygen at times of strenuous exercise. As a result, more oxygen is transported to the muscles via the red blood corpuscles and an increased rate of aerobic respiration takes place. The production of lactic acid therefore decreases. So to avoid a stitch either avoid stenuous exercise, or get fit. RON SUMNER, HARDWICK, CAMBRIDGESHIRE.

621: Where is the most powerful computer in the world, and what is its purpose?

The liquid-cooled Cray-T3D, built early in 1993, in Minneapolis, is the world's most powerful computer. Now based in Pittsburgh Supercomputer Centre, Pennsylvania, it is used primarily for biomedical research. It is capable of dealing with 300 billion calculations per second. To get an idea of the power of the Cray-T3D, imagine someone using a hand-held calculator to add 1+1=2, 2+1=3, 3+1=4, 4+1=5 etc. If they continue this process without stopping for 1,500 years they would still have done less calculations than the computer can do in one second. STEVE CONWAY, CRAY RESEARCH, MINNEAPOLIS, USA.

622: What is 'shortnin' bread' that Mama's little baby loves so much?

According to the American Dictionary of Food & Drink, shortnin' bread is an American deep south quick-bread made with a shortening such as butter or lard. The recipe goes: Mix two cups of flour with half a cup of brown sugar and blend until crumbly. Work in $^1/4$lb of butter until the dough is smooth. Divide and pat into a circle, $^1/2$in thick. Prick the top. Cook in an ungreased pan at 35°F for about 30 minutes. STEVE DIXON, COOKERY WRITER, LONDON.

623: Why does Father Christmas indulge in the risky business of getting into houses down the chimney?

Santa Claus's origins can be traced not just to St Nicholas, a one-time bishop of Antioch known for his charity, but also to the travelling shaman or medicine man of pre-Christian times who acted as priest in the cultures of Northern America and Europe. In those days the people lived in huts, partly sunk in the ground for warmth, made of branches, leaves and mud, to which the only opening was a hole in the apex of the rounded roof. This doubled as an entrance to the hut and a 'chimney' to let out smoke from the fire. The shaman was obliged to enter the hut through the chimney which gave rise to our tradition of Santa coming down the chimney. CHRISTOPHER ROYCROFT-DAVIS, LONDON E1.

In Scotland we were told Santa's custom of coming down the chimney had its origins in the fact that early Scottish houses had no windows, just a hole in the roof known as the 'lum', from the French *lumiere,* through which light entered the house and smoke from the fire escaped. While in France and other European countries, St Nicholas left gifts by putting them through bedroom windows, in Scotland Father Christmas brings presents down the lum, or chimney, and bairns still tell him what they want by 'crying up the lum.'   BILL FYFE HENDRIE, TORPHICHEN, WEST LOTHIAN.

Santa's association with the chimney dates back to the time of St Nicholas. A poor family were going to bed on Christmas Eve with very little money left and nothing to eat. Mother finished washing her children's stockings and hung them to dry above the fireplace. St Nicholas is said to have come in the night and dropped food, presents and money down the chimney so they landed in the stockings and ever since, children have hung up their stockings by the fireplace.

CHLOE SMITH (AGED 11), SOUTHFIELDS, LONDON.

624: Why is a yawn infectious?

The fact that yawns are 'infectious' nicely demonstrates the difference between Direct and Indirect Suggestion. If you say to someone: 'You are feeling tired,' the suggestion is consciously perceived and may be refuted. A yawn is a suggestion of tiredness but, being indirect, it bypasses the conscious censor to a certain extent and is therefore more readily accepted by the subconscious mind and thence absorbed into that person's thinking. Indirect Suggestion is much more powerful than Direct Suggestion and the most powerful form is Subliminal Suggestion which bypasses the conscious censor altogether. Subliminal advertising is banned in this country for this reason.   A. B. KING, CONSULTING HYPNOTHERAPIST, WATERLOOVILLE, HANTS.

625: Does someone have to stand on the roof of the Met office on Christmas Day to watch out for the two snow flakes which would trigger a 'white Christmas' payout by bookmakers?

The duty observer does indeed stand on the roof observation area on top of the Met office, though he/she is not on the roof all the time. Three trained observers, from a team of nine, share the 24-hour duty on Christmas Day, as on all other 364 days a year. Their duties include visiting the roof each hour, surveying the sky and recording visibility, cloud height and type, type of weather, weight of snow if any, etc. We have to be particularly vigilant because of the large number of bets placed on a 'white Christmas.' Just one snowflake seen to fall on the Weather Centre roof is enough for our office to confirm snow falling.

GRAHAM JOHNSON, HEAD OF LONDON WEATHER CENTRE.

626: At what time in the evening is the Daily Mail 'put to bed' and who says when it is bedtime?

Bedtime on the Daily Mail is about 10pm. That's when the first edition starts coming off the presses at printing plants around the country. After that, various pages may be changed several times for later editions before printing stops at about 4am – in time for more than 2,000,000 papers to be delivered before breakfast. Who decides when? On the Daily Mail, the Editor decides everything. HUGH DAWSON, DAILY MAIL PRODUCTION EDITOR.

627: At what stage in man's development did he become aware of the connection between the act of coition and childbirth?

Humankind has evolved over many thousands of years and, although our physical evolution followed a universal pattern, our social and cultural evolution was very different. Although we all had a natural instinct for the sex act at different times, we have imagined different reasons for its purpose. As far back as history is documented people have understood the link between coition and childbirth and our limited, and hotly debated, anthropological knowledge doesn't allow us at present to answer precisely when this awareness first dawned. EUNICE JEFFERSON, CANTERBURY, KENT.

628: What were the names of Jesus's sisters?

Jesus's sisters are mentioned in Mark's Gospel but no names are given. The names of his brothers are listed as James, Joseph, Simon and Judas (not Iscariot). The Roman Catholic faith adheres to the Doctrine of the Perpetual Virginity of Mary, which argues against the possibility of Jesus having any complete brothers or sisters, so those mentioned are taken to be close relatives of Our Lord. PATRICK FORBES, CHURCH ENQUIRY BUREAU, LONDON.

629: Where did Dustin Hoffman get his unusual first name?

The inspiration for Hoffman's name was provided by Dustin Farnum, which was appropriate because Farnum helped create Hollywood. In 1913 he starred in the film of his Broadway success, The Squaw Man. Its novice director Cecil B. De Mille hired a barn in a little Californian town and turned out the first major movie made in Hollywood. The film's backers, former glove salesman Sam Goldfish (later Goldwyn) and his brother-in-law Jesse Lasky, offered Farnum shares in their company but he insisted on a cash fee. The holding he turned down came to be worth $1 million. R. CROSS, CHELMSFORD.

630: Why is the Press called the 'Fourth Estate'? What are the other three?

From the Middle Ages, the 'Three Estates of the Realm' are the Lords Spiritual, the Lords Temporal and the Commons, gathered together to form Parliament. Edmund Burke is credited with having invented the expression 'Fourth Estate' to refer to the Press in the late 18th century. Rising to speak in the House on one occasion and looking up to the crowded Press gallery, he remarked: 'I see we now have a Fourth Estate.' The first written instance belongs to historian Thomas Babington Macaulay, who wrote in 1828: 'The gallery where the reporters sit has become a fourth estate of the realm.' In recent years, the BBC has been called the Fifth Estate.   BRIAN LICHFIELD, OLDBURY, WEST MIDLANDS.

631: What percentage of Britain's population has a criminal record?

Full national figures on people with criminal records have been available only since 1953, so we can base our conclusions only on people below the age of 44. Given that, 35 per cent of males in England and Wales will have at least one criminal conviction against them before their 35th birthday, compared with just 8 per cent of females. The peak age for offending males is 18 and for females 15. Of the 35 per cent of males who have offended, 7 per cent have at least one conviction for violence and 6 per cent have spent some time in custody before the age of 31.
                    ROBERT BANNER, NORWICH.

632: Three people pay a £25 restaurant bill by each giving the waiter a £10 note. He returns with £5 change, keeps £2 as a tip and gives £1 change to each customer. So they've paid £9 each. 3 x £9 = £27, plus the waiter's £2 = £29. What's happened to the other £1?

This is a hoary old conundrum which aptly illustrates how figures can be made to lie, a clear example of the way in which numbers can be manipulated. The apparent arithmetical contradiction arises from focusing attention on the refund. When the transaction is properly stated there is no missing pound: £30 tendered to pay a £25 bill to which is added a £2 tip, leaving £3 change. For the best practice of this financial sleight-of-hand, study the presentation of most modern Budgets.
                    R. JACOBS, WINCHESTER, HANTS.

This fake problem reminds me of the old story about the Arab sheik who died and left his 17 camels to his three sons, half to the eldest, a third to the second son and one ninth to the youngest. This was very awkward and the sons quarrelled about it and eventually went to a wise man for help in solving the problem. He said: 'Go and get my camel and add it to the herd, making the number 18. Now half to the eldest equals nine, one third to the second son equals six and one ninth to the youngest equals two. Total: 17. Now take the remaining camel back to my field.'

LEONARD JOHNSON, WORCESTER.

633: Who composed the music of The Last Post and when and where was it first played?

The beginnings of the piece derive from the military campaigns in the Low Countries in the late 17th century, when the Tattoo, the traditional drumbeat, summoned soldiers to their quarters at night. The drummer would play the First Post as a warning to tavern owners to stop serving ale and for the soldiers to return to barracks. The Last Post, usually played after sunset, was the final tattoo or warning for the men to return. The word tattoo comes from the Dutch *taptoe* meaning 'turn off all taps.' The German equivalent is *Zapenstreiche,* where *Zapsen* means bung and *Streiche* was the chalk line put over the bung in a barrel to ensure no more ale was served once the last post had been sounded. In the late 18th Century the British Army copied the Germans in starting to use bugles for communication. In 1764 the English Light Dragoons adopted the Bugle Horn, followed in 1772 by the Grenadier Guards. In 1814 the Light Infantry and Rifle Regiments were granted the bugle horn as regimental badges. From 1812, the bugle was adopted by the whole British Army for sending signals. The full list of calls used by the army was not officially published until 1895 but the piece we know as The Last Post existed much earlier. Kneller Hall was established in 1857 to deliver uniform training and standards to British military bands.

MAJOR WATTS, SENIOR INSTRUCTOR, ROYAL MILITARY SCHOOL OF MUSIC, TWICKENHAM.

The Last Post is made up from a number of bugle calls which soldiers would hear almost every working day. It starts off with 'lights out' followed by the triple four note descending call of the fire warning. My father told me that in World War I the soldiers had words for the bugle calls to help new recruits remember them, for example: 'Come to the cookhouse door, boys.' The call for a cancelled parade was: 'There's no parade today, there's no parade today, the colonel's got the bellyache and the adjutant's away.' I'm ex-RAF where the calls were made by trumpet but in 1946 trumpet calls were seldom used and we erks just got our ears blistered over the Tannoy.

E. SMITH, WALTON-ON-THAMES, SURREY.

As a 15-year-old trumpeter in the Royal Horse Artillery in World War I,

I learned to do all the calls, from reveille to lights out, on horseback, at Wellington Barracks, Woolwich. I started with the Royal Horse Artillery call for which our words were: 'The Royal Horse Artillery, the pride of the army, the first in the field and the last to come out.' Then came reveille for which the words were: 'Rise, soldiers, rise and put your armour on!'   G. Anscombe, Hurstpierpoint, Sussex.

Trumpets which are still playable were found in the tomb of the Egyptian Pharaoh Tutankhamen. They can play only a few notes but could certainly perform The Last Post.   Herbert F. Taylor, Bedford Park, London.

634: Now that the Darracq car from the film Genevieve has been bought by the Dutch National Motor Museum at Rotterdam, where is its rival, the Spyker?

The Spyker used in the film was built in 1904 at the Trompenberg factory in Holland where the Dutch Queen's golden carriage and several aeroplanes were also made. It comprised a Dutch engine and mechanical parts on an English frame. Only a couple of hundred Spyker cars were built and we are proud to have seven cars, including the film star, in our collection here at Autotron, a leisure park/museum themed around transport, south of Amsterdam in a town called Rosmalen. The car has been with us since 1964 when we bought it from the Reece family in England. In its 30 years with us we have restored it to its original condition and entered it in rallies all over the world, most notably the 1992 Australian Rally from Perth to Albany, where it met the Genevieve Darracq again and that time didn't get beaten. In Britain, the car has taken part in the 1,000-mile London to Peebles and back again rally.
                    Maraka Russ Van Mook, Autotron Theme Park, Rosmalen, Netherlands.

Both my parents were veteran car enthusiasts when we lived in Boston Vale, Middlesex. My father, Frank Reece, owner of a London taxi-cab firm, found the Spyker in a garage in Hounslow and bought it for £20. He spent a lot of time lovingly restoring the car which had been neglected. Then in 1953, his big Spyker was chosen to rival the little Darracq in the film Genevieve. My mother and father featured in the film as extras and that year, at the age of five, I became the youngest ever person to take part in the London to Brighton veteran car rally. My father donated his proceeds from the film to the Veteran Car Club of Great Britain though there seems to have been some resentment in the club that my father's car was chosen to be in the film. The Spyker was originally green which didn't photograph well so my father allowed the film company to paint the car yellow for the film provided it was repainted green afterwards. For some reason, despite the fact that the Spyker was built in 1904, it was re-dated by the club to 1905, making it ineligible for the London to Brighton race. After my father's death in 1963, my mother Minnie found the Spyker too heavy to drive and sold it to a Dutch motor museum for £3,000. My last memory of our beloved Spyker was of it being loaded onto a lorry for transport to Holland. Even now, I cannot watch the film without tears.   ELAINE LEMON (NEE REECE), WINDSOR, BERKS.

635: Why do we pour brandy over the Christmas pudding and set it alight?

Traditionally, the brandy poured over the pudding and lit to form a halo of flames represents Christ's passion. The sprig of holly stuck on top represents the crown of thorns and a protection against evil. Plum Pudding, or Christmas Pudding, belongs entirely to Britain and has been carried to other parts of the world by ex-patriates. Puddings should be made by the Sunday nearest to St Andrew's Day, the 25th sunday after Trinity, known as 'Stir-up-Sunday' from the opening lines of the Prayer Book collect for the day: 'Stir up, we beseech thee, oh Lord, the wills of thy faithful people...' In well organised households, each member of the family should take a turn at stirring the pudding with a wooden spoon.
                                    ANGELA BLACKLEY, ROBERTSONS FOODS, LONDON.

636: Does life really begin at 40?

This idea goes back to ancient Roman times when it was considered an honour for a family to send their 10-year-old daughter to enter service at the Temple of Vesta. The girl would live a simple life of prayer and abstinence as a Vestal Virgin at the temple for the next 30 years. Even setting eyes on a man was forbidden and would result in expulsion. On her 40th birthday she would be released and was no doubt eager to begin her new life as soon as possible.   JANET BEVERIDGE, DULVERTON, SOMERSET.

637: Why is the motto of the Duke of Marlborough's family 'Fiel Pero Desdichado' shown on the coat of arms at Blenheim Palace, in Spanish?

This motto, meaning 'Faithful but unfortunate', was chosen by the 1st Duke's father, Colonel Churchill, in 1661, when Charles II, after his restoration, awarded him an 'augmentation of honour' to his coat of arms for his services to Charles I and loyalty as an MP – but didn't restore to him his lands lost during the Civil War. None of the scholars who have studied the early history of the Churchills know why the motto is in Spanish though Col Churchill, later knighted, was an educated man who knew both French and Latin and may have felt the Spanish phrase most precisely and elegantly portrayed his feelings. Historian A. L. Rowse, author of The Early Churchills and The Later Churchills, said of the motto: 'Faithful, certainly, but never was the cant of heraldry more belied than in the second epithet "unfortunate".'

PAUL DUFFIE, BLENHEIM PALACE, OXON.

638: My surname is Prince and some people are called King. Are we descended from royalty?

Sorry, but almost certainly not. The children of royalty born in wedlock were automatically given titles in addition to their family name. The original hereditary royal surnames are historically known as Plantagenet, followed by the houses of Lancaster, York, Tudor and Stuart and, from 1714, Hanover. Since the Middle Ages, with the honourable exception of Charles II who rewarded his (at least) 13 natural offspring with dukedoms and earldoms etc., children born to royalty out of wedlock have been 'farmed out' and forgotten. They were given the surname of their foster family. Surnames such as King, Prince, Queen, Princess, Duke, Earl, Baron, Pope or Bishop are theatrical nicknames given to actors who played these parts. The only status surnames whose original owners were what their surnames suggest them to be are Knight and Squire, the mounted soldiers and shield bearers bound, by feudal agreement, to serve their lord, who later achieved minor nobile rank.

MICHAEL J. BROOK, RARE SURNAME REGISTER, YORK.

639: Why is the belt worn over an Army officer's right shoulder called a Sam Browne?

The belt was invented by General Sir Samuel James Browne, VC. Like many other Victorian Army officers, Sam Browne found the official Army waistbelt and slings highly unsuitable for carrying a sword and revolver in action; so he devised a brown leather belt to carry his weapons. Its shoulder brace distributed the load more comfortably and its waistbelt hitched up his sword and included space for a holster. Other officers appreciated the practicality of the design and began to adopt it, until this equipment became regulation for officers. Sam Browne won the Victoria Cross for his actions in the 1858 Indian Mutiny when, despite being severely wounded and losing his left arm, he charged and captured a rebel gun. Tradition had it that he designed the belt as a result of his disability but Browne wrote that he first thought of it in 1852, six years before he lost his arm. Sam Browne's original belt is on display at the National Army Museum, Chelsea, London, in the gallery dedicated to The Victorian Soldier, including relics such as Florence Nightingale's jewellery and Kitchener's and Baden-Powell's uniforms.

JULIAN HUMPHRYS, NATIONAL ARMY MUSEUM, LONDON.

640: Does the expression 'it's too cold for snow' have any basis in science?

This phrase really applies only to maritime countries such as the British Isles. Most of our snow falls from westerly winds which have travelled over the comparatively warm oceans and arrive at temperatures between -3 and +3 degrees Celsius. When the temperature drops to below -5C, it is normally the result of easterlies which have travelled over the cold European land mass; and we rarely get snow from them. Snow in this country tends to be wet and heavy, because Britain is surrounded by comparatively warm seas with winter temperatures of between +7C and +9C. On the Continent, where temperatures go lower, snow tends to be more dry and powdery. Because of lower temperatures, salt is less effective at dispersing Continental snow; but 'snow blowers' can be used because the snow is drier.

MALCOLM BROOKES, MET OFFICE, LONDON.

In the winter of 1990-91, British Rail was having problems clearing snow from railway lines and Radio 4's Today programme presenter Peter Hobday asked BR operations director Terry Worrall if it was the 'wrong type of snow.' Mr Worrall said it was, which resulted in British Rail becoming the butt of many jokes. But the snow was indeed different from the type we normally experience and presented problems for BR equipment trying to clear it.

BOB FENTON, BRITISH RAIL, LONDON.

641: Why are there many Friday Streets but few streets named after other days of the week?

Most Friday Streets are in market towns and areas where fish was available for sale. Streets named after days of the week usually got their names by staging markets on those days. Fish markets were, and still are, distinct from other food markets and the sale of fish, particularly on Fridays under early Christian custom and law, has given those streets their name.

W. S. JONES, SELBY, NORTH YORKSHIRE.

There are 27 Friday streets, road, avenues etc. throughout the UK. Next most popular is Monday, with four listings throughout the country. Saturday has three and there's one mention each for Sunday, Tuesday and Wednesday. Thursday has no mention in street names.

MATTHEW TRIGG, GEOGRAPHERS A-Z MAP CO, SEVENOAKS, KENT.

642: 'Thirty days hath September...' goes the well-known rhyme. But who was its author, or what was its origin?

This verse first appeared as a nursery rhyme in 1555, attributed to M. S. Stevins: 'Thirty days hath September, April, June and November, all the rest have thirty-one, Excepting February alone, And that has twenty-eight days clear, And twenty-nine in each leap year.'

In 1570, Richard Grafton published his Abridgement To The Chronicles Of England containing the version: 'Thirty days hath November, April, June and September. February hath twenty-eight alone, And all the rest have thirty-one.' LAWRENCE KING, BLANDFORD FORUM, DORSET.

643: Why do Americans use the term 'Victorian'? Why not McKinlean or whatever?

For a short woman, the Widow of Osborne cast a very long historical shadow. Americans as well as Britons describe Queen Victoria's reign (1837 to 1901) as The Victorian Age, referring to its values, sexual morality, architecture and other 19th Century social trends. The term 'antebellum' is used to describe the years before the American Civil War (1861 to 1865), while the late 19th century is often called 'The Gilded Age' and the early 20th century 'The Progressive Era', rather than the Edwardian period. America remained a 'cultural colony' of Britain long after gaining independence in 1776 and copied Victorian Britain in many things from self-help to imperialism and crinolines to mutton-chop whiskers. Even the anti-slavery and early women's movements took some of their inspiration from British Victorians. Few Americans realise that Victoria's impact extends to their modern lives in a most personal way. Believing the British to be 'the lost tribes of Israel', Victoria had her sons circumcised, a practice which became fashionable among the British upper classes and in America where, to this day, the majority of boys are circumcised. TERRY FLEMING, DEPT OF HISTORY, MICHIGAN STATE UNIVERSITY, U.S.

644: What makes a street a street and a road a road?

In present use, the name 'street' describes a thoroughfare confined to a town or village, lined on either side by dwellings or other buildings, while a 'road' is a highway going from place to place. The Romans classed their roads in order of priority as Iter I, Iter II, before their now familiar names of Watling Street, Ermine Street, Stane Street etc. It seems contradictory for the Anglo-Saxons to have called them streets but as they went from place to place in straight lines they used the Old English word *straet,* derived from the Latin *strata,* meaning straight, or *strata via,* a paved way. Later, a street used for wheeled traffic became known as a *ragweg,* or wheelway, and this was curtailed to *rad,* from which our word 'road' is derived.   JOHN BANNISTER, PRESTON.

645: How is wind-chill factor worked out? What difference does it make to the true temperature?

The term wind-chill has been used and abused for many years to describe the common experience of a person feeling colder when the wind blows than when it doesn't. Animate bodies must maintain a fixed body core temperature to survive. When the wind blows it removes heat from the surface of a body more quickly than still air and physiological processes try to maintain body core temperature at the expense of more superficial areas such as hands and feet. Many formulae exist to calculate wind-chill since a lot of work was done on it in Antarctica in the 1940s. All include elements such as air temperature, wind speed, skin temperature and clothing. Wind-chill equivalent temperatures quoted in weather forecasts try to give an indication of how cold a person might feel. The same amount of chilling might be brought about by a lower temperature in calm conditions, though this depends on age, metabolism, clothes etc. Wind speed has no effect on air temperature, only on how cold we feel. So beware of anti-freeze adverts which misquote wind-chill temperatures to encourage you to protect your car engine down to ridiculously low temperatures. A switched off engine will cool towards the air temperature, as measured on a thermometer, not below it.   JILL DIXON, THE METEOROLOGICAL OFFICE, BRACKNELL, BERKSHIRE.

646: My first two fridges were silent absorption units. Why are they not obtainable now?

Most refrigerators today work by compression, using a small electric motor to circulate coolant around an appliance. This motor creates the slight humming noise you can sometimes hear. The absorption system works on heat transfer and because it does not use a motor, and has no moving parts, it is virtually silent. The technology involved makes it more expensive than the compression system.   SIMON EWART, ELECTROLUX, LONDON.

647: Does the British Army have a serving sergeant 'major', sergeant 'sergeant' or major 'major'?

During my National Service in the RAF from 1951-53, mainly on detachment with the Royal Artillery, the NCO in charge of our small unit was Sergeant Danny Sergeant.   2505866 LAC BRIAN HOPE (RTD), MANCHESTER.

My brother and I are both Sergeant Sargent in the British Army. Our father only made it to corporal during his National Service and our sister was a private in the Queen Alexandra Royal Army Nursing Corps. I'm a clerk in the Adjutant General's Corps at the Ministry of Defence, and my brother Paul is an ammunition technician, sometimes in Germany with the Royal Logistics Corps. When I announce my name, people generally think I've got a very bad stutter – but they get used to it very quickly.   SGT PETE SARGENT, WHETSTONE, N. LONDON.

My son is Major Major and was also Sergeant Major Major and we are very proud of him.   MRS M. MAJOR, WELLING, KENT.

When I joined No 12 Squadron, flying Lancasters, in May 1943, my pilot was Sergeant Sargent. All seven crew members were sergeants and we were known as Sergeant Sargent's Sergeants.   D. OLIVER, BROADSTAIRS, KENT.

648: What was the 'big ship' and what was it doing sailing on the 'Alley-Alley-O'?

There are two versions of this ancient children's rhyme. In the English version, she is a 'good' ship and sails 'from' the Alley-Alley-O on the '20th of September'. In the Irish version she is a 'big' ship and sails 'through' the Alley-Alley-O on the '14th of December'. Both versions refer to the Mayflower, built at Rotherhithe and launched in Wapping Alley in 1620. Both dates are inaccurate and appear to have been included solely to make the rhyme scan. After her launch the Mayflower made a leisurely journey along the south coast to Plymouth, sailing from there for the New World on September 6, 1620.   KEITH M. BROOK, ENFIELD, MIDDLESEX.

The Big Ship Sails On The Alley-Alley-O is a singing game which involves a group of children holding hands in a line while the child at the end places one hand against a wall to form an arch. As the song is sung, the child at the other end leads the line under the arch and the aim of the game is to form a human chain with crossed arms. The game remains intact but over the years the words of the song have changed and nobody really knows the original, because almost all children's games pass on over many generations by oral tradition. One claimed source of the present version is that the words celebrate the opening of the Manchester Ship Canal in 1894, which was also the year when Tower Bridge and Blackpool Tower were completed. But there is a reference to the same song emanating from New Zealand, dating back to 1870, preceding the opening of the Ship Canal by 24 years.

IONA OPIE, AUTHOR, THE SINGING GAME, OXFORD.

649: Are there any numbers which are definitely not magical, lucky, unlucky or replete with significance?

In numerology all numbers have a significance and some arrangements of numbers have more power than others. However, there are no numbers that are unlucky. Even No 13, widely believed to bring misfortune, is not unlucky. If a person chooses to believe that numbers have no meaning whatsoever, they will not harness their potential power and so numbers will have far less influence on their lives than when used as part of a holistic, spiritual approach by a student of numerology.

ANTHONY HALLISSEY, SPIRITUAL TEACHER AND ADVISER, LONDON.

650: Has anybody ever deciphered the inscriptions on the Ogham stones?

There are thought to be almost 400 Ogham (also known as Ogam, Agam or Ogum) stones in existence and these are found in areas where there was once a strong Irish or Pictish influence. Most are in Ireland and the majority of the rest in Wales. The Ogham alphabet is believed to have emerged around the fourth century AD and comprises a series of notches on the edge of a stone that make up a total of 20 letters. The key to the deciphering of the Ogham writings came with the discovery of The Maglocunus Stone in 1906. The stone was found in the walls of the church of St Brynach in Nevern, Pembrokeshire, and unlike the stones in Ireland had a Latin explanation of the meanings etched into it. The Ogham inscriptions are normally very short – a name and the possessions of that person's family.

PAMELA & VALERIE RIPLEY, CHICHESTER, WEST SUSSEX.

651: Who was the woman, mentioned by weather forecaster Michael Fish, who phoned the BBC on October 15, 1987, to say a hurricane was on the way? And what was ITV's weather forecast for that night?

Michael Fish's dismissal of a prediction by a woman caller to the BBC that Hurricane Len was heading towards the South Coast of England on that date is often regarded as the lowest point in the history of the Met Office. ITV wasn't much better. The effects of the hurricane were enormous; 20 people died, five million homes lost their electricity, millions of trees were destroyed and more than a billion pounds' worth of damage was caused. The Daily Mail traced the call to Anita Hart from Pinner, who ran a firm of solicitors in the West End. She was warned of the approaching hurricane by her amateur meteorologist son, Gaon (the name means 'genius' in Hebrew), a 21-year-old trainee lawyer. The official Met Office inquiry exonerated Michael Fish for the inaccurate forecast and blamed instead the rigid analysis of data on its computer. As a result, a new, more advanced computer system was quickly installed. French and Dutch forecasts on the night issued warnings of exceptionally violent gales and the Dutch even advised people 36 hours beforehand not to travel to the UK. KERRY HAAGEN, PORTSMOUTH.

In defence of Michael Fish, he did initially forecast the possibility of a hurricane in the weekly weather outlook on the previous Sunday but down-graded it in midweek. If he hadn't, he would now be remembered for his accurate prediction of the hurricane. V. ALLEN, COALVILLE, LEICESTERSHIRE.

652: What is inside the small oblong bag attached to the cross straps on the uniform worn by the Corps of Commissionaires?

The oblong pouch was adapted from the ammunition pouch worn by soldiers. Sgt Major Stanley Baldwin, who has completed over 30 years' service, maintains that the ammunition-style pouches were used to carry messages around the Stock Exchange in London. Nowadays, the pouches contain nothing and are only worn by supervisors. The Corps of Commissionaires was established in 1859 when a Captain Walter employed eight ex-servicemen disabled from the Crimean War. Its members were initially all ex-military personnel but today they include ex-police and fire officers. BERNARD ZEOLLER, CORPS OF COMMISSIONAIRES, LONDON.

653: Is it true that all the railings taken from buildings and parks in World War II to be melted down for munitions were never actually used? Nor the aluminium saucepans collected for aircraft manufacture? If so, what happened to them?

In the darkest days of World War II, after Dunkirk, when it became obvious that the war would last a long time and all available resources would be needed, Lord Beaverbrook, proprietor of the Daily Express and later Minister of Supply, launched his 'manifesto' on July 10, 1940, as a morale-boosting operation. More than 1,000 local councils began removing public and private metal railings from parks, gardens, cemeteries and houses to be turned into munitions, bridges and tanks, etc. Meanwhile, aluminium pots and pans were collected by members of the Women's Voluntary Service and millions of housewives to be turned into war planes. By 1943 the salvage campaign was a massive operation, with compulsory orders to collect metal from any source. But the pots and pans yielded only very low-grade aluminium, and the moral-boosting exercise failed as word got round that scrap merchants still had lots of aluminium not being used and hardware stores were still stocking large numbers of pots and pans. The railing collection campaign was more successful and amounted to more than 1,000,000 tons of scrap by September 1944, when it ceased. Of this, only about a quarter was used to make munitions. The rest lay in railway sidings or council scrap areas, and was designated for use if the war went on any longer.

ROGER McCALLUM, BASILDON, ESSEX.

654: Our not-so-young record player has four speeds: 16, 33, 45 and 78 rpm. Whatever happened to the 16 rpm record?

The 16ʳrpm record had a limited commercial life during the 'battle of the speeds' after World War II. A problem had developed with 78 rpm records, intended to carry film soundtracks, because the average length of a film reel was 11 minutes whereas a disc held only four to five minutes of recording. The 33⅓ record was born from a 1925 decision to slow down the speed at which records played. But performers couldn't be relied on not to make mistakes when recording for up to 11 minutes, and it was impossible to edit a disc. During World War II, magnetic tape was invented in Germany and later acquired by the Allies, which meant recorded material could be edited. LPs playing at 33⅓ were first introduced by Columbia records in America. RCA Victor, who first invented the 78, responded with the 45 rpm seven-inch single. This 'battle of the speeds' contributed to the demise of the 78. The idea of the 16ʳrpm originated in Eastern Europe where there was a shortage of plastic after the war, but in the West very few 16 rpm recordings were made. In Britain, the only commercially available disc was a recording of Edgar Allan Poe's Tales of Mystery and Imagination. On the whole, the 16 rpm record never really took off.

PETER COPELAND, BRITISH LIBRARY NATIONAL SOUND ARCHIVE, LONDON.

655: What is the purpose of the flat bit on a billiard cue?

Billiard players used to hit the ball with the thick end of a mace. When the cue was developed, the flat end was retained and used to keep the cue level on the table. For some time, players were allowed to use either end of the cue, but these days the flat end is mainly traditional. Many top players use it as a locating point to make sure they always hold the cue the same way up. Jimmy White often spins his cue in his hand because his cue has no flat end and he is sighting up the point of the ash grain before taking a shot.

JOHN PARRIS, PARRIS CUES, LONDON.

656: How much soil was dug out for the Channel Tunnel and where has it gone?

During the tunnelling process, 4 million cubic metres of spoil were removed on the UK side and 3 million cubic metres in France: a total which would fill Wembley stadium 13 times. Lower Shakespeare Cliff took the spoil in the UK. Removed by conveyor belt and train, it was deposited behind a permanent sea wall 1.7 km long, enlarging an existing low-lying undersea shelf. Part of the tunnel cooling and ventilation system was built on this platform while the remaining 39 hectares (89 acres) was landscaped. On the French side the spoil was mixed with water to form a slurry which was pumped into an artificial lake at Fond Pignon near the Sangatte shaft. As the slurry dried and consolidated the area was landscaped.   HOLLY BROWNE, EURO TUNNEL, LONDON.

657: When TV reporters visit famine areas, how do they feed themselves while avoiding envy and anger from the hungry people all around them?

TV teams visiting famine or disaster areas usually have transport to return to the nearest town at the end of a day's filming. In those circumstances we can avoid eating in front of the starving. When logistics mean we have to stay in stricken areas for some time, it can be terribly difficult. Like aid workers, who often spend weeks among the starving, we have to eat and drink. The fact is we are there to report, not to hand out food or share the suffering of the deprived. But many is the time our bread and bananas have supplied stomachs far more desperate than our own.
MARK AUSTEN, ASIA CORRESPONDENT, ITN, LONDON.

658: Is there a rule about '-able' or '-ible' word endings such as irresolvable and irreducible?

The Oxford English Dictionary says that in English there is a prevalent feeling for retaining '-ible' wherever there was, or might be, a Latin '-ibilis', while '-able' is used for words of distinctly French or English origin. The only easy answer is to use lists which are available in Modern English Usage or Rules for Compositors and Readers at the University Press, Oxford.   ERIC GREEN, ISLEWORTH, MIDDLESEX.

659: What would a 1933 £1 be worth after 60 years of inflation? And what was the average wage then?

Taking 60 years of inflation into account, a 1933 £1 would now be worth £35.81. Men working in the shoe trade in 1933 were paid 54 shillings a week, while women had to settle for 33 shillings. Men employed in the building trade were paid about 65 shillings a week, unless they were labourers, in which case they were lucky to get 49 shillings. The lowest paid male workers of the time were shipbuilding labourers, paid just 41 shillings a week, and agricultural workers who had to make do with 35 shillings, which translates to just over £7,000 a year with an adjustment for 60 years of inflation.

ANDY FLEMING, CENTRAL STATISTICAL OFFICE, RACHEL DUNNCHIE, DEPT OF EMPLOYMENT.

660: When was Ulster last an independent state ruled over by a monarch?

There has never been a king of Ulster ruling over an independent Ulster although there have been several minor monarchs. The closest was in 1598 when Hugh O'Neill defeated the English forces of Sir Henry Bagenal at the Battle of the Yellow Ford during the Seven Years' War, leaving him in charge of all Ulster except Carrickfergus and Newry. O'Neill was eventually defeated at Kinsale on Christmas Eve, 1601, by Lord Mountjoy and his forces and signed a treaty of surrender at Mellifont on March 30, 1603. Under its terms, O'Neill kept his lands and feudal rights and was given the title of Earl of Tyrone. But in September, O'Neill and Rory O'Donnell and 90 of their followers went into voluntary exile on the Continent. This event, known as 'the flight of the Earls', left Ulster leaderless, much to the relief of the English government.

GERRY HEALEY, LINEN HALL LIBRARY, BELFAST.

661: Does the triple intertwined ring, commonly known as a Russian wedding ring, have any connection with Russia?

The Russian wedding ring design is believed to have been created by Jean Cocteau for Cartier in 1923. The original design was of 18 carat gold, featuring three interlinking hoops of yellow, red and white gold. There is a story that the ring takes its name from the Holy Trinity Church of Russia, but the Russian Embassy has never confirmed this idea. Some believe the hoops represent the Christian Virtues of faith, hope and charity.

SALLY GOLDSBY, WORLD GOLD COUNCIL, LONDON.

662: Banknotes carry the legend: 'I promise to pay the bearer on demand the sum of X pounds.' Are these just empty words or, if I take a note to the Bank of England, will they have to give me something in exchange?

This promise has its origins in the receipts or notes given by goldsmith-bankers to those who deposited cash (ie coin) with them. When the

Bank of England was founded in 1694 it adopted the practice, making its notes payable to the depositor but adding the vital words 'or bearer,' thus allowing its notes to circulate. People accepted them knowing they could always change them back into coin. Originally notes were hand-signed by one of the Bank's cashiers but the printed signature of the Chief Cashier first appeared in 1870. Nowadays, if you were to come to the Bank of England and ask for payment of, say, a £5 note, you would receive five £1 coins; if it were a £10 note payment could be made with two £5 notes or ten £1 coins or a combination of notes and coin. Any exchange could also be for another note of the same value. The Bank will always exchange genuine notes that are no longer legal tender for new notes at the same face value. CATHERINE HAYES, BANK OF ENGLAND, LONDON.

663: Why do butchers wear straw boaters?

The custom originates from the turn of the century. Through most of history the headwear for most working men has been determined by the fashion of the day. In a picture from 1851 a butcher is shown wearing the top hat, then considered essential wear for any decent gentleman, working or otherwise. The straw boater achieved popularity around the late 19th century, initially for informal and sporting wear but soon generally as a summer hat. The British boater is of straw and has the qualities of being lightweight and cool but, due to its varnished surface, is also waterproof. The boater was probably adopted by butchers purely because of its very acceptability as an all round summer hat.
JILL DRAPER, KEEPER OF COSTUME AND TEXTILES, LUTON MUSEUM SERVICE, LUTON.

664: Racing drivers used to practise something called 'four-wheel drift' through curves. What was it for and is it used in today's racing?

Racing drivers aim to use the full width of the track at bends. They approach a right-hand bend from the left, effecting any braking and/or gear change before turning into the corner then accelerating as the car turns through the corner. Because of the racing car's momentum, it heads towards the apex of the bend on the right-hand side and drifts out again to the left of the track. This practice ensures that the car is not held too tightly through the bend and the tyres are not overloaded, creating too much friction which 'scrubs off' speed. This was, and still is, known as 'four-wheel drift' because the car appears to go round the corner without the front wheels changing direction. A racing car can also be made to change direction with little use of the steering wheel by left-foot braking while the accelerator is still down. This upsets the balance of the car and turns it in more violently with the addition of almost 'hopping' it into four-wheel drift, once the brake is released.   TIM MARTIN, BECKENHAM, KENT.

Modern, high-grip grand prix cars don't use four-wheel drift and a modern racing car is never set up to change direction with left foot braking. Four-wheel drift effect occurs when a car is sliding at an angle to its direction of travel, with the front wheels aligned straight ahead. It is a finely balanced state, only achieved in low-grip conditions. If the front wheels are turned against the direction of a corner then the car is oversteering and being held on the opposite lock. If the front wheels are turned excessively in the same direction as the corner, the car is understeering and tends to go straight on. The fine line between these is the four-wheel drift. Years ago, top racing drivers like Stirling Moss used to entertain crowds with four-wheel drifts but in grand prix it is now a thing of the past, left to rally drivers to demonstrate.

TIFF NEEDELL, RACING DRIVER AND TV PRESENTER, PETERSFIELD.

665: Where do hiccoughs come from, and how does one get rid of them?

Hiccoughs are caused by a sudden, involuntary contraction of the diaphragm, coupled with a rapid closure of the vocal cords, which produces the sound. People usually get hiccoughs through an irritation of the diaphragm or phrenic nerves, rarely through a medical condition, though hiccoughs can be caused by stomach disorders, pleurisy, hepatitis, pancreatitis, alcohol poisoning or a disorder in the oesophagus. Numerous popular remedies include holding one's breath, drinking cold water or trying to sneeze. Drugs or surgery may be prescribed in severe cases. The longest recorded attack of hiccoughing affected an American called Charles Osborne of Anthon, Iowa, who began hiccoughing in 1922 while trying to weigh a hog, and continued every one-and-a-half seconds until February 1990. Despite his affliction, he had two wives and eight children. He died on May 1, 1991.   DAVID FARMER, CARLISLE, CUMBRIA.

You can cure hiccoughs by bending forward while standing and, at the same time, drinking water from the far side of a glass. This certainly does work.   DAVID JEFFREYS, SUTTON COLDFIELD.

Expand your lungs and breathe in slowly, as deeply as possible. Hold that breath as long as possible. Breathe out slowly and the hiccoughs should have gone. If not, repeat the process.   MISS E. M. CULL, GLOUCESTER.

A non-acrobatic and water torture-free cure for hiccoughs is simply to chew a teaspoonful of granulated sugar.   L. M. WILSON, CYNCOED, CARDIFF.

Simple cures, including being frightened by someone, drinking water from the wrong side of a glass or holding the breath, always work for me. More scientific remedies include carbon dioxide inhalation, pulling the tongue forward with reasonable force or taking certain drugs.

STEPHANIE SHEPPARD, NATURAL SCIENCES STUDENT, CAMBRIDGE UNIVERSITY.

Drink a glass of water slowly while someone places their index fingers in your ears. It never fails.
PAUL ROACH, PEVENSEY, SUSSEX.

My husband always gives me a long, passionate kiss. It works every time.
N. STOT, PINNER, MIDDLESEX.

666: When we write to people, even those we don't know or dislike, why do we address them as 'Dear'?

The word 'dear' at the head of a letter is an accepted convention which has nothing to do with our relationship with a particular correspondent. The word *deore* or *diore* in Old English meant glorious, honourable, noble, worthy. Initially an adjective, it was used throughout the 13th, 14th and 15th centuries when addressing somebody. The first recorded reference of the word 'dear' in a letter comes from 1450 when Queen Margaret of Scotland wrote a letter beginning 'Right dere and wel beloved… ' Since the 17th century 'dear' has been used as a polite term of addressing an equal when writing to them.

LAURENCE URDANG, EDITOR, VERBATIM, AYLESBURY, BUCKS.

667: Where does the expression 'a round robin' come from?

This term is a corruption of the old French *rond* (round) and *ruban* (ribbon). It refers to a method used by sailors who wanted to sign a petition of protest without identifying ringleaders who might be singled out for punishment. Signatures were arranged like the spokes on a wheel to show all the men united with no one name at the head of the list. The phrase is used now in tournaments when contestants play each other in turn, rather than being drawn against particular opponents.

TRACY HURST, OLDHAM.

668: What do the initials JCB stand for?

JCB has, over the years, become so much a part of the landscape and language of the country that it now appears in both Oxford English and Collins English Dictionaries. JCB is in fact the initials of the manufacturer's founder, Joseph Cyril Bamford, who started his company in a lock-up garage in Uttoxeter, Staffordshire. He was a skilled welder and fitter and made his first product (a farm trailer) in 1945, working with war surplus materials. The JCB Mark 1 was introduced in 1953 and later, with a loader fitted to the front, it became the first backhoe loader – the forerunner of the familiar JCBs we see today. During his career, Joseph Cyril Bamford was awarded the CBE for his services to exports. He retired in 1975, and his eldest son, Sir Anthony Bamford, took over as Chairman and Managing Director. CHRIS STONE, JC BAMFORD EXCAVATORS LTD, ROCESTER, STAFFS.

669: Has chickenpox got anything to do with chickens?

There is no connection whatsoever between chickens and chickenpox. The term chickenpox derives from the French *pois chicke* which itself evolved from the Latin *cicer,* both of which mean 'chick-pea.' This is presumably a reference to the blisters which form when someone has chickenpox and the fact that they resemble the chick-pea in appearance. Other countries have different words for this kind of 'pox.' The Germans call it 'Wind pox' while the Finns go for 'Water pox.'

DEBORAH HOLGATE, MELBOURNE, DERBYSHIRE.

670: King George V and Queen Mary had a son, John Charles Francis, born on July 12, 1905, who died on January 18, 1919. He was kept away from public gaze, in a house in Windsor Park, and Queen Mary confided to her diary on his death: 'Poor John has gone to his rest.' What was the dark secret?

There is no 'dark secret' about the fate of 'poor John.' He was the fifth and youngest son of King George V and Queen Mary. At the age of four he developed epilepsy and, on doctors' advice, lived a secluded life at Wood Farm on the Sandringham Estate. He was looked after by the family nanny, Mrs Bill, and by all accounts grew to be a handsome boy. He died in his sleep on January 18, 1919, aged 13. Of his death Queen Mary wrote: 'For him it is a great release as his malady was becoming worse as he grew older and he has thus been spared much suffering. I cannot say how grateful we feel to God for having taken him in such a peaceful way.' Prince John was buried in the graveyard of Sandringham Church.

SPOKESPERSON, BUCKINGHAM PALACE, LONDON.

671: Why is the quorum for the House of Lords only three peers?

There is no evidence to show why only three peers are needed to make up a quorum in the House of Lords. However, there have to be at least three present so that if two members have opposing points of view, the third can give the final judgment. One of the trio has to be either the Lord Chancellor or the Deputy Speaker. This rule only applies for general meetings and procedures. For divisions and debates on bills a quorum in the House of Lords has to comprise at least 30 members. The first reference to this dates back to March 22, 1889.

SPOKESPERSON, HOUSE OF LORDS, LONDON.

672: Why can't you home-freeze yogurt when you can buy yogurt ice-cream?

Chilled yogurt does not contain the stabilizers which frozen yogurt ice-cream includes. Chilled yogurt could in fact be frozen but it cannot be guaranteed that separation would not take place.

TONI HENSBY, ST IVEL LTD, SWINDON, WILTSHIRE.

673: When it's noon in Britain on January 1, 1998, what will the time be at the North and South Poles?

The short answer is that at the North and South Pole all times are the same and so it can be any time you wish. This is because as the Earth spins on its axis, the poles are in effect stationary with regard to time, as they encompass all time zones at once. Visitors to the poles, such as scientists or explorers, normally use, for practical purposes, the time in their own country. If they are a group from several nations they normally agree on a particular time zone so that they don't have problems such as one member making breakfast when others are having dinner etc. The exact time used by any British team at either pole at noon on January 1, 1998, will be exactly the same as it is in Britain though its members could, if they wish, choose any time zone they want.

HARRY FORD, PLANETARIUM LECTURER, ROYAL OBSERVATORY, GREENWICH.

674: What is the origin of the word gymkhana, and why is it associated with horse meetings?

The word gymkhana comes from the Hindi gendkhana, meaning racket house, and the Greek gymnasium, school for gymnastics, and dates back to the days of the Army in India. British cavalry officers stationed in India used mounted games to improve their riding and athletic skills and to entertain themselves. Polo was another of the games they played, a very ancient game which is believed to date back to Persia in 5000 BC. A gymkhana nowadays is an event made up of different mounted games – bending races, musical chairs, potato races etc, usually for younger riders. There are gymkhana games at most local horse shows. Every year Pony Club teams compete in the Pony Club Mounted Games Championships for the Prince Philip Cup, decided at the Horse of the Year Show at Wembley. ALISON BRIDGE, EDITOR OF HORSE & RIDER, SURBITON, SURREY.

675: We hear of barristers being called to the Bar, joining Inns of Court and dining a required number of times. Why should a lawyer be so involved with food and drink?

As with most of the older professions, the process of becoming a barrister is steeped in a great number of traditions which established themselves over a long period. Every student barrister has to be a member of one of the four Inns of Court, the Inner Temple, Middle Temple, Lincoln's Inn or Gray's Inn. They are called inns after the older meaning of an inn as a hostel or lodging rather than any association with the modern pub. One of the essential elements in the process of qualifying as a barrister is for the student to be called to the degree of an 'Utter Barrister' ('called to the Bar' for short) by his or her Inn, in a ceremony comparable with graduation days at universities. This expression is derived from the time centuries ago when junior barristers took their places 'outside' the bar which divided them from senior members of the Inn on formal occasions. There is no connection with the provision of liquid refreshment. To be called to the bar, the student is required to eat 18 dinners at the Inn. This tradition may seem odd to the public but it is a long established part of what can be regarded as a form of apprenticeship. The students acquire academic and practical qualifications during three- or four-year university degree courses and a year's further vocational course at the Inns of Court School of Law. During dining terms they are given the chance both of getting to know their contemporaries and mixing with senior members of the Inn – judges and barristers – to learn from their experience in a more informal and personal way than is possible from lectures or books. The Inns arrange debates, mock trials and talks after the dinners, all of which are part of the student's education. The apprenticeship is continued after the call to the Bar while they serve a 12-month 'pupillage' under an experienced, practising barrister.

T. DAVID MACHIN, UNDER TREASURER, THE HONOURABLE SOCIETY OF GRAY'S INN, LONDON.

676: Why is a hot-dog so called?

In 1904, Anton Feuchtwanger asked his brother-in-law to bake buns for sausages he was selling at the St Louis Exhibition. Before that he had been lending gloves to customers to wear while they held the hot sausages. In April 1906, Tad Dorgan, a cartoonist, caricatured the new snack, called the 'dachshund,' by drawing a snapping Sausage Dog. He was unsure how to spell dachshund, so he wrote 'hot dog' instead. Today, our company supplies about 80 million hot dog frankfurters a year.

IAIN MELDRUM, WESTLER FOODS, MALTON, NORTH YORKSHIRE.

Like many people of my generation, growing up in the Fifties and

Sixties, I first came across hot dogs at fairgrounds, the seaside and the cinema. But the link between entertainment and this slightly dubious sausage produce goes back more than 100 years to Coney Island, near Brooklyn, New York. During the second half of the 19th century, three great amusement parks were built there and they became America's national playground. One of the attractions was 'electric bathing.' Under primitive arc lamps, daring bathers swam in the cold waters of the Hudson River, after which they could warm up with a novel kind of fast food, basically, sausage and chilli peppers, invented by Charles Feltman and available from his shoreline restaurant. He called them Coney Island Red Hots while others, less certain of their ingredients, called them 'hot dogs.' In America they were so well liked that 'hot dog' became a popular slang expression of approval.   JONATHAN HILL, BAMPTON MUSEUM, DEVON.

677: When was the writing of music invented and by whom?

There's no definite answer to this question. Musical notation seems to have begun at the start of the 9th century with the use of 'neumes' – graphic signs indicating melodic movement. These signs were quite general and didn't show specific pitch. The person regarded as being responsible for developing musical notation as we know it was Guido D'Arezzo, a Benedictine Monk at Pompoza, near Ferrara. He established a form of notation that did show a specific pitch and is also believed to have invented the staff or stave.   DEBBIE WARREN, ROYAL COLLEGE OF MUSIC, LONDON.

678: American film star Audie Murphy was said to be the most decorated U.S. serviceman of World War II. Who was, or is, his UK equivalent?

It is difficult to answer this question because medals are not attached to a points system, so you can't realistically tot up the awards made to an individual and then compare the findings against the medals of other recipients. But some British servicemen are certainly candidates for the title of 'most decorated.' In World War I, Captain Noel Chavasse, of the Royal Army Medical Corps, was awarded the Victoria Cross twice for two separate acts of bravery. In effect, this is known as 'VC and Bar' – not actually receiving two Victoria Crosses. In World War II, Group Captain Leonard Cheshire is most likely to have been decorated the most often. He was awarded the Distinguished Service Order and Two Bars (the equivalent of three DSOs), the Distinguished Flying Cross and the Victoria Cross. Interestingly his VC, awarded in 1944, was not for a specific action but to mark his 100th bombing mission against German targets. Cheshire was the 'pathfinder' with responsibility to mark targets for other bombers. A year later he was one of the official British observers to visit Nagasaki to witness the devastation caused by the dropping of the atomic bomb. This left a lasting impression on him and he devoted the rest of his life to aiding the suffering of others, setting up the Cheshire Foundation Homes for the incurably ill. His wife, Baroness Sue Ryder, was involved in very similar work and was responsible for the Sue Ryder Foundation for sick and disabled people.   IMPERIAL WAR MUSEUM, LONDON.

Probably the most decorated RAF officer was Group Captain J. R. D. 'Bob' Braham, a fighter pilot who received at least six foreign decorations in World War II and was awarded further decorations after the war, in addition to his British accolades. He was given the DSO and two bars, the DFC and two bars, the Belgian Croix de Guerre 1940 with Palm, and the Belgian Order of the Crown with Palm. Post-war, he was awarded the AFC and Canadian Forces decoration. The Guinness Book of Air Facts and Feats says he was the only man ever to win seven British gallantry decorations. Group Captain Braham was a most gallant and courageous officer but is almost unknown to the general public. He destroyed at least 29 enemy aircraft in the air and also bombed and straffed targets on the ground and at sea. He was shot down in 1944 and spent 11 months as a prisoner of war. He died in Canada in 1974 at the age of 53 and his awards and decorations can be seen at the RAF Museum in Hendon, London. I had the honour of serving under him as armourer to 141 Squadron.   DON ARIS, RICHMOND, SURREY.

679: What is 'extra virgin' olive oil? Surely it is either virgin or not?

In the UK olive oil is divided into several categories dependent on the level of acidity found in the oil. The one with the lowest acidity is the most highly prized and therefore the most expensive. It is known as 'extra virgin olive oil' and has a maximum acidity of 1 per cent. Following this are 'virgin olive oil', which has a maximum acidity of 2 per cent, and plain old 'olive oil', which has various categories. 'Pure' olive oil is nearly always refined, which means it will have been cleaned, filtered – and even deodorised. The level of quality for olive oil generally comes from the point at which it was pressed from the olives – the first pressing being the best and giving 'extra virgin olive oil', the second pressing giving 'virgin olive oil', the third and further pressings giving 'olive oil' and 'pure olive oil.' As for olive oil being 'virgin' or not, there are moves within the EC to standardise the labelling due to massive variations from country to country. It is hoped that this will lead to just 'virgin olive oil' and 'pure olive oil', with acidity levels being displayed.   MICHELLE LEWIS, SAINSBURY'S, LONDON.

680: Why are rechargeable batteries not recommended for use in appliances such as clocks and camera flash units?

The recommendation concerns rechargeable nickel cadmium batteries. As a rule of thumb, a good-quality alkaline manganese throwaway battery will have around three to four times the amount of energy of an equivalent-sized rechargeable battery. In addition, and probably more importantly, the self-charge characteristics of the rechargeable battery – the rate at which it will lose its stored charge – is very much worse than the alkaline battery. A rechargeable would be almost discharged in a few months, as opposed to several years for the alkaline (if you are anything like me the camera is used only for birthdays, holidays, etc.). The rechargeable comes into its own for high-power repetitive use, for example camcorders and portable computers.

KEITH WILD, TECHNICAL SALES ENGINEER, VARTA BATTERIES, CREWKERNE, SOMERSET.

Nickel-cadmium batteries are capable of producing a greater flow of electrical current than alkaline or zinc-carbon ones and would cause irreparable damage to some small electronic flashguns. However, if you regularly use a flashgun, it would be worthwhile checking whether rechargeable ni-cad cells can be safely used because they are a better choice in terms of performance and economy. Ni-cads have a slightly lower nominal voltage than ordinary cells, even when fully charged. Electric clocks consume very little current but require a constant voltage and it would be inconvenient to use ni-cad cells in them.

K. R. TERRY, ASHFORD, KENT.

681: Why is it harmful to leave fingerprints on a replacement bulb for a car headlamp?

Car headlamp bulbs are made from vitreous silica, which is produced by fusing high-purity sand (silicon dioxide or silica) at high temperatures to form glass. In this glassy state, however, silica is less stable than it is in its more normal crystalline state. Handling the bulb contaminates its surface with small amounts of sodium from the salt in sweat. When the bulb is hot, these points of contamination (called nucleation sites) become centres from which the glass surface is able to begin to revert to the more stable crystalline form of silica. This process produces an opaque, white surface layer which progressively impairs the optical performance of the bulb and also weakens it. If a bulb has been marked it should be wiped with a clean cloth moistened with methylated spirit.

D. T. EVANS, GE LIGHTING LTD, TECHNOLOGY DIVISION, LEICESTER.

682: How do chocolate manufacturers completely cover items like Brazil nuts, and leave no sign of any blemish on the surface?

There are several ways of coating nuts such as Brazils. The simplest is to pass them on a mesh belt under a curtain of flowing chocolate – to 'enrobe' them. Excess chocolate is shaken off and the finish can be very good but there is always a clear discernible flat bottom where the nuts rested on the belt. To achieve a perfect symmetrical coating, nuts are tumbled in a revolving pan, something that looks like a concrete mixer. This technique is used for our Tasters product. Chocolate is trickled slowly onto the nuts and the temperature is carefully controlled to make the chocolate stick to the nuts (and not to the pan). It can take four to five hours for sufficient thickness of chocolate to build up. Finally an edible glaze is added to help stop the chocolate melting in the hand. Panned chocolates seem to be increasing in popularity. Last year we sold 45 million bags of Tasters, representing nearly one billion chocolate pieces.

RICHARD FROST, CADBURY LTD, BOURNEVILLE, BIRMINGHAM.

683: Diamonds apparently have a Knoop number of 8,400 and tooth enamel one of 300. But what is a Knoop number?

This 'Knoop value' is a measure of the hardness of a material. The Knoop test is only one of a number of methods which can be used to determine the static hardness of materials. Many, but not all, of these methods involve measuring the material's resistance to plastic deformation under static loads. Other typical methods are Brinell, Vickers, and Rockwell hardness tests. In each of these tests an indenter is pressed into the surface of the material being tested, using a known load. The hardness of the material can then be calculated from the size of the indentation produced. The indenters are made from hard materials such as hardened steel, tungsten carbide or diamond. The Knoop tests, developed in 1939 for testing very hard materials such as diamond, use a diamond indenter in a variety of shapes. Typical Knoop hardness values for diamond range from 6,000 to 10,000.

P. R. DUTTON BSc, CEng, MIM, CoMech LTD, DERBY.

684: Who were Mutt 'n' Jeff?

'Mutt 'n' Jeff' is cockney rhyming slang for 'deaf.' The saying comes from two comic strip characters created by the American cartoonist Bud Fishcher (1884-1954). Mutt was a tall, thin character while Jeff was short and fat. The saying can also apply to two friends, or a married couple, who are very unalike in physical appearance. SIMON ROUSE, SHROPSHIRE.

685: How did the saying 'at sixes and sevens' come about?

It's commonly thought that this comes from dice playing. The numbers in dice were said in French with the five, *cinque,* being easily mistaken, when Anglicised, for the word six – so the real six would have to be seven. More likely though is that the expression dates from the rivalry between two of London's Livery Companies, the Merchant Taylors and the Skinners. Both companies had been given a charter in 1327 and, 150 years later, could not agree as to which of them should go in sixth place, and which in seventh, during the annual procession through the City. The dispute was quite fierce and was resolved by the mayor of London only in 1484 when it was decided that they would each take turns at being sixth and seventh on a yearly basis.   KIMBARA KEITH DAVIS, LONDON.

686: How are snooker balls made so that they are perfectly spherical and from what material are they made?

Nothing is 'perfectly' spherical; there's a tolerance (margin of error) in all things. However, parts such as billiards and snooker balls can be produced to a very low out-of-sphericity tolerance by centreless grinding. The centreless grinding machine uses a generative process in which the principles are complex and involve many variables. A rough shape is produced and has the excess material removed by grinding. As the rough part moves between the two profile-shaped wheels of the machine, the centreless principles cause the part to feed on its own errors to infinite accuracy. The limiting factors to the degree of spherical accuracy produced are the time spent revolving between the wheels and the dynamic stiffness of the machine. Other less accurate methods to produce spherical shapes such as snooker balls include plate lapping and diamond turning. Some low grade pool balls are sold as they come from the mould. Early snooker balls were made of ivory and modern balls are made from either fired ceramics or plastic composites. The manufacture of snooker balls in this country is now a thing of the past. The last factory was dismantled and shipped to Belgium in 1990.

IAN WILEMAN, SANDY, BEDS.

687: Why are magistrates called beaks?

One idea is that the word 'beak' originates from an old Celtic word meaning judgement. However, the most likely reason for its inclusion in today's language dates back to the 16th century and is quite simply a reference to the nose and 'nosiness'. If one considers the intrusive nature of our institutions of authority, especially magistrates, it becomes easy to understand that they may have been regarded as 'nosey', sticking their 'beaks' into other people's affairs. The word is not exclusive to magistrates and has long been used by public schoolboys when referring to their schoolmasters. As recently as 1989 the magazine Tatler reported that 'beak' was the standard slang term used by the boys in reference to the masters. ANTHONY EDWARDS, BRISTOL.

688: Where does the expression 'he's got a lot of bottle' come from?

The word 'bottle' as used in the sense of 'having plenty of bottle' is a corruption of the cockney phrase 'bottle and glass', referring to one's derriere. The inference is to keeping control of oneself in moments of great stress or danger. This is another of the numerous occasions when the less than tasteful words in rhyming slang have passed into the language with their eventual users being unaware of the true strength of their actual meaning. Another that immediately springs to mind is to 'blow a raspberry' – from raspberry tart. J. RANDALL, ROMFORD, ESSEX.

My East End upbringing of more than 60 years leads me to understand that 'bottle and glass' in Cockney rhyming slang means 'class', social standing, rather than one's derriere. 'Bottle' therefore has a wider interpretation. It was quite usual to describe people who had improved their status in society through discipline and hard work and had pride in themselves as having 'plenty of bottle'. Rhyming slang was much used in the Forces and when a man lost his nerve on the battlefield he was no longer held in esteem and had therefore 'lost his bottle' or social standing. The rhyming slang for one's derriere is Khyber Pass. The admonition for a youngster who had transgressed was 'You'll get a kick up the Khyber' not 'up your bottle.' The idea that 'raspberry tart' is rhyming slang for breaking wind is also inaccurate. Cockneys had a far more polite approach to this bodily function which was referred to as a 'D'Oyly' from the D'Oyly Carte Opera Company. GEORGE SHAW, SOUTHEND, ESSEX.

In Medieval times it was the custom to hang a bottle containing a spool of thread outside the door of a house to ward off evil spirits. The theory was that the spirit would feel obliged to unravel the thread and would be so busy doing this that it would refrain from entering the house to harm the occupants. So to lose one's bottle was to be in a state of fear and trepidation. REGINALD KNAPP, RUISLIP, MIDDX.

I believe this use of 'bottle' comes from the bottle used to collect money at open air fairs, markets or on beaches. Wherever there were performers, money was collected in a sealed bottle so the artists could see how much there was and nobody could take anything out until the whole company saw it fairly distributed. The 'bottler' would go into the crowds and was supposed to approach everyone, even those who were heckling, so the best 'bottlers' had to have nerve. The great Max Miller learned to 'bottle' with concert parties on the South Coast and said the expression arose during his time there.   JACK PURVIS, CHATHAM, KENT.

689: If temperatures all over the world were averaged out, would we all be warm or cold?

The average global temperature is around 14 degrees Celsius. This does however, include the two polar regions. The average temperature in England and Wales is around 9.5 degrees Celsius and for Scotland it's about 8 degrees Celsius.   MALCOLM BROOKS, THE MET OFFICE, BRACKNELL, BERKS.

690: Is it true that all racing thoroughbreds are descended from two Arab horses?

The word 'thoroughbred' derives from the Arabic *kehilan,* purebred. Today's English thoroughbred race horses are indeed descended from two Arab stallions, the Darley Arabian and the Godolphin Arabian and possibly a third stallion, about which there is some argument but which is generally believed to also have been an Arabian, the Byerley Turk. These horses were brought to this country during the latter half of the 17th century by Richard Darley, Edward Coke and Captain Robert Byerley. The female foundation stock used is less well documented but seems likely to have included English mares of Arabic origin. The Arabian horse has been the foundation of many breeds and 'arab blood' was also introduced into other breeds to improve intelligence, stamina, and beauty.   DEBORAH NEALE, STEEPLE MORDEN, HERTS.

691: Where did the Order of the Bath originate and what does the bath refer to?

In 1399, at his coronation, Henry IV conferred the dignity of knighthood upon 46 men and it is recorded that he was attended by these Knights of the Bath but not Knights of an Order, thus the Order was founded at that time. As far back as the 11th century, the candidate for knighthood had to submit to many symbolic rituals of which absolution was one, as a symbol of purity and washing away sin and it is from this that the name would appear to be derived. It was not until May 25, 1725, that the order was founded in its present form. It was remodelled in 1815 and subsequently enlarged 13 times.

J. A. CROSBY JP, ORDERS AND MEDALS RESEARCH SOCIETY, NORTH WEALD, ESSEX.

692: Did the small Shropshire town of Much Wenlock hold a forerunner of the Olympic Games?

Much Wenlock held the Olympian Games, forerunner of the Modern Olympics, in 1850, and has continued to hold them intermittently ever since. The founder was Dr William Penny Brookes, the son of the local doctor. In 1831, after studying medicine in London and Paris, Brookes returned to Much Wenlock to take over his father's practice and became involved in local affairs. He was responsible for the introduction of the railway and a public gas service in the town. In 1841 he founded the Agricultural Reading Society and it was from this base that in 1850 he founded the Wenlock Olympian Society with the intention of promoting 'the moral, physical and intellectual improvement of the town and neighbourhood of Wenlock.' His aim was to hold outdoor sporting events for the local people. The first games, including old country sports and athletics, as well as cricket, football, putting the stone and a ladies' race, were held in October 1850. By 1859, Dr Brookes had persuaded the King of Greece to introduce an Olympian Games in Greece but this turned out to be a one-off. He was also at the forefront in the formation in 1865 of the National Olympic Association which held its first games at Crystal Palace the next year, attracting 10,000 spectators. Dr Brookes was hopeful of reviving the Olympic Games in Greece but, despite strenuous efforts, failed to make much headway with the Greek authorities. It was a Frenchman, Baron Pierre de Coubertin, who had enough wealth and political contacts to get them off the ground with the First Modern games in Athens in 1896. The Baron had been in contact with Dr Brookes and visited the Much Wenlock Games in 1890. Brookes was invited to the 1894 congress that set up the Modern Games but was by this time an old man and unable to attend. Sadly he died in 1895 and missed his dream becoming a reality by one year. Although there have been gaps in the staging of the Much Wenlock Olympian Games – for example, during the two world wars – they survive today and now encompass arts events. In 1986, the 100th Games were visited by members of the British Olympic Association, the International Olympic Committee and Geoffrey de Navacelle, grand-nephew of Baron Pierre de Coubertin. Her Royal Highness The Princess Royal has also visited the Games. As for how Britain fared in the 1850 Games – we won everything.

NORMAN WOOD, SECRETARY, WENLOCK OLYMPIAN SOCIETY, SHROPSHIRE.

As a born and bred Salopian, I am very interested in the origins of the Wenlock Olympian Society. At the games held on June 5, 1906, my grandfather, Roderick Thomas Jervis, then aged 18, won first prize for Tilting With Rings Over Hurdles and was presented with a 14-carat gold pocket watch, engraved to mark his achievement. The watch, which still keeps excellent time, is still owned by his family, having been handed down on my grandfather's death in 1972 aged 84. The case bears the name Jones & Co, of Foregate Street, Worcester, with the inscription 'Proprietors of the National Clubs'. My grandfather's mother, Mrs T. A. S. Jervis, was proprietress of the Gaskell Arms Hotel in Much Wenlock. The hotel remained in the family and was owned by my grandfather's brother Thomas, until a few years before his death at the age of 91 in 1981.

PHILIP S. GIBBS, DENHAM, BUCKS.

693: Why do starlings chatter so noisily when they gather in the late afternoons in winter before flying to their roosting places?

Starlings are renowned for their communal roosts when hundreds, even tens of thousands, may gather together in one place. These flocks provide the birds with greater security against predators which find it difficult to select a target among a large group. Smaller gatherings often take place on the way to large roosts and at all stages these flocks are usually very noisy. As the birds flock together, the noise from the singing increases gradually until this reaches a crescendo. There is then a deafening silence which is immediately followed by the whole flock leaving the area at the same time on its way to the final roosting place for the night. Similar noisy song occurs at dawn before the birds leave their roost. The exact reason for this behaviour is not clearly known, but it is probably linked to the birds' remarkable ability to all leave at once. The volume of song and the number of birds singing might be the trigger which enables the flock to leave simultaneously.

CHRIS HARBARD, ROYAL SOCIETY FOR THE PROTECTION OF BIRDS, SANDY, BEDS.

694: How do old soldiers qualify to be Chelsea Pensioners?

There are a number of conditions that a soldier has to satisfy to become a Chelsea Pensioner. First, he has to be an Army pensioner, either through long service or because of disability caused by military service. He must also be aged 65 or over and be of good character. There is a provision to allow in soldiers younger than 65 if they are unable to work because of a disability caused while in military service. We also expect applicants to be reasonably fit as we want them to enjoy their time at the hospital. The final qualification is that the soldier be single. Most of our 'in-pensioners' are widowers. It is possible for a Chelsea Pensioner to leave the hospital and live somewhere else but he then cannot use the title. The Royal Hospital where the pensioners live was founded in 1682 by Charles II and was opened by William and Mary.

MAJOR GENERAL FRANCIS SUGDEN, LIEUTENANT-GOVERNOR,
ROYAL HOSPITAL, CHELSEA, LONDON.

695: Who was Miss Resistor, the slightly-built stage artiste who used to defy the strongmen volunteers from the audience to lift her in the air? What was the basis of the trick in her act?

She was married to my uncle, Jack Belfield, a variety artiste going by the name of Jack Volta. I still have several pieces of memorabilia from his and Miss Resistor's heyday on the stage. Miss Resistor (sometimes spelt Resista or Resister) was Lillian Ellis before marrying my uncle. She was born in 1906 in the Holbeck Moor area of Leeds and took to the stage in 1924 and had immediate success through her ability to hold herself firmly to the ground, regardless of how strong – or even how many – people tried to lift her mere seven stone. Her act toured the UK and by 1926 she was always the top of the bill whenever she revisited her home town. At one point, even the 11 members of Leeds United football team failed to defy her resistance to being lifted. Despite the efforts of local historian Sam Wood and Yorkshire Evening Post journalist John Thorpe to discover her present whereabouts, any record of her or my uncle ended with the advent of World War II.   Mary Myers, Leeds, West Yorks.

Miss Resistor was not the originator of the art of defying strongmen to pick her up – that title goes to another American lady whose stage name was Little Georgia Magnet. The young, and by all accounts beautiful, lady took the country by storm when she appeared at the Alhambra Theatre, Leicester Square, London in 1891. The basis to the trick in her act was that there are certain ways in which the body can be positioned, which make the lifting off the ground by another person almost impossible. The modern version of the trick is to electromagnetise the stage artist's feet to a magnet below the stage.   Carla Barnsfather, Bristol.

696: What is the origin of the saying: 'The apple of his eye'?

The pupil of the eye was traditionally thought to be solid and was thought to be in the shape of an apple. As the eye is one of the most important parts of the body, then the pupil was even more so. To compare someone to the apple of the eye, thus meant to cherish especially that person. There are several references to the saying in the Bible, for example: 'He kept him as the apple of his eye' (Deuteronomy 32:10).

Rebecca Stevens, Great Yarmouth.

697: What is the original context of the often quoted expression 'charity begins at home'?

The actual quotation as we know it today comes from the Religio Medici part II, written by the English physician and writer, Sir Thomas Browne

(1605-82). Its true implication requires the full quotation: 'Charity begins at home, is the voice of the world.' Unfortunately it has since been put to misuse as a quote by smug individuals who take it to mean: 'I'm all right Jack.'

M. TURNER, BLACKBURN, LANCS.

698: When did the unnatural practice of shaving start?

Shaving began with cavemen. The first shaver probably realised that the removal of a beard would cause less restriction and, at the same time, make him perhaps look different to others – therefore possibly more dangerous to a potential foe. Early man is thought to have used a sharp rock to cut the beard and rubbed a coarse stone against the face to get a close shave. Several razors used by primitive Italian tribes have been found by archaeologists. The Egyptians are known to have used razors, the Greeks used them to shave off moustaches, and the razor is even mentioned in Homer's Iliad. The Romans were mainly unshaven until around the third century BC, when it was observed that Scipio Africanus was the first to have his beard shaved daily. The big change in shaving came when the safety razor was invented in 1895 by King C. Gillette. It was marketed for the first time in 1903 when 51 razors and 168 blades were sold. Sales increased dramatically from that year and in 1917 more than one million razors were sold and 120 million blades. Compare that to today when last year alone our company sold 115 million razors and 7.8 billion blades.

GWENDOLINE RAWLINGS, GILLETTE UK LTD, ISLEWORTH, MIDDX.

699: Why haven't zebras been domesticated and used by man?

Zebras may not be suitable for several reasons – the most obvious being that they are smaller than horses and do not have such an affable and reliable temperament. Horses have been domesticated all over the world and are therefore already doing the job so the drive to seriously domesticate the zebra has never really been there. Historically, attempts have been made to try and tame, train and ride individual captive animals but these have met with limited success.

SARA FORD, PRODUCER BBC NATURAL HISTORY UNIT, BRISTOL.

My great-grandfather Alfred Thrower was landlord of the Kings Head, Burr Street, Norwich, and trained horses for trap and cart work. He is said to have won a bet with a customer with circus links by training a zebra to pull a trap which he drove through the streets.

TIM COLE, RUISLIP, MIDDLESEX.

The South African mountain zebra proved too hard to train but in 1892 Burchalls Zebra was found to be easily trained for draught and Messrs Zeesberg used up to five pairs to pull their coaches.

MRS D. KIRKMAN, MAYBOLE, AYRSHIRE.

Dr Rosendo Ribeiro, the first doctor in Nairobi, Kenya, bought a zebra in 1907 and soon became a familiar sight riding the animal around the straggling township visiting patients. SUSAN WOOD, WITHAM, ESSEX.

700: There's been a Wessex in the West, Sussex in the South, Essex in the East and Middlesex in the middle. Was there ever a Norsex, and if not, why not?

After the fall of the Roman Empire various peoples from Northern Europe began to settle in the British Isles during the 4th, 5th and 6th centuries. Among these settlers were the Saxons, from the Rhine area of what is now Germany, who settled in southern England along the Thames and the Angles and Jutes, from what is now Denmark, who settled further north. The word 'sex' as used in Essex, Middlesex, etc, represents the word Saxon and is used to show what areas of southern England were the Saxons', Middlesex being the centre of the Thames area under their control, Wessex the area to the west of that, Sussex the area to the south and Essex the area to the east. The area north of the Thames did not come under the influence of the Saxons but instead was settled mainly by Angles and Jutes. The area that one might think should be called Norsex, was therefore not Saxon and instead became Anglia, after the Angles. They named their areas of control the North Folk (Norfolk) and South Folk (Suffolk). With the coming of the Normans in 1066 the area known as Wessex ceased to exist as a name, only finding new life in the novels of Thomas Hardy. JULIAN RICHARDS, CAMBRIDGE.

701: Why is an English police force based at Scotland Yard?

Traditionally, the buildings that originated around Scotland Yard formed part of the old Royal Palaces of Westminster and was used by the Royal Family of Scotland when they visited the English court. According to an Act of Parliament of 1531, the boundaries of this palace were referred to as Scotland or Scotsland so that in time, the headquarters became known as Scotland Yard. The plan of the Palace of Westminster shows a yard with the name 'Scotland Yard.' The site is also associated with an area of land called scottes grounde bequeathed from the contents of Cicilie Selly's will, dated August 10, 1472, to her daughter. The land was at one time adjacent to the river Thames at a site named 'Scots wharf', so called because the people using it avoided a local tax, and were therefore said to have got off 'scot free.'

ROBIN GILLIS, CURATOR OF THE METROPOLITAN POLICE MUSEUM, LONDON.

702: Pork is considerably cheaper than beef. Why then are pork sausages more expensive than pork and beef mixed?

Sausage legislation states that a pork sausage must contain at least 65% meat while a beef sausage (or a pork and beef sausage) should contain at least 50% meat and it is on this basis that prices vary by variety. Historically, the difference in legislation occurred because of the different natures of the meat when made into a sausage, beef being both more fatty and most costly than pork.

ANDREW CARPENTER, VAN DEN BERGH FOODS LTD, BURGESS HILL, WEST SUSSEX.

703: Why did Eric Sykes direct and star in two different versions of the silent film The Plank?

The first film was with Tommy Cooper and was a feature film made for the cinema. Thames TV then approached me to make another, this time with Arthur Lowe.

ERIC SYKES.

704: If something is shot at close quarters it is called point-blank range. What does the expression mean – and how far away would it need to be, so that it was no longer point-blank?

The term was originally applied to early artillery when weapons were very crude. Around 1500 came the first gunnery instrument, the gunner's quadrant, reputedly invented by Emperor Maximilian I. It was no more than a 90-degree quadrant with one side extended, carrying a plumb bob. Since degrees were then not known, the quadrant was arbitrarily marked off in 'points.' By placing the extended side in the gun's bore, the weapon could then be elevated or depressed until the plumb-bob indicated the desired point to achieve the desired range. With the gun horizontal, the plumb-bob reached the end of the scale, whence comes the term 'point-blank.'

MICHAEL NORFOLK, PORTSLADE, SUSSEX.

The expression is believed to have originated from a French phrase meaning 'point of contact,' a reference to the old duelling days when the point of a sword such as a foil could actually touch an opponent at the start of a duel. The armed forces generally refer to a distance of up to five metres as being point-blank, in the case of firearms. As a general rule, therefore, point-blank is the distance from which the opponent can be physically touched with the weapon.

SPOKESPERSON, GREATER MANCHESTER POLICE FIREARMS DIVISION, MANCHESTER.

The term pre-dates guns and refers to the 'point of aim' when shooting an arrow from a bow. For long-range shooting, the tip of the arrow is sighted above the target, while for short range, the tip of the arrow is sighted below the target. At some place between the two is a distance at which the point of aim will be directly positioned on the target. This is point-blank, where the arrow blanks out the target. The point-blank distance is not a fixed length but varies for each bow, its drawn length and the strength of the archer. Modern bows have sophisticated sights to compensate.   E. MITCHELL, BLETSOE, BEDFORD.

Early gunners fought alongside archers and picked up many archery terms, among them 'point-blank.' A piece of white cloth (*blanc,* French for white) was pinned to the butt as a target and the distance at which the point of aim, using the point as a sight, was on target was called point-blank. The Oxford Dictionary suggests the origin of the actual term 'point blanc', is the white spot at the centre of a target used on the rifle range. It says point-blank is 'the distance within which a gun may be aimed horizontally.'   KENNETH MILL, (EX ROYAL ARTILLERY), NOTTINGHAM.

705: Why is it supposed to be lucky to have a gap between your front two teeth?

This is often put down to superstition but really the 'beauty spot' syndrome applies. This simply means some physical characteristic which is uncommon, being regarded as potentially significant. Family and friends of those with gappy teeth or beauty spots rally round and express the difference in a positive light so as not to make the person feel stigmatised. In the case of a facial mole, society refers to it as a beauty spot and gap teeth are de-stigmatised by being considered a sign of good luck. Some societies believe people with a gap between their teeth will travel far and be blessed with good fortune, wealth and longevity. Conversely, those with teeth positioned closely together are predicted to remain near to home. In Norway, those with a gap are said to be untruthful. The loss of teeth plays an important role in superstition, often being connected with death. So if a mourner were to eat bread at a funeral, or look at the deceased while eating, his teeth were supposed to fall out. And if a woman bit the thread while sewing a burial dress, her teeth were also supposed to be doomed.   MICHAEL WATSON, BRITISH DENTAL ASSOCIATION, LONDON.

706: Why is a person with expert knowledge sometimes termed the 'cat's whiskers'?

Don't be tempted to think this has anything to do with old-fashioned crystal wireless sets. The 'cat's whiskers' is a deliberate piece of early-century nonsense that became popular in the U.S. in the Twenties when such expressions as 'the cat's pyjamas' and 'the bee's knees' were also the craze – all three phrases meaning excellent, ideal, or perfect.

                    NIGEL WILCOCKSON, BREWER'S PHRASE AND FABLE, CASSELL PLC.

707: What is the plural of moose?

There is an example 'mooses' from the 18th century but the standard plural listed in the Concise Oxford Dictionary is just 'moose'. Examples quoted without an 's' are 'the moose are driven' and 'moose are plentiful'. English words that don't add an 's' for their plural number more than 300 and include 'carp', 'sheep', 'hovercraft', 'quid', and 'loris'.

EDMUND WEINER, DEPUTY CHIEF EDITOR, OXFORD ENGLISH DICTIONARY, OXFORD.

708: Boats sail and aircraft fly. What do submarines do?

When the submarine is on the surface the general term is the same as for any other seagoing vessel: 'sailing.' When the submarine travels under the surface the term used by most submariners, in the absence of any other given, adapted, or adopted word, is 'proceeding.' The Oxford English Dictionary has no word to describe a submarine travelling below the surface at a steady depth, speed, and direction, though it's possible that words such as 'sailing', 'swimming', 'steaming', or even 'flying' could have valid claims for use, and The Admiralty also has no specific word. Like all other Royal Navy vessels, submarines travel under 'sailing orders', regardless of whether they are above or below the surface. This question has shown a small gap in our language. Among suggestions I have thought up are 'subsailing', 'flailing', 'slying' and 'aquaflying.'

LIEUT TOM NOLAN, ROYAL NAVY, MANCHESTER.

I was surprised to read in an earlier answer that the Admiralty doesn't have a term to describe the passage of a submarine when under water. I thought the word 'marinating' could be appropriately applied, or has this already been rejected as too saucily obvious? MRS D. SIMON, SOUTHEND, ESSEX.

My husband, a submariner for 30 years, tells me a sub 'transits' to or is 'on passage' to an area, and once there 'patrols' it. MRS MANDY TROW, DEVON.

709: How do we catch a cold? Can we catch one from simply being cold?

There is, as yet, no evidence to suggest that just by being cold one is any more likely to catch a cold. We catch a cold by being infected by viruses which grow in the cells of the nose. The virus gets to the nose either when somebody sneezes, sending out droplets of mucus containing the virus, infecting other people near them, or by getting mucus on one's fingers and touching the inside of the nose or the wet part of the eye. From the eye, germs find their way to the lining of the nose. To prevent spreading the virus, people who have colds should sneeze into a handkerchief, and try to stay away from others when sneezing. Although it is possible to relieve the symptoms with medication, at the moment there is no known cure.

DR DAVID TYRELL, FORMER DIRECTOR OF THE COMMON COLD UNIT, SALISBURY.

710: Is it true that if a corpse for burial is taken along a farm road, the road cannot remain a private road?

Yes. A classic example exists near my home. In the 18th century, the body of a highwayman hanged in Derby prison was being conveyed by a company of soldiers to the hamlet where his crime had been committed, to be hung there on a gibbet and the young cornet in charge of the cavalry decided to take a short cut through the Duke of Devonshire's Chatsworth Park. He was stopped by the lodgekeeper who told him it was the Duke's private road. 'Duke he may be, but I have the King's Commission,' replied the young officer and ordered his men to carry on through. The road has been a public highway ever since.

E. D. CHAMBERS, SHEFFIELD.

What if the corpse is a royal one? My great-uncle lived in Kingsway, Chandlers Ford, Eastleigh, in Hampshire, and was one of the first – if not the first – to have a house built there. At that time the road was not made up. Just after the war the local council sent an order for him and the few other householders along that road to pay £100 each for the road to be properly made up. My uncle consulted the Domesday Book and found that the road was called Kingsway because the body of King William Rufus was carried along that road after he was killed in the New Forest. Therefore, he argued, the road was no longer a private road, and the council was responsible for having it made up. However, in his book The Killing Of William Rufus, Duncan Grinnell-Milne, writes that the King's last journey was via Ower, Romsey, Ampfield and Hursley to Winchester, which doesn't touch Chandler's Ford. Whatever happened, my great-uncle and his neighbours did not have to pay the £100 each.

SISTER MILLICENT BECKETT, CLAPHAM, LONDON.

When I was a police officer dealing with a complaint of trespass, an elderly occupant of a cottage near the land in question told me that as a boy he had been gathering blackberries there when he was approached by two women from the nearby Hall. He asked if he was trespassing but one of them said: 'No, my husband's body was carried over this land so it is now a public footpath.' I also know of an incident in which a funeral procession was refused permission to cross a toll bridge because to have allowed it over would have freed the bridge from tolls in future.

C. GILBERT, COVENTRY.

The law doesn't regard the passage of a funeral in itself as being sufficient to create a right of way. It's difficult to improve upon the explanation in the Dornford Yates novel The Berry Scene. 'There's an odd belief,' said Berry, 'that where a funeral has passed, there will forever be a right of way. In fact, it's bad in law. But such beliefs die hard.'

ARTHUR H. MOIR, REGISTRAR OF TITLES, H.M. LAND REGISTRY, BELFAST.

711: When the clocks go back, does Big Ben stop for an hour or is it wound back? And does it chime the same hour twice?

What most people think of as Big Ben is actually the Great Clock of Westminster. Big Ben is the name of its hour bell, so called because it weighs 13 tons. When the clocks go forward in spring the process is as follows: at 9.45pm we stop the strike and chimes and shut off the clockface lighting. We then run the hands on to 12 o'clock, so they are in the upright position, avoiding confusion for the public. Then we stop the 'going train', the clock's drive mechanism. At 23.00 Greenwich Mean Time, 00.00 British Summer Time, we restart the clock but leave the strike and chimes off until just after 00.45 GMT (01.45 BST). At 00.58 GMT (01.58 BST) the clockface lights are switched on and at 01.00 GMT (02.00 BST) the clock chimes and strikes the hour. For the autumn change the process is the same in reverse.

BRIAN O'BOYLE, DEPUTY WORKS MANAGER, PALACE OF WESTMINSTER, LONDON.

712: Did anyone actually use the famous threat: 'This town ain't big enough for the both of us'?

In the 1948 Bugs Bunny cartoon Bugs Bunny Rides Again those exact words are screamed at Bugs Bunny by his old enemy Yosemite Sam.

LISA BRODY, NATIONAL ARCHIVE FOR FILM PRESERVATION, WASHINGTON DC, USA.

The saying probably came to modern fame through the song of the same name sung by the U.S. group Sparks which reached the top ten here in 1974.

JANET HUTTON, LITTLE LEVER, LANCS.

There's a much-mistaken chain of thought that these words were spoken in almost every feature and B-western by mischievous villains encountering some gallant defender of justice. My records show the threat was rarely used: its earliest mention was when ace Western baddy Charles King said it to singing cowboy Tex Ritter in a 1936 film made by Grand National Pictures in the Boots And Saddles series. What a pity that today's TV companies fail to recognise the wide interest in this genre.

R. FRANK MOORE-COLTMAN, B-WESTERN FILM HISTORIAN, MELTON MOWBRAY, LEICS.

713: Would a gyroscope in space, outside earth's gravity, always have its axis pointing in the same direction? If so, in what direction does it point and why? Has the Universe some notional centre of gravity?

A gyroscope is a rotating mass of material. As every galaxy, star, planet and particle of dust has some rotational component to its movement, it too can therefore be said to be acting like a gyroscope. The question assumes gravity has a major influence upon the behaviour of a gyroscope but gravity is in fact an example of gyroscopic behaviour. A gyroscope's behaviour is influenced by its own internal movement and by external forces. In the absence of external forces (i.e. the vacuum of outer space) the gyroscope will remain spinning with its axis pointing in the direction it was in when it started. However, the gravitational attraction of other spinning bodies (in the example of outer space) will have an influence upon the gyroscope. When stars and planets fall together to form galaxies, they develop a rotation around a single centre of gravity. In an attempt to conserve energy, the gyroscope will realign itself so that its axis is lined up with the rotational axis of the whole system. As for the whole universe, as it has a mass it also has a notional centre of gravity. Directly it would not have any influence upon the gyroscope in space, but it is the main factor which has determined the behaviour of those things which will have an influence upon the gyroscope.

R. D. HUGHES BSc (HONS), CHESTER.

714: When do a bride and bridegroom begin and finish being so called?

There are no rules. Technically, the titles should apply only on the day of the marriage ceremony. However, once a couple are engaged, they often come to be known as the bride and bridegroom. The couple should stop being known by these titles the moment they leave for their honeymoon.

KATHLEEN BAIRD-MURRAY, YOU AND YOUR WEDDING MAGAZINE, LONDON.

715: Who first had the idea to train guide-dogs for the blind?

Dogs have been used as guides and protectors of the blind for at least 1,000 years, as can be seen from the many examples in European art of blind people being accompanied by dogs. The Textbook For Teaching The Blind, published in Vienna in 1819, describes training a dog with a rigid leash to lead the blind. After World War I, a centre in Potsdam did much pioneering work in training dogs to work with the blind but the person who did most to spread the use of guide-dogs was wealthy American Mrs Dorothy Harrison Eustis. She was a dog breeder for the

Swiss Customs service who visited the Potsdam centre in 1927 and went on to set up The Seeing Eye guide-dog centre in Vevey, Switzerland. She later opened a branch in America and the first American to own a trained guide-dog was Frank Morris whose dog was called Buddy. The link with Britain was established via Rosamund Bond and Muriel Crooke of Wallasey, Cheshire, who, with Mrs Eustis, set up a trial programme in 1930. The first permanent British guide-dog trainer was Captain Nicolai Liakhoff, a former officer in the Russian Imperial Guard. Having trained with Mrs Eustis, he started work in 1933 and trained guide dogs until his death in 1962. The name Guide Dogs for the Blind Association was adopted in 1934. The association is a registered charity, supported entirely by public donations and legacies. Annual guide-dog week acts as a focus for the association's publicity, with advertising and fundraising events. Nearly 500 voluntary branches all around the UK help raise funds.

ALISON RADEVSKY, GUIDE DOGS FOR THE BLIND ASSOCIATION, READING.

716: As tyres wear out, where does the used material go to and is it harmful to the environment?

The 25 million licensed vehicles that use our roads each day leave minute particles of their tyres on road surfaces. These billions of particles are washed by rainwater or blown by wind to the side of roads, ending up in fields, gardens, pavements, road gullies or sewer systems. Tyres are made of many materials which can damage our environment. Among the most harmful are copper, cadmium and zinc which can be washed into roadside sewers and carried to wherever outlet pipes are, often not far from the food chain. Some of these minerals are also released into the atmosphere and breathed in by pedestrians at the roadside, other drivers or people with homes near busy roads. Many environmentally harmful materials are dispersed from tyres into roadside fields where they may also enter the food chain. Much effort is being made to minimise the harmful effects of tyre breakdown. Guidelines have been drawn up by the European Community on tyre gauges' pressure and better control of sewer outlets into rivers and lakes. Measures have been taken to prevent tyres which have ended their life being used for landfilling, which is where 50% of them currently end up. It is planned to make better use of the mineral waste by the year 2000.

DEBORAH HOLGATE, HALE, CHESHIRE.

717: Which days in Britain commonly have the highest and lowest recorded temperatures?

There are two different answers to this question. Looking at different places between 1961 and 1990, London (at Heathrow) and Sheffield both had their highest daily average maximum temperature on July 30 and lowest on February 15. Glasgow (at Abbotsinch) had its highest daily average maximum on July 20 and its lowest on February 16. Alternatively, examining the records for each year, the most frequent dates to have the extreme annual temperatures. taking each year since 1972 for weather stations in Britain, are July 11 for highest maximum and January 13 for the lowest minimum. But in that period both dates occur only twice. Martin Allwright, The Met Office, Bracknell, Berkshire.

718: If Prince William were to renounce Anglicanism for another faith, would his right to the throne be affected or would the Archbishop of Canterbury be obliged to switch denominations?

The reigning monarch is required to join in communion with the Church of England. In the unlikely event of Prince William leaving the Church of England, there could be several outcomes. If he joined another Trinitarian Church (one that believes in the Father, the Son and the Holy Spirit), his right to the throne might not be affected provided that from time to time he received communion according to the rites of the Church of England. If he joined a non-Trinitarian Church, or became a Roman Catholic, Moslem or a Jew, for example, then he could not join in communion with the Church of England. Technically, therefore, he would be unable to become King of England and Defender of the Faith. The next in line of succession to the throne who could join in communion with the Church of England would be crowned sovereign. In all cases, the Archbishop of Canterbury would remain within the Church of England and would not be obliged to change denominations. Rev Eric Shegog, director of communications, General Synod of the Church of England.

Were Prince William to become a Roman Catholic the title Defender of the Faith would be more appropriate than at present as it was conferred by the Pope on the Roman Catholic Henry VIII, before his excommunication and when, before his fall from grace, he was regarded as a devout Roman Catholic. E. F. Thorpe, Bradford, West Yorks.

719: Why is a 'cock and bull' story so called?

The phrase originated during the 18th-century heyday of the coaching industry. The Cock and The Bull were inns on the High Street in Stony Stratford, Bucks. Coach passengers bound for London changed at The Bull and Birmingham-bound passengers at The Cock. A fierce rivalry grew up between the two hostelries as to which was the best, and the tall and fantastic tales bandied between the passengers, coachmen and innkeepers became known as 'Cock and Bull' stories. Both inns thrived on the competition – and they still stand today.   D. G. EDMONDS, BUCKINGHAM, BUCKS.

720: What is the origin of the phrase 'swinging the lead', meaning feigning illness to avoid work?

There are two claimed origins for this saying. The first, and least commonly known, is that it comes from the military saying 'swing the leg', which meant that a malingerer was feigning an injury by pretending to have a limp. The muddling of 'swing the leg' into 'swinging the lead' arose due to a misunderstanding of the original meaning when the phrase entered general speech. The second claimed origin comes from the days of sailing ships when a piece of lead on the end of a long line was used to discover the depth of water. It is thought that the job of 'swinging the lead' was given to the less physically able members of the ship's crew, and thus came to be used to refer to someone not considered a full working member.   SAMUEL BRIARS, CAMBRIDGE.

The naval origin of this phrase is more complicated than has been suggested. The sounding method of measuring the depth of water with a lead weight and line continued to be used on ships until the 1930s. This method, known as 'heaving the lead', required the leadsman to display considerable strength and skill and was certainly not a task given to less competent members of the crew. Admiralty instructions were to 'swing the lead as a pendulum to obtain impetus, then swing it over the head in a circle by bending the arms smartly in at the elbow as the lead is rising and letting the arm go out again after the lead has passed the perpendicular. After completing two or three circles, slip the line after the lead has passed the water and before it comes to the horizontal.' It goes on: 'In shallow water or if the ship is moving slowly, time is saved by using only the under hand swing.' This last instruction was used by unskilled or lazy seamen as an excuse to 'swing' the lead instead of 'heaving' it.   G. BROMHEAD, TONBRIDGE, KENT.

721: How can I stop my shoes from squeaking?

The sole of a shoe is made of three parts: the outer sole, in contact with the ground, the inner sole, in contact with the foot, and, acting as a brace between the two, the shank which can be of either wood or metal. If the shank becomes unattached from the shoe at one end it will start to move independently from the remainder of the sole, causing a squeak. This can be corrected by repair work, re-fixing the shank at both ends. If new shoes squeak, it is the result of the leather creasing as the shoe moves when you walk. The greater the amount of creasing, the more squeak you will get. This will stop happening as the shoe is worn and the leather becomes 'worn in'. It can be overcome by polishing or oiling the leather, but you may not wish to do this with a pair of new shoes.

BRIAN HENSMAN, BOOT AND SHOE COLLECTION, NORTHAMPTON CENTRAL MUSEUM.

While I bow to the technical expertise of Brian Hensman, of the Boot And Shoe Museum, who says that shoe squeaking is related to problems with construction and wear, I cannot forget that in my youth it was generally understood that squeaking shoes was a sure sign that they hadn't been paid for.

JACK TINSON, SOLIHULL, WEST MIDLANDS.

722: What is gorm? Surely, if one is gorm-less, then gorm must be some desired thing to have?

There doesn't seem to be an actual modern word 'gorm' but the derivation comes from a word meaning 'heed.' For 'heed', Collins English Dictionary gives the following definition: 'heed: n. 1. close and careful attention; notice (often in the phrases give, pay or take heed) – "heedful" adj'. This would mean that the historical opposite of 'gormless' would have to be 'heedful', although the meaning has changed somewhat. The noun by itself has not survived. The chief lexicographer confirms this but also points out that if you actually started using the word 'gorm' you could start a vogue. An example of this is 'gruntled' (meaning 'happy or contented; satisfied') which is a back formation from 'disgruntled' and only made it into the Collins Dictionary because somebody suddenly started using it.

BIRTE TWISSELMANN, COLLINS ENGLISH DICTIONARY, LONDON.

Strictly speaking, gormless is a misspelling of 'gaumless', which is how Emily Brontë, a Yorkshirewoman, spelled it in Wuthering Heights in 1847. Gaumless was originally a North Country word which can be traced back to the 18th century, a compound of 'gaum' and 'less'. Gaum, not used in the south but still in use in Yorkshire, is a very old word which originally meant 'attention, heed, care' but has come to mean 'sense, wit, tact.' The Oxford English Dictionary cites the 1877 Holderness Glossary which gives this meaning for the word, as do a number of books on North Country dialect.

EDMUND WEINER, CO-EDITOR, OXFORD ENGLISH DICTIONARY.

'Gormless' is a comparatively recent spelling of 'gaumless' meaning 'lack of understanding'. Gaum means understanding, while to gaum means to understand. Daniel Peggotty uses the word 'gormed' in Charles Dickens's David Copperfield.

ERIC THOMAS, PURLEY, SURREY.

Fifty years ago, my Lincolnshire born and bred neighbour used gorm as a verb meaning 'to take notice': 'Mrs Smith passed me in the street and never gormed me.' In Yorkshire, an unmarried man and woman living together were said to be living gormless, sackless or dateless; meanings rarely heard nowadays. Mrs J. Davies, Scunthorpe, South Humberside.

In broad Yorkshire, if you were advising someone to ignore something, you would say 'Tak' n' gorm on't.'

W. H. Metcalfe, Hebden Bridge, West Yorkshire.

'Gorm', meaning to ignore or take no notice, was commonly used where I lived in Leeds before the war. Alec Taylor, Walton, North Yorkshire.

In my part of the country, gormless was originally applied to a farm cart without its 'gormers', the front and back upright extensions. These were wooden, ladderlike structures used to hold bulky, loose loads such as hay or straw. Without them, the cart would be next to useless. Hence a useless person is gormless. Andrew Broadbent, Buxton, Derbyshire.

723: How do you iron and fold a fitted sheet so that it retains some semblance of having been ironed?

Fold in half widthwise with wrong side of sheet inside. Tuck corners inside each other. Iron, fitting corners and sides over ironing board easily. Fold again ending up with all four corners tucked inside each other. Fold in sides and corners to lay straight inside sheet, then fold again to make neat square. Elizabeth Norwood, Bellingdon, Buckinghamshire.

Having struggled with this problem for some years, I now leave the sheet un-ironed until it is needed. I then stretch it over the mattress (with a flat sheet underneath), take the extention lead and iron up to the bedroom and iron the sheet on the bed. Mrs Sandra Price, Hornchurch, Essex.

724: How were the famous London hospitals, such as Bart's, Guys, St Thomas's and Charing Cross, financed before the NHS came into being in 1948?

Before 1948, the major teaching hospitals in London relied on private and charitable income to finance their work. Bart's Hospital and St Thomas's received money from endowments, legacies and wills as well as from estates they owned. All hospitals relied on charitable donations plus money given by their governors. In the 19th century, someone who donated two guineas to St Mary's Hospital could become a hospital governor, or a life governor for 10 guineas. Until 1892, governors had the right to attend any meeting on the day-to-day running of the hospital and were given tickets for inpatient and outpatient care to send their servants, tenants and friends to the hospital for treatment. They also helped select medical staff and consultants. After 1892, the governors elected a board of management to run the hospital. In the 1920s, St Mary's introduced a form of means testing and charged patients according to their means for their keep, though not for their treatment.

KEVIN BROWN, ARCHIVIST, ST MARY'S, LONDON.

The Hospital Savings Association was very important in helping both patients and hospitals. Seventy years ago, when I was a schoolboy, my father, among his other duties for the community in New Cross, south east London, was honorary secretary of the local HSA branch. For 3d a week paid to the hospital, the HSA provided a voucher for hospital treatment.

E. PACKER HARDMAN, TONBRIDGE, KENT.

725: Why are dockers called stevedores?

The word 'stevedore' initially related to a particular type of dock worker who worked on board a ship loading the cargo into the hold or removing it. The word itself derives from the Latin *stipare* meaning 'to cram.' Men who worked on the quayside discharging the cargo from ship to shore were known as dockers. The distinction between the two roles seems to have been recognised in the London docks though not in other parts of the country. However, as time went on there was a merging of the two roles and the general term 'docker' was applied to all dock workers.

JOHN CONNOLLY, NATIONAL SECRETARY, DOCKS AND WATERWAYS GROUP, TGWU, LONDON.

726: How did the Romans build their roads from fort to fort, and city to city, in straight lines, over hills and dales, without the use of modern surveying instruments?

Roman roads are not always straight. Like modern road builders, they tended to go from A to B by a direct route because it is the shortest distance and the cheapest to build. Roman roads curved to avoid hills and bogs just as we try to do today. Still, the Romans were very competent civil engineers. They used an instrument called a groma, like a modern-day theodolite, to map out the line of a road. A groma consists of a pole on which sit four arms at right angles to each other. From the arms hang weights which, when aligned, enabled the engineer to plan straight ahead. There is a reconstruction of a groma in the Science Museum in London. But a groma cannot approach the accuracy of today's surveying equipment. When French and British engineers building the Channel Tunnel finally joined the UK to the Continent, they were just 4mm (less than a quarter of an inch) off target.

JOHN HALL, GEORGE WIMPEY PLC, LONDON.

The Romans have been credited for straight roads in this country but often they merely paved existing tracks and improved upon what had already been marked out by the Dod-men of Neolithic times. These early surveyors carried two stakes, and used them to line up the straightest route between bases, moving, or 'doddering', about until the best line was achieved. The routes were marked with stones and huge mounds of earth, and coincide with the powerful lines of Earth energy, offering strength and protection to the traveller. Military encampments, hospitals, mental institutions, churches and colleges were often built on these locations, to gain advantage of the natural healing and spiritual energies. A picture of a prehistoric surveyor is to be found cut into the turf at Wilmington, Sussex. Known as The Long Man, and measuring 240ft from head to toe, he appears to be in normal proportion when viewed from below the Downs but can be seen to be highly elongated when viewed 'straight on' from the air.

KEITH GULLIFORD, CHANDLER'S FORD, HAMPSHIRE.

727: How did Lyme get its Regis and Leamington Spa its Royal?

According to The Short Story Of Lyme Regis by John Fowles: 'In 1284, Edward I gave Lyme Regis or King's Lyme a Royal Charter. This was in no way a special honour but a matter of policy. Edward wanted to make England a conscious nation, centred on the Crown. One way he chose to do that was to increase both national prosperity and royal income from it. He was therefore free with such charters (he granted seven others in the same year as Lyme's). Although still kept firmly under the local eye of central administration, in the person of the King's bailiff or Reeve, these new local boroughs were allowed considerable trading privileges, a degree of self-government and their own minor courts. They could also send two Members to Parliament – a right Lyme enjoyed (or abused) from 1295 until 1832. In return they had to pay an annual rent and other taxes to the Exchequer.'

COUNCILLOR TED STREET, LYME REGIS.

Despite adding Regis to its name – derived from the Saxon name of the little river Lym – the town has not been notable for adherence to the royal cause. Lyme was one of the few West Country towns which backed Parliament against the King in the Civil War, successfully withstanding a six-week siege by Royalist forces under Prince Maurice in 1644. And in 1685, the Duke of Monmouth chose to land there at the start of his ill-fated attempt to win the English crown.

LIZ-ANNE BAWDEN, LYME REGIS PHILPOT MUSEUM, DORSET.

Queen Victoria visited Leamington Spa just before her coronation and was so impressed with the town and its environment that she felt it deserved royal recognition. Immediately after her coronation as Queen of England in 1838 she instructed that it be granted the prefix Royal and it has been known as Royal Leamington Spa since then.

TREVOR ASHBOURNE, CLERK OF THE CHARTER TRUSTEES OF ROYAL LEAMINGTON SPA.

Queen Victoria may have visited Leamington Spa just before her coronation but another story claims the town acquired its title through the bad manners of Henry Jephson. Dr Jephson was presented to Queen Victoria's court by Lord Eastnor and the Queen knighted him but on leaving he turned his back on her instead of backing away as protocol demanded. She didn't like this and I believe her exact words were: 'Royal Leamington Spa certainly, plain Henry Jephson.' Thus the knighthood was withdrawn and Leamington Spa became Royal.

MRS M. C. SHERRIFF, LEAMINGTON SPA, WARWICKSHIRE.

728: What do weather forecasters mean when they say there is a 10 per cent chance of rain?

All forecasters assess the chances of certain weather conditions in percentage terms, i.e. definitely going to rain, 100 per cent; no chance at all, 0pc. When giving the percentage chance of particular weather conditions occurring, we consider individual locations, towns and cities, not general areas. Percentages are particularly useful when describing the chance of showers, which are often random. A showery westerly wind might give Manchester a 70pc chance of getting a shower (i.e. more likely than not) whereas Leeds, sheltered by the Pennines, could have a 10pc chance of seeing a shower.

BILL GILES, HEAD OF BBC WEATHER CENTRE, LONDON.

729: Has any person who returned a 'No' reply envelope to a Reader's Digest offer and competition, ever won a prize with their allocated numbers?

You do not have to purchase anything to enter the Readers Digest prize draw. All you have to do is return your allocated entry numbers to us in either the Yes or the No envelope, as you prefer. We use Yes and No envelopes so that we can identify and service orders more quickly. Colin Brown, from Southport, who was presented with a cheque for £250,000 in our Prize Draw in September 1992 after returning the No envelope, is only one among thousands every year who win by declining our offer. Entry to our competitions, on the other hand, may well be dependent on purchase.

ELEANOR WORDSWORTH, READERS DIGEST, LONDON.

A few weeks ago a friend invited me and my husband to accompany him to a presentation in London's West End. We were met at the station and taken by chauffeur-driven limousine to a Readers Digest champagne lunch and reception. Three people were given prizes, presented by Hannah Gordon, including our friend who got £31,000. He gave us £100 for going with him, as he would have been too shy to go on his own. He had not bought a book or subscription and had put No on his return letter.   MRS E. KEMP, RAYLEIGH, ESSEX.

For two years, I was bombarded by letters about the Reader's Digest Prize Draw with affirmations that I was successfully through the first stage of the draw, followed by indications that I was through the second stage and several that I was now in the final stage, all accompanied by offers of goods I would find it difficult to resist. I returned most of the certificates in the 'No' envelopes. Then came a letter containing 'Yes' and 'No' cards on whether I could attend a presentation ceremony. My hopes of a substantial win were sky high, especially when a letter arrived from P & O announcing they had been informed of my imminent win and asking if I would be interested in booking one of their cruises. Then came a further offer of a book, which I purchased, then not another word about the prize draw. I wrote a letter of protest to Reader's Digest, pointing out the mental cruelty to which their selling methods had subjected me and others. Since then, I have received three more indications that I am in the final stages of the draw, a letter noting my wish to be removed from their mailing list and a communication from Guy Salmon Chauffeur Service, telling me they provide winners with transport to the award ceremony etc. In conclusion, I have bought a large number of books but, as far as any prize draw is concerned, I have received only egg on my face.   L. G. WRIGHT, BOURNEMOUTH, DORSET.

730: Why are toes angled off the longitudinal axis of the foot so that sprinters have to turn their feet inwards to achieve maximum push off the ground?

The foot, during motion, acts in two different capacities. As it strikes the floor, it behaves as a mobile adaptor to adjust the step for uneven surfaces and soak up the stress of heel strike. This movement is called pronation. Then, as the body moves over the fixed foot, the leg rotates externally and the foot becomes a rigid lever. This is called supination. One of the effects of supination is that the fore-foot is twisted inward to the mid-line of the body. The more supinated, the more rigid the foot and the more effective it is in transferring power from the muscles to provide motion. The angle of the toes away from the longitudinal axis of the foot increases its stability but it is supination which provides the means for the transfer of power.   ERNEST ROWBOTTOM, CHIROPODIST, OLDHAM AREA HEALTH AUTHORITY.

731: In French addresses, what do 'Cedx' and 'bis' mean? And there are many Blvd/Ave Gambetta – who was he?

'Cedx' is an abbreviation of *Courrier d'enterprise à distribution exceptionelle*, the French Postal System's express distribution service for large bulk mailers. The English version of this is 'Mailsort.' 'Bis' is the word normally used to signify what we in this country call 'a' addresses. For example, if somebody who lived in a typical street in this country had the address 24a The Street, in France this would be 24bis The Street. Leon Michel Gambetta (1838-82), whose name figures in hundreds of streets in France, was a French liberal politician who took part in the proclamation of the Third Republic after the surrender of Napoleon III to Prussian forces in 1870. He escaped by balloon from the German siege of Paris and was virtually in control of France for several months. He is regarded as one of France's greatest ever leaders. — PHOEBE JONES, CARDIFF.

732: Can anyone complete the rhyme for remembering the Kings and Queens of England in correct order, which begins: 'Willy, Willy, Harry, Steve; Harry, Dick, John, Harry three; One, two, three Neds, Richard two; Henry four, five, six –' then who?

Yes, the rhyme is fresh to me, as I taught it each day in History. It continues: 'Edwards, four, five, Dick the Bad, Harries twain, and Ned the Lad, Mary, Bessie, James the Vain, Charles one, two, then James again, William and Mary, Anna Gloria, Four Georges, William and Victoria, Edward the seventh and George the fifth, Edward the eighth, and George the sixth, Now we have Elizabeth.' And for the future? 'Liz the Second, and Charles her son, Let's hope the Monarchy's not done.' — MR I. HAY, FRIERN BARNET, LONDON.

This rhyme omits the unfortunate Queen Jane, Lady Jane Grey, who reigned for nine days in 1553. — J. B. MURRAY, DORKING, SURREY.

733: When I visited the Great Wall of China recently, the guide said it was one of the Seven Wonders Of The World and one of only two constructions on earth which could be identified from the moon. Is this true and what is the other one?

This long-standing claim, going back at least as far as 1909, is incorrect. I researched this subject exhaustively in 1989, even asking no less than five Apollo astronauts. I concluded that the Great North Wall certainly cannot be seen from the Moon with the unaided human eye. James Lovell, of Apollos 8 and 13, said the idea was absurd. The wall is, at best, eight to ten metres wide, and my calculations showed that seeing the wall from the Moon is roughly comparable to seeing an ice-lolly stick in Glasgow when you are in Birmingham. The wall can be seen only with difficulty from close orbit around the Earth. Astronauts who are good map readers might then pick it out, using binoculars. The only things on Earth you can see from the Moon with the unaided eye are continents, oceans, other large water areas and cloud masses. The Great Wall claim is a myth which won't go away. And it's not one of the Seven Wonders of the World either.   H. J. P. ARNOLD, SPACE FRONTIERS LTD, HAVANT, HANTS.

734: Where does the expression 'left to carry the can' originate?

'Carry the can', meaning to take the blame or be the scapegoat for another's mistake or misdemeanour, is said to have originated in military circles. It is supposed to relate to the tradition of one man, often the newest recruit, being responsible for fetching the beer for the rest of the group. He would have to carry a container or can of beer to the rest of the men and then take it back again when it was empty.

MALCOLM KNIGHT, EDINBURGH.

735: What system is used to establish the date of Easter each year?

Most Christian religious festivals are held on what were previously pagan feast days. Early Christian church leaders chose the dates when people were used to celebrating. Though nobody knew the true date of the birth of Christ, Christmas Day, signifying hope in the depths of winter, was fixed at the time of the Roman Saturnalia. Easter was linked to the Jewish Passover. The exact method of calculating the date of Easter was decided in AD325 at the Synod at Nicea. Easter falls on the Sunday following the first full moon on or after the Vernal Equinox, March 21. So it can be on any date between March 21 and April 25. The Venerable Bede thought it important to retain the symbolism in Britain of the days being seen to get lighter after Easter.   FELICITY ROGERS, NOTTINGHAM.

736: Has the word camera, as used for taking photographs, anything to do with holding meetings 'in camera'?

Here at Foredown Tower we have a large camera obscura which means 'darkened chamber', optical equipment which projects the image of the outside scene on to a screen in a darkened room using a mirror and lens. The 'camera' part of the name means chamber, as it does for 'in camera' meetings or 'in chambers' for something which a judge does other than in open court. The word was taken and used to refer to the darkened apparatus that takes a photograph: which became the camera.

MIKE FEIST, INTERPRETATIVE RANGER, FOREDOWN TOWER, BRIGHTON.

737: Where in the world of photography do the words 'watch the birdie' originate?

This saying originated in Victorian studios during the early days of photography. Our collection includes a little whistling bird, common at the time, which makes a noise when you fill it with water and blow it. It dates from the 1890s and photographers used them to make subjects look up at a focal point, relax and smile.

PENNY FELL, NATIONAL MUSEUM OF PHOTOGRAPHY FILM & TELEVISION, PICTUREVILLE, BRADFORD.

738: What became of the Russian space dogs used in the early stages of the Sputnik programme?

The first living creature to travel in space was a dog called Laika, sent up in Soviet space craft, Sputnik 2, launched on November 3, 1957. Unfortunately Laika died during the flight. The second and third dogs in space were Strelka, meaning 'arrow' or 'pointer', and Belka, meaning 'squirrel', who went up together in Sputnik 5, launched on August 19, 1960. Both dogs were recovered alive after orbiting the earth a total of 18 times and lived out their lives as national heroes in the Russian Academy of Sciences. A press conference on March 28, 1961, announced that Strelka had given birth to several puppies.

RALPH GIBSON, RUSSIAN INFORMATION AGENCY, LONDON.

739: In 1941 our train to Manchester was sent back to Blackpool by police, who told us there were food riots in Manchester and many civilians had been shot. Was this all hushed up?

I worked as a bank clerk in Manchester throughout the war years and I know of no food riots. Manchester suffered greatly at the hands of German bombers, the worst raid being on the night of December 22-23, 1940, when Victoria station, among a lot of other places, was almost demolished. The bank in the Corn Exchange where I was employed was completely destroyed when a land-mine dropped down the lift shaft and blew a hole in the wall of the strongroom causing millions of pounds' worth of damage to cash, ledgers and safe deposit boxes. Fires raged for five days. In the same raid the fish and poultry supplier Goulburns, in the Old Shambles, took a direct hit and thousands of turkeys and chickens ready for collection and distribution for Christmas were ruined. The putrid stench of the rotting flesh made it advisable to avoid the area for weeks afterwards.

NETA ALDHOUSE, ABERGELE, CLWYD.

I can find no reference to food riots in Manchester in 1941. It's often difficult to obtain details of 'home front' incidents from the war but I doubt if such a public incident could have been hushed up for more than 50 years. The train may have been turned back to Blackpool because of either of the two serious air-raids on Manchester in 1941, the first on March 11, which lasted three hours, and the second on June 1 and 2, which was the heaviest raid since the Christmas blitz of 1940. Destruction and loss of life were on a heavy scale. On October 26, 1941, there was a large scale 'invasion' exercise in Manchester and Salford which included civilians and may have involved the use of tear-gas.

DAVID TAYLOR, RESEARCH OFFICER, MANCHESTER CENTRAL LIBRARY LOCAL STUDIES UNIT.

Trains were diverted when the four main stations in the city were inaccessible after the Christmas blitz. The reference to food riots could be a result of the fact that the Eccles, Salford and Manchester Home Guard battalions went onto the streets with live ammunition to deter looting. Within two hours of these patrols commencing, and a number of rounds being fired, all disturbances had ceased. There were no reported casualties. I was a Home Guard sergeant at the time, serving with the Eccles Battalion.

H. F. HINDSHAW, 42 COUNTY OF LANCASTER BATTALION, LANCS.

740: Is there any land not registered, or not officially owned, by anybody in this country and if so how do I claim it?

Technically, all land in England and Wales is deemed to be owned by the Crown and held either freehold or leasehold by its current owner. Anyone who believes a piece of land has no current owner and wants to claim it, should seek legal advice. Compulsory registration of 'title on sale' in England and Wales was completed on December 1, 1990, when it became compulsory to register the ownership of any land sold in England and Wales. Voluntary land registration began in 1862 and the compulsory process started in 1899 in the old County of London. Her Majesty's Land Registry, responsible for the register, has details of 14.5 million registered properties, about two thirds of the estimated number of land titles in England and Wales. About one third of all potential titles remains unregistered but this number is steadily reducing. To find out if land is registered, an individual can apply to the registry enclosing a map of the extent of land concerned and, for a fee of £5, we will make an official inspection of the large scale Ordnance Survey maps which show all registered land.

TONY MARR, H.M. LAND REGISTRY, LONDON.

As Marshland Rural District Health Inspector in the late Fifties, I was involved in the case of an infestation of rabbits along the defunct Wisbech-Upwell Canal and called in the Ministry of Agriculture to deal with them. They asked 'Who owns the land?' and were told 'Nobody.' The Canal Company had obtained a 'Bill of Abandonment' and the share certificates were given away to gentlemen of the road, who used them to light fires etc. Some time later the need for refuse disposal space led to the idea of filling in the canal and a considerable sum of money had to be deposited with the Government in case any rightful owner appeared.

ARTHUR NUNN, RIPON, NORTH YORKSHIRE.

741: Who was the highwayman who liked to dress up as a woman and demand jewellery from his victims?

This sounds like Thomas Sympson, from Romsey, Hants, better known as Old Mobb, who enjoyed a 45-year career, starting during the Civil War, before meeting his end at Tyburn in 1690. The story goes that Old Mobb was at Bath when he chose to rob a particular lord who was known as a lecherous fellow. Mobb disguised himself as a woman and galloped after the lord, who was accompanied by a small army of retainers on the route to London. His lordship was very drunk and Mobb's make-up job (he was still in his youth at the time) and determined flirtation were very good. After several suggestions for a closer rendezvous, Mobb seized his chance and suggested they went into the woods away from the view of the others. In the woods, Mobb pulled his pistol, bound and gagged the nobleman and relieved him of 100 guineas, a gold watch, gold snuff box and two diamond rings.

ROGER EATON, HATFIELD, HERTS.

742: Why are spectacles known in slang as 'bins'?

Contrary to popular belief, the term 'bins' has nothing to do with cockney rhyming slang. It is the plural of an abbreviation of 'binocular', meaning for the use of two eyes, a direct derivative of 'binary ocular', binary meaning two, or dual, and ocular meaning 'of the eye.' Strictly speaking, the words 'spectacles' and 'glasses' refer only to the lenses, so 'bins', though regarded as slang, may be a more accurate description of the everyday tools of the visually impaired.

MICHAEL AND RUBY SOLOMAN, BINNS SUNGLASS DISTRIBUTORS, BRIGHTON.

743: Why are some people said to be 'as fit as a fiddle'?

Fit has been used to mean 'healthy' only since the 19th century. Before then it meant 'right and proper.' There are two equally likely, and probably connected, explanations as to why the fiddle was chosen for this phrase. A violin had to be made by a highly skilled craftsman and a good violin would be constructed to a high degree of precision. The admiration for such a well-made instrument lent itself well to explaining the condition of the human body. Folk music played on a violin can be very fast and frantic, demanding great skill and dexterity from the player and making it an ideal metaphor for fitness and health.   BARBARA FREEMAN, LONDON.

The original saying was 'as fit as a fiddler', because many fiddlers danced to their own music as street entertainers and had to be fit to do that.
H. JONES, LEICESTER.

The 'fiddler' on a farm carried the seed tray or 'fiddle', like an usherette's ice-cream tray but wider and filled with seeds, with a handle on the side which was turned to release the seeds evenly through holes in the bottom of the tray as the fiddler walked. If you had to walk a 40-acre field, you certainly needed to be fit.   PETER BELLAMY, CHELMSFORD, ESSEX.

744: If the heart is dependent upon an electrical impulse, where does this impulse come from and how is electricity made?

The electrical impulse originates in a specialised area of the heart, the sinu-atrial node, and is produced by the movement of sodium and potassium ions (which carry a positive charge) in and out of the muscle cells in the sinu-atrial node. The wave of electricity spreads through the entire heart, eliciting a rhythmical contraction at around 70 times per minute in the resting state. This process continues throughout life, and this electrical activity can be traced using the ECG heart-tracing scan.
DR PHILIP BELL MB, DIP SPORTS MED, LONDON BRIDGE CLINIC, LONDON.

745: What is the machine used to record events in court, and how does it work? The 'typist' seems to have only a few keys and types rather slowly.

Two types of machine are used in courtrooms in this country: the British Palantype and the American Stenograph. Both type phonetically by a technique more akin to playing a piano than using a typewriter. A number of keys can be hit at the same time to type in syllables, words and phrases. The machines can be linked to a computer which converts the information into standard English. For example, an operator may type in the letters f.r.i.mt, shorthand for 'from time to time.' Operators of these machines in court are normally top-grade typists who can input at least 180 words per minute, with some typing 200-250 words per minute.
CHRIS ASHLEY, COURT REPORTER, THE OLD BAILEY, LONDON.

746: Why say: 'The game is not worth the candle'? What game and why candle?

Card games were a very popular source of entertainment for the middle and upper classes during the 18th and 19th centuries and candles were used to light them, when played in the evening. But candles were expensive and if a game was not going well, or was being played for low stakes, it was said to be not worth the cost of lighting it.

CAROLE MULLINEAUX, MICKLEOVER, DERBYS.

The word candle in this context is a corruption of 'caddle', a West Country expression denoting a paltry job. Old timers in Somerset would say: 'It's a main caddlin' job, a fiddlin' job.' The game refers not to a sporting game but to a 'fiddling game', a tedious job with little or no return.

C. G. TRASK, MAIDSTONE, KENT.

747: You can run a clock by wiring it to a potato. How many would you need for a lightbulb?

Just two potatoes, connected in series, are needed to power a potato clock, which requires about one volt. So, in theory, though we can't find anyone who has tried it, it would require at least 480 potatoes to power an electric light bulb. However, potatoes are a very efficient source of nutritional energy and a much better way to light a bulb using potatoes would be to eat them and use the resulting energy to pedal a bicycle equipped with a dynamo.

ROS WEHNER, POTATO MARKETING BOARD, OXFORD.

748: What is the average life expectancy of doctors compared with the rest of the population?

The latest data published in this country which can shed some light on this subject is more than 15 years old and shows deaths only up to the age of 65 so does not account for the mortality of doctors compared with other pensioners. This aside, the average life expectancy of a male doctor is two to five years greater than that of the male population as a whole. The data available for female doctors is insufficient to be able to draw any conclusion. One of the interesting points in the last study was the higher rate of suicide within the medical profession compared with the population as a whole. A new study is now being conducted.

ALAN PAVELIN, GOVERNMENT ACTUARY'S DEPARTMENT.

749: Why did Teddy Tail tie a knot in his tail and when and why did he disappear from the Daily Mail?

In the Daily Mail's Adventures Of Teddy Tail Annual, which I was given in 1916 when I was ten, Teddy's friend Dr Beetle is knocked down a hole in the floor when the cork explodes from a champagne bottle. He threatens he'll set the cat on Teddy if he doesn't get him out. Teddy says: 'I made a little knot in my tail for him to hold on to, slipped it down the hole and pulled him out.' But a dreadful thing happened: they couldn't get the knot undone. Dr Beetle poured oil on it and Teddy says: 'I don't think much of Dr Beetle as a doctor. He oiled it and patted it but it was no good. My beauty has gone forever.'   J. R. WATKIN, EARLSDON, COVENTRY.

Teddy Tail, created by Charles Folkard, who named him Teddy after his son, was 'born' in April 1915 and appeared regularly in the Daily Mail, except during World War II, until October 1960. In that time he was drawn by several artists and often changed in appearance. In 1933 a Teddy Tail League was formed and acquired more than 800,000 members within five years. Members received a birthday card each year and tips on hobbies. Rule 1 stated: 'Members must be interested in either a hobby or a pet.' There is a secret sign for members, which I am not at liberty to divulge. Charles Folkard died in 1963, aged 84.

KEITH NOTT, DAILY MAIL.

750: What did they do with all the lashings of boiling water demanded during childbirth, as described in old books and films, or was it just a way to keep the men out of the way?

The use of boiling water during childbirth relates to the period when nearly all mothers had their babies at home and the midwife used the hot water to sterilise her medical instruments. Once the water had cooled sufficiently, it could then be used to wash both mother and child. The water was also useful to make a well-earned cup of tea for everybody after the baby had been born. Nowadays, the medical staff involved in childbirth use sterile cold water and pre-packed sterilised instruments, and the hot water is saved exclusively for that cuppa.

JOHN FRIEND, CONSULTANT OBSTETRICIAN AND GYNAECOLOGIST,
MATERNITY UNIT, DERRIFORD HOSPITAL, PLYMOUTH.

751: Why are there so many spelling mistakes in TV and film subtitles?

Subtitling errors occur rarely when programmes are available in advance of transmission and material can be pre-prepared. However, the BBC subtitles many live programmes, including national news, Westminster Live, Crimewatch and Blue Peter. For these, the BBC uses a technique called stenocaptioning, employing phonetic machine-written shorthand, like that used in courts, and the subtitles are translated directly onto air by computer. Sometimes, particularly with news programmes, words may be used which are not in the computer's dictionary and the machine will use the nearest phonetic equivalent. Also, the sheer speed at which the stenographers work, sometimes up to 220 words per minute, means that occasionally a finger will fall in the wrong place.

PATRICK BARROW, BBC NEWS AND CURRENT AFFAIRS, LONDON.

752: The removal firm Hudsons used to carry the word Ecoscevepheron in block capitals across the front of its vans. What did it mean?

Twenty years ago, as I walked past Hudson's Depository, beside London's Victoria Station, I puzzled over the strange word which appeared on all its vehicles and wrote to the company to find out what it meant. It replied: The word is supposed to mean 'We carry to the farthest point.' It was coined by classics scholar Mr Hudson when he founded the company in 1857. He took the first part from Xenophon, who used the common Greek word *economia* to describe the way in which the Spartans systematically loaded their baggage carts with provisions and arms. In Liddell and Scott's Lexicon he found *skeue,* latinized as *sceve,* meaning the contents of a dwelling, including farmyard stock, kitchen utensils and equipment. And he added phoron, like the Latin *fero,* to carry, as used by Sophocles in his epic drams, by Artistophanes in his satirical comedies and Herodotus in his Histories. As far as I am aware, the company is no longer in existence.

MARTIN BEALE, WHITSTABLE, KENT.

753: What are the oldest man-made structures in the world and where are they?

The earliest known human structure is a rough circle of loosely piled lava blocks found on the lowest cultural level at the lower palaeolithic site at Olduvai Gorge, Tanzania, revealed by Dr Mary Leakey in January 1960. The structure was associated with artefacts and bones on a work floor dating from about 1,750,000 BC. The oldest free-standing structures in the world are believed to be the megalithic temples at Mgarr and Skorba on Malta, and those at Ggantija on nearby Gozo, dating from around 3,250 BC – that is 350 years before the earliest Egyptian pyramids. Twelve small stone clusters, associated with broken bones and charcoal at the early palaeolithic site at Hoxne, near Eye, Suffolk, are regarded as Britain's earliest structural remains, dating from 250,000 BC. Stonehenge, a site commonly thought to be the oldest, seems to have been in use only from around 3,100 to 1,100BC.

CAROLE JONES, GUINNESS BOOK OF RECORDS.

754: Why do we refer to a 'slap-up' meal?

'Slap-up' and 'bang-up', both meaning 'excellent', were in use in England by the early 19th century and could be used to describe anything, not just food. Nowadays, however, we tend only to use 'slap-up' when we are talking about a meal. Quite why this should be isn't clear, but the connection between 'slap-up' and food may have something to do with the fact that there is also an old northern dialect verb 'to slap up' which means 'to eat hurriedly.'

NIGEL WILCOCKSON, BREWER'S PHRASE AND FABLE, CASSELL PUBLISHING, LONDON.

755: How does a blind pianist learn the score of a piece of music?

Louis Braille (1809-1852) officially unveiled his system of raised dot notation for both alphabet and music in 1829. Several other music notation systems were devised, using embossed letters and numbers but these could not be reproduced by blind people themselves, barring them from composing their own music. Printed music is pictorial but the Braille system relies on the same symbols used for reading and writing. Unlike printed music which relies on lines, symbols and spaces to denote pitch, value and length, in Braille the name and value of the note are represented by the same symbol with pitch designated by another series of signs so Braille music is read in the same way as Braille writing. Music can also be learned by ear. The Royal National Institute for the Blind is the only organisation in the UK currently producing music in Braille and it has hosted symposia to explore how music can be transcribed onto audio tape for blind and partially sighted people who cannot read Braille.

ROGER FIRMAN, MUSIC SERVICES MANAGER,
ROYAL NATIONAL INSTITUTE FOR THE BLIND, LONDON.

My father, who was blind from birth, was a church organist and choirmaster for 30 years. He would spend hours each night learning a particular score from Braille books, and checking it on his piano until he was note perfect. All musical works, from a simple hymn to Handel's Messiah, were processed in this manner.   R. THOMPSON, KIRKCUDBRIGHT.

In 1958, I taught the first movement of the Schumann piano concerto, note by note, to a blind musician because he had a concert engagement and could not get the Braille music score in time. He mastered it within a week.   ANNETTE SAVILLE, LONDON NW4.

756: Is Britain, with a population of 57 million in 94,249 square miles, the most densely populated country in Europe?

The present population density of Great Britain and Northern Ireland is

613 people per square mile which is the sixth highest in Europe. Monaco is the most densely populated country in Europe with a density of 49,520 people per square mile, followed by Vatican City, whose 802 citizens get a rating of 4,717 people per square mile. We then have Malta with 2,901 per square mile, The Netherlands with 95 per square mile and finally, just ahead of us, Belgium with 84 per square mile. Gibraltar, a colony rather than a country, has a density of 11,860 people per square mile, which would make it the second highest in Europe. Population densities per square mile for the constituent parts of the UK are England 962; Wales 349; Northern Ireland 286 and Scotland 162. The lowest population densities in Europe are Iceland with just six people per square mile, followed by Russia with 22.

JULIET THOMPSON, WORLD ALMANAC AND BOOK OF FACTS, MACMILLAN, LONDON.

757: When Buddy Holly was killed in a plane crash in 1959, his wife was expecting a baby. What happened to his offspring?

Some weeks after the plane crash in which Buddy was killed, his wife, Maria Elena Holly, suffered a miscarriage and lost her baby. She did, however, re-marry and became Maria Elena Diaz. Although married for many years she is now divorced, which she has attributed to never being able to let Buddy's memory go. Her new family now broken up, Maria travels the world as a very enthusiastic ambassador for her first husband's music.

MARC ROBINSON, LEAD SINGER WITH BOOTLEG BUDDY AND THE CRICKETS, TIPTREE, ESSEX.

758: In what year was the present AD/BC calendar introduced? Who implemented it and why – and in which countries?

It's something of a fluke that most of the world now uses Christian-era dating. In AD525, an influential monk called Dionysius Exiguus was given the task of constructing a mathematical table from which the date of Easter for any year could be calculated. The system required a base date and Dionysius decided it should be the birth of Christ. He had to set this in a recognised framework and chose the Roman *ab urbe* condita (AUC) listing years since Rome was founded. He concluded that Christ was born in 753 AUC, making the first year of the newly devised Easter cycle the Roman year 754 AUC. It didn't occur to anyone at the time that a new era had been inaugurated. It was not until 1087 that the Roman Church finally officially adopted the Anno Domini (AD) designation of the Christian era. But the Venerable Bede had already welcomed the idea and introduced AD dating in England in the 8th century. Anterior dating, designated Before Christ (BC) did not begin until the Reformation in the 16th century.

S. W. WHITFIELD, NEW ROMNEY, KENT.

759: Why, when human skin constantly dies and renews itself, do tattoos remain?

Human skin has four layers, the outermost of which is the epidermis, which is constantly renewing itself. Beneath the epidermis is the basal layer, the part which renews the cells which migrate to the surface in a continuous process. Below the basal layer is the papillary dermis and finally the reticular dermis.

In the tattooing process, the needle pierces the epidermis and carries small particles of colour to the papillary dermis and reticular dermis. These particles are thereby fixed to the spot and the tattoo remains impervious to anything except injury or alteration which could obliterate these deeper layers.   LOUIS MOLLOY, UK TATTOO ARTIST OF THE YEAR, MIDDLETON, MANCHESTER.

760: Did convicted criminals ever wear the broad arrow uniforms depicted in old films? If so, where and when?

Broad arrow uniforms were issued to prisoners who had committed serious felonies and were held in government prisons in Britain from the early 19th century. Prisoners held in local authority jails did not wear these uniforms, but whatever design the local jail favoured. Variations included blue at Holloway, bright scarlet, grey, or even yellow and brown stripes at others. The broad arrow mark denoted prison clothing as 'Property of HM Government' and was stamped on a wide number of government items. It is still in use as a benchmark on Ordnance Survey maps and could be seen until recently stamped on Ministry of Defence pencils. In at least one prison, the soles of the prisoners' shoes were also nailed with the broad arrow design to help in tracking them down on escape. When local authority and government prisons were combined in 1878, the broad arrow uniform was retained for the most dangerous prisoners and this regime remained until 1921.

DR PETER DAVIES, CURATOR, PRISON SERVICE MUSEUM, NEWBOLD REVEL, RUGBY.

761: Leeds United nearly did it in the 1993/94 season, but has any league football team played a full season unbeaten at home while failing to win away in the league?

Five English clubs have come close to achieving this dubious footballing honour but none has actually done it. The most recent was Gateshead, back in the 1935/36 season. The others were: Blackburn in 1933/34; Northampton in 1932/33; Orient in 1913/14; and Grimsby in 1903/04. In all five cases the clubs were undefeated at home but won two of their away games. In Scotland, however, Ayr FC in 1900/01 and Port Glasgow

Athletic in 1894/95 were both unbeaten at home and yet failed to win a single away game. In both these instances, though, the season consisted of only 18 games.

RAY SPILLER, SECRETARY, ASSOCIATION OF FOOTBALL STATISTICIANS, BASILDON, ESSEX.

762: Excerpt From A Teenage Opera was a hit in the Sixties. Were any further excerpts issued or, for that matter, was the entire Teenage Opera ever finished?

The Teenage Opera was the brainchild of songwriter Mark Wirtz who enlisted the help of Keith West, lead singer of the group Tomorrow who recorded the original version of Nazareth's hit My White Bicycle. Together, they wrote Excerpt From A Teenage Opera under the pseudonyms Philwit and Hopkins. Recorded by West, this tale of the life and death of a village grocer was a big hit, reaching Number Two in the charts in 1967. Continuing the theme of songs about ordinary people, West released a follow-up second extract, Sam, about an engine driver but this was only a minor success, reaching Number 38. At this point, West decided to end his association with the Teenage Opera. Undaunted, Wirtz released a third extract, He's Our Dear Old Weatherman, under his own name but it was a flop. The record-buying public had clearly lost interest and the idea for the opera was quietly allowed to die.

HOWARD PIZZEY, STAPLEHURST, KENT.

763: Who hijacked the word gay and applied it to homosexuals?

The word gay was 'hijacked' considerably earlier than most people imagine. When it came into wide circulation in the late Sixties it had already been used in its contemporary context for several decades. In his Dictionary Of The British And American Underworld, Eric Partridge defines a 'gay cat' as 'a homosexual boy', tracing his source to Noel Ersine's Glossary Of Prison Slang, published in America in 1933. I have traced this meaning of the word as far back as 1929 in Noel Coward's lyrics for Green Carnation from the operetta, Bitter Sweet. A quartet of young men sing: 'Faded boys, jaded boys, come what may Art is our inspiration And as we are the reason for the Nineties being gay We all wear a green carnation.' Such blooms were worn by Oscar Wilde and his circle of male friends as a way of proclaiming their homosexuality to other initiates. Language transmutes, grows and becomes richer. Words can't be hijacked, but they can change.

PETER BURTON, FEATURES AND REVIEWS EDITOR, GAY TIMES, BRIGHTON.

764: What is the area like at the top of Everest? Does it go to a point or is there a few feet of flat ground?

The actual summit, which I sat on in 1993, was a horizontal bank of snow about the size of three average dining tables. There was room for six of us to stand or sit but not much more. One end overhung a 9,000-ft drop into Tibet and when Ramon Blanco (the oldest man ever to climb Everest) started backing towards it to get a shot of five of us, we all screamed at him to come back. If the overhang had fallen under his weight we would never have found his body. The view was astounding – over the whole of Nepal and into India to the south; northwards we could see well over a hundred miles into Tibet. In winter the summit may be pointed, flat or sloping; the winds are so strong that the snow there is always changing shape and therefore changing the height of the mountain as well.   GRAHAM HOYLAND, MEMBER OF THE 1993 DAILY MAIL/HIMALAYAN KINGDOMS EVEREST EXPEDITION.

765: Why is the actors' waiting room in the theatre always referred to as the Green Room?

The term 'green room', first referred to in Thomas Shadwell's play The True Widow (1678), has been used since at least the Restoration. The original green room may have been in the Theatre Royal, Drury Lane, built to Christopher Wren's design in 1674; it has been suggested it may have been painted or hung with green but the Oxford Companion To The Theatre says green room is merely a corruption of 'scene room.' 'The green' has long been an actor's term for the stage, probably because of the 'tragic carpet', a green cloth which, from the 17th to 19th centuries, traditionally covered the stage during a tragedy.
          MARTIN HARRISON, AUTHOR: THEATRE: A BOOK OF WORDS, MANCHESTER.

This comes from Cockney rhyming slang: stage – greengage, shortened to 'green.' To this day, more mature artistes will leave the dressing room saying 'see you on the green.'   MARRION WELLS, HASTINGS, SUSSEX.

766: Who and what were spivs seen in and around London during the war, and when did they disappear?

The word 'spiv' originated in the 1890s about 50 years before its World War II heyday when it was used by racecourse gangs of crooks and conmen. It is probably derived from the word 'spiffing', meaning smartly dressed or dandified. By 1940 the 'spiv' was firmly established as a flashily-dressed, shady, fast-talker, making money by selling items such as chocolate, nylon stockings, petrol or anything which was rationed, on the wartime black market. Dad's Army's Private Walker is the epitome of the type. Spivs haven't gone: there seem to be more Arthur Daleys and Del Trotters around than ever these days.   GEORGE FIRMAN, ROTHERHITHE, LONDON.

The abbreviation 'spiv' stood for Suspected Person or Itinerant Vagrant, noted in police records. They were found everywhere, not only London.
R. SANDBACH, STOCKPORT.

Spivs were characters at the opposite end of the scale from important, high-ranking establishment figures, referred to as 'VIPs.' The term 'SPIV' is a reversal of 'VIPS,' characterising the difference between low life and Very Important People.   E. T. DAVIS, GARSTON, HERTS.

767: The claim has been made for Blackpool, Godalming, Lynton, and Douglas but which was the first to have electric street lighting?

According to the Electricity Council, electric lighting in the UK started in December 1878 when street lighting trials were held at the same time in Westgate-on-Sea and London. In September 1879 electric 'illuminations' were first tried in Blackpool using six lamps. From 1881 on, continuous use of electric street lighting began in a number of places: London, Cockermouth, Godalming and Chesterfield. Chesterfield had a valid claim at the time to being the only town in the country wholly illuminated by electricity. Godalming was the first town to combine public and private lighting in a commercial venture.
DR ALAN WILSON, CURATOR OF ENERGY DIRECT,
MUSEUM OF SCIENCE AND INDUSTRY, MANCHESTER.

Godalming was one of the first towns in Britain to be lit by electricity, in 1881, despite critics claiming horses would be frightened, insects would be attracted to the town and human eyes would be at risk. The innovation was powered by the water wheel of John Pullman's mill and attracted visitors to the town in the evenings to see the lights. Neither the town council nor the contractors had permission to dig up the roads so the cables had to be laid in the gutters. There were frequent power failures and the lights always fused after heavy rain. After four years Godalming abandoned its 25s-apiece electric lights and reverted to gas.
AUDREY SIMMONS, WELWYN, HERTS.

768: What is the origin of the horrid terms 'soccer' and 'rugger' for the two forms of what is commonly known as football?

Use of the suffix '-er' to create nicknames for Association and Rugby football was started by pupils at Rugby School around 1863 and passed into general Oxford University slang about 1875. From Oxford the words came into common use throughout the country. This style of slang was used to make familiar formations on words by curtailing them and adding '-er' to the remaining part. Earliest instances include 'footer' (1863), 'socker' (1891), 'rugger' (1893) and 'togger' (1897). The use of '-er' continues today in a limited way. In the Twenties almost every word uttered at Oxford was changed: Mr Gladstone became 'Gladders', breakfast became 'brekker' etc. Several words made up then have remained in the language, a good example being 'bedsitter' for a student's room.

EDMUND WEINER, OXFORD ENGLISH DICTIONARY, OXFORD.

769: Is it true that the Waffen SS attempted to form a British SS unit from PoWs?

Originally known as the Legion of St George, the Britische Freikorps was formed mainly from Mosley's blackshirts and British ex-servicemen with divided loyalties due to German parentage. The concept was originated by John Amery, disowned son of Leo Amery, wartime Secretary of State for India and Burma. John Amery had long been a Nazi sympathiser and, in 1942, began making broadcasts from Berlin. By 1943 he had persuaded the head of the SS, Himmler, to allow him to set up an anti-Bolshevik 'British Free Corps.' He began recruiting at the British internee camp at St Denis before attempting to persuade British PoWs to join. One of the earliest recruits was 'Frank Wood' (all members used pseudonyms) a former pharmacist who wrote a recruiting leaflet distributed at many PoW camps. At least 300 took up the offer of a trip to Berlin but many of these were ordered to join by their own officers to gather information. Only 58 became full members of the unit, most of these were caught at the end of the war, court martialled, and imprisoned. Amery was tried for treason in London and was hanged in December 1945.   MATT MANNERS, ABBEY WOOD, LONDON.

In November 1945, I was instructed to attend the trial of John Heller-Cooper who was charged with treason at the Old Bailey. I recall the unfolding of the prosecution case by the Attorney General, Sir Hartley Shawcross, alleging the visits of Heller-Cooper to PoW camps, attempting to recruit British prisoners for the Freikorps. Heller-Cooper was found guilty and sentenced to death by Lord Justice Oliver.

COL. BRIAN B. G. JONES, WEYMOUTH, DORSET.

I was a PoW of the Germans from June 1940 to May 1945 and did not hear of the Waffen SS trying to form a British SS from PoWs. While I was in Stalag XXIB, at Fort Reich, Posen, attempts were made by the Germans to enlist PoWs in what they called the 'British Free Corps', offering almost complete freedom and excellent accommodation. To my knowledge there were no recruits. In 1943 we were informed that Corps members were outside the camp gates, wishing to talk to the prisoners. They were told by the assembled PoWs that if they ventured inside the camp gates their safety could not be vouched for, so they made a quick retreat.

W. McBAIN, LONDON W3.

I was taken prisoner at Dunkirk and spent almost five years at Stalag XXA, in Torun, Poland, and the last two years in Fort XIII which was surrounded by a moat. One morning we found leaflets everywhere, supposedly dropped by Allied planes, asking us to join the British Corps to be used against the Russians on the Eastern Front. They were supposedly signed by the British High Command. But the Germans who had made the delivery made the mistake of depositing some of the leaflets in places where they couldn't possibly have come from aircraft. We even found stones on some of them to stop them blowing away!

TOM WOODWARD, TILSDOWN, GLOUCS.

An attempt was made to form as SS unit from volunteer PoWs. Named the Britisches Freikorps, or Legion of St George, it never consisted of more than two platoons and saw no action. Its value was more for propaganda than military use: the men caused the Germans headaches with their demands for women and drink. The Germans eventually formed units of Waffen ('fighting') SS from most occupied nations, including France, Belgium and the Soviet states. PoW volunteers helped form units of Indian and Cossack SS but most were torn to pieces on the Russian front. Surviving members were returned to their respective nations for punishment when the war ended. MICHAEL MURPHY, SOUTH CROYDON, SURREY.

770: Is it true that a German plane bombed Plymouth on September 2, 1939, the day before war was declared?

The city was rife with rumours and there was great military activity but there is no evidence of a bombing raid at that time. As elsewhere in the country, air-raid sirens wailed over Plymouth within minutes of Chamberlain's broadcast announcing the war but the all-clear soon followed. Those sirens eventually signalled the death knell of the old city. The first bombs fell on Plymouth in July 1940 and by the end of October, Plymouth had been hit in 21 raids. The King and Queen visited to give moral support on March 20, 1941, and there was another alert before they left. That night and the next night, the heart of Plymouth was wiped out with 336 civilians killed and 20,000 properties destroyed or damaged. Then, for five nights at the end of April, bombers completed the destruction of central Plymouth, flattening Devonport and killing 590 civilians. Many more were injured and an unknown number were lost without trace. Some 1,500 dwellings were destroyed or damaged beyond repair and another 15,000 damaged. By VE Day, May 8 1945 Plymouth had endured 59 bombing attacks, 1,172 civilians had been killed and 4,448 injured. Apart from the two main shopping centres, two guildhalls, a theatre, six hotels, eight cinemas, 26 schools, 41 churches and 100 pubs, 3,754 houses had gone and another 18,389 were in need of major repair. All told, 72,102 houses were damaged. So many people had been forced to find homes outside the city that the population was down from 208,000 to 127,000.   CRISPIN GILL, PLYMOUTH.

I was 11 at the time and on holiday at my uncle's house, opposite the gates of Devonport Naval barracks. On the day in question, a German Heinkel 111 flew low over the barracks, so low that I could see the crew members. No bombs were dropped. The anti-aircraft guns on the barracks could be seen following the flight but did not open fire.
                                        RAY HALES, BARNSTABLE, DEVON.

771: Why is the Cornish village of London Apprentice so named?

London Apprentice, Cornwall, just south of St Austell (pop: 90) was first recorded as a village in 1747. The name comes from a village pub which took it from a contemporary ballad, The Honour of an Apprentice of London Wherein He Declared His Matchless Manhood and Brave Adventures Done by Him in Turkey and by What Means He Married the King's Daughter of that Same Country. The pub no longer exists.
                        DR OLIVER PADEL, CORNWALL RECORD OFFICE, TRURO.

According to the book, Roseland, Mevagissey Driveabout, a Cornwall Heritage Project, the name of this Cornish village is based on the story of a young lad who came from London to Polgooth to be apprenticed to a blacksmith. He worked hard and succeeded his master but was always known as 'the London apprentice.'   CHRISTINE HINDS, ST AUSTELL, CORNWALL.

772: What are the regulations regarding ramps from the roadway across pavements to the front of houses? Does a ramp give a householder parking rights to the area of roadway in front of the ramp?

Nobody has an automatic right to park on the highway outside his or her property. However, if another driver parks obstructing entry or exit from the drive, then the resident has the right to complain to the police. Ramps from the roadway and parking rights on any road they lead to are subject to borough by-laws and need permission from the local authority.
                        LYNN ACKROYD, STOCKPORT METROPOLITAN BOROUGH.

773: Who holds the title for youngest Prime Minister of Britain, Tony Blair or Pitt the younger?

The title 'Prime Minister', meaning the monarch's principal or first minister, has been an acknowledged term only since 1878, was given a royal warrant as a title only in 1905 and has its first statutory mention in 1917. Before this, the role of Prime Minister was generally known as First Lord of the Treasury. So the youngest person officially recognised as Prime Minister is indeed Tony Blair, born on May 6, 1953, elected at the head of a Labour General Election victory on May 1, 1997, at the age of 43 years and 360 days. In doing so he upstaged his predecessor John Major, who took over from Margaret Thatcher as Prime Minister on November 28, 1990, aged 47 years and 244 days. However, examining the records of those who performed the function of Prime Minister, without necessarily holding the title, the youngest by far is William Pitt (Pitt the Younger), born in 1759, who became Prime Minister on December 19, 1783, aged 24 years and 205 days. He could actually have been Prime Minister at the age of 23 but declined the earlier offer.

JULIAN POWELL, GRAVESEND, KENT.

774: What is the origin of the lullaby Rock-a-bye-baby? Is there a sinister story behind it?

One possibility is that a pilgrim youth on the Mayflower was influenced by the way Red Indians hung their birch bark cradles on branches of trees and so wrote the words of the song. But the most likely derivation comes from a nursery song published in 1797 called Oh Can Ye Sew Cushions. The second verse goes: 'I've placed my cradle on yon holly top, and aye as the wind blows my cradle did rock, Oh hush a bye baby...' The song's author is unknown but there doesn't appear to be a sinister origin. IONA OPIE, CO-AUTHOR, OXFORD DICTIONARY OF NURSERY RHYMES, HANTS.

This lullaby is in fact not Rock a By Baby but Hush a By Baby, a nursery song from about 1820 which goes: 'Rock a By Baby, Puss is a Lady, Mousey has gone to the mill. She'll come by and by, So hush a by baby lie still.' According to the 1951 Oxford Dictionary of Nursery Rhymes, Hush a By Baby is a warning to the proud and ambitious who climb so high that they generally fall in the end. Some imaginative minds have stretched this to ancient Eygpt, the baby being Horus etc.

PAUL LEGGETT, NORWICH, NORFOLK.

This nursery rhyme was a political lampoon against James II from a time when open criticism of the king was forbidden. After the death of his first wife, James II married a young Catholic princess and was thought to be taking instruction in that faith. When their son was born ('on the tree top' – the highest baby in the land) the Protestant parliament invited William of Orange and his wife Mary, James's elder daughter to invade England and oust James from the throne. The Dutch fleet waited for the east wind to bring them over ('when the wind blows, the cradle will rock'). The invasion was joined by a Protestant uprising ('when the bough breaks, the cradle will fall'). 'Down will come baby, cradle and all' refers to the throne and James's rule. James sent his wife and small son, later The Old Pretender, to France and secretly joined them.

A. DOWNES, EAST CARLETON, NORWICH.

775: Shareholders have enjoyed large profits from privatisations and stock market booms. The money must come from somewhere. Who are the losers?

People who buy and sell shares can make a profit when the price of their shares increases after they have bought them. In this case, the losers are those who have sold their shares for less than their real value or less than they could have if they had held on to them longer. Most people who bought shares in privatised industries found their shares went up rapidly after buying them; the losers were the Government and, therefore, the taxpayer. Shareholders can also enjoy a higher payout when the company they hold shares in pays out more of its profits in dividends (payments to shareholders) and so keeps less for investment. The dividend share increased from 23 per cent in 1985 to 61 per cent in 1992 (TUC calculations based on Central Statistical Office data). The loser here is the long-term future of the company and potentially any employees who may lose jobs because of an investment squeeze. Overall, there does not have to be a loser for everyone who enjoys a higher profit. In most years the cake gets bigger as wealth is created and companies grow.

BOB LANDERS, TUC, LONDON.

776: How is it we no longer see wheel-tappers at work when trains pull into stations?

Today's train wheels are built to a far higher standard of engineering and don't need the regular checks required in the past. In the early years, train wheels consisted of an inner wheel, sometimes made of wood on carriages, with a hard steel 'tyre' around the outside. The wheeltapper hit the wheels and could tell by the 'ring' whether they were in good condition. By the late Fifties and early Sixties, wheels were marked by a series of four white blocks to show if the wheel and tyre were out of line so the checks could be done by shunting or platform staff. Modern trains have one-piece 'monoblock' wheels made of forged steel, though the heavy demands made on them in terms of running speeds and miles travelled still necessitate regular and thorough examination, now done with ultra-sound scanning and hi-tec wheel profiling equipment when trains are overhauled.   BOB FENTON, BRITISH RAILWAYS BOARD, LONDON.

777: What celebrations were there at the end of the first millennium?

The word millennium was not used in the way we understand it (a period of 1,000 years) at the turn of the 10th and 11th centuries. The Oxford English Dictionary says our present meaning of millennium became current only in the 18th century; before that it described the period of 1,000 years during which Christ would reign in person after the Second Coming. A thousand years ago there was no universal system of dating and no standard way of describing the days December 31, 999 to January 1, 1000. In parts of the British Isles it was customary for the educated and legal classes to use regnal years which means that around the year 1000 people would have thought of themselves as living, for example, in the 22nd year of the reign of King Ethelred (known as 'the Unready.') It's very difficult to determine how, if at all, the general populace would have classified the years at that time and people would have had no conception of the significance of what to us would have been the end of the first millennium. Any contemporary accounts of celebrations or commemorations are unlikely to have been documented. In short it seems that the first real millennium celebrations are the ones coming up at the end of this century.   DR BART SMITH, THE BRITISH LIBRARY, LONDON.

There is documentary evidence that some people sold their homes and made the pilgrimage to Jerusalem so they could be in the Holy City when the trumpet sounded for the Day of Judgement. At home, thousands spent the last night of the century sitting and praying on hill tops to await the final dawn, and Christ's coming. But when the sun rose, the birds sang in the trees and it was just another day.
                              C. BRACEGIRDLE, SALE, CHESHIRE.

778: How can a tiny frail plant force its way upwards through a tarmac surface?

Small annual weeds, such as the hairy bittercress and thale cress can live in the cracks between tarmac particles, anchored in accumulated dust and organic debris. Since tarmac is not solid, once the roots of small plants start penetrating it, water can seep down and the surface start breaking up, especially in frosty weather. Once started, the process accelerates and suitable homes for larger plants are created. Tarmac can, however, be penetrated from below by tree suckers and vigorous shoots from plants which spread underground. Japanese knotweed and certain bamboos are very good at this. Thin or poor-quality tarmac laid over soil in which the roots of perennial weeds such as dandelions or bindweed have been left is also prone to penetration. ADRIAN WHITELEY, BOTANY DEPARTMENT, THE ROYAL HORTICULTURAL SOCIETY, WOKING, SURREY.

779: Was the large table in the hall of Gray's Inn made from the wood of Drake's ship?

The hall of Gray's Inn contains a large screen known as the Armada Screen and it is suggested that the timber used was presented to the Inn by Lord Howard of Effingham, commander-in-chief of the English fleet at the time of the Spanish Armada in 1588 and was taken from the frame of a Spanish galleon. There is no proof of this though some of the wood is certainly Spanish chestnut and carbon dating tests have shown that it does date from the right period. There is no evidence to suggest that the table in Gray's Inn comes from any ship of Drake's.

DAVID MACHIN, UNDER TREASURER, THE HONOURABLE SOCIETY OF GRAY'S INN, LONDON.

The table made of the timber of Sir Francis Drake's ship The Golden Hind stands not in the hall of Gray's Inn but in the Middle Temple. It's a ceremonial table, used by the Inn for calling students to the bar. Known as 'Drake's cupboard', it measures 6ft by 4ft and was constructed sometime in the late 16th century from wood given to the Middle Temple by Drake, himself a member of the Middle Temple, after it was brought to dry dock at Deptford for repairs following the defeat of the Armada.

BILL KEOGH, HEAD PORTER, THE HONOURABLE SOCIETY OF MIDDLE TEMPLE, LONDON.

780: What is the origin of the saying 'born with a silver spoon in his or her mouth'?

This saying is associated with the idea of being born into good luck or hereditary wealth. It derives from the Victorian tradition of godparents giving a gift of a silver spoon, or set of spoons. The child who is born with a silver spoon already in his or her mouth doesn't have to wait until baptism to be blessed with fortune or wealth. A single silver spoon would normally have a figure of one of the apostles on the handle. Occasionally 12 spoons, representing all the apostles, would be given, or four, depicting the four evangelists. Later spoons simply had the name 'Master Spoon' or 'Lady Spoon.' DELIA KINGSTON, DEWSBURY.

781: Who was the original Buggins who had his turn?

This phrase is common slang for the promotion or appointment of somebody either due to their length of service where merit or qualifications are not considered. The saying gained popularity in the civil service, a profession well known for this sort of practice. The first recorded use of this disparaging term is credited to Admiral Fisher (later First Sea Lord) in 1901. The name 'Buggins' is not thought to be based on a real person but was used because it sounded dull.   THOMAS DERBYSHIRE, LINCOLN.

782: What is the origin and meaning of the expression 'Beware of Greeks bearing gifts'?

This is a loose translation of the famous line 49 from Book II of Virgil's Aeneid: 'Timeo Danaos et dona ferentes,' meaning 'I fear the Greeks, even when they bring gifts.' In his epic of the fall of Troy, Virgil has the Trojan priest Laocoon say these words of warning when the Trojans are considering dragging into their city the wooden horse left on the plain by the apparently departed Greeks after a ten-year siege. Unfortunately for Troy, Laocoon was killed by a sea serpent sent by gods favourable to the Greeks before anyone would listen to him. And as everyone knows, the horse turned out to be a far-from-genuine gift to the brave city. It contained a small force of men who, once within the walls, waited for night to fall, left the wooden horse, overpowered the guards and opened the gates of the city to admit the returning Greeks.   JOSH McMURDO, DUNDEE.

783: Why is there a large German cemetery in Cannock, Staffordshire? Our dead are buried in cemeteries where they were killed, so why are German soldiers buried here in large numbers?

High on the heathland plateau of Cannock Chase is the last resting place of almost 5,000 German servicemen who died in both World Wars, the only German military cemetery in Britain. The cemetery, dating from World War I, when the Chase was temporary home to thousands of British and Commonwealth troops as well as German prisoners of war, was laid out by the prisoners. Along with British and New Zealanders from World War I, some 222 Germans were buried in the cemetery, many of whom died as prisoners in the great influenza epidemic of 1918/19. Following World War II, the cemetery was enlarged to accommodate all German servicemen who died in Britain. Some 4,929 bodies were brought to the Chase from other graveyards, including the crews of four Zeppelins shot down between 1914-1918. The new cemetery was consecrated in 1967, since when it has been a destination for many

German visitors. In recent years, further bodies of German pilots have been found and these men, too, have been buried on the Chase.

KEN PEDEN, VALLEY HERITAGE CENTRE, HEDNESFORD, STAFFS.

There was a large World War I PoW camp in the area and before the prisoners could be repatriated, the camp was hit by the virulent flu epidemic which swept the country in late 1918 to early 1919. Conditions in such a camp were ideal for the spread of the disease. It's heartbreaking to walk along row after row of graves and see that, almost without exception, every death occurred between December 1918 and March 1919 – they survived the horrors of war and succumbed to illness with freedom in sight. Adjacent to this cemetery is a similar British one telling the same sad story.

S. H. YOUNG, MICKLEOVER, DERBY.

784: What are the books between the two boxes behind the mace in the House of Commons? Do they have any significance to the running of Parliament?

The books between the despatch boxes are recent volumes of the Public General Acts, that is, the laws that Parliament has passed over the past decade. They are very relevant indeed to the work of the House, especially where an existing Act may be repealed or amended by a Bill the House is considering.

DR CHRIS POND, HEAD OF PUBLIC INFORMATION OFFICE, HOUSE OF COMMONS.

785: Which bird flies the highest and what is the uppermost sighting of any bird?

A combination of radar, birds colliding with planes and direct observation shows that most birds fly below 500ft. During migration, some will fly higher to take advantage of winds but they usually stay below 5,000ft. Some birds may be forced to fly high – bar-headed geese have been seen flying over the Himalayas at altitudes of about 29,000ft. One of the highest known sightings of birds over the UK concerns a flock of whooper swans seen by a pilot over the Inner Hebrides at 27,000ft. Their altitude was confirmed by radar which also recorded their speed at 86mph. The world record is held by a Ruppell's griffon vulture which collided with an aircraft at 37,000ft over the Ivory Coast, West Africa. The plane landed safely but the bird was identified from feathers.

CHRIS HARBARD, RSPB, SANDY, BEDS.

786: What happened to the vanished Roman IXth Legion?

The history of the IXth Legion is more obscure than that of other legions but we do know that it was not destroyed in present-day Scotland around AD117, as proposed by Rosemary Sutcliff in her delightful story The Eagle Of The Ninth. The IXth landed in Britain with three other legions for the invasion of AD43 and inscriptions and other archaeological evidence place its headquarters at what is now Lincoln until around AD71, then at York until AD122, and near Carlisle for a few years thereafter. We now believe the IXth was transferred from Britain to Lower Germany some time before AD130 and subsequently posted to the East, where it may have been destroyed by the Parthians in AD161. A list in Rome of all the legions of the Roman Army which can be dated to the period AD161-180 makes no mention of the IXth, suggesting that by then something very drastic had happened to it. The mystery of the IXth Legion was celebrated in verse some years ago: 'The fate of the IXth still engages, The minds of nitwits and of sages. But that problem, one fears, Will be with us for years, And for ages and ages and ages.'

H. J. P. ARNOLD, LEGIO SECUNDA AUGUSTO, HAVANT, HANTS.

787: Our son Kevin was born on March 5th, 1957, Pancake Tuesday. His birthday has never fallen on Pancake Tuesday since. When will it fall on Pancake Tuesday again?

Shrove Tuesday (Pancake Day) and March 5 have not coincided since 1957 when Kevin was born. The next time this will happen will be in 2019 when Kevin will be 62 years old. Shrove Tuesday will also be on March 5 in 2030, 2041 and 2052, then not again in that century. It always comes 41 days before Easter, a movable celebration based around the first Sunday following the first full moon on or after the vernal equinox (March 21). KAY GOODALL, CHARLES LETTS DIARIES, DALKEITH, MIDLOTHIAN.

788: Why did young children like those in the Railway Children wear red flannel petticoats?

Many young girls and adult women in Victorian times wore red petticoats to keep themselves warm. Petticoats were made of flannel and it was believed at the time that red flannel was warmer than cream flannel. Red flannel petticoats were common throughout the second half of the 19th century when ladies commonly wore more than one petticoat. They wore white cotton or linen ones next to the skin with another, warmer one – often red – over the top of it.

RICHARD ROBSON, COSTUME COLLECTION, CASTLE HOWARD, YORKS.

789: Does the turning off of lights to save power apply to fluorescent lighting, or is it better left on because the starting charge is heavy?

Many people are under the mistaken impression that it's better to leave a fluorescent tube on all the time because the energy required when switching it on is so high. When a tube is switched on there is a momentary increase in electric current which can be several times greater than the running current, but it only lasts a fraction of a second and switching fluorescent tubes off when not required will certainly save energy. However, the tube may fail prematurely if switched on and off every few minutes. GRAHAM SKELDON, OSRAM LIGHTING, WEMBLEY, MIDDLESEX.

790: Apart from being the Queen, what was her name and where was Sheba?

Known in the Bible as the powerful Queen who visited Solomon in Jerusalem (I Kings X), the Queen of Saba (translated in Hebrew as Sheba) is known to the Arabs as Balkis. She is thought to have ruled, around the 10th century BC, an area roughly corresponding to modern-day Yemen, from a capital known as Marib. The Saba nation had highly advanced engineering skills, exemplified by the building of a large dam, and were thought to be excellent traders, controlling most of the trade around the Red Sea and Indian Ocean and dealing with nations as far north as Syria. JOSEPH CHEVELSON, DERBY.

791: When was the very last farthing minted and what was the final date that they were legal tender?

Farthings first appeared in 1279 in the reign of Edward I. He ordered a round farthing after the common practice of giving change from a silver penny was to simply cut it into halves for halfpennies or quarters to give 'four things' (farthings). The last farthing was minted at the Royal Mint, then near Tower Hill, in 1956 and the final date when they were legal tender was proclaimed by the Queen under Section 11 of the Coinage Act, 1870, as being December 31, 1960.

DEREK SLARK, ROYAL MINT, LLANTRISANT, MID GLAMORGAN.

South Africa struck them until 1960 and Ireland until 1966.

BRIAN BRINDLE, ACCRINGTON.

792: Would one arrive in Scotland more rapidly by the High Road or the Low Road? Did the composer of The Bonny, Bonny Banks of Loch Lomond have reason to know?

The song refers to the spiritual roads to heaven. Later verses suggest the lovers have parted and will not meet until they reach their final resting place. The High Road is followed by High Church folk while the Low Road is used by those with an evangelical leaning. Nonconformist Scottish churches would naturally find the Low Road quicker.

PAUL DAVIES, BRITISH ASSOCIATION OF BARBERSHOP SINGERS, CAMBRIDGE.

In 1745, Bonnie Prince Charlie was in retreat from England and some of his wounded had to be left behind in Carlisle where they fell into English hands. The song refers to two of them, one to be released and the other to be executed at the same hour. According to Celtic belief, the spirit of the dead prisoner, travelling by the 'Low Road' back to his birthplace would reach Scotland before his comrade, who would have to trudge many miles there by the 'High Road' of the living.

J. M. GRAHAM, STANMORE, MIDDLESEX.

Loch Lomond was composed by a MacGregor, a native of Glen Endrick, south east of Loch Lomond, under sentence of death in Carlisle Castle in 1746. It represents a Celtic belief that the ghosts of the slain travelled under earth to haunt the place dearest in memory.

D. F. McGREGOR, ST ANDREWS, FIFE.

793: How did the triple jump originate in modern international athletics?

References to multiple jumps go back in the days of the ancient Greeks and a Spartan chap called Chionis is recorded as having jumped a tremendous distance though the number of jumps he used isn't known. During the 15th and 16th centuries multiple jump events were popular at local events and fairs, particularly in Germany, and most comprised three hops. By the 18th and 19th centuries a form of multiple jumping was popular in Scotland and Ireland. Three jumps were usual though in some instances up to five jumps were used. The event became very popular in Greece in the 19th century and when the first Olympic Games were held in 1896 it was included. American James Connolly was the first winner of the Olympic event, becoming the first ever modern Olympic gold medallist because the triple jump (then known as the hop, step and jump) was the first event finished during the Games. The event had no tight rules until the Twenties and its name was changed from hop, step, and jump to triple jump in the Fifties without any significant change to the rules. STAN GREENBERG, BRITISH ATHLETICS FEDERATION HONORARY STATISTICIAN, FRIERN BARNET, LONDON.

794: Why can't I record Teletext?

Most domestic VCRs will not record Teletext because the text is broadcast in the first 20 or so scan lines of the 625 lines which send the pictures. These 20 lines were originally left blank in the early days when television sets needed to settle down between the end of one scan (picture) and the next. As TV sets improved this problem disappeared and, rather than cause difficulties for existing owners, broadcasters use the spare lines for extra services, including Teletext. Most video recorders still use the top 20 lines to re-synchronise their mechanisms between recording each picture. They use a mechanical scanning process to achieve the necessary head-to-tape speeds and so cannot record continuously enough to capture the spare lines. Only a small proportion of video recorders presently in use can show Teletext.

CHRIS HALL, LECTURER, BBC ENGINEERING TRAINING, WOOD NORTON, WORCS.

795: What is the origin of the Three Wise Monkeys, Hear No Evil, See No Evil, and Speak No Evil?

They are based on an old Japanese pun. The Japanese for monkey is *saru* or *zaru* and *zaru* is also a negative verb ending. The saying *mizaru, kikazaru, iwazaru* (one who sees nothing, one who hears nothing, one who says nothing) can thus be illustrated by three monkeys in appropriate attitudes. Since *mi* also means three, *mizaru* can mean three monkeys. The best known set of these figures in Japan is the charming painted woodcarving at the Toshogu Shrine at Nikko, north of Tokyo.

GRAHAM HEALEY, SCHOOL OF EAST ASIAN STUDIES, UNIVERSITY OF SHEFFIELD.

796: What is the 'gunge' used on programmes like Noel's House Party made of?

It consists of a thickening powder which forms a non-sticky, paste-like substance when mixed with water. Its trade name is Natrusol and a non-toxic dye is used with different colours each week, depending on who is under the tank and the clothes they are wearing. It is all mixed together with hot water which has reached a comfortably warm temperature by the time the gunge is used. We start mixing on Saturday afternoon and make about 12 gallons for one good gungeing. Careful filling of the header tank just before the show ensures multiple colours don't mix. The gunge is released by an electric button just behind the stage, pressed by one of the visual effects team. We haven't missed yet.

STEVE LUCAS, BBC VISUAL EFFECTS DESIGNER, TV CENTRE, LONDON.

797: What happens to supermarket foodstuffs not sold by the 'sell by' date?

Very little perishable stock is normally left unsold or unused by the end of its shelf life but if there is any left we must follow the law, which clearly states it should be destroyed. No one wants to see food wasted, least of all supermarket companies. Our policy aims to sell all products several days before the 'use-by' date and our stock ordering system is geared to ensure this happens. We carefully monitor the food ordered for stores and barcode scanning at checkouts helps us identify quantities sold in an hour, day or week and minimise potential wastage. Goods close to their use-by date are reduced in price for sale or may be used in the staff restaurant. With 300 to 500 people working in an average store, much can be consumed.   MICHELLE LEWIS, SAINSBURY HQ, LONDON.

A lot of the food goes to institutions, prisons and other outlets and what's then left often goes to Merchant Navy ships. I was served food which was more than two years past the printed use-by date and, when I complained, became a marked man who was eventually sacked for being a trouble-maker. During the Forties, an advert appeared in a West Country newspaper which stated: 'Five tons of potatoes, fit for pigs or Merchant Seamen.'   J. J. THOMAS, NEWTON ABBOT, DEVON.

798: Whatever happened to Prince Len and Princess Shirl of Hutt River Province, Australia, who had a Buckhurst Hill publican as ambassador and knighted Alan Whicker on one of his travel programmes?

It caused quite a fuss in 1970 when my fellow citizens of Hutt River Province, Princess Shirley and I seceded from the Commonwealth of Australia. It was tough but we worked hard, fought many battles and now have a nation to be proud of. Our 29 square miles (roughly the same size as Hongkong), now has a total citizenship of 13,000 people, though only 30 of them reside in the country. After 24 years, the Australian Government seems to have finally decided it can no longer bully us into being a part of its commonwealth and clashes with the authorities have become less frequent. The infrastructure of our fledgling nation is nearing completion. Our application to the Postal Union should have been accepted by now and a deal with a large Australian Telecommunications company should provide for future needs. We're planning a large 'city of the future' for when our citizens return to our land. I have carried out extensive royal visits to other parts of the world, using my Hutt River Province Passport and was especially delighted to be personally invited to the Vatican. Sadly our UK Ambassador, Reginald Pash, died a few years ago and one of our royal knights passed away in New Guinea. But I, at 71, and Princess Shirley, 69, are in fine form and enjoying meeting the thousands of visitors from all over the world who come to visit every year. My eldest son, Prince Ian, will be able to take the country forward when he takes over. My other six children (three Princes and three Princesses) are all well and our citizens content. Thank you, Britain, for your kind interest in my welfare. On behalf of the people of Hutt River Province I would like to convey my respects to your Queen and good citizens. Should any of you wish to apply for nationality, our committee will be pleased to welcome your applications via Northampton Post Office, Western Australia 6535.

HRH Prince Leonard, Hutt River Province.

799: My grandfather, my father and myself were all born with an extra finger on the left hand. Anne Boleyn had a similar deformity. But this has not recurred in my son or grandsons. Can I assume it has disappeared from our family?

Extra digits are often inherited in the manner described (known as autosomal dominant) where an affected person has a 50-50 chance of passing it on. Sometimes the 'extra digit' appears as a tiny 'nubbin' on the outside of the little finger, which can easily be overlooked. If there are no signs for two generations, it has almost certainly disappeared.

Prof. Marcus Pembrey, Mothercare Professor of Paediatric Genetics, Institute of Child Health, London.

800: Is it true that when a group of Americans bought London Bridge they thought they were getting Tower Bridge?

The first London Bridge was a wooden construction built over the Thames around AD43 by the Romans. The initial stone bridge was constructed in roughly the same location from 1176 onwards and had a great many piers with tall narrow houses on it. However, it was replaced in 1831 by the bridge designed by John Rennie. This bridge was dismantled in 1968 and shipped to Arizona and reconstructed at Lake Havasu. Replacing it is the present London Bridge, which was completed in 1972. When I asked George McCulloch, of the McCulloch Oil Corporation of America, the man who gave the order to buy the bridge, this question, his reply was: 'You don't get to be head of a major corporation by not knowing what you're buying.'

Chris Stevens, bridge master, Tower Bridge, London.

Not the entire London Bridge was shipped to Lake Havasu, only a seven-inch veneer of granite, together with balustrades and parapets. A five-arch reinforced concrete structure forms the main body of the Arizona bridge. The remainder, some 100,000 tons of mainly Cornish and Scottish granite, was stored in Cambridge. I was employed by John Mowlem Ltd, who demolished the old bridge and built the new one, to continue marketing the London Bridge granite after its demolition in the late Sixties and early Seventies. We produced ash trays, book-ends, paperweights, table-lighters and many more products.

DOUGLAS W. RUDDOCK, KINGSBRIDGE, DEVON.

Ordinary Americans clearly thought they were getting Tower Bridge. At Long Beach, California, just after they had purchased the bridge, I overheard an American say: 'We thought we were getting Tower Bridge, but all we got was a lump of concrete.'   MISS J. LONG, GRAVESEND, KENT.

801: In what way, if any, is moon rock different from rocks found on earth?

Rock is rock wherever it's found, but the history of earth and moon is different and the processes which created and shaped the physical and chemical format of rocks show some differences. Earth's atmosphere and radiation belts protect it from bombardment from most outer space material but the rock is affected by weathering and erosion. Moon rock has no protective atmosphere, constantly exposed to radiation and bombardment. Scientists have discovered some chemical differences between moon rock and earth rock, including a great abundance of the lunar isotope Helium-3, not found on earth and used for nuclear fusion. Oxford and Princeton University recently succeeded in achieving a reaction for a second but the ability to create power by nuclear fusion remains decades away. A power station working by nuclear fusion would need one shuttle load of Helium-3 to provide all the energy to power America for a year. Another element found in lunar rock is Ilmenite, which contains large amounts of hydrogen and oxygen, the 'building blocks' of life.   BRIAN WELCH, JOHNSON'S SPACE CENTRE, HOUSTON, TEXAS, USA.

802: How did the pilot's position in an aircraft come to be called the 'cockpit'?

The small enclosed arena used for cock fighting gave rise to this expression. This was literally an open circular pit into which birds were lowered to face each other. The term then applied to other enclosed spaces, including junior officers' quarters on ships and the steering wheel well on sailing vessels. Early fighter aircraft provided cramped space for the pilot which rapidly became known as the cockpit.   NICK MANN, LONDON.

803: Is it true that if you marry on a Saturday, your silver wedding will be on a Tuesday?

Generally yes, with two exceptions. If the marriage takes place, or took place, on a Saturday in January or February of a leap year, the silver wedding anniversary would fall on a Wednesday. If the 25-year-period of marriage spans, or spanned, the beginning of a century which is, or was, an exception to the basic leap year rule – not 2000 – and the marriage takes place, or took place, on a Saturday between March and December, the silver wedding would fall on a Monday.

D. MARTIN STEWART, SUNBURY-ON-THAMES, MIDDX.

It worked in reverse for us. We married on Tuesday, July 8, 1947, to suit my father-in-law who was a publican. Our daughter Elizabeth was married on our silver wedding day on Saturday, July 8, 1972.

OLIVE GREEN, NORTHAMPTON.

The answer is simply yes, unless you marry on a Saturday in a year preceding a leap year when your Silver Wedding will be on Wednesday – as ours was: 1959 to 1984. MRS E. BROUGHTON, CHESTER.

Theoretically the mendiological calendar (from the Latin *mensis,* month and *dies,* day) works on a recurring cycle of seven years, with a regular pattern of dates and days, starting on Sunday, January 1. In practice it is a six-year cycle because the intervening leap year combines two years into one, eg 1994 is year seven, 1995 year one, 1996 years two/three. They move up one day each year, two in leap year after Leap Day. Seven leap years ensure Leap Day covers all the days and including them all takes a 28-year cycle, called a solar cycle, starting at year one, following a leap year: 1989 or 2017. Each year has a fixed position which only recurs every 28 years in the cycle, e.g. 1994, year seven, was the even number year between leap years, its previous such position being in 1966. Thus anyone marrying that year will have their most exact anniversary in 2222, not only on the same day of the week but in the same cycle position too. Incidentally, the proper mendiological anniversary of D-Day is 2000, year 7/1, as in 1944. ROBERT MURRAY, SWINDON, WILTS.

804: Who was the last official holder of the world record for the 100-yard sprint and will he be in the record books for ever?

On August 1, 1976, the International Amateur Athletic Federation listed Ivory Crockett and Houston McTear, both Americans, as having run the 100-yard dash in a world record 9 seconds. Crockett's time was set in Knoxville, Tennessee, on May 11, 1974, and McTear's was achieved at the Winter Park, Florida, on May 9, 1975. However, 1977 saw the deletion from official schedules of all hand-timed sprinting records and those for non-metric distances other than the mile. Thus the IAAF list for August 15, 1977, excluded any reference to the 100 yards. The last female 100-yard record holder was Taiwan's Chi Chieng who recorded 10 seconds at Portland, Oregon, on June 13, 1970.   Tim Mickleburgh, Grimsby, Lincs.

805: What is the origin of the expression OK?

Of all the expressions in the English language the origin of this word has been the most fiercely debated. Most sources agree the first usage of OK in print was in the Boston Morning Post of March 23, 1839, by C. G. Greene as a reference to 'Old Kinderhook', nickname for then President Martin van Buren, taken from the name of his home town. Before this it is thought that the initials OK were used by another President, Andrew Jackson, to stand for 'Orl Korrect.' Jackson may, like many Americans of the time, have purposely mis-spelled words to make them more American or the expression may have been spuriously attributed to him in mockery of his lack of learning. Other theories for the origin of OK include: with African slaves in the US whose mother tongue was Ewe or Wolof, both of which used a word 'okay' to mean good; from the Greek *ola kala,* meaning all is well; from the Finnish *oikea,* meaning correct, from the Scottish Och Aye or from Omnes Korrectes marked on students' test sheets. Some people maintain it originated with early railroad clerk Obadiah Kelly who marked with his initials every parcel that passed through his hands. Any of these explanations may have contributed to the expression becoming so universal but the most plausible reason for its original use is the existence of a similar term in the Choctaw language, a native American tongue.   George Lambatti, Guildford, Surrey.

806: Is it cheaper to boil three pints of water in an electric kettle or on a gas ring?

Gas costs less than 2p per kilowatt-hour while electricity is about 8p per kWh so, generally speaking, it's cheaper to boil water on a gas ring rather than in an electric kettle, but certain points need to be taken into account. The thermal efficiency of an electric kettle is roughly 80% while that of a gas hob is only about 45%. Variations in quality and efficiency of both electric kettles and gas cookers may alter the comparison as will the position of the pan on the cooker and whether it is covered with a lid. The performances we work on are based on new appliances: older models may not be as reliable for making a relative cost comparison.

Dr Marcus Newborough, School of Mechanical Engineering, Bedford.

807: Who invented bar billiards?

Bar billiards, sometimes known as Billiard Russe (Russian Billiards) was played in the cafes and bars of Belgium and northern France in the late Twenties. It is thought to have been a development of the Flemish game *schuiftafel*, still played in northern Belgium, which involves striking flat wooden discs with a cue into holes protected by pegs or skittles on a wooden table. English businessman David Gill came across Billiard Russe while on a walking holiday on the Belgian-French border in the early Thirties. Back in Britain he persuaded billiard table manufacturer Jelks of London to make an attractive and exacting British version of the Belgian table and christened the game Bar Billiards. The first pub to take one of Gill's tables was the Rose And Crown at Elham, near Canterbury, and the game proved so popular that by 1936 the first Bar Billiard League in Britain was organised in Oxford, soon followed by leagues in Reading, Canterbury and High Wycombe. LAURENCE KING, BLANDFORD FORUM, DORSET.

808: Why does Israel take part in the Eurovision Song Contest?

Israel can take part in the Eurovision Song Contest because it is a member of the European Broadcasting Union, which set up the event. There were 30 members of the EBU at first, including the geographically non-European countries Jordan, Libya, Morocco, Israel and Turkey. This figure has now increased to 46 members because of the division of Eastern Europe. All 46 countries are eligible for the contest, so there has to be an elimination process to reduce competitors to 25. Israel first participated in 1973 and first won in 1978 with A-Ba-Ni-Bi, performed by Izhar Cohen and Alpha Beta. The following year they were also successful with the song Hallelujah, by Milk and Honey.
ANN ROSENBERG, BBC TELEVISION, LONDON.

809: Why do we say 'have a decko' for 'have a look'?

This is another of the many words we took from Urdu, during our long rule of the Indian sub-continent. These words found their way back to Britain with returning forces and local administrators. The word *dekho* is Urdu for 'see' or 'look.' GRAEME COBB, SALTCOATS, AYRSHIRE.

Dekho is the imperative of the Hindi verb *dekhna,* to look or glance. 'Dekho, sahib', could be heard on the lips of many stall-holders in the bazaars of the sub-continent. A. V. JONES, BRIDGWATER, SOMERSET.

810: What was the Sonning Cutting disaster?

The Sonning Cutting disaster, on Christmas Eve 1841, was the first major railway disaster and happened when a train travelling from Paddington to Bristol ploughed into a land-slip caused by heavy rain. The full weight of the 17 goods wagons at the rear of the train crushed the two third-class passenger carriages against the engine, Hecla. Eight passengers were killed and 17 injured. Most of the casualties were workmen returning home for Christmas from building the new Houses of Parliament. The Great Western Railway Company was fined £1,000, but successfully appealed against the fine when a Board of Trade report cleared it of any blame. The fine was reduced to a nominal sum. The company was criticised, however, for its treatment of the passengers. The wrecked coaches were open-sided with no spring buffers and the passengers had to endure the harsh winter weather for the 9½ hours it took to make the journey. The practice of carrying third-class passengers on a goods train was also criticised. Later carriages were enclosed, fitted with spring buffers and never placed directly behind the engine in a goods train.

MICHAEL BLAKEMORE, YORK RAILWAY MUSEUM.

811: Has the name proved an advantage to those not employed as 007 but called James Bond?

There's no doubt that the name Bond has been a distinct advantage to me. In the early Sixties when the name first acquired its romantic aura, I did a bit of dinghy sailing. When I was introduced to lassies available for crewing they were suitably impressed and responded favourably to my completely spurious image. On the other hand, during a visit to Paris, when I was countersigning some traveller's cheques in a bank, the cashier remarked with a smile: '*Monsieur, vous avez un nom terrible.*'

ANTHONY JAMES BOND, RICHMOND, SURREY.

812: Why were learners allowed to drive on their own during the Suez Crisis in 1956?

Driving tests began in this country in June 1935, but during World War II, from 1939 until 1946, petrol was rationed, driving examiners were seconded to the Civil Service role of Petrol Coupon Officers and no civilian driving tests were carried out. Similar provisions were applied when the Suez Crisis began. Petrol was rationed and driving tests abandoned. The Government allowed learner drivers to go unaccompanied for the duration of petrol rationing, which lasted into 1957, eighteen months after the Suez conflict. The business-use ration was about four gallons a week. By the time rationing ended I had used all my school's allocation until 1960.

PETER RUSSELL, DRIVING INSTRUCTORS ASSOC, CROYDON.

813: Why is an argument often called a 'barney'?

The origins of this expression stem from the 19th century and the nickname of Barnabas, a common Christian name among Irish settlers in England at the time. The expression was an allusion to the reputation of the Irish for having a fiery temperament. In a more modern context, many people now know the expression 'barney' as rhyming slang for The Flintstones' character, Barney Rubble; ie. trouble.　　　D. C. Seeley, Kidderminster, Worcs.

814: As the Ancient Romans are supposed to have brought apples, pears, plums, peas, beans, carrots and onions to these islands, with tomatoes and potatoes coming from the New World hundreds of years later, what fruit and vegetables did the Ancient Britons eat?

Our pre-Christian Celtic predecessors used to eat many wild plants which we would look upon today as mere weeds. The leaves of 'Fat Hen' *(Chenopodium Album)*, which has been used as a food since Neolithic times, contain more iron and protein than cabbage or spinach. 'Good King Henry' *(Chenopodium Bonus Henricus)* is another wild plant once much used by the ancient Britons as a green vegetable. Fruits such as wild raspberries and dewberries have been found in ancient Celtic encampment sites. A barrow-load of sloe stones was collected during excavations of a neolithic lake village at Glastonbury, though it's possible the sloes had been used for dyeing. Before the Romans arrived, Silverweed *(Potentilla Anserina)* was widely cultivated as a root crop and boiled like a potato or made into a type of gruel. Apparently, it tasted not unlike a parsnip. The early Celtic folk had rich and wholesome diets from which modern man could do well to learn.　　　Patrick Regan, Southport.

815: In the John Leyton recording of the song Johnny Remember Me, who was the female with the ghostly voice in the background singing 'Johnny, remember me', and where is she now?

The lady with the ethereal voice providing background vocals was Lissa Gray, who sang on many hits of the Sixties, including Cliff Richard, Billy Fury and Tom Jones singles. Now married with two children, she gives classical recitals and teaches music, as well as being involved with county council music education projects in Hampshire.

Kim Pavey, Wolverton, Milton Keynes.

816: Many modern homes have several items – cooker, microwave, hi-fi, video, radio alarm clocks – with constant time displays. If a family has, say, six such items, how much would these add to their electricity bill in a year?

The circuit driving a digital clock takes only a few millionths of an amp, which can be ignored and the same is true of the non-luminous (LCD) type of display. Where luminous (LED) circuits are used, appreciable current is taken from a 5V dc supply. Each figure of the display consists of seven segments. Each segment takes 10mA. All are on only for the figure 8. Assuming an average of 20 segments 'on', current is 200mA (0.2A). So, the wattage is 0.2 x 5, i.e. 1 watt. For six displays running for a year, the total number of units used is 6 x 24 x 365/1000, ie 52.56 units. At a price of 7.5p per unit, the total cost of 52.56 x 7.5/100, i.e. £3.94. This figure assumes an average number of illuminated segments of 20, which closer analysis may show to be somewhat different. Even so, the annual cost will not be much above £2.   G. Read, Southampton.

While the displays themselves require only milliwatts, the appliances still draw five or six watts, due to power loss in transforming the mains voltage. For example, my micro-wave uses five watts to power a digital display and my video uses almost ten watts. An appliance constantly drawing five watts will consume 5W x 24 hours x 365 days/1,000 = 43.8KWhrs (units) a year. Six such appliances will consume 262.8 units. If one unit costs 7.5p, this corresponds to an addition of £19.71 to an annual electricity bill. If I use my video for two hours per day for a year, more than 80% of the power used will be for the display when the video is not in use.   N. A. Hunt, Maidenhead, Berks.

817: In 1870, an ancestor of mine was baptised 'Amnessin.' I have not been able to trace this anywhere as a Christian name. He was apparently born on board a ship between Cork and Portsmouth, but I have not found any trace of a ship of that name. Has anyone any ideas as to the origin of this name?

It's difficult to assign a specific source for the name Amnessin. People were often named after ships if they were born on them. However, in this case, there isn't a ship registered under this name. 'Amnis' is the poetic Latin form for water and is normally associated with the sea or rivers. There's a good chance the name of your ancestor comes from this Latin word, particularly as he was born at sea.   Anthony Camp, Director of the Society of Genealogists, London.

Many ancient Greek words are used in English as Christian names e.g.

Iris – Rainbow, (E)Irene – Peace. The Greek word *mnesis* means memories or remembrance and the letter 'a' as a prefix has several senses, one being negative and the other intensive. Amnesis therefore, could be either forgetfulness or intense remembrance, the personification of 'never again' or 'happy memories' – take your choice. HAROLD MITCHELL, CLEVELAND.

818: Why were the Lillehammer Winter Olympics only two years after the ones at Albertville, instead of the usual four?

The amount of time and financial commitment involved in preparing for the Olympic Games in any one year has steadily increased over the years, so in October 1986 the International Olympic Committee decided to change the pattern of the four-yearly Games and separate the summer and winter events so that only one Olympic Games would occur in one year. To launch the new cycle, it was agreed that, for one time only, there would be a two-year gap between one Olympic Winter Games and the next. The last Summer Games were held in 1996 in Atlanta, Georgia and the next Winter Games will be in 1998 in Japan.

JILL BEAGLEY, PUBLIC AFFAIRS DEPARTMENT, BRITISH OLYMPIC ASSOCIATION.

819: Where and when was the first set of traffic lights installed and did the idea meet with general approval?

Traffic problems are nothing new: in ancient Rome Julius Caesar banned chariots from the city centre during trading hours and this was probably the first traffic regulation order. On December 7, 1868, the world's first robot traffic signal was installed in London at the corner of Westminster Bridge and Great George Street to enable pedestrians to cross the road, particularly peers of the realm and MPs trying to get into Parliament. Designed by railway signalling engineers Saxby and Farrar, it was based on railway signals with red and green gas lamps and semaphore arms. The system was controlled by a policeman from a signal box beside the road. Unfortunately the system blew up after just one week and was never replaced. The next traffic lights in this country were erected in 1926, again in London, at the junction of James Street and Piccadilly. They had red and green electric lamps operated by a policeman standing in a control box. On November 4, 1927, the first automatic electric signals, controlled by clockwork, were installed in Wolverhampton and the amber light was included for the first time.

L. ROBERTSON, CHIEF ENGINEER, WEST YORKSHIRE H.E.T.S., URBAN TRAFFIC CONTROL, LEEDS.

I remember cycling one Saturday afternoon in 1928 to see the new wonder, traffic lights, installed in the City of London at the north-west corner of the Bank of England at the junction of Lothbury, Gresham Street and Moorgate. R. E. BAZIN, FALMOUTH, CORNWALL.

The world's first three-coloured traffic light was erected in Detroit, Michigan, in 1919. The first electronically-interlocked traffic signals appeared in Houston, Texas, in 1922.

TONY BEADLE, EDITOR, AMERICAN CAR WORLD, TADWORTH, SURREY.

820: Why do black cab drivers call the slack time after Christmas the 'kipper season'?

The quietest period for the London taxi trade has always been the months of January and February. In past times, when money was short, the only food taxi drivers could afford to eat was kippers. As a result of this kipper diet when business was bad, taxi drivers always refer to a quiet period as a 'kipper season.' ALLEN TOGWELL, DIAL-A-CAB, LONDON.

Use of this word reminds me of the expression 'all kippers and curtains.' Regularly heard in immediate post-war days when money and food were scarce, it described someone whose home looked superior from the outside when inside they were eating kippers, the cheapest food around.

JANET ROBERTS, GREAT BARR, BIRMINGHAM.

When I recently asked a cabbie this question he replied that it was when business was flat and full of bones. PETER ELEMENT, BEDFORD.

821: The building industry has nicknames for various tradesmen, such as chippies, sparks, plumbobs, brickies, all of which speak for themselves. But an old name for painters and decorators was 'skibs.' What is the meaning and origin of this word?

This word probably comes from 'skibbereen', taken from the town in Ireland which suffered badly during the great potato famine of 1845-49. Since then it has been used as slang to describe someone living in a state of poverty. This use dates from the influx of poor Irish workers to the mainland. Anyone who was considered to be lowly was referred to as a 'skib' and builders used the word as a reference to the lowest in their trade, the poor old housepainters. GILLIAN HANDWELL, LANCASTER.

I agree the word 'skib' was introduced to the English vernacular by those fleeing the ravages of the great Irish Famine in 1845-49 but I feel it probably derives from the native Irish *scwab,* brush, rather than from a place name. Many who escaped the famine worked in the Great Exhibition of 1851 and the colossal building programme of those decades. House painting, as well as being the poorest of the construction trades, was also very dangerous because of the lead, arsenic and mercury widely used in paint. SEAN MacNEILL, WEMBLEY, MIDDLESEX.

822: Why is a ship's captain called 'skipper'?

'Skipper' is the English variation of the earlier Dutch word *schipper*, a ship person or sailor. The word has expanded from its nautical roots to include the chief pilot of an aircraft, captain of a team or leader in almost any context, from bus driver to head of a multi-national corporation.

JOSEPH HARDY, WINCHESTER.

823: Who is the most successful female pop star of all time, in terms of records sold?

Diana Ross is the most successful, with more than 50 UK solo and accompanied hit singles, 35 albums and 12 Number One U.S. singles. Madonna, however, holds the record for the largest contract for a female artist – £40 million with Time Warner in 1992.

CAROLE JONES, GUINNESS BOOK OF RECORDS, ENFIELD, MIDDX.

Other suggestions are victims of the usual modern pop music hype. The answer is neither Madonna nor Diana Ross. Connie Francis is arguably the world's top-selling female singer with total sales of more than 75 million since her first hit in 1958, followed by Brenda Lee with around 60 million sales since the same year. Both these singers, though they have not had a major hit single for many a year, have continued to enjoy huge worldwide sales via frequent re-issues of their vast back catalogue and they are still recording. They scored their hit singles at a time when it was necessary to sell 250,000 records a week to get into the Top Ten, unlike the paltry chart sales figures of recent years.   CHRIS WHITE, BALHAM, LONDON.

824: Most of my friends are ex-sailors, yet not one knows why the dogwatch is so-called.

The term was in use aboard ship in the 18th century. The first written record I've come across is in the translation from the Dutch of Fryke and Schweitzer's Voyage To The East Indies, published in London in 1700. The word was defined but no origin given, in Dana's Two Years Before The Mast in 1840. In the old days, a ship's crew was divided into two watches, a starboard and port, each being alternately on watch for four hours. To avoid the same men being on the same watch every day, two two-hour watches were instituted, creating seven watches instead of six in each 24 hours. These short watches were called the first dogwatch and the last dogwatch (only landlubbers called it the second dogwatch). One ingenious but unlikely punning explanation for the origin of the 'dog' part of the word is that the short watches had been 'cur-tailed'. The word was probably a corruption of 'dodge-watch' which described this method of shuffling watches.

CAPT. PETER ELPHICK, WRITER AND HISTORIAN, EX-MASTER MARINER, LONDON.

My father, Donald Giles, in the Navy from 1946 to 1957, says the dogwatch is named after the Dog Star (Sirius), the first star sighted in the night sky in the northern hemisphere. The first dogwatch is from 1600 hours to 1800 hours; the last from 1800 hours to 2000 hours.

SALLY GILES, CHINGFORD, LONDON.

Dogwatches have to do with engineering, not animals. A 'dog' is part of an escapement wheel which breaks the movement from one side to the other.

D. R. HARVEY, POTTERS BAR, HERTFORDSHIRE.

825: What is the significance of the word 'Stoke', as in Stoke Mandeville, Stoke Hammond, etc?

'Stoke', which has found its way into many place names for towns and villages throughout the land, stems from the Old English *stoc*, meaning 'place.' It developed two distinct meanings, a religious place or an area that relied on another town, much as we use the word suburb today. The names Stoke Mandeville and Stoke Hammond probably came from the family who owned the land, meaning 'place of Hammond' and 'place of Mandeville.'

TERRY GREENAWAY, BRISTOL.

826: Why do we say 'stone deaf'?

This expression, along with many other similar ones such as 'stone-dead', 'stone-blind', 'stone-cold' and 'stone still' is used merely for figurative purposes when trying to explain any characteristic which is 'stone like.' Most other languages also express certain stone or rock-like characteristics in the same way, a good example being the German *steinalt*, 'stone-old' or 'as old as the hills.'

MAURICE KNIGHTON, LIVERPOOL.

This phrase received currency from the influence of the Cornish tin industry in the early years of the industrial revolution. Very loud and brutal steam hammers were used to smash up stone from the mines to extract the ore and anyone who worked in the vicinity of these machines for any length of time was likely to go deaf – stone-deaf.

A. SAMUELS, REDRUTH, CORNWALL.

827: Why are Marmite jars brown, making it impossible to see when all the contents have been used?

We always use brown glass to make Marmite jars because it absorbs ultra-violet light which could otherwise destroy some of the vitamins in the product. This is important because the nutritional properties of Marmite are an essential feature.

SUSAN N. FLOOK, CPC (UK) LTD, ESHER, SURREY.

828: When anyone looked untidy, my mother used to say 'You look like the wreck of the Hesperus'. What was the Hesperus, and where and when was she wrecked?

The Wreck Of The Hesperus is a poem by American Henry Wadsworth Longfellow (1807-88). His poems, including other favourites such as Hiawatha and Tales Of Wayside Inn were very popular in English schools in the first decade of this century. I can recall my mother quoting from The Wreck Of The Hesperus when I was a child. It's more than 50 years since I last read the poem but, from memory, the opening verse ran as follows: 'It was the schooner Hesperus/That sailed the wintry sea/And the skipper had taken his little daughter/To bear him company/Blue were her eyes, like the fairy flax/Her cheeks like the dawn of day/Her bosom white as hawthorn buds/That ope' in the month of May.'

AUDREY HAMILTON, LA OROTAVA, TENERIFE.

The Wreck Of The Hesperus is a long poem which ends with the ship being wrecked amid ice and snow on the reef of Norman's Woe. Both skipper and daughter perished. The last but one verse says: 'Her hair like brown seaweed floated in the waves' and my mother used to say I looked like the wreck of the Hesperus when my long hair was untidy when I was a child.

EVELYN COLLEDGE, MARKFIELD, LEICESTER.

A clipper ship by the name of the Hesperus operated between the UK and Australia as a cadet ship under a training scheme of Lord Brassey. She was built in 1873 and appears to have been named after Longfellow's poem which was published in 1841. The Hesperus was dismantled in 1923 after spending her later life in the service of the Russians.

R. BARNET, CREW MEMBER M.V. TANKERMAN.

829: Is there any truth in the story that if a shingles rash meets around your torso, that is the end of you?

Shingles *(Herpes zoster)* is a common disease caused by the chickenpox virus. The virus lies dormant in the nerve roots around the spinal cord following an attack of chickenpox and may erupt as shingles at a later stage in life. The shingles rash is characterised by itchy and painful vesicles in the area supplied by the nerve root. Initially there is pain and redness, followed by eruption of the vesicles. Although shingles most commonly affects only the distribution of one nerve root, occasionally more than one is affected. If two nerve roots at the same level are simultaneously affected the rash can circumvent the trunk and meet in the middle. The condition is particularly unpleasant and painful but it is not fatal.

DR JACQUELINE V. JOLLEYS, UNIVERSITY OF NOTTINGHAM.

830: What is the origin of the word 'moniker', meaning name or face?

First use of this expression is in Mayhew's classic work on poverty, London Labour, published in 1851, where the word is spelt 'monekeer' and was regarded as a common slang word in the underworld. The reason for its original use as a word meaning 'spoken name' is unclear and may have been some form of rhyming slang or even been taken from another language. It has only recently gained recognition to mean signature or face, so it has had several different spellings including 'monica', 'monicker' and 'monniker' as well as 'moniker'.

EDMUND WEINER, OXFORD ENGLISH DICTIONARY.

831: For 45 years the size of wallpaper rolls has been the same at 20½ins by 33 feet. Why these obscure dimensions?

The first wallpapers were made by block printing on large rectangular pieces of paper. It was difficult to align the print accurately from one square to another so, in the 18th century, printers started sticking the rectangles together to make a 'piece', now referred to as a roll. The length of a roll was about 11½ yards, or just over 33 feet, dictated by the dimensions of the rectangles which were either an 'elephant', 38ins long, or a 'double demi', 35ins long. Each of these pieces of paper was normally 22ins wide, said to be derived from half the medieval width of a standard piece of cloth which was about 45ins, known as an 'el.' Until about 1960, British wallpapers were normally supplied untrimmed at about 22in widths. From around that time they were adapted to European standards with a 10.04m (33ft) roll length and trimmed width of 20½ins.

GEORGE ZACAL, CROWN WALLCOVERINGS.

832: Did native North Americans really use smoke to communicate or is this just another myth?

Horse-mounted plains peoples, such as the Comanche, often carried out war raids over distances of 300 or 400 miles, the scouts riding as much as a day ahead of the main body. To communicate over long distances, they would use smoke signals meaning, for example, 'enemy in sight,' 'buffalo,' 'danger,' 'come,' 'stop' or 'all clear.' Colonel Richard Irving Dodge describes the method in his 1882 book Our Wild Indians: 33 Years' Personal Experience Among The Red Men Of The Great West. He wrote: 'A small fire is built on which is placed damp grass, creating a large volume of smoke. As it begins to ascend, a blanket is held horizontally above it and when the space beneath is quite full, the blanket is slipped off sideways and then quickly brought back to its place. Smoke managed in this way ascends in round puffs, miniature clouds, one meaning one thing, two another. A single smoke, ascending naturally, is a warning that there are strangers in the country. Every military command passing through Indian country will be preceded and flanked by these signal smokes.'

GRAHAM HEALEY, SHEFFIELD.

833: Has any Registrar of Births ever refused to register a child with the name parents wanted?

When I worked at Caxton Hall, Westminster, as Registrar of Births and Deaths I encountered parents who wanted to call their little boy Weedoff. I thought this might be offensive for the child when he went to school so I contacted the Registrar General for guidance and was told that if the parents couldn't think of a different name, I should register the child without a first name. This was done. Other parents wanted to call their baby daughter Velvet, Cotton Wool or Silk but this was also refused by the Registrar General. On another occasion a couple wanted to register a child with a football team's first names, which I agreed to, though I had a job fitting all the names in the small box on the birth certificate.

MRS AVERIL WILKINSON, LONDON.

When I was registered on October 4, 1905, Registrar John Farrow, of Ilford, refused to allow my parents to name me Kitty. He said it was a nickname, though my mother had an aunt and a cousin named Kitty. My parents were told I had to be Kate, but I was christened Kitty and became a Deputy Registrar in another district for 19 years, never once refusing a name chosen by parents.

KITTY M. BALL, BOURNEMOUTH.

On March 24, 1967, at Kelty Registrar Office, Fife, the Registrar refused to use the spelling of the name we had chosen for our first daughter. We wanted to call her Sheri but were told to go away and think of another more acceptable name. After two hours of argument and pressure we eventually agreed on Cherrie. This was in the year Ringo Starr named his son Zak.

M. C. WALTHO, WATERLOOVILLE, HANTS.

834: Ancient Greeks and Romans diluted their wine with water, added herbs for flavour and even heated it up. What exactly were they drinking?

The Ancient Greeks produced *melitites,* or honey wine, by heating honey, salt and wine. A similar product was made in ancient Rome, where it was called *mulsum,* or mulled wine, a traditional drink made from wine, heated, spiced and sweetened. The Romans also had *conditum,* an aromatic, spiced wine, and *absinthites,* wine flavoured with wormwood, early ancestors of today's vermouths.

GODFREY D. SPENCE, WINE AND SPIRIT EDUCATION TRUST, LONDON.

835: Where do vets get the blood they need for transfusions during operations on animals?

There's less demand for blood transfusions in veterinary medicine than in human medicine. The need for transfusions is mostly limited to dogs. Other animals cause a problem because of their small size, though transfusions have been carried out on cats. There is no organised donor system or central blood bank but each veterinary practice has informal arrangements with owners of large, placid and healthy dogs. Donor pets are taken to the practice and a small amount of blood is taken for immediate use. This is no more unpleasant or harmful than the similar procedure in humans. There are only two dog blood types (A+ and A-), making finding donors less of a problem than for humans.

BRADLEY VINER, BRITISH SMALL ANIMAL VET. ASSOC, CHELTENHAM.

Holly Blood Donor Appeal for dogs has set up a national register of donors. The list, detailing more than 1,100 dogs and owners, is sent annually free to all veterinary practices in Britain. Donor dogs should be between two and 10 years old, large and in good health. The pedigree is immaterial but a donor needs to be capable of sitting or lying under command for up to 15 minutes while blood is taken in a procedure similar to a human donation. Owners should be aware that there is a risk of rejection because dogs' blood has not yet been fully classified. Holly, the cocker spaniel which gave its name to the charity, died from rejection effects. Holly's charity is raising £150,000 (less than 3p for every dog-owning household) to finance a research programme to identify canine blood groups. HARRY HIBBEN, HOLLY BLOOD DONOR APPEAL, PO BOX 95, DARTFORD, KENT.

836: What happens to the clothes left in shops when the sales end? Are they recycled, sent to charity or destroyed?

Fashion retailing is a seasonal business and very few styles or colours are carried forward. Sales are our main opportunity to clear end-of-season merchandise to make way for the new ranges. Price reductions are set to ensure items become attractive enough to find customers. We go on reducing the price until all the items are cleared.

JOHN GREENE, HEAD OF CORPORATE COMMUNICATIONS, C & A, LONDON.

No merchandise is destroyed. Goods which are soiled or damaged to such an extent that we are unable to sell them, even at a reduced price, are donated to charity. SUE SADLER, MARKS & SPENCER HQ, LONDON.

Many clothes left when the sales are over are shipped to South America. On a visit to my son's family in Venezuela, I bought a number of chain store garments for £3, which would have sold here at a sale price for £8 to £12.

ANGELA KIRBY, SOLIHULL, WEST MIDLANDS.

Some shops donate end-of-sale clothing to the WRVS clothing stores where they are issued free of charge to the needy.

BARRY GRUNDON, WOMEN'S ROYAL VOLUNTARY SERVICE, TRURO, CORNWALL.

837: If the two World Wars and the consequent loss of life hadn't happened, would the population of the UK be substantially different from today?

Whether the rate of growth would have been the same or greater is open to speculation because the course of history would be different. What certainly was affected was the age structure of the population, both by the war deaths (750,000 in World War I and 400,000 in World War II) and by the fall in the number of births during the war years, which were followed each time by a dramatic increase immediately afterwards. Without the wars, these births would have been more evenly spread and we would not have had the baby booms of 1920 and 1947.

SPOKESMAN, OFFICE OF POPULATION, CENSUSES AND SURVEYS, LONDON.

838: Why 'kangaroo courts'? Do kangaroos pass unceremonious judgment on their peers?

First use of this expression is found not in Australia but in the U.S. prison system during the last century. It has nothing to do with the social habits of the kangaroo, though they are known to be aggressive. 'Kangaroo' in this context is thought to be an allusion to 'jumping out of line' for which a prisoner was tried in summary fashion by other inmates.

JAMES HARRISON, TORQUAY.

839: Is there a sure-fire way of winning at solitaire?

I was taught this as a child and the drawback is that, once you know how it is done, the game ceases to have any attraction except as an occasional demonstration of skill. AUDREY HARDMAN, RUSHDEN, NORTHANTS.

I'm no mathematician and there are no doubt many other ways of winning but the solution I found is as follows: The letters N, E, S, and W represent the directions in which to move the pegs and the numbers 1 to 33 represent the holes from which to move the pegs. The holes are numbered from left to right, and from top to bottom so that the top row is numbered 1, 2, and 3 from left to right, and the bottom row is numbered 31, 32, and 33. The central hole is number 17. Make the following 31 moves: 15E, 4S, 7E, 21N, 10W, 7E, 16N, 1S, 2S, 10W, 12W, 3S, 11W, 8E, 25N, 10E, 13W, 20W, 27W, 24E, 11S, 26W, 23E, 32N, 31N, 24E, 33N, 26W, 17S, 22E, 29N. At the end of this you should have an empty board with just a peg in the middle. SIMON FOY, PADBURY, BUCKS.

The sure-fire way of completing Solitaire takes me about 65 seconds, two seconds per move, and no doubt could be done in less than a minute. There are many other challenges in a Solitaire board, for example, start with any hole, taken at random and finish with the last remaining peg in that hole. I've kept a notebook over the years of procedures for every hole, except the middle one at the end of each of the four wings, which still beats me.   DOUGLAS THOMPSON, HASSOCKS, WEST SUSSEX.

Having spent my O-level revision time mastering the solitaire board, I can help Douglas Thompson. Numbering the board as above, and starting with a peg-less hole at No 2, the moves are as follows: 10 to 2, 24 to 10, 19 to 17, 30 to 18, 27 to 25, 13 to 27, 18 to 30, 33 to 25, 32 to 24, 24 to 26, 27 to 25, 22 to 24, 31 to 23, 24 to 22, 21 to 23, 16 to 28, 8 to 22, 7 to 21, 21 to 23, 28 to 16, 10 to 8, 1 to 9, 6 to 18, 25 to 11, 16 to 4, 3 to 1, 1 to 9, 8 to 10, 17 to 5, 12 to 10 and 10 to 2. The same moves, transposed, work for holes 14, 20 and 32. Needless to say, my O-level results were mediocre but I got enough passes to enter the sixth form and passed my A-level two years later.   JEAN CARTWRIGHT, BALBY, DONCASTER.

840: It used to be possible to tell where a car was first registered by the three letters on the number plate. Why doesn't this apply now?

It's still possible to identify where a vehicle was first registered by the last two letters on the number plate. Our practice for issuing registration marks is to assign to each Vehicle Registration Office throughout the country a number of prime index letters, which form the second and third letter of the current registration format. But since the introduction of the Agency's sale of attractive registrations, it is possible to select certain letters and numbers of one's choice within defined limits.
                                    BARBARA WILLIAMS, DVLA, SWANSEA.

The overall picture can be distorted by the fact that large fleet operators tend to use one Vehicle Registration Office for all their registrations. Every one of British Telecom's thousands of vehicles carries a Birmingham registration.   F. H. GILLETT, SUNDERLAND.

841: Whatever happened to Betty Hutton, the original 'Blonde Bombshell'?

Leggy Betty starred in Annie Get Your Gun, The Fleet's In and The Greatest Show On Earth. But her career petered out in the Fifties and despite having earned at least £3 million in her heyday, she went bankrupt in 1967. The last of four marriages, to trumpeter Peter

Candoli, ended in divorce in 1971. Ms Hutton 'disappeared', cutting herself off from her three daughters and hitting rock-bottom through alcoholism and drugs. On release from hospital in 1972, weighing just six stone, she worked for several years, incognito, as housekeeper to a Roman Catholic priest at Portsmouth, Rhode Island. Father Peter Maguire (who, when she revealed her identity, had never heard of Betty Hutton), helped her rehabilitation and in 1980, reunited with her daughters, she made a triumphant Broadway comeback in the musical Annie. Following that, she enrolled as a literature and psychology student at a New England college before settling in Los Angeles to be near her family, which included five granddaughters. Hollywood came up with no more roles – but, at 68, Betty Hutton did take part in the 1989 Academy Awards ceremony.   U. SHEARER, STOKE-ON-TRENT.

842: Is the infamous rugby song She Was Poor But She Was Honest, with the refrain 'It's the same the whole world over', based on any actual historical characters?

In most versions, the song has seven verses with an extra four possible. Modesty forbids the lyrics appearing here. It began life in the music halls around 1875 and was popularised by troops in World War I. It is thought to be based around the story of Aimee McPherson, a lady of the street, who met rich gentlemen, fell in love, fell pregnant, was rejected and had to return to her miserable life on the streets. Ms McPherson travelled to London where her unfortunate experiences were repeated at the hands of a politician, leading to the refrain: 'It's the same the whole world over.' The song has been changed and added to several times during its life. At different times the protagonists' identities were tagged to whatever scandal was occurring at the time. The politician has been identified with individuals of all parties and, most popularly in the States, with a former governor of Arkansas, long before the days of Bill Clinton.
                                          MIKE WILLIAMS, AXMINSTER.

843: Who were the Phoenicians? Did they ever visit Britain?

The Phoenicians were a Semitic people who settled around 3000 BC in what is now Lebanon and parts of western Syria. Best known as the first people to use an alphabet, which they subsequently passed on to us, the Phoenicians were organised in small city states including Sidon, Tyre, Ugarit, Arvad, Berytus, and Byblos. They were great traders who, at the height of their power in 1200-800 BC, traded goods including glass, cedar wood, metal, ivory and weapons and set up colony trading posts around the Mediterranean, including the cities of Carthage and Cadiz, making the Mediterranean the greatest trading area in the world. They circumnavigated the continent of Africa and travelled north along the Atlantic coast of Europe. They are thought to have not only visited Britain on at least one occasion, but also travelled as far north as Scandinavia. Around 600BC the Phoenicians were conquered by the Persians, who used their skills as craftsmen and seafarers to further their own empire building.   JOE OZMAN, CHELMSFORD, ESSEX.

It may be recalled that Sherlock Holmes, whose passion for detailed investigations extended far beyond mere crime, was at one point studying books on philology to follow up his idea that the ancient Cornish language was akin to the Chaldean and had been largely derived from Phoenician tin traders. Needless to say, these studies were interrupted by a case, The Devil's Foot, and Dr Watson doesn't tell us of their eventual results but it seems likely that Holmes had some positive basis for his theory.   M. FOLEY, AYLESBURY, BUCKS.

844: Greenfly and whitefly always return to my greenhouse each summer, but where do the little devils go for the rest of the year?

Insect pests remain dormant over winter, concealed in cracks and crevices. Aphids, of which there are around 500 species in northern Europe alone, can survive as adults, or more commonly as eggs wrapped in leaves, buried beneath flakes of bark – or in cracks and crevices around the garden, greenhouse, etc. Ideally they find a warm glasshouse or conservatory full of plants so that they can continue breeding without a winter break. Whitefly are different. There are basically two types, those of tropical origin that can survive only in somewhere well protected, and the hardy north European native variety that withstands severe conditions. Both whitefly can also winter as scales and pupa fixed to the underside of leaves. Adults emerge in the spring to start the next breeding cycle which continues throughout the summer.   PAUL PATTON, ICI GARDEN PRODUCTS, HASLEMERE, SURREY.

845: In the Gulf War, a number of Iraqi aircraft escaped to Iran. What has happened to these aircraft? Were they kept or returned?

During the conflict, 115 Iraqi Air Force combat aircraft fled to Iran, including 24 Mirage F1EQ strike aircraft, 24 Su-24 swing-wing bombers and four MiG-29 fighters. In addition, 32 Iraqi civilian registered aircraft were flown to Iran by their crews. These were returned in 1991-92. None of the combat aircraft has been returned to Iraq and all but two have been reduced to spare parts, scrapped or pressed into Iranian Air Force service. Two MiG-29 fighters were sent from Iran to Pakistan for testing and evaluation, these aircraft being identical to those used by the Indian Air Force. PAUL BEAVER, GULF STATES REGIONAL SECURITY ASSESSMENT, JANE'S INFORMATION GROUP, LONDON.

846: Why was the conflict between Britain and Spain (1739-1741) called The War of Jenkins's Ear?

On April 9, 1731, Spanish coastguards boarded the brig Rebecca, off Havana, supposedly to carry out a search of the vessel, accused of illegal trading with Spanish American possessions. The ship was set adrift with its captain, Robert Jenkins, tied to the mast after one of his ears had been cut off. He survived and initially complained to his own government without success but in 1738 he was called to the bar of the House of Commons to repeat his accusation and produce what he claimed was the ear in question, pickled in brine. His story lost nothing in the telling but caused great popular indignation and provided a motive for a naval trade war with Spain from 1739 to 1742. Conduct of this war merged into the war of the Austrian Succession (1740-48) which ended with the Treaty of Aix-la-Chapelle. LAURENCE KING, MILBORNE ST ANDREW, DORSET.

847: What prevents modern-day welded and continuous railway lines, with no expansion joints, from buckling in a heatwave?

Traditionally, rail was laid in 60ft lengths, joined with fishplates which allowed for expansion and meant the trains emitted that familiar clickety-clack sound. Most modern lines have continuous welded rail. Any length can be installed, giving a smoother ride and reducing wear and tear. To prevent buckling in heat, it is stretched to the length it would be at 27°C and firmly clipped under tension to baseplates on concrete sleepers. Expansion of the rail will start only above 27°C when modern sleepers, bedded in stone ballast, are of sufficient quality and weight to prevent lateral movement. BRIAN MORRIS, INFRASTRUCTURE MANAGER, INTERCITY EAST COAST.

848: What is the origin of the expression 'everything is all Sir Garnet' when things are neat and tidy?

This expression began in the British Army during the late 19th century and refers to the meticulous and skilful planning and organising abilities of the 1st Viscount Garnet Joseph Wolseley. Born in Dublin in 1833, Wolseley joined the Army in 1852, was wounded in the Burmese War of 1852-53 and served in the Crimea, where he lost an eye. He fought the Indian Mutiny in 1857-58 and served in the Chinese war of 1860. Ten years later, he put down the Red River Rebellion in Canada without losing a man. He was also in command of British troops during the West African Ashanti War of 1873-74, and was granted a large sum of money by a grateful Parliament for the work he had done. In Natal and the Transvaal, his flair for simplifying all aspects of operations gained him a reputation as a great planner. In 1882 he was Commander-in-Chief of the expedition to Egypt which beat Arabi Pasha against great odds at the Battle of Tel el Kebir but in 1884 his expedition to the Sudan arrived too late to save Gordon at Khartoum. He was highly influential in effecting the reorganisation of the Army onto a professional footing, with proper supply lines and an integrated command structure. At the age of 56 he was given command of the entire British Army, a post he held for the next six years. Queen Victoria used to refer to him as 'our only soldier.' He died in 1913, happy in the knowledge that his expertise, ideas and planning abilities had been passed on to future generations of the British Army.

JOHN CARMICHAEL, ALDERSHOT.

Sir Garnet Wolseley was also the original for Gilbert and Sullivan's 'very model of a modern Major General' in Iolanthe.

D. W. S. FLETCHER, WYMONDHAM, NORFOLK.

During his reforms of the British army, my relative Sir Garnet Wolseley accidentally gave the British soldier his nickname 'Tommy.' When drawing up his new enlistment form for joining the army, Wolseley inserted the sample 'Tommy Atkins' as the new recruit's name. He also helped establish the famous Wolseley car company, started by his youngest brother, Frederick York, by supporting him with money when cash flow proved problematic.

GEORGE J. C. WOLSELEY, FINMERE, BUCKS.

George Wolseley's view that his ancestor Sir Garnet Wolseley gave the British soldier his nickname 'Tommy Atkins' is open to question. Colonel Newham-Davis records that the Duke of Wellington, in his last few days as Commander in Chief, was asked by a young staff officer to approve the issue of the new Army pay book which included guidance for soldiers on how to fill in personal details. The Iron Duke was asked to suggest a suitable name as an example and gave the name Thomas Atkins, a soldier of the 33rd Regiment of Foot he had seen die bravely in Germany at the end of the 18th century. Most soldiers were illiterate and many filled in their pay books (effectively their identity cards) from the example provided, including the name Thomas Atkins. Virtually every soldier in the British Army had the same name in his pay book. I prefer this origin for the British 'Tommy' though it's just possible that the staff officer involved was the young Garnet Wolseley, who joined the Army in 1852, the year the Iron Duke died.

D. P. MACDONALD, CROWTHORNE, BERKS.

849: In childhood games we crossed our fingers and said 'fainites'. What does it mean?

The word 'fainites' is used by children in the schoolyard when a child wants a temporary absence from a game or a truce in the rules. It could be used to re-tie a shoelace in a game of tag or to speak with another child not involved in the game. When my husband and I were researching the book The Lore And Language Of Schoolchildren (Oxford University Press) we discovered that this particular word was found more commonly in London and southern England. Fainites dates from the 14th century, from the Old English *faine,* the modern equivalent being 'feign.' It was used to mean back out or hold back, especially in battles or jousts when admitting defeat. Equivalent words found in other parts of the country include: barleys, ballies, creases, cree, skinch, kings, keys and scribs.   IONA OPIE, LISS, HAMPSHIRE.

I understood the term to derive from the French *fais neant,* meaning 'do nothing', because your opponent had to immediately stop what he was doing.   MRS I. D. LUTLEY, HEMYOCK, DEVON.

850: On the credits of many television documentary programmes are references to Mary Evans Picture Library. Who is Mary Evans and what is her picture library?

The Mary Evans Picture Library was started in London 30 years ago by Mary Evans and her husband Hilary from a small collection of pictures they had in their possession. Reputedly the collection was first stored in a clothes cupboard. An initial inquiry from the BBC, wanting images of 'horses throwing their riders', was the first of what turned out to be tens of thousands of requests for a particular image from hundreds of different types of company. The collection of images has now built up to contain several million prints, drawings, photographs and ephemera in colour and monochrome covering almost every subject. Mary Evans still runs the library with her husband and several workers, including myself, sourcing new pictures all the time.   TERRY FORSHAW, MARY EVANS PICTURE LIBRARY, LONDON.

851: How can skaters and dancers spin so quickly and yet not appear to become dizzy?

It does seem remarkable that professional skaters can move at tremendous speed and execute spins of up to 20 revolutions while maintaining perfect balance and coordination and not be affected by dizziness. The key to this lies in the natural ability of the skater or dancer to maintain a good balance while getting used to the sensation of spinning and, in strict training, learning how to maintain eye contact with fixed points while the body is revolving and moving the head round sharply between those points. Skaters with natural ability to avoid dizziness are spotted at the beginning of their careers and can quickly become accustomed to the sensation of spinning. Skating and dancing routines are practised many times so the performer knows every movement he or she must make and can automatically move the body on to its next position even while feeling mildly dizzy.   EILEEN ANDERSON, NATIONAL ICE SKATING ASSOCIATION, LONDON.

852: It used to be common to see the sign 'Running in, please pass' in the rear window of new cars. Why is it no longer necessary to 'run in' new cars?

Advances in design and manufacture of engines, with much more precise tolerances, have almost entirely removed the need for running in. Improvements in synthetic engine oils mean there is no longer any necessity for special running in oil, which used to be replaced after the first 1,000 miles. Nowadays, we normally recommend owners use only 4,000rpm and two thirds full throttle for the first 1,200 miles, which is enough to allow cruising at motorway speeds. This encourages mechanical sympathy and can improve the life of the components.

SCOTT MELVILLE BROWNLEE, BMW(GB) LTD, BRACKNELL, BERKS.

853: How are the recipients of Maundy Money chosen?

Maundy Thursday, the day before Good Friday, gets its name from the first words of the antiphon for that day 'Mandatum novum do vobis,' which initiates the ceremony of the washing of the feet. This ceremony, which has existed since the days when sovereigns, Popes and priests washed the feet of the poor in imitation of Christ washing his disciples' feet, was last practised in England by James II. In Elizabeth I's time, gifts of cloth, bread, fish and wine were given to the poor by the monarch and, from 1725 onwards, money was distributed. Personal distribution by the monarch ceased in 1688 but was restarted in 1932 by George V. Recipients are nominated by members of the clergy from among those aged over 65 living in the local diocese who are of humble means and have performed some service in the community. The number of people taking part relates to the monarch's age, so this in 1997 there were 71 men and 71 women. Maundy Money is the only silver coinage still minted, consisting of 1, 2, 3 and 4 penny pieces with a total value of 10p for each person. They are legal tender and are also given to others taking part in the ceremony.   PRESS OFFICE, BUCKINGHAM PALACE, LONDON.

854: What does the saying 'gone to see a man about a dog' mean?

This American expression probably dates from the late 19th century, and is a deliberate piece of nonsense used by people who wish to leave a conversation but are anxious to conceal their destination or are embarrassed at what they are doing. During the Prohibition era in the U.S., for example, 'going to see a man about a dog' meant going to buy illegal alcohol from a bootlegger.

NIGEL WILCOCKSON, BREWER'S PHRASE AND FABLE, CASSELL BOOKS, LONDON.

I believe this is not an American expression but rhyming slang, meaning quite simply 'going to the lavatory'. Dog is rhyming slang for 'bog': slang for lavatory.

H. E. DAVEY, CRANLEIGH, SURREY.

855: Do the radiowaves from dozens of TV channels, scores of radio stations, etc., which can penetrate brick and mortar and human bodies, do any harm to us?

The National Radiological Protection Board (NRPB) has advised that there is no evidence that exposure to radiowaves (or RF radiation) emitted by radio and TV transmitters has any effect on health at the levels of exposure experienced by the public.

GILL WILKINSON, NATIONAL RADIOLOGICAL PROTECTION BOARD, DIDCOT, OXON.

Frequencies used by radio, TV, radar, microwave transmitters, etc., do penetrate the body but there is controversy over how harmful they may be. There's evidence of increased cancer rates near powerful radar sources and in the U.S. recently there has been a number of lawsuits over a link between police radar guns and testicular cancer among police officers. The new generation of mobile phones use digital (pulsed) signals and the new microwave antenna/transmitters being erected on blocks of flats, schools, etc to serve them are also raising concern. Research is being carried out both here and in the U.S. into possible harmful effects from this radiation. SIMON BEST, EDITOR, ELECTROMAGNETICS AND VDU NEWS, LIPHOOK, HANTS.

856: What is the origin of the many 'cold harbour' lanes dotted around the country?

The name Cold Harbour means 'shelter from the cold' and originally referred to a lane offering some protection or shelter in an inhospitable place. There are 35 Cold Harbour Lanes and Coldharbour Lanes in Great Britain plus many more roads, streets, etc.

MATTHEW TRIGG, GEOGRAPHERS' A-Z MAP COMPANY LTD, SEVENOAKS, KENT.

It's probable there was once a Roman villa or small station on these roads which had fallen into ruin but was roughly repaired to furnish a temporary shelter for travellers. Shelters of this kind, consisting of bare walls as a minimal defence against bad weather, were termed *cealb hepebepza* or cold harbours, which would account for the great number of places in different parts of Britain bearing this name, almost all on Roman sites. PAT WILKINSON, THIRSK, NORTH YORKSHIRE.

I believe 'Cold harbour' is a corruption of the French *col d'arbres,* a hill with trees, dating from Norman times. It was first applied not to a road but to a settlement or steading in the vicinity of such a natural feature. J. WEBSTER, SIDMOUTH, DEVON.

857: Why are cups given to the winners of so many sporting events?

Cups in the form of such things as coconut shells, horns, and eggshells of large birds have been used by all known societies as drinking vessels on cultural, social and religious occasions. From ancient Greek and Roman times, a cup was synonymous with celebration. Sharing a drink or sharing food showed friendship and hospitality. Significance came to be attached to the cup from which everyone drank. Pursuit of a particular cup was important in mythology, such as the story of the Holy Grail, the chalice supposedly used by Jesus at the Last Supper. Cups came to be presented as sporting prizes in the last century to signify the high regard in which they are held in our culture, as lasting, substantial, portable and visible awards. MARIE OAKLEY, COVENTRY SILVERCRAFT, WEST MIDLANDS.

858: Why were so many snooker halls established above Burton's stores?

Initially, it was the policy of founder Montague Burton to lease the upper floors of his shops wherever possible to other retailers of anything other than food, which might attract mice to the detriment of his cloth stocks. Where no suitable retailer could be found, the upper floors were turned into billiard saloons to attract young men, who would have to pass Burton's windows on their way upstairs and might be tempted into the shop to buy. Burton, a teetotaller, was particularly pleased at the idea of keeping these potential customers out of public houses. The billiard halls were so successful that in 1930 Montague Burton bought his own billiard company, Bright Billiard Halls Ltd, to run the upper-floor businesses. When the popularity of the sport declined, many of the halls were closed. Although the games of billiards and snooker have regained popularity, due in part to TV coverage, the Burton Group has no plans to revive this method of tempting customers into its shops. JENNY SCOTT, BURTON GROUP, LONDON.

859: Why does my touch on/off table lamp not work when I'm wearing gloves?

Several different types of switch are used in domestic table lamps, including rubber-protected push switches, dimmer switches, infra-red remote control or sensor switches and touch switches. The touch switch works by use of a finally balanced electrical 'trigger' which turns the light on or off by contact with the electrical capacitance of the human body – the energy released by the finger on contact with the switch plate. The resistance to electrical current between the finger and the switch is critical and wearing a glove, particularly if it is made of a high-resistance material, will affect the operation of the switch.

TED GLENNY, TECHNICAL MANAGER, PHILIPS LIGHTING LTD, LONDON.

860: Where does the expression 'a night on the tiles' originate?

This 19th-century expression, meaning to go out on a late night spree of drinking and debauchery, started life as a rather unflattering reflection on the nocturnal roof-top habits of the household cat.

NIGEL WILCOCKSON, BREWER'S PHRASE AND FABLE, CASSELL BOOKS, LONDON.

861: What is a laugh and why do we do it?

If we hear a joke or see something funny we experience a sudden sense of awareness which releases tension in an articulated form. This release is a basic physiological function for reducing tension in the body, known as laughing. Laughter can be used to try to manipulate people, or to win them over to our point of view, or to ingratiate ourselves if we are an outsider in a social setting. We've all heard professional comedians tell of their schooldays when they became class jester to avoid being bullied or when struggling academically. Someone watching something on their own is less likely to laugh at something than when watching with friends because, although laughter is an initial physiological response to a situation, laughing is a social activity which we want to share.

JIM BOWEN, ONE-TIME COMEDIAN AND GAME-SHOW HOST.

862: What exactly is a dimple and is it hereditary?

A dimple is a depression in subcutaneous fat and is caused by a slight defect between the fat and the muscle which shows in the skin as a little hollow. These are most commonly visible in the chin, cheeks and knee. This irregular clumping of fat may be genetically passed on from one generation to another. 'Dimple' is probably an Old English word, stemming from the Old German *tumphilo,* which meant a deep place in water.

KATE SHAW, PECKHAM RYE, LONDON.

863: Has a computer ever made an error?

Computers, regardless of make, type or function, are complex combinations of electronic and mechanical parts which can produce errors through the effects of natural background radiation or everyday electrical interference. Mechanical parts can fail from normal wear and tear. So computers can make errors, though they are built to detect and correct these before they become a problem. The number of mistakes generated by computers pales into insignificance compared with the number made by the people who program or use them. A rough comparison would be to consider how many times your video recorder needs repairing against how often you manage to record the wrong programme.   MARK FERGUSON, SOFTWEAR ENGINEERING CONSULTANT, MAGOR, GWENT.

Many people can quote examples of gas bills for millions of pounds or final demands for zero pence but these are all caused by human mistakes. When I was involved in the development of a computerised fund transfer system for banks, I encountered a computer which 'forgot' how to do arithmetic. The computer had to calculate the money in various bank accounts and we found it was using incorrect account numbers. Fortunately, checks within the destination banks' computer systems detected the error and stopped the transactions. Detailed investigation showed the computer was 'forgetting' how to multiply and generating wrong numbers about once in every million calculations. The fault was traced to a cracked printed circuit, which had to be replaced.

RON LOCK, JENBRY DATA SERVICES, HEMEL HEMPSTEAD, HERTS.

I queried a few extra noughts in the total on my electricity bill and was told that this was 'a computer error.' When I contacted our local newspaper, it printed a cartoon of two white-coated men puzzling over a computer, with the caption: 'It's gone on strike. It was getting blamed far too often for other people's mistakes.'   JEAN F. SKINNER, BIRSTALL, LEICS.

864: Why does eating rhubarb make your teeth feel furry?

The tongue has more highly sensitive nerve endings per square centimetre than almost any other area of the body and these are affected by food and drink. Rhubarb contains the astringent tannin, which causes a tightening or shrinking feeling of the tongue. The teeth may feel different, even 'furry', while eating particular things because the tongue's nerves are responding in a particular way.

PETER GODON, SCIENTIFIC ADVISOR, BRITISH DENTAL ASSOCIATION.

865: Is there a word, the opposite of 'mysogyny', meaning hatred of men?

The opposite of mysogyny is 'misandry', from the Greek *miso,* hatred, and *andrea,* from *aner,* a man.

BIRTE TWISSELMANN, COLLINS ENGLISH DICTIONARY, LONDON.

I would like to think that the opposite of mysogyny is 'misterogyny' but I suspect that is a misnomer.   JANET BURHOLT, DORCHESTER, DORSET.

866: Is there a special way to place one's cutlery on the plate at the end of a course to indicate that a second helping is desired?

As a finalist in the 1993 Head Waiter of the Year contest, I can state that leaving one's cutlery apart instead of together on an empty plate indicates that the customer hasn't finished the meal and an observant waiter should then ask if a further helping is required.

NEIL WILLIAMS, NOEL ARMS HOTEL, CHIPPING CAMPDEN, GLOUCS.

When I worked as dining hall maid at Repton public school at the tender age of 14, I was taught that the knife and fork should be placed together after a meal but that if another helping was required the fork should be placed upside down.   MARGARET BELL, BELPER, DERBYS.

To date, there is no standard method of indicating through the use of cutlery that a second helping is desired. Customers simply make verbal requests. At the Ritz, we encourage arranging the cutlery in the opposite way to the 'I have finished my meal; please clear my plate away' signal, which is to place the cutlery between the three and four o'clock position, with the handles near the edge of the plate. The signal indicating a desire for a second helping is to place the cutlery roughly at the quarter to nine position, with the cutlery handles on the left hand edge of the plate.

PETER ROMERIO, RESTAURANT MANAGER, RITZ HOTEL, LONDON.

I was always taught to leave the fork and knife together on the plate in the 12 o'clock position, with the points of the fork upwards to signify I had finished. Leaving them any other way, particularly if the points of the fork are facing down, indicates otherwise. It is impolite of a waiter to ask 'Do you require more?' but permissible for him to ask 'Have you finished?' giving the diner the opportunity to ask for more. The horizontal position for knife and fork at the end of a meal was adopted after a royal lady caught her lace cuff on the cutlery in the original 12 o'clock position and so took up the habit of leaving the handles to the right hand side. Alas, many of these table manners have since gone by the board.   K. ANDERSON, WARRINGTON, CHESHIRE.

867: I understand that some stamps produced in the Channel Islands for the Germans during World War II had some form of pro-Allied message. Can anyone confirm this?

In 1941-43 Jersey Postal Service stamps, printed on the presses of the Jersey Evening Post, when the Channel Islands were occupied by the Germans, incorporated a pro-Allied secret message. The stamps' designer Major N. V. L. Rybot defied the German occupation by using four letter As, standing for the Latin *ad avernum Adolf atrox* ('To hell with atrocious Adolf') on the 1d stamp and AA, BB, standing for 'Atrocious Adolf' and 'Bloody Benito' in the four corners of the halfpenny stamp.

HOWARD PIZZEY, STAPLEHURST, KENT.

Stamps issued in Guernsey between 1941 and 1944, designed by E. W. Vaudin and printed by the Guernsey Press, had small 'V' for victory signs in each corner.   J. W. GREENHALGH, CLITHEROE, LANCS.

On holiday in the Channel Islands more than 35 years ago, my wife and I stayed at a guest house in St Martins whose proprietor was called Blampied. He told us a relative of his, a well-known Jersey artist, was ordered by the Germans to design the occupation stamps. He said that, unknown to the Germans, Blampied interwove 'GRVI' (Georgius Rex VI) in the design so that it was not readily apparent.   PETER NORVILLE, BEXHILL, SUSSEX.

These 'morale-boosting' pro-Allied messages incorporated in new designs for wartime Channel Islands stamps eluded not only the Germans but also the vast majority of islanders until long after the war. It's tempting to think the covert messages in the designs had more to do with the designers' desire to avoid any later charges of collaboration than with bolstering the defiance of the population at large.   P. STEPHENS, REDRUTH, CORNWALL.

868: Why do we say that Eve gave Adam an apple, when the fruit isn't specified in Genesis?

An apple isn't mentioned in this context in Genesis or in any part of the Old or New Testaments. It's probable that the apple wasn't even grown in Biblical lands because of the hot climate there. References to an apple in the Garden of Eden probably stem from the association in Latin of the words *malus,* meaning bad and *malum,* meaning apple. These words can be regarded as some form of Latin pun. Many people still refer to the apple in Eden in a metaphorical sense.   REV ERIC SHEGOG, GENERAL SYNOD, LONDON.

The apple first appears in medieval carols such as When Adam Lay Ybounden. The idea really took off after Milton's Paradise Lost, standard literature for any educated Englishman until recent times.

JEFFREY WOOD, UPMINSTER, ESSEX.

869: How do you start the engines of a jumbo jet? Does the pilot have an ignition key?

When an aeroplane is delivered from manufacturer to purchaser, a symbolic key is handed over but this is purely a traditional gesture. No key is required to start the engines. Each engine is started by compressed air delivered from a smaller engine at the rear of the aircraft. At the flick of a switch, a simple valve opens to allow the compressed air to turn the blades of each engine via a gearbox and shaft. At a predetermined point, fuel is introduced and subjected to high-energy ignition. When the engine becomes self-sustaining, the ignition is automatically terminated and the start valve closes, completing the start sequence.

TONY HAMPSON, BA DUTY ENGINEER, BRUSSELS.

870: If leaves on trees produce oxygen, is there less oxygen in the air in winter when there are no leaves on the trees?

Seasonal changes in oxygen levels are too small to detect. The winter reduction is a few parts per million, hardly noticeable in air which is 21 per cent oxygen. There is, however, a more noticeable difference in carbon dioxide, the increase of which, by a similar level to the oxygen lost, is proportionally greater, because it makes up only 0.03 per cent of the air we breathe. When the trees are bare in winter, light they would have absorbed penetrates to plants such as grass and moss, which are shaded in summer, and there is little net loss of plant activity. Oxygen-producing photosynthesis slows down in winter but so does plant respiration, which uses oxygen. Cold-blooded animals, hibernating mammals and plants use less oxygen in winter. The sea doesn't cool as much as the land and millions of tonnes of green, oxygen-producing, algae live on as usual.

DR SEAN EDWARDS, THE MANCHESTER MUSEUM.

871: Why can a crab grow a new limb when it loses one, whereas a human, who is higher up on the evolutionary scale, is unable to duplicate this useful ability?

The 10,000 species of crab, along with other crustaceans as well as insects and arachnids, are arthropods, having some ability to regrow severed limbs. Crabs have an external skeleton which they shed and replace with a new one at regular intervals. When this occurs, any limb which has been lost can be fully or partially grown back as part of the regeneration process. Humans cannot do this but have other regenerative processes, such as being able to regrow burned skin. Humans, being 'higher up the evolutionary scale,' are far more complex than crabs and more difficult to repair.

DAVE CLARKE. INVERTEBRATES CONSERVATION CENTRE, LONDON ZOO.

872: Why is an eagle, a bird of prey, on the front of the lectern in churches? The dove, which signifies peace, would be more appropriate.

The eagle has become the traditional model for the lectern because it was considered the strongest and highest-flying bird, best able to carry the Word of God to the greatest number of places. The dove is a symbol of peace and represents the Holy Spirit. Though not used on lecterns, it is widely found in religious art. Some lecterns are modelled on the pelican because of the myth that the pelican fed its young with blood from its own breast, something early church leaders liked to compare with the way Jesus fed his followers with the Word of God.

STEVE JENKINS, GENERAL SYNOD OF THE CHURCH OF ENGLAND.

The eagle carries the Bible because it was believed it was the only bird that could look up to heaven without a lid dropping over the eye.

M. J. FEATHER, LEAMINGTON, WARKS.

The eagle is the symbol of St John, the apostle who characterised Jesus as The Word, and is thus uniquely appropriate to carry the Word of God in church.

A. SMART, HASTINGS.

873: In Middlemarch, the Garth family 'received nine costly letters for which the postman was paid three and twopence.' At what point did it cease to be customary to pay for letters on receipt instead of when sending them?

The obligation of recipients to pay postal charges started in 1635 when Charles I opened the facilities of the Royal Posts to the public. It ended in 1840 when the Post Office reformed the service with the introduction of a uniform rate of one penny throughout the country and adhesive postage stamps (the famous Penny Black). It had been considered socially undesirable for the sender to pay the postage because it implied that the recipient might be too poor to pay. Today, most people think it's bad form not to put a stamp on a letter. Before the reforms, postage rates determined by distance and the number of sheets making up the letter were both high and inconsistent. In 1820, sending a two page letter from London to Manchester could cost 1 shilling (5p), equivalent to about £2.18 at today's values, with no guarantee of delivery date. Now, a letter sent first class anywhere in the UK costs 26p and has a 90% chance of being delivered the next working day after posting.

KEVIN SQUELCH, POST OFFICE ARCHIVES, MOUNT PLEASANT, LONDON.

Remembering his poverty-stricken childhood, Rowland Hill wrote in his journal: 'My mother was afraid the postman might bring a letter while she had no money to pay for it.' Three years after he invented the Penny Post, following a change of government, he was dismissed amid great public outcry. He went on to become a director of the London and Brighton railway company and, to the disgust of wealthy Brighton residents, introduced cheap day return fares and monthly season tickets. He virtually invented commuting to work by train.   GLENDA CLARKE, HOVE, SUSSEX.

874: Has any cow from a so-called organic herd died of 'mad cow disease'?

The Soil Association's symbol scheme which inspects and certifies 70% of the organic farms in Britain, recorded eight deaths from Bovine Spongiform Encephalopathy (BSE or Mad Cow Disease) in a period of two years. These animals were either in herds which had converted to an organic regime in the previous few years or had been bought in as replacements. They may have been given feedstuffs which contained animal by-products before conversion to an organic regime. The Soil Association's Standards for Organic Food and Farming have never permitted the use of animal by-products in livestock feed. They also require that the offspring of infected animals be removed from organic herds to minimise the possibility of the disease recurring. Organic farms are subject to an EU regulation and UK law which requires rigorous inspections by an approved body.   JOHN DALBY, SOIL ASSOCIATION ORGANIC MARKETING CO LTD.

875: Were there no horses in the Americas before the Spanish conquest?

There do not seem to have been any horses in the Americas when the Spanish arrived in the 15th and 16th centuries but it is possible to trace ancestors of the modern horse to the American continent during the Eocene age, about 60 million years ago. An ancient skeleton of a horse-like creature the size of a fox – the 'Eohippus' Dawn Horse – was found 120 years ago in Wyoming. The American continent was joined to Asia and Europe by land bridges until the end of the Ice Age and ancestors of the horse are believed to have migrated from the Americas into Asia, Europe and Africa. The land bridges disappeared by the end of the Ice Age, leaving America isolated. For unknown reasons, the horse appears to have become extinct in America 8,000 years ago.
                ELWEYN HARTLEY EDWARDS, AUTHOR OF THE ULTIMATE HORSE BOOK, NORTH WALES.

876: Is it true that potatoes with a slight greenish colour are bad for us?

Potatoes go green when exposed to light for too long. A group of substances form, called glycoalkaloids, which are harmful if eaten in large quantities. High concentrations of them taste bitter. Slightly green potatoes shouldn't do a lot of harm but it's wise to cut any green parts out or throw the whole vegetable away if it's discoloured throughout. To avoid potatoes turning green, they should be stored in a cool, dry, dark place.

ROS WEHNER, POTATO MARKETING BOARD, COWLEY, OXFORD.

Potatoes are members of the solanum family, which includes deadly nightshade and henbane. Green potatoes have an accumulation of solanine which can cause gastro-intestinal problems or affect the nervous system. Many foods contain natural toxins – fortunately our bodies can deal with the doses normally present.

PETER L. G. BATEMAN, SOCIETY OF FOOD HYGIENE TECHNOLOGY, LYMINGTON, HAMPSHIRE.

877: What is the origin of the 'Desiderata'?

This poem – which opens with the lines 'Go placidly amid the noise and haste, and remember what peace there may be in silence' – was once a popular poster. It is often incorrectly thought to have been found on a 1692 gravestone at Old St Paul's church, Baltimore, Maryland. In fact, it was written and copyrighted in 1927 by Indiana poet, Max Ehrman, a Harvard-educated lawyer who gave up his career to concentrate on his artistic abilities. He was socially aware, speaking out about the ills he saw in the world. He died in 1945, years before his work was recognised. The copyright on the 'Desiderata' was renewed in 1954 by Bertha K. Ehrman and the work was published in a book entitled The Poems Of Max Ehrman. This wasn't a great seller but was noticed by the Rev Frederick Kates at St Paul's, Baltimore, who was putting together a booklet of inspirational poems. He included the 'Desiderata' which was later extracted by a poster publisher. Somewhere along the line, the author's name and dates went missing and were replaced by the tombstone myth, plus the date 1692, the year of St Paul's foundation.   ERIC GREEN, ISLEWORTH, LONDON.

878: When a person is cremated, are the ashes of the coffin included in the urn and, if not, where are all the coffins – up for resale?

The Code of Cremation Practice requires that the coffin remains intact and sealed when placed in the cremator. In no circumstances are bodies removed from coffins before cremation. The deceased is placed by the funeral director in the coffin chosen by the family, dressed in accordance with the wishes of the next of kin. The coffin is sealed and taken to the crematorium where a religious or a non-religious service takes place, and the coffin containing the deceased is cremated. All remains, primarily bones and timber ash from the coffin, are collected in a tray beneath the cremator and reduced to a coarse ash which is placed in an urn or box for final disposal. Metal parts such as handles, screws, nails etc are removed by magnet. Disposal of the ashes can be done in various ways but the most common are by scattering, burial in a grave or niche or they are kept by the family. Coffins are generally made of solid timber or timber veneer, though lately there has been an increase in demand for environmentally friendly coffins made from processed cardboard.

MRS D. R. PALMER, FUNERAL SERVICES CONTROLLER,
UNITED NORWEST FUNERAL SERVICE, HANLEY, STOKE-ON-TRENT.

879: What is the origin of the famous John Bull in Union Jack waistcoat, and how did England come to be known as Perfidious Albion?

John Bull originated in a series of five satirical pamphlets written by Dr John Arbuthnot in 1712, originally entitled Law Is A Bottomless Pit, later changed to The History Of John Bull. John Bull represented England, the French were represented by Lewis Baboon and the Dutch by Nicholas Frog. In the late 19th century the character of John Bull was elaborated by Punch magazine, giving him his Union Jack waistcoat and faithful bulldog. This portly, hard-working, decent, jolly fellow has been an inspiration and example in times of crisis, especially during two world wars. The top hat and riding jacket and breeches may be a bit outdated now, but the spirit of stubbornness and lack of fear keeps him close to our hearts. Coincidentally, the music for our national anthem was written by a John Bull.   JOSEPH D.J. MELBOURNE, LICHFIELD, STAFFS.

Albion is an ancient and poetic name for Britain. The first person to ascribe treachery and faithlessness to Britain by using the term 'perfidious Albion' was the Frenchman, Augustin, Marquess of Ximenez whose poem of 1793 urges the French to attack perfide Albion at sea. The term became popular in France and was used in the recruiting drive to attract men to the French forces during the Napoleonic Wars.   SARAH THOMAS, BOLTON, LANCS.

880: Why is canned beer commonly sold in 440ml cans which don't appear to have any rationale in either metric or imperial terms?

Britain uses 440ml beer cans because when canning became popular in the Sixties, the technology had to be imported from the U.S. where the largest cans contained a U.S. pint (473ml) of 16 U.S. fluid ounces. This became standardised as 15.5 Imperial fluid ounces or 440ml, which ended up being our most popular size as technology allowed more variations.

JOHN HUNT, SCOTTISH AND NEWCASTLE BREWERY, EDINBURGH.

881: How many Indian restaurants are there in the United Kingdom, and when and where was the first one opened?

There are currently around 25,000 'Indian' restaurants in the UK, most of which are family owned, employing about 150,000 people. Most of these 'Indian' restaurants are run, not by people whose origins are in the modern state of India, but by people from Bangladesh, in particular from the area called Sylhet.　David Harrold, Restaurateurs Association of Great Britain, London.

Our restaurant, the Veeraswamy, is the oldest Indian restaurant in the country. It was founded in 1927 by Edward Palmer, grandson of Lieut. Gen. William Palmer and great-grandson of the Nizam of Hyderabad. Palmer was born in India in 1860 and came to live in England at the age of 20, where he established E. P. Veeraswamy & Co, purveyors of aromatic Indian spice and produce. He soon built up a reputation as an expert on curries, chutneys and pickles and was put in charge of the Indian catering at the famous 1924 Wembley Exhibition. After the success of the exhibition he went on to set up, at the age of 67, the first Indian restaurant in the country, on its present site in Regent Street. His idea for the restaurant was that people could try out the sumptuous dishes found at the Royal Palace of Hyderabad, the recipes of which he had learnt from his grandmother. In 1934 the restaurant was bought by Sir William Steward who maintained its high standards of Indian culinary art for thousands of servicemen and women returning from the East.

Paul Baretto, Manager, The Veeraswamy Restaurant, London.

882: How does the label on Cussons Imperial Leather soap withstand washing until the bar is a tiny sliver? Can this attachment be used in other fields?

Precise details of the adhesive formulation used to attach the special Imperial Leather badge to the soap are a closely-guarded secret. The label has been an enduring symbol of Imperial Leather's quality, which no rival has been able to imitate. While the adhesive contains some elements that are common to ordinary glue, the combination of ingredients and the temperature of the glue and soap at the moment they are joined form a unique process. The badge also has the practical advantage of enabling the soap to be laid label-down, allowing residual water to drain off to help keep the soap dry. However, our own research has shown that most people prefer to leave the soap badge up.　Gavin Walker, Cussons (UK) Ltd, Kersal Vale, Manchester.

883: Where did the saying 'Heavens to Murgatroyd' originate? Who was Murgatroyd?

This saying originated with the genial, orange-furred cartoon lion known as Snagglepuss. He is always in a state of calamity and prone to saying either 'Heavens to Murgatroyd!' or the equally popular 'Exit stage left …better yet, exit stage right!' as he sought to avoid capture by the pith-helmeted hunter. Snagglepuss was created by the legendary Hanna-Barbera animation studio in 1960. There's no ready identity for Murgatroyd. The expression was simply created by the writers and not based on anyone in particular. DANIELA SCALA, CARTOON NETWORK, LONDON.

884: Is it possible to compile crossword puzzles in Chinese, Japanese, Hindi, Arabic, Burmese or Tamil?

Apart from its 2,000 complex Chinese characters, Japanese writing uses two sets of simple phonetic letters called kana. Each letter represents a complete syllable so, broadly speaking, a four syllable word will be written with four letters, a five syllable word with five letters, and so on. For example, the word Hiroshima can be written with the letters for 'hi', 'ro', 'shi', and 'ma'. (In normal Japanese the word would be written with the use of only two Chinese characters). Thus, it is possible to compose crossword puzzles with one syllable to each square. Japanese crossword puzzles are fairly simple in comparison with those found in English-speaking countries, and the more elaborate ones such as the cryptic clue type have not caught on at all.

GRAHAM HEALEY, SCHOOL OF EAST ASIAN STUDIES, UNIVERSITY OF SHEFFIELD.

Crosswords are very popular in the Arab world and almost all newspapers and magazines publish them. But the puzzles differ from English ones in various ways. The grid is numbered horizontally at the top, from left to right, and vertically, downwards, on the right. Under any number, across or down, more than one clue may be listed. Clues are not followed by the number of letters required, but only by the number of words, if more than one features in the answer. Because some answers are written backwards and others are scrambled words, and since the letters 'h' and 't' are easily interchangeable, Arabic crosswords have fewer black squares. DR S. HANY, ROCHDALE, LANCS.

885: How many London Roads/Streets/Ways etc are there in Britain?

The Royal Mail's address file, containing 25 million UK addresses, lists 1,250 London Roads, plus 150 London Streets, 15 London Lanes, three London Avenues, two London Ways, and one London Walk. There are no London Parades, Gardens, Rises or Crescents. London Roads can be found in Northern Ireland, Scotland and Wales as well as England.

ALAN BREWER, NATIONAL POSTCODES CENTRE, PORTSMOUTH.

886: What is the origin of the word 'tad' meaning a tiny amount of something?

This word originated in the mid 20th century in the US and Canada from the word tadpole.   BIRTE TWISSELMANN, COLLINS DICTIONARY, LONDON.

887: Is it correct that the Hippocratic oath, embodying the code of medical ethics, is no longer sworn by doctors and, if not, why not?

The Hippocratic oath is in full: 'I swear by Apollo the physician and Aesculapius and all the gods and goddesses that, according to my ability and judgment, I will keep this oath and this stipulation, to reckon him who taught me this art equally dear to me as my parents, to share my substance with him and relieve his necessities if required; to look upon his offspring on the same footing as my own brothers and to teach them this art if they shall wish to learn it, without fee or stipulation; and that by precept, lecture and every other mode of instruction, I will impart a knowledge of the art to my own sons, and those of my teachers, and to disciples bound by a stipulation and oath according to the law of medicine, but to none other.

'I will follow that system of regimen which, according to my ability and judgment, I consider for the benefit of my patients and abstain from whatever is deleterious and mischievous. I will give no deadly medicine to anyone if asked, nor suggest any such counsel; and in like manner I will not give to a woman a pessary to produce abortion. 'With purity and with holiness I will pass my life and practise my art. I will not cut persons labouring under the stone, but will leave this to be done by men who are practitioners of this work. Into whatever houses I enter, I will go into them for the benefit of the sick, and will abstain from every voluntary act of mischief and corruption; and, further, from the seduction of females, or males, of freemen or slaves.

'Whatever, in connection with my professional practice, not in connection with it, I see or hear, in the life of men, which ought not to be spoken of abroad, I will not divulge, as reckoning that all such should be kept secret. While I continue to keep this oath unviolated, may it be granted to me to enjoy life and practice of the art, respected by all men, in all times. But should I trespass and violate this oath, may the reverse be my lot.'

The oath is thought to have originated with the Greek physician Hippocrates and has embodied the fundamental principles throughout the recorded history of medicine. The oath is not obligatory and has gradually fallen into disuse largely because, although the principles are relevant, the terms are out of date. However, about 50 per cent of new doctors still swear the oath or something similar, for example the Declaration of Geneva, drawn up by the World Medical Association in 1947.   SIMON BARBER, GENERAL MEDICAL COUNCIL, LONDON.

The British Medical Association annual meeting in Edinburgh in July 1997 considered using a new 10-paragraph oath, drawn up by a doctors' committee, but voted it worthy but too dull and boring. It will be submitted, for consideration, to the World Medical Association but meanwhile doctors' leaders are considering asking a poet to come up with a more interesting version.   P. RAMMEL, LONDON N5.

888: Are any members of the original Temperance Seven still going strong and, if so, where are they and what are they doing now?

The Twenties-style jazz group Temperance Seven had a string of hits in the early Sixties, including Pasadena, Hard Hearted Hannah, and their most famous hit, You're Driving Me Crazy, which was also Beatles producer George Martin's first number one. The group was formed by friends at the Royal College of Art who chose the name Temperance Seven although there were nine of them. All now pursue different interests. They are: Brian Innes (percussion), in publishing and living in Islington; John Watson (banjo), a graphic designer living in Teddington; Phillip Harrison (saxophone), a film set designer in Hollywood; Major Cephas-Howard (trumpet and euphonium), the owner of Arreton Manor craft centre on the Isle of Wight; John R. T. Davis (alto sax, trumpet and trombone), a collector and dealer in 78rpm records in Burnham, Bucks; Paul McDowall (singer), scriptwriter and actor, has been seen in EastEnders; Martin Fry (sousaphone), who owns an antique shop in Brighton; and Alan Cooper (clarinet and bass clarinet), retired after teaching sculpture and living in London. The ninth member, Colin Bowles (piano and harmonium) passed away several years ago.
                       JOHN WATSON, EX-MEMBER OF TEMPERANCE SEVEN, TEDDINGTON, MIDDLESEX.

The Temperance Seven were first called Paul McDowall's Jazzmen, but I renamed them after an appalling evening on the bottle.
                       DOUGLAS GRAY, SEDGEFORD, NORFOLK.

889: Will a letter get to the right address if I give only the name of the addressee and the correct postcode?

Royal Mail delivery staff cannot easily identify the exact address from the postcode alone. We do our best to deliver every one of the 63 million letters we handle every day as efficiently as possible and postcodes mean letters can be automatically sorted 20 times faster and more accurately than by hand. But they can only pinpoint a row of houses down to an average of 15 addresses. The Royal Mail has invested millions in a special centre in Belfast which tries to find a destination for every undeliverable letter, but giving the full address makes sure your mail gets there swiftly.

ALAN BREWER, NATIONAL POSTCODE CENTRE, PORTSMOUTH.

In theory a letter can be addressed with name and postcode only: in practice, you'll be lucky. A letter addressed to me from the U.S. had my name, town and correct postcode, with only the district in the town omitted. It was returned to sender marked 'insufficient address.' On complaining, I was told my postcode referred to one of 17 even-numbered houses and my postman didn't know which house it was for.

F. STANLEY, HEDGE END, SOUTHAMPTON.

If this gets printed, I would suggest it will.   J. BROWN, SLOUGH, BERKSHIRE.

890: Does anyone know a good alternative to the violent expression 'killing two birds with one stone'?

How about 'take down two ministers with one scandal' or, with the recent focus on passive smoking, 'give two people cancer with one cigarette.'

MICHAEL FRY, TONBRIDGE, KENT.

A reasonable alternative might be 'hitting two MPs with one egg.'

LES ABRAHAM, MABLETHORPE, LINCS.

891: Why do we 'clutch at straws'?

To 'clutch at straws', meaning 'to be desperate enough to take any form of help or assistance' is a 19th century phrase taken from a much earlier proverb which ran 'a drowning man will catch at a straw.' It's thought the original proverb dates from the 16th century and in other forms may have been said as 'a drowning man will catch at a twig.'

WILLIAM GYLES, BLACKPOOL, LANCS.

892: How did the QWERTY typewriter keyboard layout originate?

All the letters needed to type the word 'typewriter' are in the top line of the Qwerty layout, and some people believe this was intended to help non-skilled sales staff perform an easy demonstration of the machine. But this is an old secretaries' tale. The Qwerty layout was designed to slow down typing and prevent jamming of the keys in the relatively crude mechanics of early machines. The idea was to keep alternating between opposite sides of the keyboard to stop adjacent keys jamming. The first typewriter was invented by American William Burt in 1829, but the first commercially successful version wasn't produced by Remington and Sons until 1873, also in America. This adopted the anti-jamming Qwerty keyboard designed by the Americans, Scholes and Glidden, which beat all its potential competitors in both speed and ease of use in a speed-typing competition in 1877. The Qwerty layout remained the dominant one in the world for 55 years until 1932, when jamming problems had been overcome and Dr August Dvorak introduced his Dvorak layout, claiming it could increase typing speeds by 35 per cent. But the Qwerty layout was so well-established Dvorak's alternative didn't catch on. Qwerty is still going strong, although as computers become more demanding and RSI more of an issue, there's a growing demand for different types of keyboard, including the Dvorak layout. Companies at the forefront of technology can pay for staff to have personalised keyboards with layouts and keyshapes individually fashioned to an operator's hand. SALLY WHITWORTH, BRIGHTON.

893: Why are chefs' hats such a daft shape?

The chef's hat or 'toque' was thought to have been invented by Leonardo da Vinci, the inventor and artist who was also a great but unconventional cook. Its pleats were originally folds, created to hold in the long hair of the period and the hat resembled a floppy deerstalker. Antonin Careme (1784-1883), chef to the Prince Regent at the beginning of the 19th century who was responsible for streamlining the operation of the kitchens, thought the old design looked like a nightcap and redesigned it to hold the hair inside the hat. It was Alexis Soyer (1809-1858), however, who began to starch the pleats so the hat stayed erect, allowing it to remain open for ventilation. SARA JAYNE, ACADEMIE CULINAIRE DE FRANCE, LONDON.

894: Why do companies offering promotional competitions state 'no purchase necessary' when clearly they would like to increase sales of their product or service?

Section 14 of the Lotteries and Amusements Acts 1976 makes it illegal to conduct a lottery associated with the sale of any article to the public. In all competitions of this nature, the rules provide for an alternative entry method and tokens can be obtained by sending off for them. To be legal, competitions where a purchase is required must involve a reasonable degree of skill, like spot-the-ball and the football pools, where winning is held to be not just a matter of chance, but depends upon the skill of the entrant. However, small lotteries held for social and charitable purposes are allowed for in the law. The spate of lotteries by people unable to sell their houses who decided to raffle them off were illegal and a number of people were prosecuted. PAUL DREW, BUTTON AND JONES SOLICITORS, COVENTRY.

895: When grilling someone, we give them the 'third degree'. What happened to the first and second degrees?

Despite its association with grilling, the expression 'third degree' has nothing to do with the term used to describe burn damage to the body but stems from Freemasonry. Freemasons have three degrees of rituals which must be endured before a person is fully qualified as a member. The third degree is the highest and most difficult part of the initiation process. DAVID BANKS, STREATHAM, LONDON.

896: What do 'nap' and 'nb' mean when used by racing tipsters?

To go 'nap' is to risk everything on a single bet, from the abbreviation of Napoleon after whom the card game which hinges on the turn of one card is named. Don't be misled into thinking 'nb' stands for 'next best.' When I don't back an 'nb' it means 'not beatable' but when I do put my cash down it's short for 'no bloody good.' ROGER VINCE, BOURNEMOUTH, DORSET.

897: Why 'tell it to the Marines'? Are they more sceptical than anyone else?

The most common story told about the origin of the saying is that when the diarist Pepys was re-telling stories of the Royal Navy's travels to Charles II he mentioned shoals of flying fish. The courtiers had difficulty believing this and the matter was put to an officer of the Maritime Regiment of Foot. He confirmed the story and the King accepted his evidence, noting at the time that whenever any further dispute over something that seemed to lack possibility occurred, we should 'tell it to the Marines.' Unfortunately, this most glamorous of stories was merely a well-spun yarn. The reality of the origins will never really be known as there are two differing opinions. The first is that only the Marines – a constant butt for sailors' jokes – would be credulous enough to believe anything. The other being that only the Marines, with their wide-ranging service and experience, could verify or negate any tall story. As for whether or not the Marines are more sceptical than anyone else, the answer must be Yes and wouldn't you be after enduring the longest, toughest training of any service?

ED BARTHOLOMEW, THE ROYAL MARINES MUSEUM, SOUTHSEA, HANTS.

898: What is the significance of the tears which clowns paint under their eyes?

Clowns and clowning can be traced to earliest history but the appearance of modern clowns owes much to the *commedia dell'arte* of late medieval Italy, which developed the characters of Harlequin, Pulcinella, Pantalone etc. The clown with a tear on his face is Pierrot and first appeared with troupes touring France in the early 18th century. With his wan complexion and long white peasant smock, his roots lie among the apprentice bakers who made merry once a year, fooling around with flour. As his character developed, the naive and vulnerable Pierrot became a symbol of unrequited love; always too shy to win his sweetheart, who invariably went off with Harlequin. His humour lay in his being thwarted and depressed. The stylised tear represents the converse side of happiness, the point where sadness becomes ludicrous.

ELIZABETH MORGAN (CLOWN FIZZIE LIZZIE),
CLOWNS INTERNATIONAL GALLERY AND ARCHIVE CO-ORDINATOR, LONDON.

899: Is there really an even chance that two people out of 24 at a party have their birthday on the same day?

The answer is Yes. In fact, you only need 23 people, not 24, at your party to give you an even chance, if you omit people born on a leap year. The trick is to imagine the people arriving one by one at the party and to calculate the chance that the birthday of each new arrival is not the same as those already there. The first person arrives and has nobody to compare with. The second person arrives and since one birthday in a 365 day year is already taken he has a 364 in 365 chance that his birthday is different. When the third person arrives there are two birthdays taken, so he has a chance of 363 in 365 that his birthday is not the same. The fourth person has a chance of 362 in 365, and so on. The last to arrive at the party, the 23rd person has a chance of 343 in 365. Now the chance that they all have different birthdays is obtained by multiplying the individual chances together, giving a value of 36997978566217959340182499134166757044383351847256064 in 75091883268515350125426207425223147563269805908203125, otherwise known as 0.493. This tells us that for 49.3 per cent of the time the birthdays are all different, from which it follows that 50.7 per cent of the time two or more of the birthdays will be the same. Just above an even chance.

DR ALAN F. JONES, DEPARTMENT OF MATHEMATICS, UNIVERSITY OF MANCHESTER.

900: Why does February have only 28 days? Wouldn't it be better to have January, February and March 30 days long, so that even in leap years all the months would be 30 or 31 days?

The old Roman calendar started in March. September, October, November and December were so named because they were the seventh, eighth, ninth and tenth months. February, the last month, had to make do with fewer days because Julius Caesar decided to name the fifth month after himself and lengthen it by stealing a day from February. His successor, Augustus Caesar, followed his example, renaming and lengthening the sixth month. Despite the change from the Julian to Gregorian calendar, the lengths of the months remained unchanged, except for the provision of the extra day for February in leap years.   BARBARA-ANNE EDDY, VANCOUVER, CANADA.

The civil year of 365.25 days was invented during the rule of Julius Caesar, a close approximation to the astronomical year – the time it takes the earth to revolve once around the sun: 365 days, 5 hours, 48 minutes and 46 seconds. The Julian calendar ensured that the most important astronomical events of the year, like the spring and autumn equinoxes and the two solstices, fell on, or near, the same day every year. To account for the extra quarter day of 365.25 days, Julius decreed that every four years an extra day would be added to the end of the Roman year or the last month before the spring equinox, which took place in mid-March. This brought the civil year in line with the astronomical year.
      LAURA WESTON, ROYAL OBSERVATORY, GREENWICH.

The best idea for calendar reform, suggested a few years ago, was that there should be eight months of 30 days each and four of 31. January, February and March would have 30 days, followed by April with 31, then May, June and July at 30 days and August 31 days, September, October and November at 30 days, and December, 31. That leaves an odd day besides the four-yearly leap year day. This could be a public holiday called World Day, between June and July. The leap year day would also be a public holiday, between December and January. The scheme should begin on a New Year's Day that falls on a Monday, then in all future years the same days would fall on the same dates.
      L. DALLANEGRA, MITCHAM, SURREY.

With tongue in cheek I refer you to W. S. Gilbert's Pirates Of Penzance, where the pirate king sings: 'For some ridiculous reason, to which, however, I've no desire to be disloyal. Some person in authority, I don't know who, very like the Astronomer Royal, Has decided that, although for such a beastly month as February, twenty-eight days as a rule are plenty, One year in every four his days shall be reckoned as nine and twenty.'
      RON BARRETT, TORQUAY, DEVON.

901: When did we start giving Easter eggs and what is behind this practice?

The association of eggs with the Christian festival of Easter can be traced to the early days of the church. Eggs are, to a great extent, survivals or adaptations of more ancient practices as Easter was closely associated with the pagan spring rites. The first chocolate eggs did not feature as part of Easter celebrations until the late 1800s. For centuries the egg has been a symbol of rebirth, fertility or beginning. With the rise of Christianity in Western Europe, the early church adapted many pagan customs and the egg came to represent the Resurrection. Some Christians regarded the egg as a symbol of the stone being rolled away from the sepulchre. Consecrated eggs featured in church ceremonies until the fourth century when eggs became forbidden during Lent. As hens came to the peak of their laying-time in spring, the practice of hard boiling and decorating eggs developed. These were presented as gifts on Easter Sunday – the end of Lenten fasting. The 17th and 18th centuries saw egg-shaped toys given to children at Easter. John Cadbury launched the first chocolate Easter eggs in the UK in 1875. The smooth, dark chocolate eggs were made of dragees and decorated by chocolate piping and marzipan flowers. We now spend more than £230 million on chocolate at Easter with more than 80 million eggs bought every year.

DEBORAH RISBY, CADBURY LTD, BIRMINGHAM.

902: Did the Three Musketeers ever use muskets? Why are they always depicted as swordsmen?

The Three Musketeers, Aramis, Porthos and Athos and their companion D'Artagnan are characters from the novels of Andre Dumas. Though always depicted using swords, in a time of war they would have used muskets, as their name suggests. The musketeers were a mounted guard of gentlemen in the service of the kings of France from 1661 until 1791 when the Revolution caused their abolition. There were two companies of musketeers, the Greys and the Blacks, named after the colour of their horses. The uniform was scarlet which led to their quarters being known as La Maison Rouge. During periods of war the regiment of musketeers fought with the army but in peace time they formed the King's bodyguard. The musketeers are usually seen in films using swords, rather than muskets because a musket took at least 20 seconds to reload and fire – not exactly the ingredients for the most exciting of action scenes in a feature film.

DAVID RYAN, EDITOR, ENGLISH CIVIL WAR NOTES AND QUERIES, LEIGH-ON-SEA, ESSEX.

903: Why is it that when the first sub-four-minute mile is remembered, the fourth man of Roger Bannister's squad, Alan Gordon, is rarely included?

Roger Bannister ran the first sub-four-minute mile on May 6, 1954. His historic run of 3 minutes 59.4 seconds took place at Oxford in the Annual Night Match between the University and the Amateur Athletic Association. Bannister was running on behalf of the AAA, along with Chris Brasher, Chris Chattaway and W. T. Hewlett. Alan D. Gordon was representing Oxford along with G. T. Dole and T. N. Miller. Athletics Weekly has a full report of the race in its issue of May 15, 1954. It states that Brasher led the race for the first two laps. By the end of the third lap Chattaway had taken over only to be passed by Bannister with a final burst to win the race and a place in history. Chattaway finished second and third was Hewlett. The reason few of the other athletes, including Alan Gordon, are rarely mentioned is that they were simply not fast enough and never shared the lead.

TREVOR FRECKNALL, NEWS EDITOR, ATHLETICS WEEKLY, PETERBOROUGH.

904: Are there any words in English which rhyme with 'pint' or 'orange'? If not, are there any other words with no rhymes?

I can recall no rhymes for the word pint and other words which pose a rhyming problem are further, film, restaurant, oblige and fugue. Many words have only proper nouns as full rhyming partners. The nearest rhyme I know for orange is syringe but this offers a different metrical balance in a line of poetry as it is iambic rather than trochaic – an unstressed syllable followed by a stressed one, rather than a stressed syllable followed by an unstressed. To use orange in a rhymed poem, I would suggest the near-rhyme porridge or, better still, say tangerine which is far more poetic.

ALISON CHISHOLM, AUTHOR: THE CRAFT OF WRITING POETRY, SOUTHPORT, MERSEYSIDE.

There are about 160 words in the English language that end 'int' like pint, including point, faint, dint etc. But there are no well-known rhyming words among them. Perhaps 'cuckoopint', a type of flower, would make a good rhyme though as it ends in 'pint' it would to a certain extent be cheating. In the case of orange, there are roughly 30 words that end 'ange', such as strange, change, range, etc. Once again it is a case of same letter ending with different pronunciation. Words that sound very similar and could possibly be accepted as rhyming might be hinge or mange though purists would disagree. There are many other words in our language for which there are no other rhyming words. Ones that spring to mind are skeleton, limited, ninth and – ironically – poem, although the word 'proem' is still in the dictionary.

EDMUND WEINER, OXFORD ENGLISH DICTIONARY, OXFORD.

It would indeed be cheating, as suggested, to attempt to rhyme cuckoopint with pint. The 'pint' in cuckoopint is pronounced to rhyme with flint, mint, etc, being derived from the old English *pintel,* meaning penis. Anyone who has seen a cuckoopint – also known as cuckoo-pintle – can see why it was so named.   ERIC THOMAS, PURLEY, SURREY.

There was an old man named Geraint Went into a pub in Pumpsaint. He talked for an hour Of Owen Glendower And left without buying a pint. (Pumpsaint, in Dyfed, is pronounced 'Pimp-signt.') The master of metre, W. S. Gilbert, suggested inventors could help rhymesters by giving their inventions names to rhyme to some of our many common words with few or no rhymes. Gilbert, like many a lyricist before and since, lamented the paucity of rhymes to 'love', 'above' and 'dove' being sadly overworked, while 'glove' has its limitations. Rose-Marie was too romantic for its hero to have wooed with the words: 'Rose-Marie, I love you. I'll never kick or shove you.' Gilbert also noted that 'revenge' and 'avenge' could muster only Penge and Stonehenge: A sacked young curator from Penge Determined to have his revenge, So one day, in malice, He burnt down Kew Palace And wrote naughty words on Stonehenge. Those who cavil at 'malice' and 'palace' are reminded that A. A. Milne's Christopher Robin went down with Alice to Buckingham Palace.

GEOFFREY WILSON, LONDON.

Years ago a magazine ran a competition for the best limerick composed to rhyme with a given word. One month they tested readers with the word 'silver' and the winning limerick went: There was an old man who said 'wilver', And 'bilver' and 'gilver' and 'nilver', His daughter said 'Dad, You've gone suddenly mad', He said 'No, but what does rhyme with silver?'   BRUCE REDDINGTON, SURBITON, SURREY.

There is a single syllable English word which I believe to be rhyme-free: the word month.   G. S. TUCKER, MODBURY, DEVON.

905: What is the history of hot cross buns? How many are eaten in the UK every year?

The distinctively marked hot cross bun at Eastertime is known to have been a fundamental part of the Christian culture since at least AD1361. It is suggested that at St Albans Abbey at this time the monks used dough left over from making the sacramental bread for Good Friday to create small buns for the poor. They marked the buns with the cross to represent the crucifixion. However, buns or cakes marked with a cross have been with us during spring since at least the Roman and Greek periods. Both ancient societies ate small wheat buns around the time of the spring equinox. And Britain's own pagan festivals used similar buns during the worship of the goddess Eaostre, using a cross to represent the four quarters of the moon. LOUISE PLATT, J. SAINSBURY PLC, LONDON.

906: What do the inscriptions on the edge of £1 coins mean?

The £1 coins minted in 1983 and 1993 (with the 'Ensigns Armorial of Our United Kingdom of Great Britain and Northern Ireland') have the edge inscription *Decus et tutamen.* These Latin words also appear on the 1988 UK £1 coin (with the 'Shield of Our Royal Arms ensigned by representation of the Royal Crown'), the 1986 and 1991 Northern Ireland £1 coins (with the 'Flax Plant eradicated enfiling a representation of Our Royal Diadem') and the 1987 and 1992 England £1 coins (with 'Oak Tree enfiling a representation of Our Royal Diadem') and mean: 'An ornament and a safeguard.' The Scotland £1 coin, minted in 1984 and 1989 (with the 'Thistle eradicated enfiling a representation of Our Royal Diadem') has the Latin inscription *Nemo me impune lacessit* meaning: 'No-one provokes me with impunity'. The Wales £1 coin, minted in 1985 and 1990, (with the 'Leek eradicated enfiling a representation of Our Royal Diadem') is inscribed with the Welsh *Pleidiol wyf i'm gwlad,* which translates as: 'True am I to my country'. The Latin inscription *Sic vos non vobis* which appears on the edge of the £2 coin, struck this year to commemorate the tercentenary of the Bank of England, means: 'Thus you labour, but not for yourselves'. It was the motto of William Paterson, the colourful entrepreneur who suggested the plan on which the bank was established in 1694. DEREK SLARK, THE ROYAL MINT, LLANTRISANT, GLAMORGAN.

907: What became of the leading lady of British silent films, Flora Le Breton?

Flora Le Breton was born in 1898 and became a leading stage and film actress during the era of silent movies. She was a pretty English actress, typical of her time, whose last known film was an early sound version of Charley's Aunt, made in America in 1930. The film also starred Charles Ruggles, June Collier and Hugh Williams. Possibly another victim of the advent of 'talkies', she was last heard of as living in New York in 1935 but research has found no mention of her since that date. JANET AMBROSE, CAMBRIDGE.

908: My index fingers are shorter, my wife's longer, than our respective ring fingers. Is one of us normal and the other abnormal, or is the human race divided 50-50 in this matter?

In most cases the three central fingers on the hand are approximately the same length. However, there is variation within the normal range. It's not unusual for one person to have a slightly longer ring finger than index finger and vice versa. Neither can be said to be abnormal though it's most unlikely that the human race is divided equally in this matter.

DR A. KESSLING, GENETICIST, ST MARY'S HOSPITAL SCHOOL OF MEDICINE, LONDON.

Most glove companies manufacture their gloves with the index and ring fingers exactly the same length. And who would know better?

GERRY DAVIDSON, COVENTRY.

The third finger is longer than the first on most hands, though it's also common to find these fingers of equal length. Far fewer hands possess a longer index finger. It's said that Napoleon's index finger was slightly longer than his second finger, a combination which, in 25 years as a palmist, I have yet to see.

DAVID A. CANTELLO, KILGETTY, PEMBROKESHIRE.

909: How much of the famous Cape to Cairo railway was actually completed?

The Cape to Cairo railway was the brainchild of British statesman and Empire builder Cecil Rhodes, who made it his goal to encourage the expansion of British power throughout Africa and the entire world. One of the ways in which he aimed to achieve this was to build a railway from Capetown in South Africa to Cairo in Egypt. Although his railway ended in Bulawayo in 1897, five years before his death, he was very happy to have reached so far. Within South Africa, Sir Cecil succeeded in helping to extend the Cape Railways to Johannesburg, through the Orange Free State. It's possible today to travel from South Africa as far as Tanzania by rail. This route is taken on Rovos Rail's Edwardian Train Safari between Capetown and Dar Es Salaam on one of the most luxurious trains in the world, The Pride Of Africa.

ALISON WHITFIELD, SOUTH AFRICA TOURISM OFFICE, LONDON.

910: When soldiers fire their guns in the air, is there any danger from the falling bullets?

Experiments on this specific question and many others regarding bullet speed and velocity were conducted before World War I by ballistics expert R. L. Tippins on tidal mud on the Suffolk side of the River Stour. Similar experiments took place in Germany and the U.S. Tippins discovered that the Lee Enfield .303 mark VII, later used in both world wars, had a muzzle velocity of 2,350ft per second and that a bullet fired exactly vertically would rise for 19 seconds to a height of 9,000ft. Its maximum returning velocity would be 300ft per second, taking another 36 seconds to hit the ground. On landing, the bullet would have 30ft/lbs energy. Estimates at the time suggested it would need around 60ft/lbs to injure anyone. On a soft pine roof board at the launch point, the bullet would cause only a one-sixteenth inch dent, like a light tap with a hammer. The bullets were very unstable in flight, depending on air conditions, and hardly ever fell at the spot from which they were fired.

BILL CURTIS, NATIONAL RIFLE ASSOC MUSEUM, BISLEY, SURREY.

When a salute is fired, members of the armed forces fire blank rounds into the air, brass cases containing a charge only, so there's no danger from falling bullets. ANTHONY FAIRBANKS WESTON, ARMY HEADQUARTERS, COLCHESTER.

In many countries where firing of live rounds has occurred as part of some informal celebration there have been numerous confirmed deaths from descending bullets. An example closer to home would be the significant number of deaths caused during World War II from returning anti-aircraft fire. LIAM MARTIN, STREATHAM, LONDON.

During Battle Of Britain over southern England in 1940, I was looking skywards at the many aerial dogfights when I was wounded by a falling bullet shot from the ground at one of the planes. It lodged in my neck, just missing the main artery and a small operation and five nights in the hospital soon put things right. A similar thing happen to my father during the Blitz but he was wearing his tin hat and avoided being killed or injured. EDWIN NICE, BETCHWORTH.

911: Why do Americans have to take a blood test before marriage? Has anyone been prevented from marrying because of the results?

It depends on the state in which you wish to be married, as each has its own laws, regulations and systems. Some require blood tests, others require medical information, some simply require identification before you can marry on the spot. A total of 35 states require some form of medical test or, at least, medical information about the couple. But only 33 request a blood test. The tests are generally to determine if the couple are compatible should they wish to have children. Other tests may be for venereal disease, rubella, TB, sickle cell anaemia, AIDS (optional) or even mental competence. In the case of partners being found to be unsuitable, the couple are made aware of this information but not normally prevented from marriage. In other cases, a marriage licence will not be given until an infection found has been treated. But this cannot stop the couple travelling to another state with different laws and marrying there.

JUDITH MCCARTHY, SENIOR REGISTRAR, BOSTON REGISTRY OFFICE, MASSACHUSETTS.

912: What powered ornamental fountains before steam or electric pumps were available?

The simple answer is gravity but, as with most things in life, it's not quite that easy. The ornamental waterworks at Chatsworth, Derbyshire, are a classic example. Two systems of valves, streams and pipes control various fountains and waterfalls, one high pressure the other low. The high pressure system was installed by Sir Joseph Paxton in the 1840s for the 6th Duke of Devonshire and harnesses a 400ft head of water to produce a jet capable of rising to 296ft. The system consists of a catchment area of five square miles with seven miles of streams carrying the water to three linked lakes, which have a combined capacity of more than 30 million gallons. The water is then delivered from the Emperor Lake to the fountain through 880 yards of 15in-diameter, cast-iron pipe. When the fountain is not in use during the winter, this system drives a water turbine to produce electricity for Chatsworth House. The low pressure system makes the water work equally hard. It flows through pipes and streams down two waterfalls, through the cascade then on to the Sea Horse Fountain and another in the West Front Garden. They finally flow into the River Derwent. The main feature of this system is the newly-restored Cascade, built in 1703 by Thomas Archer. Water runs down the roof then reappears, pouring through vases and dolphins' mouths to tumble on stone trays, which deflect it away from the building, creating a shower of droplets. The water then flows down 24 flights of stairs, each designed to make a different sound as the water rushes over them: what a feat of engineering. JOHN OLIVER, ASSISTANT COMPTROLLER, CHATSWORTH HOUSE, DERBYS.

913: Did Sir Arthur Conan Doyle invent the name Sherlock for his famous detective or was it already in use?

The name Sherlock has some pedigree as a surname in Ireland – Doyle's parents were Irish – and a fellow student of his at Stoneyhurst College had that surname but it was unknown as a Christian name. When Doyle wrote his first Sherlock Holmes story, A Study In Scarlet in 1886, he considered calling his detective Sherrinford Holmes before settling on Sherlock. Much later, in October 1921, Doyle told an audience gathered to celebrate the first film version of Sherlock Holmes that playing cricket for the United Services against the MCC, 'The MCC brought down against us two fine bowlers in Atwell and Sherlock…and I think the name Sherlock impressed itself on my mind.' But Lilleywhite's Cricketer's Companion and local newspaper reports show Doyle's memory was at fault. It wasn't until 1890, four years after the first Sherlock Holmes story, that he scored 20 runs for the United Services against the MCC and caught out a player called Shacklock. Doyle would also have known Sherwin, another famous cricketer of the time. A further MCC player of that era was Mycroft, the Christian name Doyle gave to Sherlock's brother. JOHN MICHAEL GIBSON, GREAT BOOKHAM, SURREY.

914: How did the saying 'not by a long chalk' come about?

'A long chalk' means by a long way or a large amount, so an athlete may beat somebody 'by a long chalk' if they have a convincing win. Conversely 'not by a long chalk' means by a short distance or small amount. These sayings almost certainly date from the time before pencils and pens were in common use and chalk marks were used to keep score in a game or sporting event. The custom of using chalk still survives in the game of darts. ANN MCGUINNESS, MANCHESTER.

Though it's in all the reference books there's no evidence to support the idea that this expression comes from a game in which the length of a chalk mark reflected the comparative standing of the players. The earliest references are to instances where no such scoring took place. In horseracing, R. H. Barham's 1837 Ingoldsby Legends includes: 'Alured's steed is by long chalks the best of the party.' In boxing, Charles Selby's 1844 London By Night has: '…which will come off second best by long chalks.' And Rolf Boldrewood's Robbery Under Arms has: 'Isn't it easy?' 'Not by a long chalk.' In fact, no one knows this expression's origin but a good guess is that the old use of 'chalk' meaning 'to score', as in cutting a groove, is involved, with a punning reference to scoring in games. This meaning appears in nautical use for a scratch or scar, as in Marryat's 1840 Poor Jack: 'I got this chalk…' and in thieves' argot as 'to strike.' This gave us The Chalkers, the Irish equivalent of London's 18th century Mohocks, who walked the streets indiscriminately slashing ('chalking') with a knife the faces of passers-by. The 'long' part may be like the old 'long' or 'royal' count whereby a 'long hundred' was 120 and a 'long score' 24. So 'a long chalk' is simply an intensifier, bearing no relation to the length of a mark or to a stick of chalk. DR TIM HEALEY, BARNSLEY, SOUTH YORKS.

915: One and twopenny pieces minted after 1991 are magnetic, while those minted during and before are not. Why has the iron content increased?

The first 1p and 2p coins, introduced on February 15, 1971, with the advent of decimal coinage, were made of bronze. This continued until September 1992, by which time the bronze content of the coins was worth more than their face value and the metal had to be changed. From that date, all 1p and 2p coins are made of copper-plated steel, which has magnetic properties. The older bronze coins are not being taken out of circulation and continue to be used alongside the newer ones. There are approximately 3,700 million 2p pieces and 6,000 million 1p pieces in circulation.   DEREK SLARK, ROYAL MINT, LLANTRISANT, MID GLAMORGAN.

916: Is it true that in Britain, more people go to church on Sunday than attend football matches on Saturday?

A fair proportion of our worshipping population don't actually have Sunday as their sabbath day. Two examples are the Jewish community, who have a national attendance figure at synagogues throughout the country of around 50,000 people on a typical Saturday, and the Moslems, with a figure of around 350,000 on a typical Friday. The breakdown for churchgoers on a typical Sunday is: 1.56 million Roman Catholics, 1.24 million Anglicans, 400,000 Methodists, 200,000 Baptists, 550,000 Church of Scotland, 120,000 United Reformed, 300,000 Independent, 100,000 Pentecostal, 80,000 Afro-Caribbean, 10,000 Orthodox, and about 100,000 others, a total in Britain of 4,660,000. Taking the Association of Football Statisticians' figures for attendance at professional football games on a typical Saturday in January they were broken down as follows: 559,193 at all 45 Football League and FA Premier League games in England and Wales; 61,179 at all 19 Scottish League games; and 14,632 at all ten GM Vauxhall Conference games: a total attendance of 635,004. Comparing church and football attendance, it's plain to see that in Britain as a whole, for every one person who goes to a football match on a Saturday, roughly seven others will go to church on a Sunday.   PATRICIA HARDING, DURHAM.

917: Did the escape by the Army expedition in Malaysia recall for anyone a similarly incredible escape by a British soldier in a Fifties plane crash there?

In December 1956, Driver Lee, a 20-year-old National Serviceman, was the sole survivor when a Royal New Zealand Air Force Bristol freighter crashed on a 4,200 ft high steep ridge in deepest jungle in central Malaya. Driver Lee was an air-dispatcher with 55 Company, Royal Army Service Corps, now amalgamated into the Royal Logistical Corps, who were dropping supplies by air to soldiers fighting the communist terrorists in the Malayan jungle. The wreckage could only be reached by SAS soldiers from the air and so thick was the jungle, it took two and half days for the SAS to hack their way 2,000 yards to the wreck site. It appeared that the whole crew had perished and Driver Lee's parents were informed that he had been killed in action. But a fighting patrol of the 4th Malay Regiment remained in the area in case terrorist scavengers came upon the wreckage. Deeper in the jungle, they came across a makeshift shelter, reporting their findings by radio. But it might have been an abandoned terrorist camp. So the Malay patrol began following the rough track and camps, which they found 1,000 yards apart. In the meantime, Driver Lee was aware that the terrorists might attempt to capture him as a prize hostage. On the morning of the 12th day after the crash, a ragged figure was seen crossing a river by a rough rope bridge left by the Malay patrol. The ragged figure made it known to the Malay soldiers that he was not a terrorist but a survivor of the crash. He had burned hands and arms and his left ankle was broken. He had found his own rescuers. In hospital in Kuala Lumpur, on December 23, 1956, he telephoned his parents and told them of his ordeal and flight to safety. In a straight line, Driver Lee had covered about seven miles through uncharted jungle, living on one handful of rice, twice a day. In total, he probably covered 12 miles. I was in Malaysia in the Sixties with the 8th Royal Australian Regiment and saw the cine film taken of the aircraft wreckage. You can't imagine how frightening the jungle was when you couldn't even see daylight through it. The man deserved a medal but was merely mentioned in dispatches. PETER LAIDLER, MARCHAM, OXFORDSHIRE.

918: Why do we use a water bird's name in expressions such as 'queer as a coot' and 'the old coot'?

The water-loving coot is an ungainly bird on land. Its clumsy walk, like that of a chicken, may have given rise to the belief that it is strange or stupid. It certainly looks odd, its black body contrasting with a featherless white patch on its head. As early as 1325 people in Sussex, Somerset and Gloucestershire, knew the bird as the 'bald coot', while Scots folk called it the bell kite, a dialectal variant of the same name.
DEREK NIEMANN, ROYAL SOCIETY FOR THE PROTECTION OF BIRDS, SANDY, BEDS.

919: What is it about storks and gooseberry bushes that got them associated with the arrival of babies?

The idea of finding a baby under a gooseberry bush probably stems from the ancient practice of 'exposing' sickly or unwanted babies to the elements as a way of getting rid of them without having to murder them outright. Killing an unwanted child was thought immoral but leaving it to fate was not a crime. The practice is best-known through the Spartans, but it most certainly also happened in Britain and the rest of Europe until only a few hundred years ago. The reason a gooseberry bush was used was that in many cases of 'exposing' where the child was not sickly, it was a place where for a while it would be safe for long enough for it to be found by a passer-by and passed on to a couple who genuinely wanted a child. The gooseberry has very sharp and long thorns that would protect a child from any likely predator, thus giving the child a chance of survival. The modern explanantion of 'finding a child under a gooseberry bush' began during the Victorian era to answer the sort of 'Daddy, where did I come from?' questions that embarrassed parents in those less open days. HEATHER WINTERHOLME, LEEDS.

Storks have been highly regarded for centuries and long associated with the arrival of babies. They have always had the reputation of being caring – parent birds look after their young and the young, in turn, are believed to look after their parents in old age. Storks were linked with virtues such as gratitude and temperance and described as omens of harmony and fertility. In continental Europe, storks often nest on roofs of houses and are regarded as the bringers of good luck. In the 16th century, it was a common belief that a stork nesting on a house left one of its own young in gratitude to the owner. So the stork became a symbol of generosity and its arrival linked with the gift of a child. But beware: a good child arrives on the back of the stork, while a naughty one will be brought in its beak. CHRIS HARBARD, ROYAL SOCIETY FOR THE PROTECTION OF BIRDS, SANDY, BEDS.

920: Could burning joss sticks or scented candles be as bad for one's health as passive smoking?

Tobacco smoke contains at least 42 cancer-causing chemicals, which is why about 35,000 smokers and 300 non-smokers affected by passive smoking die from lung cancer every year. Passive smoking can also cause respiratory and other diseases in children, exacerbate asthma and may cause heart disease. There have so far been no studies of the effects of breathing the smoke from joss sticks or scented candles. However, although it is known that smoke and fumes from any source and the human body don't really mix, it seems unlikely they would cause damage on a comparable scale. AMANDA SANDFORD, ACTION ON SMOKING AND HEALTH (ASH), LONDON.

A study published in The Science Of The Total Environment in 1991 showed that candles, wax lights and incense – the latter a source of polycyclic aromatic hydrocarbons – were important contributors of soot. Earlier studies have postulated open lamps and candles caused pneumoconiosis among Scottish coalminers. However, under reasonable ventilation conditions, one ought still to be able to enjoy an anxiety-free candlelit dinner for two followed by coffee, liqueurs and a Virginia or Havana. A. A. WOOD, AMERSHAM, BUCKS.

921: Is it possible to live on vitamin pills and water and nothing else?

No. Vitamins are essential for good health but we also need other nutrients such as protein, carbohydrate, small amounts of fat and minerals. There's no substitute for a balanced diet of fruit and vegetables, wholegrains, dairy products, lean meat and fish.

GEN ANDREW, ROCHE PRODUCTS LTD, WELWYN GARDEN CITY.

922: Is the width of the pockets on professional snooker tables, used on TV, wider than those at my snooker club?

The width of pockets on all full-sized snooker tables should conform to specifications laid down by the Snooker and Billiards Control Council. It supplies each member with a standard template which is stamped each year. The width of each pocket should be 3½ins at the fall where the ball drops. If a maximum 147 break is to be ratified, the table has to be remeasured with the official template. There is no difference between the size of pockets on the snooker tables seen on TV and those at local snooker clubs: it's just the high calibre of play that makes it look that way.

PETER LUDGATE, HUBBLE AND FREEMAN SNOOKER TABLES, MAIDSTONE, KENT.

While there's no difference on the entry width of the pockets, the contour of a cross-section through the cushion on a professional table shows that it is radiused to the shape of the ball. This means the ball will still go into the pocket after a greater degree of error in the 'pot.' The diameter of a snooker ball is 2 and one sixteenth inches and, because the cushion height is above the centre of the ball, it fits further under the cushion due to the radius of the cushion. I believe the true pocket width is therefore greater on professional tables.

J. KNOWLES, LUTON, BEDS.

923: Who was the man who broke the bank at Monte Carlo?

Charles De Ville Wells emptied the Monaco Casino's cash reserves not once, but six times in three days, during an extraordinary run of luck in July 1891. Playing roulette, and using a version of the Martingale System in which a gambler doubles his stake every time he loses, the 50-year-old London businessman turned his initial £400 into £40,000. Later that year he won another £10,000 at the casino. However, Wells was later jailed for false pretences over his English business ventures, losing his reputation and his fortune. He died penniless in 1926.

KEVIN HANDS, NO MAN'S LAND, CORNWALL.

The man who really broke the bank at Monte Carlo was Joseph Hobson Jagger (1830-1892), from Shelf, outside Bradford. Jagger was a textile engineer with a natural flair for statistics and a belief that roulette wheels were bound to be biased if they spun on wooden spindles, which were the basis of his fortune. After several days of watching, he realised one particular roulette wheel had a bias towards certain numbers and his bets on this wheel paid dividends. Although Jagger was cautious, the management changed the wheels around the following morning. That evening Jagger guessed what had happened and located the faulty wheel. Realising his time was now limited, he bet enormous sums, eventually winning more than two million French francs, about £500,000 in today's values. His success led to the temporary closure of the casino and the introduction of ball bearings instead of wooden spindles in all the wheels. The song The Man Who Broke The Bank At Monte Carlo was written in the year he died. His grave, with an impressive monument, can be seen at Bethel Churchyard, Shelf.   A. AMBLER, PUDSEY, WEST YORKS.

924: Was the children's author Dr Seuss a medical doctor and is he/she still alive?

Dr Seuss's real name was Theodor Seuss Giesel. Born in 1904 at Springfield, Massachusetts, he later studied at Lincoln College, Oxford. For his first adult novel, Seven Lady Godivas, published in 1939, he added the authoritative-sounding 'Dr' to his name, as a way of distinguishing between his adult works and the books he was writing for children. He was responsible for 48 children's titles, his most famous being the Cat In The Hat series, first published in 1958. Most of his children's books are still in print. Seuss was also a playwright and cartoonist and illustrated his own work. He was never a qualified doctor but was given an honorary doctorate in the Seventies and died in September 1991.

ANN SOHN-RETHEL, CHILDREN'S LIBRARIAN, YOUNG BOOK TRUST, LONDON.

925: I have an engraving of George II entitled 'King of Great Britain, France and Ireland.' By what right did he claim to be King of France? Who was the last English monarch to use that title?

The claim to the title of Monarch of France was officially in existence from 1340 until 1801. It originated in 1328 when Edward III's uncle, Charles IV of France, died without leaving an heir and Edward claimed the French throne through his mother Isabella, Charles's sister. Conflicts with France ensued and, even though at one point his forces reached the gates of Paris, Edward's claims on France were ultimately unsuccessful. The 1801 Act Of Union with Ireland declared that the title of the new state should be the United Kingdom of Great Britain and Ireland, dropping the claim to the throne of France, so the last English monarch to carry this title was George III. DAVID JOHNSON, HOUSE OF LORDS RECORD OFFICE, LONDON.

926: Would Shakespeare have had personal experience of black people when he wrote Othello?

There would have been a distinct black population in London when Shakespeare wrote Othello in 1603. The earliest documented black person in London was a trumpeter at the court of Henry VII in 1507, though there had been black soldiers serving with the Roman army in Britain many centuries earlier. As the slave trade with West Africa developed in the second half of the 16th century, black people were brought to England as slave-servants for the aristocracy or as entertainers at court. Peter Fryer's book, Staying Power: The History Of Black People In Britain (Pluto Press, 1984), notes a 'lytle Blackamore' at court around 1577 and a picture of around 1575, depicting Queen Elizabeth I and her Court at Kenilworth Castle, shows a group of black musicians and dancers. As someone who was familiar with the court, Shakespeare would almost certainly have had personal experience of a number of black people. In the Gray's Inn Christmas revels of 1594, one of the parts was played by a woman called Lucy Negro, who was almost certainly black. Some have even suggested that she was Shakespeare's 'Dark Lady' of the sonnets. DR NICK MERRIMAN, MUSEUM OF LONDON.

927: Can anyone complete the clever wartime parody of Lewis Carroll's Jabberwocky poem which begins: 'Twas Munich and the Nazi hordes, Did heil and Hitler in the Reich...'?

The wartime parody of Lewis Carroll's Jabberwocky that came into my hands during the World War II is known as The Song Of The Grabberwoch and goes:

'Twas Danzig and the Swastikoves
Did heil and hittle in the reich,
All Nazi were the lindengroves
And the neuraths julesstreich.

'Beware the Grabberwoch, my son,
The plans that spawn, the plots that hatch,
Beware the Jewjew burd and shun
The fuhrious Bundersnatch.

'He took his Aryan horde in hand.
Long time the Gestapo he taught,

Then rested at the Baltic Sea,
And stood a while in thought.

'And as a Polish oath he swore,
The Grabberwoch with lies aflame
Came Goering down the Corridor,
And goebbled as he came.

'Ein Zwei, Ein Zwei, one in the eye
For Polska folk, alas, alack!
He left them dread, and as their head
He came meinkampfing back.

'And hast thou ta'en their lebensraum?
Come to my arms, my rhinish boy.
O, grabjous day, sing heil, be gay!
He strengthened in his joy.'

R. V. Lyle, Witney, Oxfordshire.

928: Vera Lynn and Ann Shelton were 'forces sweethearts' for men in the armed forces during World War II, but there were tens of thousands of women also serving. Were there any forces sweethearts for them?

English romantic vocalist Denny Dennis certainly was; he made several hundred recordings, first with the bands of Jack Jackson, Roy Fox and Ambrose in the Thirties and at the outbreak of the war worked for the BBC's light music and variety departments, which were then based in Bristol, where he broadcast sometimes as often as six times a day, appearing as a guest artist on programmes like ITMA and Much Binding In The Marsh. In 1940 he enlisted in the RAF, serving until 1945 and entertaining troops not only in this country but in Iceland. In addition to his own commercial recordings, he made many others for Overseas Recorded Broadcast Services. These were a mixture of solo recordings and live shows with the Skyrockets Orchestra and were shipped out to Europe, the Middle and Fast East for rebroadcasting to troops. As a result, Denny's fan club received many letters from serving women and he became known as the man who sang a thousand love songs. After the war his solo career continued, he sang with the Tommy Dorsey band in America in 1948/49 and he continued to make records, broadcast and tour with bands like Harry Leader, Sid Phillips, Frank Weir and Vic Lewis until the music scene changed drastically in the late Fifties. Denny died in November 1994 on the day after his 80th birthday. As a mark of their appreciation of his contribution to music The British Academy of

Songwriters, Composers and Authors, gave him one of their coveted gold badge awards the previous month. In his home city of Derby he has been honoured by the erection of a plaque on the house where he was born, the only one of its kind in the city.   MIKE CAREY, DARLEY ABBEY, DERBY.

The U.S. Government put Clark Gable in Air Force officer's uniform – and very handsome he looked – and sent him to England and elsewhere. He hated it.   JACK KEIGHTLEY, PEACEHAVEN, SUSSEX.

Clark Gable volunteered for U.S. Army Air Force service in August 1942 after being devastated by the death in a plane crash of his film-star wife Carole Lombard that year. The Pentagon decided to make a film of his life as an air gunner, as a recruiting aid, and he was sent for officer training. In January 1943, as a First Lieutenant, he was awarded his gunner's wings and assigned to 508 Bomb Squadron, 351st Bombardment Group (Heavy), which flew B-17 Flying Fortresses. In April 1943 the group was based at Polebrook, Northants. Gable, at 41, was twice the age of most other aircrew, some of whom called him 'Pappy' behind his back. By June that year, Gable was a captain and flew five missions over France, Germany and Norway. He was scared that if he was shot down and captured he would be put in a cage as an exhibit, on Hitler's orders. He was awarded the Air Medal for operational services, and the Europe-Africa-Middle Eastern Campaign Medal with Bronze Star. In October Gable was posted back to the U.S., and in May 1944 he was promoted to Major. In June 1944 he was honourably discharged. The gunnery film, Combat America, was ready for exhibition in October.   GEORGE H. FOX, ENFIELD, MIDDLESEX.

929: What did the ordinary British family drink with their meals before tea, coffee, or cocoa were brought here?

The introduction of the first coffee house in 1652 was to a certain extent the beginning of the end for a lot of the traditional drinking habits of the typical British family. This great new interest in coffee was followed five years later with the first recorded sale of tea and about the same time the first introduction of cocoa. All three drinks went on to become, very quickly, the standard drinks of the nation, eradicating many of the traditional liquids that had been popular before. Until this time the average family would have drunk either water, milk, an ale of some kind, wine, cider, or a mix of hot or cold water with various herbs, fruits, honey etc. The drinks available were all normally made from whatever could be found locally, and would have included drinks such as nettle juice, elderberry juice, apple juice, sloe juice, goat's milk, rye wine, wheat wine, barley wine, grape juice and a myriad of combinations of some natural ingredient mixed with water. The idea of tea or coffee was not exactly alien to the typical British family either, as it is known that many families would have infused various leaves to make a hot leaf tea of some kind, or dug up dandelion roots, roast and ground them, and then had dandelion coffee. Today there is a resurgence in many of these earlier drinks as can be witnessed in the many new 'old drinks' that have come on to the market, the growth in beer and wine making, and herbalism and homeopathic remedies. PATRICK REGAN, PAGAN AND CELTIC HISTORIAN, SOUTHPORT.

930: When and where did the practice of wearing heels on our shoes start in Western society?

For at least the past 2,000 years it is known that our footwear has generally been equipped with some form of small heel; even the invading Romans used heels on their shoes. These heels were only very small, in most cases only a few millimetres thick, because it was believed a heel made a shoe more comfortable to wear. By contrast, in most eastern societies the use of a heel has never played a part in any of their fashions. The fashion for heels as we know them today began in the late 16th century. The heel size fluctuated from this point onwards but was always prominent, and by the 1770s had shot up to a point where some heels were as high, although not as narrow, as the typical stiletto heel found today. Just ten years later, in the 1780s, the fashion for heels in women's shoes virtually disappeared and this continued to be the case for the next hundred years. The reintroduction of the female heel in the 1870s has kept the heel firmly with us, although the sizes have been varying constantly ever since at a far quicker rate. The two most notable periods were the 1970s and today when the fashion for excessively high heels has been prominent – although these are not as high as the fashion in Italy in the 16th century for footwear known as *chopines,* which were more like slippers on stilts and were generally over 8ins high, ensuring the wearer had to be escorted everywhere in case they fell off.

AVRIL HART, TEXTILES AND FASHION SECT, VICTORIA & ALBERT MUSEUM, LONDON.

931: What is the origin of what, in the playground, we used to call 'chewing up' as a way of choosing individuals?

The practice of 'chewing up', also known as 'chinging up', 'ching chang cholly', 'flee fly flo bank', 'hik hak hok', 'dib dab dob' and many other names, has been used for centuries all over the world as a fair method of choosing an individual for a particular task. Though thought to have originated in the Orient where examples are common in Hong Kong, China and Japan as methods of betting, settling disputes or even deciding who is going to buy the next round, there is evidence of the practice of this type of game in ancient Egypt in 2,000 BC. In Rome in AD60, Calpurnius Siculus described how a similar type of game was used to see who would perform first in a singing competition. The game may have come to Britain with the Roman occupation, though later British contacts with the Far East are a more likely source for the present day playground practice. IONA OPIE, PETERSFIELD, HANTS.

932: Why are Bath chairs so called?

They are simply named after the spa town of Bath, the first town to use them. The Bath chair was invented by James Heath of Bath in the mid-18th century. At first it was associated only with invalids but by the 1830s it had replaced the sedan chair (which had no wheels and was carried by two men, one behind and one in front) as a conventional means of transport. The Bath chair had one seat enclosed in a panelled chassis with a hood. Some had glazed windows to keep out the draughts. The chairs had three iron or wooden wheels and were pulled with a tow-bar by a 'chair-man'. Chairs were manufactured in Bath by a number of companies including James Heath, Austin Dawson and W. Monk and Co but used by invalids everywhere. In the 19th century, Bath chairs were used in particular to carry the sick from their lodgings to receive treatment in the spa water or drink the waters from the Pump Room. Contemporary photographs shows rows of Bath chairs with their chair-men, dapper in frock coats and bowler hats, awaiting fares. By 1937 only six chairs were operating in Bath and the last run by a Bath chair-man was made by Ernest Ball in 1939.

JANE BIRCHER, KEEPER OF COLLECTIONS, ROMAN BATHS MUSEUM AND PUMP ROOM, BATH.

933: Why are 'pea' jackets worn by sailors in the U.S. Navy and why are they so called?

According to Naval Ceremonies, Customs, and Traditions, by William P. Mack and Royal W. Connell, the origin of 'pea-coat' is thought to be the Dutch word pij, which means a coarse, woollen cloth. The name has been with the U.S. Navy for 200 years and is applied to the heavier top coat worn by seafaring men in cold weather. The coat was originally made of a material called pilot cloth.

WENDY D. GALLAND, PUBLIC AFFAIRS OFFICE, U.S. NAVAL FORCES EUROPE.

934: How much gas, and at what cost, does a pilot light which is left on permanently use?

Pilot lights are a feature of some types and models of gas appliance, particularly central heating boilers and water heaters. They perform an important safety function and provide a convenient source of ignition. It's difficult to give a precise figure, as models and types of appliance vary but, on average, the cost is a few pence each week or a few pounds a year.

MARTIN LARKIN, BRITISH GAS, LONDON.

Over a 79-hour period, when no other gas was used, my hot water/central heating pilot light used an amount of gas equal to 59.89 cubic feet over a full year. Using British Gas instructions for calculating the number of therms: 59.89 multiplied by 1016 (calorific value), divided by 1000 gives 60.85 therms. At 45.9p per therm the annual cost would be £27.93. With a year's total bill of £260, this represents around 10 per cent of the full cost. There must be a more efficient method.

A. C. ENGLISH, ACLE, NORFOLK.

935: Why are the navigational terms port and starboard still used at sea when it would appear far simpler to use left and right?

The reason for the retention of the terms port and starboard is that they define the respective sides of a vessel, regardless of the direction in which one is facing, whereas right and left relate solely to the direction faced. Thus, the starboard side of a vessel's cargo hatch, for instance, would be the right-hand side for someone facing for'ard but the left side for someone looking aft, eliminating misunderstandings in carrying out instructions etc. When considering the many communications needed between converging ships, or aircraft, and between people looking at the same situation from different viewpoints, the potential confusions caused by the simple terms left and right could easily become highly dangerous.   CAPT W. R. HOUGHTON BOREHAM, BLUE STAR SHIP MANAGEMENT LTD, LONDON.

A red light to port and green light to starboard were officially adopted by the Royal Navy in April 1873, after a two-year trial period, as self-indicating helm signals to prevent accidents at sea. This system was the invention of my great grandfather, George Read. Other countries copied it and Mr Read received many commendations, including medals from Queen Victoria, the US President and Chancellor Bismarck of Germany. The Royal Navy gave him £200 on taking up his invention. These signals are still used throughout the world, especially on aircraft at night.

C. W. EASTMAN, DINAS POWIS, SOUTH GLAMORGAN.

The term 'starboard' dates from the Viking age when ships were steered by a specially-shaped oar, vertically displaced on the right-hand side towards the stern. The Old Norse word *ster-bord,* literally a board for steering with, came to mean that side of the ship. The other side was called the *leer-bord* or left board. At the end of the Viking age, major ports built piers and jetties to facilitate loading and unloading. Ships would be moored with the left-board to the port wall to avoid damage to the steering oar so around this period it became the custom to refer to the starboard and port sides. In the 12th century the practice of building ships with a stern rudder caught on. However, the terms for the right- and left-hand sides of a ship were by that time fixed by a fiercely traditionally-minded profession. It's also true that it avoids any confusion about whether a person is facing forward or backward on a ship; port and starboard are absolutes. J. K. SIDDORN, BRISTOL.

936: I have a postcard dated January 1917, referring to an awful explosion in London which shook doors and windows in St Albans. Is there a record of such an explosion?

A huge blast took place at the Silvertown Chemical Plant in North Woolwich on January 19, 1917. The plants was owned by Brunner Mond & Co and had been opened in 1894 to produce soda crystals from ammonia crystals. The plant later produced caustic soda from the same raw material. For the initial part of World War I the Silvertown plant lay idle but when the Ministry of Munitions was established in 1915 it was reopened to process and purify trinitrotoluene (TNT) for weapons. There was a small fire at the plant in 1915 but this was brought under control and TNT processing continued there until the explosion in January 1917. This explosion seems to have been caused by a fire which broke out in the melting-pot room. It happened at 6.52pm and was so great that buildings up to 400 yards from the plant, including a flour mill and, ironically, the local fire station, were completely demolished. A ship on the Thames, the SS Italia, was also destroyed. Locals reported molten metal, stones, bricks and earth raining down on them. Official figures say 69 people were killed, 98 seriously injured and 328 slightly injured while between 500 and 600 people suffered minor injuries. ALLISON DUFFIELD, IMPERIAL WAR MUSEUM, LONDON.

When the Brunner Mond Chemical Works exploded on Friday, January 19, 1917, in Silvertown, the entire building vanished. The flames were seen 30 miles away and windows were broken in Kings Lynn, Norfolk, 87 miles away. There was a huge crater where the factory had stood and roads, homes and buildings for six acres around were a tangled mass of wood, iron, bricks and mortar. MISS J. BUNCE, CROXLEY GREEN, HERTFORDSHIRE.

Prime Minister Lloyd George ordered an inquiry into the disaster but then 'did a Matrix Churchill' and slapped a 40-year ban on its findings. They finally emerged from the Public Records Office in 1974. In 1915, TNT was urgently needed for the war effort. Lloyd George, then

Chancellor, and Lord Moulton agreed to the disued Brunner Mond's chemical plant at Silvertown being used to refine raw TNT into crystals for shells and bombs – despite knowing of explosions at three other TNT plants. The report showed there were 83 tons of TNT on site at the time of the explosion despite the fact that only nine tons a day were manufactured, and should have been taken away daily. The TNT was made unstable by the presence of caustic soda – previously made at the plant – though Lloyd George and Moulton didn't tell the chemist in charge about the earlier explosions. King George V was at Sandringham at the time and is said to have rung the War Office having seen the red glow in the sky over London. The shock wave was felt as far away as Cambridge.   BRIAN BATEMAN, ROMFORD, ESSEX.

The Silvertown explosion had a lasting effect on all who experienced it. My mother, living in Forest Gate at the time, for many years afterwards would work out the ages of my cousins by saying: 'Now let's see, so-and-so was four in the year of the Silvertown explosion.'
MARGERY LANCASTER, HIGH WYCOMBE, BUCKINGHAMSHIRE.

Extract from the diary of the then Lord Chamberlain, Viscount Sandhurst: 'A terrible and terrific explosion took place at Brunner & Mond's Munition Works on January 19. The immense sheet of flame was seen to shoot into the sky, an explosion shook all London and then all was still. I believe rows of houses in the neighbourhood were entirely demolished, about 100 killed and a similar number wounded. I hear a window was broken in Buckingham Palace, ten or 12 miles from the scene, and windows in Carlton House Terrace. The cause is not accurately known and I suppose never will be.' January 22: 'The devastation resulting from the explosion, though not so great as at first rumoured, is immense; now they say some 60 lives were lost and some 100 injured; many killed and injured, including some soldiers at Blackheath, by falling houses, walls, projectiles of iron and brick and no doubt, I fear, many children killed and buried in the debris. Many casualties occurred because workers remained gaping at the fire which began the whole thing. There was some ten minutes' interval between the fire alarm and the explosion: of the factory itself nothing remains, a two-ton boiler was moved up like a paper bag, a mill blown up and burnt which contained 2,000 tons of flour (a serious loss), the big gasometer near by had the roof blown up with the result the gas escaped, caught alight, glared for a few moments and subsided instead of exploding. Had the wind been blowing from the west instead of from the east it is thought nothing could have saved Woolwich. The head chemist, Dr Angell, and the firemen behaved with the greatest heroism, the former, after getting the workers out, returning to help fight the flames.'   LORD SANDHURST, ST BRELADE, JERSEY.

My wife's grandmother was cooking sausages at the time of the explosion on her open range in Canning Town. The sausages disappeared up the chimney and were never seen again.   Alan C. Cooke, Winchester, Hampshire.

We lived near Crystal Palace and when the explosion occurred my father, who was cleaning his teeth, dropped his dentures into the basin and broke them, much to the amusement of us children.

Mrs M. B. West, St Austell, Cornwall.

I clearly recall the frightening Silvertown explosion, although I was only three at the time. We lived in Hilly Field Crescent, Brockley, and the family used to take shelter under the dining room table, with a mattress on top, during air raids. My father was overseas at the time and the explosion was enough to persuade my scared mother to move with her five youngsters to the more peaceful environs of Eastbourne, Sussex.

Ian Leitch, Malvern, Worcestershire.

937: It is generally recognised that the beach between high and low tides belongs to the Crown and is a public right of way. How far up a tidal creek or river does this rule apply?

The principle which gives the shore to the Crown is that it is land not capable of ordinary cultivation or occupation and so is in the nature of unappropriated soil. It has been held the the the 'foreshore' means the whole of the shore that is from time to time exposed by the receding tide, the shore and bed of the sea and of any tidal water below the line of the median high tide between the spring and neap tides. This includes any channel, creek, bay, estuary and navigable river as far up as the tide flows.

Eric Davies, H. M. Land Registry, London.

938: Why are top tennis players called 'seeds'?

We use the term 'seeds' because the selection process used in most tennis tournaments spreads the higher-ranked players evenly through the tournament, 'seeding' them as a farmer or horticulturalist would space out planted seeds, rather than clumping them together, and allowing them to reach their full and natural growth.

Linda Maguire, Wimbledon Tennis Museum, London.

This word isn't really 'seeds' but 'cedes', from the Latin *cedere,* meaning to hand over or yield. It indicates something yielded up, given or allotted, and is used in tennis to indicate positions given up to others in accordance with form and performance.   Mrs J. M. Crickmore, Mitcham, Surrey.

939: How many different ways are there to perm the batting order of the 11 cricket players?

Incredibly, the answer is close to 40 million. Batsman No 1 can be chosen from any of the 11 players, so there are 11 ways of filling this position. For each of these 11 ways the No 2 spot can be filled by any of the remaining ten players. The number of ways of choosing Nos 1 and 2 is therefore 11 x 10. Similarly, the No 3 batsman can be chosen in nine ways, giving a total for the first three positions of 11 x 10 x 9. Proceeding in this fashion, the number of ways for the entire team is 11 x 10 x 9 x 8 x 7 x 6 x 5 x 4 x 3 x 2 x 1. This works out at 39,916,800 different permutations for the batting order – as if the selectors hadn't got enough to think about already.   F. M. JEPSON, LANCASTER, LANCASHIRE.

940: How long would it take an army of one million soldiers to march past a given point, non-stop, in single file, at normal marching pace?

Normal marching speeds of the various regiments in the British Army differ considerably. The Guards, for example, generally march at 120 paces a minute while the Light Infantry manage 160 paces a minute. The only constant is the fact that the step is exactly 30in long and the gap between the rows of soldiers is also 30in. If we were to take an average of 140 paces a minute, this would mean that 70 soldiers (if in single file) would pass a given point every minute. Thus, for one million soldiers to pass this same point would take 14,286 minutes, or just over 238 hours – nearly ten days.   PHIL HUTTON, ASHTON-UNDER-LYNE, MANCHESTER.

An accurate method to assess this is contained in the formula used to calculate the adequacy of the means of escape from a building in case of fire. An exit 525mm wide is reckoned to allow people to pass through in single file at a rate of 40 persons a minute. Under this formula, it would take 17 days and eight hours to evacuate a million people from one door, though the logistics of forming the queue might dictate that it took considerably longer. The formula was originally worked out by the French Army to enable it to calculate troop movements in confined spaces when designing the fortifications of the Maginot Line.
                                      R. C. BAILEY, ST AUSTELL, CORNWALL.

941: Why is it considered bad luck to carry a box of Swan Vestas matches aboard a boat or ship?

It was not actually considered bad luck. Swan Vestas weren't allowed on boats or ships because the matches were very easy to ignite. Anyone taking matches aboard was asked to carry the Bryant and May safety match instead, which had been approved for use on boats and ships. Any measure that could reduce the risk of fire was gladly taken up by the sailors – fire of course, being sailors' worst enemy at sea.

ROGER N. WILLIAMS, MASTER AT ARMS (RETD), PORTLAND, DORSET.

It is certainly considered bad luck on fishing boats. I was given a dressing-down for carrying Swan Vestas while at sea and was told the swan on the box is held to represent the unfortunate albatross from Coleridge's epic poem The Rime Of The Ancient Mariner. In some extreme cases, the skipper will throw them over the side, circle them three times and return to port. PHILIP HANVEY, SEAHOUSES, NORTHUMBERLAND.

942: Why is a V-shaped hairline known as a widow's peak?

The V-shaped hairline is so named due to its resemblance to a form of headwear commonly worn by widows from the 16th to the early 20th century. The mourning dress of widows was considered from earliest times to be of the utmost importance. Strict conventions for court mourning were laid down as early as the 15th century, based on principles of modesty and tradition. An essential part of mourning apparel was the enveloping headdress, usually comprising a black hood, inner cap and a veil. Mary, Queen of Scots, widowed at the ages of 16 and 36, wore a wired mourning veil, a shadow (or gauze veil) and a close-fitting cap with a peak at the forehead. Although not an innovation, from this time a peaked headdress became associated with a widow and such a headdress was generally referred to as a Marie Stuart hood. The peak was usually a flap projecting from the headdress, falling over the forehead in anything from a gentle V to a sharp zig-zag. In the 19th century, Queen Victoria, in mourning for the death of her husband, Prince Albert, wore a cap with a front peak, based on a mourning headdress shown in a portrait of Mary, Queen of Scots.

JILL DRAPER, KEEPER OF COSTUME AND TEXTILES, LUTON MUSEUM SERVICE.

943: Why is it said of people who fail to do something that they cannot do it 'for toffee'?

The saying has nothing to do with other familiar expressions such as 'toffee-nosed', 'toff', or even 'toffee' as a word for empty flattery. It comes simply from the normal use of toffee, a type of sweet. In other words, even the knowledge of a small reward at the end of a task still wouldn't have any effect on the person's ability to perform, thus showing them to be hopeless even when presented with an incentive.

RUTH MARKS, CAMBERLEY, SURREY.

944: When listening to the wireless in the Twenties and Thirties, reception was not as efficient in daylight as after dark, when distant stations were clear due to the effects of the 'heavyside layer'. We do not hear anything about this now. Was it a theoretical fallacy?

The Heaviside-Kennelly layer, as it was called when discovered, affects radio propagation. It is part of the ionosphere, also called the E-layer, and plays a part in reflecting medium waves. During daylight a lower layer – the D-layer – absorbs medium wave signals, limiting reception to about 200 miles. The D-layer vanishes at night, when there's no radiation from the sun, and radio waves can travel to the E-layer and beyond that to the F-layer – the Appleton Layer. These layers act as mirrors so that signals can be heard from thousands of miles away. A negative side is that domestic medium wave stations can distort badly when direct surface transmission conflicts with reflected skywaves. Developments in TV and satellite mean that this subject is now largely ignored.

S. J. MASON, HULL, HUMBERSIDE.

The Heaviside Layer was discovered by Oliver Heaviside (1850-1925), a distant relative of mine. In his book Oliver Heaviside And The Mathematical Theory Of Electrical Communication, Sir George Lee, chairman of the Radio Research Board from 1928-47, writes 'the electrical density of the layers (Heaviside) varies with the time of day and the season of the year.' Differing reception on radios is due to this varying density.

JAMES OLIVER HEAVISIDE, RETFORD, NOTTS.

945: Who was the Royal Navy hero depicted on the front of the John Player cigarette packet?

My grandfather, Joe Simpson, claimed to have designed the original Player's Navy Cut packet. He was a commercial artist from Nottingham and said the sailor he drew was a figment of his imagination.

MRS L. F. ROBINS, SKELMERSDALE, LANCS.

The sailor on the cigarette packet was my grandfather, Charles Samuel Merrey, who invented and blended the first Navy Cut tobacco mixture. Different pictures have been used since but he was the first.

MRS NEWSTEAD, ASPLEY LANE, NOTTINGHAM.

Contrary to popular belief, the figure did not represent any particular individual, though his hat referred to a ship's name. The sailor picture was simply an artist's conception for an advertising design, used as the firm's trade mark. The name of the ship appeared on the sailor's cap ribbon without the letters HMS because they were forgotten in the original drawing and the trade mark was registered without them. HMS Hero was a cruiser built in 1885, and the other ship, on the left, is HMS Britannia, a wooden three-decker with 120 guns. The name Navy Cut derived from tobacco rolled and pressed by coiling a thin rope tightly round it. To smoke, the sailors would unwind the rope a turn and slice off a pipeful of pressed plug. MRS SUE WALTERS, IMPERIAL TOBACCO, NOTTINGHAM.

During the Fifties there were many claims from old salts to having been the original Player's sailor but they were all probably too young to have a valid claim. My great uncle Charles Francis, who was born in the 1850s and died before World War I, was one model for the painting, though I suspect there may have been others. Charles and his brother Tom, my grandfather, both served in the Victorian navy before the turn of the century and both bore a striking resemblance to the Player's sailor. When my great uncle's ship was in harbour the Player's artist came on board looking for volunteers to be painted. Charles, who was a handsome man with a full set of red hair, moustache and beard, sat for the artist and was given a pint of beer and a half-crown for his services. He may not have been exactly the person in the picture of this 'imaginary' sailor, but he most certainly was the main inspiration for the artist.

ROSEMARY NIMMO, BOTLEY, SOUTHAMPTON.

In 1885 John Player came across a canvas of an unknown bearded sailor, painted by Wright of Clapham, being used by the Parkins of Chester tobacco company to advertise their Jack's Glory tobacco. Player's bought and registered the painting as a trademark for their Navy Cut cigarettes, adding a lifebelt in 1888 and two ships, HMS Britannia and HMS Hero, in 1891. During these early years many variations of background and frame appeared, including one of a boy seaman and another of the back of a sailor's head. In November 1927, Player's bought a similar portrait of a sailor, by Arthur D. McCormick RA, which they have since used for advertising. This sailor wore the cap tally HMS Invincible until 1933, then it was changed to HMS Excellent, the shore establishment at Whale Island, Portsmouth. The painting was presented by John Player and Sons to HMS Excellent in June 1980 and hangs in the wardroom Mess.

COMMANDER ALLAN ADAIR, ROYAL NAVY, THE COMMANDER, HMS EXCELLENT.

The sailor on the Player's cigarette packet is my husband's grandfather, Chief Petty Officer Thomas Huntley-Wood. He was serving on HMS Edinburgh when a photographer took a picture for a magazine in 1897. The picture appeared in the tobacco advertisement the following year. His part in the Player's trademark has been acknowledged by the company and it is his portrait which hangs in the Mess at HMS Excellent.

MRS VERA D. ROBINSON (WIFE OF ALBERT EDWARD ROBINSON, GRANDSON OF MR WOOD), BRIGHTON, EAST SUSSEX.

As a boy, I remember walking with my father in North Street, Portslade-by-Sea, and meeting a nautical gentleman who chatted with my father and was obviously a good friend. When I asked who he was, my dad said many people carried his picture in their pockets. He was the sitter for the picture on all the Player's cigarette packets. This was in the late Twenties, and my father said the man's name was Tom Wood.

E. J. WOODMAN, BRIGHTON, SUSSEX.

946: What happened to Clark Gable's son? Why wasn't he considered for a part in the remake of Gone With The Wind?

John Clark Gable initially became a racing driver in America but then became involved in acting, appearing in Bad Jim, a low-budget Western. He was turned down for the part of Rhett Butler because, at 33, he was the same age his father had been when Gone With The Wind was filmed but the sequel, Scarlett, required Rhett to be at least ten years older. Gable Junior is married to Sindy O'Hara.

CAROLE WATTS, BRACKNELL, BERKS.

947: When Barbara Stanwyck was asked, in an old film, to choose a card from a pack, she replied with a shrug: 'Ish Kabibble.' The well-known post-war band of Kay Kyser had a singer named Ish Kabibble. What is the meaning of this phrase or name?

'Ish kabibble' is a Yiddish term, normally used with a shrug of the shoulders, meaning 'I should worry' or 'I don't care.' The term belongs to American English and is a polite way of letting somebody know you have little interest in what they are saying.

DON RAINGER, MANCHESTER JEWISH MUSEUM.

Ziegfield follies comedienne Fanny Brice, the original 'funny girl,' introduced 'Ish Kabbible' – meaning 'So what?' or 'Who cares?' in her radio show Baby Snooks. The name Ish Kabbible was also adopted by a trumpet-playing comic and was heard on the Phil Silvers Show, where many other formerly Yiddish words – often spoken by New Yorkers at the time – featured.

PHILIP FOX, LEEDS.

948: What is the origin of marmalade and why does it have a long association with Britain, bearing in mind that this country is not noted for growing oranges?

Despite quaint stories about seasickness en route to France, or illicit trips to visit Darnley – all of which turn on the phrase 'mamman est malade' – the word marmalade has nothing to do with Mary, Queen of Scots. It is derived from *marmelo,* Portuguese for quince, hence marmalade, which began as quince jam. The recorded history of marmalade goes back to 16th century Portugal where it was made from quinces and imported into England throughout this country's long association with our oldest ally. Before long English travellers to southern parts of Europe brought back recipes for this delicious preserve so it could be made here using homegrown quinces. In due course people started to experiment with alternative fruit, the most popular being oranges.

SELINE McCANN, ROBERTSON'S JAM AND MARMALADE PRODUCERS, DROYLESDEN, MANCHESTER.

949: What is the origin of the expression 'choc-a-block'?

Chock-a-block is another of the many English expressions derived from our maritime tradition. It refers to a ship's tackle when it has been pulled so tight that the pulley blocks are close to or touching one another and cannot usefully be pulled further. The idea of things being squeezed or jammed together in this way gave rise to the modern meaning 'crowded' or 'very full.'   NIGEL WILCOCKSON, BREWER'S PHRASE AND FABLE, CASSELL, LONDON.

950: In the Seventies, an Arab plane hijacker demanded the Vatican reveal the third secret of Fatima. What were the secrets and was the third revealed?

Three peasant children living in Fatima, Portugal, claimed to have received apparitions of the Blessed Virgin Mary in 1917. Two died shortly afterwards, but the third, Lucia, became a nun and is still alive. On July 13, 1917, the Blessed Virgin gave three secrets to the children, two of which Lucia was permitted to reveal in 1927. The first was that World War I, still in progress at the time of the message, would end but that 'if people do not stop offending God a worse one will break out during the pontificate of Pius XI.' The second secret was that war could be prevented if people made a special effort to receive Holy Communion on the first Sunday of each month and that Russia would be prevented from spreading communism through the world if the Pope, in union with all bishops, consecrated that country to the Immaculate Heart of the Blessed Virgin. Acts of consecration were made by the Pope alone in 1942 and 1952 but not in union with most of the world's bishops until 1984 by which time changes in the Soviet Union over the past decade are well known. The third secret was made known to Pope John XXIII in 1960 and subsequent Popes and Vatican officials have been permitted to read it. Cardinal Ratzinger said in 1985 that publishing it 'would mean exposing the Church to the danger of sensationalism, exploitation of the content.' It has been speculated, however, that the third secret speaks of the apostasy of the Western World at the end of the 20th century, predicting that many will reject the Christian faith and many priests will abandon their vocations.   GARETH LEYSHON, THE CATHOLIC CHAPLAINCY, ST ALDATE'S, OXFORD.

The consecration of Russia, as required by the Virgin Mary in her appearance to three children at Fatima, Portugal, in 1917, has not yet been made in accordance with Our Lady's request. The third secret spoke of apostasy among the clergy and was to be made known when its effects were beginning to show – by 1960. After 30 years of apostasy we can see the devastation it has caused. The rite of mass as we knew and loved it for more than 1,500 years has been replaced by a parish tea party.

G. MARLOW, PRESTON, LANCASHIRE.

951: Why is a large hammer called a 'sledgehammer'?

There are two nouns for sledge in the Oxford English Dictionary. The first one goes back to pre-Norman Conquest times and means a large, heavy hammer wielded with both hands. The second is the now more familiar vehicle on runners which comes from a similar Dutch word, introduced into our language in the early 17th century. Today we use the word sledgehammer when the original word was just sledge, because the later use for the vehicle has become better known. The root of the original word sledge is associated with the word to slay, as in battle, rather than sleigh as in sledge.

EDMUND WEINER, OXFORD WORD AND LANGUAGE SERVICE, OXFORD ENGLISH DICTIONARY.

The sledge and hammer were originally two distinct instruments. This is borne out by an epitaph in Oldswinford Church Yard, close to the heart of the Black Country, resting place of many old forge masters: 'My Sledge and Hammer are reclined, My bellows too have lost their wind, My fires extinct, my forge decayed, And in the dust, my vice is laid, My coal is spent, my iron gone, My anvil broke, my work is done.' – John Taylor (died 1822).   M. MELLOR, STOURBRIDGE, WEST MIDLANDS.

952: Why is Peterborough United football team known as The Posh?

Peterborough United have been called The Posh since the club was formed in 1934 from two earlier Peterborough football clubs, Fletton United, which folded in 1923, and Fletton and Peterborough United which existed between 1923 and 1932. Both played at the same council-owned London Road ground where we play today. Fletton United, managed by Pat Terrell, were commonly known as The Brickies. In the summer of 1921, after a bad season in the Northamptonshire League,

Terrell signed some new players and when they turned out for a press call it was remarked upon how 'posh' they looked. The quote appeared in the local paper and when the new season began the team was referred to as The Posh Boys. The Posh was still their nickname in 1923 when Fletton and Peterborough United was established and carried on after the demise of that club and establishment of Peterborough United. We have been known by that name ever since. A recent conversation with Pat Terrell confirms that this story is the correct origin of the name.

KIM SLANEY, PROGRAMME EDITOR, PETERBOROUGH UNITED FC.

Some confusion has arisen in this matter because the history of Peterborough United includes two different people with very similar names. Harry (known as Pat) Tirrell was player-manager of Fletton United and then Fletton and Peterborough United when the nickname 'The Posh' began in the 1920s. He was an amazing man who played cricket for Northants and soccer for West Ham and Northampton before starting Fletton United with two friends. He died many years ago and I feel his true role as originator of 'The Posh' should be recognised. The second person involved is myself, Frank (also known as Pat) Terrell, director of Peterborough United during the Fifties and Sixties and witness to my earlier (almost) namesake's achievements.

PAT TERRELL, PETERBOROUGH, CAMBRIDGESHIRE.

It was the local football paper 'The Pink Un' which first used the nickname. The paper gave each club in its area a nickname and caricature: Fletton United were known as The Brickies, caricatured by a cartoon working class clodhopper. On April 27, 1921, the club held a meeting to consider a better class of football for Peterborough and The Pink Un picked up on this and the following season called them 'the posh boys in a posh team from a posh town.' The clodhopper cartoon was changed to a posh man with trilby and cigar, later changed to top hat and monocle. After a run of poor results The Pink Un reverted to its original Brickies nickname, with 'ex Posh' in brackets until they defeated Kettering Town 5-1 in the FA Cup on October 7, 1922. The Posh reference then returned and continued after the merger of Peterborough and Fletton United in 1923 and has been used for the present Peterborough United FC since 1932.

MEL HOPKINS, KETTERING, NORTHAMPTONSHIRE.

953: I love the taste of garlic in cooking and the after effects do not worry me. However, my wife, my friends and my work colleagues do not feel the same way. Is there anything I can eat or drink that will make me pleasant to be with once more?

At least two divorce cases have featured garlic eating by one partner as the main reason for separation, and there are two cases of airliners being grounded until the smell of garlic cleared. Garlic, or *allium sativum,* has been a part of the human diet since written records began. Phoenicians, Romans, Greeks, ancient Chinese and Vikings all believed in its medicinal qualities, though it is only recently that we have discovered just how good garlic can be for our circulation, suppression of blood fats, reduction of heart disease and the fight against cancer. Traditionally the British dislike garlic, associating it with 'foreigners' across the Channel, but we are now eating more of it than the French. Half a million garlic pills are used every day in this country and we now export garlic to the Continent. The distasteful after-smell is caused by a sulphur compound called allicin which is released when the garlic is eaten. Traditional methods to neutralise it are chewing parsley or cardamom seeds or taking honey and lemon. Parsley is the most effective. To reduce the smell, garlic cloves should be thoroughly crushed before use. Or you can buy recently introduced Japanese or English odourless garlic. Alternatively, abandon your friends, workmates, partner or whoever else objects to the smell and move to Gilroy, California, a town so wrapped up in garlic culture they have a garlic festival every year that attracts 150,000 people, and they have been known to spray the town with essence of garlic just to make everyone feel good. KATRINA McCONNACHIE, LONDON.

954: In her obituary it was said that the father of Lady Elliot of Harwood was born in 1823 and her grandfather in 1786. Can anyone alive beat this?

I cannot beat this incredible feat of ancestral longevity but I can come very close. My grandfather was born in 1801, his brother, my great uncle, in 1787 and my father in 1859. I am 71. It's a shame my grandfather wasn't born just a couple of years earlier so we could have three generations all born in different centuries. MRS J. McSWINEY, RAMSBURY, WILTSHIRE.

955: How do you pronounce 'Bamigboye', surname of the Daily Mail's show biz star, and what does his first name 'Baz' stand for?

The correct pronunciation in the Yaruba language, from which the name stems, is best described as rhyming with 'Danny Boy' though in Britain and the US the 'g' tends to get sounded whereas in Nigeria it's the final 'e' which should be heard. Bamigboye actually means 'help me to carry this crown', a reference to a prince helping his father through the duties of being king. 'Baz' doesn't stand for anything but is a nickname which became the name everyone knew him by. All his mail, credit cards etc refer to him as 'Baz.' His full name – rarely used because he tries to shy away from its royal content – is Olufemi Bamidele Bamigboye, son of the Oba or Iresi, Nigeria.

DR BABAJIDE BAMIGBOYE, BAZ'S OLDER BROTHER, NASHVILLE, TENNESSEE.

956: When my house caught fire a neighbour said, 'Never mind, worse things happen at sea.' Where does this saying come from?

This saying, from Britain's rich nautical heritage, refers to the fact that any adverse incident, accident or minor crisis which occurs on land may have a more serious equivalent at sea. Isolation on a ship on the high seas, cramped conditions and limited facilities are liable to exacerbate any difficulty. An illness which, on land, may be bad, could prove life-threatening at sea. The expression was first recorded in this country in 1829 in the form 'worse accidents occur at sea.' Ancient Greek historian Thucydides once remarked 'A collision at sea can ruin your entire day.'

IAIN MACKENZIE, NATIONAL MARITIME MUSEUM, GREENWICH.

957: A betting colleague sings We're In The Money whenever he backs a winner. How does the song go on?

The song We're In The Money comes from the Warner film musical Gold Diggers Of 1933, directed by Mervyn Le Roy and starring Warren William, Joan Blondell, Ginger Rogers, Ruby Keeler and Dick Powell. The choreography was by Busby Berkeley and the music and lyrics by the famous partnership of Al Dubin (1891-1943) and Harry Warren (1893-1981). Other songs in the film included My Forgotten Man and Pettin' In The Park. Warren and Dubin had also written the music and lyrics for 42nd Street and went on to create the songs for a total of 20 musicals by the time their partnership ended in 1938. Their songs included massive hits such as Lullaby Of Broadway, Keep Young And Beautiful, I Only Have Eyes For You and September In The Rain. We're In The Money was further popularised when it was released as a record by Dick Powell and again when it was used in a revamp of the Gold Diggers style, in the 1951 film Painting The Clouds With Sunshine.

BETTY BARRON, SUTTON COLDFIELD MUSIC LIBRARY.

The full words of the song go: 'We're in the money, we're in the money, We've got a lot of what it takes to get along. We're in the money, each day is sunny. Old man depression you are thro', you done us wrong. We never see a headline 'bout a breadline today. And when we see the landlord we can look that guy right in the eye. We're in the money, we're in the money, Let's lend it, spend it, send it rolling along.'

E. TAYLOR, KENNINGTON, SOUTH LONDON.

958: What's the difference between an army corps and a regiment? The Duke of York and Albany's Maritime Regiment of Foot is now referred to as the Marine Corps, and the Tank Corps is now the Royal Tank Regiment. What happened to the Royal Armoured Corps?

A regiment is both an administrative and tactical unit, larger than a battalion and smaller than a brigade, in which all personnel are usually of the same arm or service, commanded by a colonel. First use of the word applied to a body of British troops came in the reign of Queen Elizabeth I. An army corps is an organisation larger than a division but smaller than a field army. It usually consists of two or more fighting divisions with supporting arms and services.

JENNIFER LEAKE, NATIONAL ARMY MUSEUM, CHELSEA.

There are two other uses for the word Corps in the British Army besides the tactical unit. Corps is a convenient term for describing a body of soldiers of any size outside a regiment or battalion. It can mean a large group of regiments engaged in the same kind of work or a body of specialists who give support to front-line regiments. The regiment is a permanent body of a more standard size, whose members are trained in warfare and policing. It differs from the specialist corps by its cultivation of battle honours and anniversaries, and usually recruits from a particular region. The Royal Tank Corps was renamed Royal Tank Regiment in 1929 so it could join other armoured regiments in the newly-formed Royal Armoured Corps.

DAVID GRIFFIN, AUTHOR OF BRITISH ARMY REGIMENTS, LEICESTER.

959: If the National Trust continues to acquire property at the current rate, how long will it take the NT to become the trustees for the entire British Isles?

The National Trust celebrated its centenary in 1995. In its first 100 years it acquired in excess of 600,000 acres, about 1 per cent of all the acres in England, Wales and Northern Ireland. There is a separate National Trust for Scotland. You can rest assured that the National Trust is unlikely to become the trustee for the whole of the British Isles in the foreseeable future. The Trust isn't an acquisitive organisation; our job is to protect coast and countryside of outstanding natural beauty and buildings of historic or architectural importance for the benefit of the nation. We prefer buildings or land to be cared for by sympathetic private owners.

WARREN DAVIS, THE NATIONAL TRUST, LONDON.

960: In most towns the main street is called High Street. In what sense is it 'high'?

Long before anyone thought of postal services or official addresses, people referred to the principal street in their town as the high street, not because of that street's altitude but because the word 'high' in this context means 'most important', as in high court or high priest.

MICHAEL HAVERTY, OFFICER RESPONSIBLE FOR STREET NAMING, SHEFFIELD CITY COUNCIL.

This may have something to do with elevation. Working in a soft sub-soil, the Romans built their roads on raised banks. Workers cleared vegetation and wood to a width of about 27ft, dug drainage ditches and filled the centre of the road with material to make a camber. Waterlogged areas were covered with brushwood, large stones and fine flint. These roads were built to high standards. After the Romans left Britain around AD410, hardly any roads were built until the Turnpike Act of 1663. Roman roads usually passed directly through the centre of towns. The main central road of a Roman colonia was the *via principalis,* main street. Hence the main street of a town is usually called the 'High' Street.

RACHEL HUGHES, LINCOLN.

961: Who now owns the island of Iwo Jima where 6,000 U.S. Marines and 20,000 Japanese perished in early 1945? Is it inhabited and can it be visited?

The eight-square mile island of Iwo Jima, won by American troops in one of the bloodiest battles of World War II, is now a restricted area under the control of the Japanese Self-Defence Agency and virtually impossible to visit. It was one of the most important strategic islands in the Pacific during the war and will be remembered for ever through the sculpture in Arlington National Cemetery, in the U.S., depicting Marines raising the flag on top of Mount Suribachi, the island's highest point, in 1945. Iwo Jima is part of the Volcanic Group of islands, roughly 750 miles south of Tokyo. It was annexed by the Japanese in 1887 and turned into a virtual fortress during the war with the deployment of 23,000 troops there. In 1945 the Americans bombarded it for seven days before sending ashore a force of 30,000 men on February 19. After five days of intense fighting the Americans took Mount Suribachi but it was not until mid-March that they had complete control of the island. The Japanese lost a total of 21,000 men with just 200 taken prisoner. The Americans lost 6,000 men, though none is now buried there. After the war the island was controlled by the U.S. Navy until it was returned to Japan in 1968. It now has about 1,000 Japanese residents, mostly involved in mining sulphur and refining sugar. It has no ferry connections and no hotels and can be visited only by special permission. TONY DIBDINE, DIDSBURY, MANCHESTER.

962: Who first thought of cooking an egg-white to make meringue?

Some cookery historians believe meringue was invented by a Swiss pastry chef named Gasparini who practised his art in the small town of Meiringen. Others maintain the word comes from the Polish *marzynlia* and that the preparation was invented by the chef Leszczynski while in the service of King Stanislas I. The king passed on the recipe to his daughter Marie who introduced it to the French. Queen Marie Antoinette had a great liking for meringue and it is said that she often made them with her own hands. Until the early 19th century, meringues cooking in the oven were shaped with a spoon. The great pastry chef Marie Antoine Careme first had the idea of using a piping bag.

MATTHEW COX, SOUS CHEF, LANGDALE HOTEL AND COUNTRY CLUB, AMBLESIDE, CUMBRIA.

963: What is a 'snook' that one may 'cock' it?

The 'snook', sometimes called a 'snoot', is the nose. We get it from the same Anglo-Saxon word which gives us 'snout'. You 'cock' a snook or snoot in the same sense that you 'cock' a firearm by pulling back the hammer. The gesture of cocking a snook is an ancient form of what anthropologists call a 'non-obscene insult gesture.' All sorts of obscure reasons are given as to why it is supposed to be offensive. One suggestion is that it is an imitation of the Sun-worshipping infidels in the Bible book of Ezekiel (chapter 18 vs16-17) who turned their backs on God and put 'the other branch to their nose.' Another suggestion is that it represents a satirised form of salute.

J. RIDDINGTON YOUNG, CONSULTANT EAR, NOSE AND THROAT SURGEON, DEVON.

964: What does the 'g' in g-string stand for?

The most likely reason as to why a small triangular piece of material held in place by a couple of narrow strings to preserve the wearer's modesty should be known as a 'g-string' is that the 'g' stands for gusset. There is some suggestion that the 'g' may stand for genitals and a more obscure but widely quoted view that the article is so called because G is the lowest string on a violin. G-strings were in common use by stage artistes before becoming a popular part of underwear and beachwear collections in recent, less modest, times. Early forms of g-string can be found in many cultures where the weather was kind enough to allow a modicum of undress. ROS MORGAN, FELIXSTOWE, SUFFOLK.

965: When did women start to iron men's clothes?

About 20 seconds after a man invented the iron.

ALAN WHITE, WANTAGE, OXFORDSHIRE.

The day they married them.   S. MURPHY, ALTRINCHAM, CHESHIRE.

The first reference to an iron in modern times is in a cottage inventory of 1635 which describes an iron container for hot stones. In earlier times, clothes were flattened by being pressed, either by their own weight in a cupboard (still known in some places as a press) or on a flat surface with a heavy roller. There were gas-fired irons by 1890 and electric irons appeared in the early 1900s. After lighting, ironing was the first household use to which electricity was applied. By 1948, 86 per cent of households had an electric iron. Today, almost every household possesses at least one iron – last year we bought 3.6 million. Modern research shows that women aren't doing all the ironing. Many men like to take care of their own clothes and marketing departments have now introduced irons targeted at males.   PETER HOTSTON, KENWOOD APPLIANCES, HAVANT, HAMPSHIRE.

966: What is the story behind the Robert Browning poem How They Brought The Good News From Ghent To Aix?

Browning explains in a letter of 1883: 'There is no specific historical incident commemorated in the poem, which I wrote with merely a general impression of the characteristic warfare and besieging which abound in the annals of Flanders. This accounts for some difficulties in the time and space occupied by the ride. The good news "which alone could save Aix from her fate" is therefore a matter for the imagination of the reader.'   LINDY CLARK, HAVERFORDWEST, DYFED.

967: Who, when and where was the first English league footballer to go on the field of play as a substitute?

Just 11 minutes into the Second Division game on Saturday, August 21, 1965, between Bolton Wanderers and Charlton Athletic, at Burnden Park, injured goalkeeper Michael Rose was taken off the field and Charlton called on substitute Keith Peacock. Until the 1965/66 season, no substitutions were allowed in English League games. Injured players had to struggle on or leave the team one man short. From the beginning of that season, League teams were allowed one substitution. Keith Peacock has his place in the record books but it wasn't Charlton's day – they went down 4-2 to Bolton. Peacock remained with Charlton as reserve team coach and his son Gavin was a Chelsea star. Eight of the 13 teams which used substitutes on that first day finished as losers, though

Barrow FC's Robert Knox became the first sub to score in a League game when he struck in the 79th minute helping his side to a 4-2 victory over Wrexham. In today's Premier and League football, clubs can have three subs on the bench, two of whom can be introduced into play.

CHRIS HULL, FOOTBALL LEAGUE, LYTHAM ST ANNES, LANCS.

The first substitute in an FA Cup final was Dennis Clarke for West Bromwich Albion against Everton on May 18, 1968, when WBA won 1-0 after extra time. The first FA Cup final goal by a substitute was by Eddie Kelly, of Arsenal, on May 8, 1971, who scored the equaliser against Liverpool in a match which Arsenal won 2-1 to complete the 'double' of FA Cup and League Championship. The goal was originally attributed to George Graham who later became Arsenal manager but TV cameras proved Graham didn't make contact with the ball.

When L. Roose, the Welsh goalkeeper, retired hurt in the England match at Wrexham, March 16, 1908, D. Davis, of Bolton Wanderers, was allowed to take his place as substitute. Wales used 12 players but England won 7-1. The first recorded use of a substitute was in 1889, Wales v. Scotland at Wrexham on April 15, when Wales's S. Gillam was injured and was replaced by A. Pugh, Rhostellyn.

OWEN LUDER CBE, WESTMINSTER, LONDON.

The league season starts with the Charity Shield match between the previous season's Cup and League winners. On August 15, 1959, I was the first substitute used in that game, between Wolverhampton Wanderers and Nottingham Forest, in front of 39,834 at the Molyneux. Because substitutes had never been used before, a lot of the press were taken by surprise and in the Sunday papers I was billed as 'Mr X, substitute for Nottingham Forest.' PETER KNIGHT, HONINGTON, SUFFOLK.

968: I have heard that the youngest British casualty in World War II was a 14-year-old Merchant Navy cadet. Is this correct?

My brother James Campbell left school at 14 and joined the Merchant Navy as a cabin-boy. His first ship SS Induna was torpedoed in the Arctic Ocean en route to Murmansk as part of a convoy. James spent five days in an open lifeboat and he and a 16-year-old seaman were the only survivors. James spent several months in a Russian hospital, where his right leg, left foot and fingers on his left hand were amputated due to the severe frostbite. I believe that at the age of 14 years and two months old he was World War II's youngest British military casualty. On his return to Glasgow he received a Hero of the Soviet Union medal. He is married with children and grandchildren. He is now retired from his post as a

District Superintendent with the New Zealand Department of Labour where he emigrated more than 30 years ago.   RONNIE CAMPBELL, LEEDS.

I understand the question is about military personnel but, having researched the war history of Harrow, where I spent my war years, I came across notification of civilian deaths caused by V1 bombs in 1944 including Alan John Michaelis who was a mere seven hours old.

K. WILLIAMS, ST ALBANS, HERTS.

969: Where is the hill that you have to accelerate down and brake when you drive up?

'Electric Brae' in Ayrshire is probably the finest example in the world of this optical illusion. A quarter-mile section of the A719 coast road, nine miles south of Ayr and 13 miles north of Girvan, locally known as Croy Brae, confuses motorists, cyclists and pedestrians by appearing to run downhill when in fact it goes up. Many a driver has stopped there to check if his car engine was okay.   MATT CONNELLY, AYRSHIRE TOURIST BOARD.

A hill with this characteristic was noted by a farmer driving his horse and cart in 1802 near Moncton, New Brunswick, Canada.

A. TELFORD, BOURNEMOUTH, DORSET.

Several places in Northern Ireland have this reputation, including the sloping side entrance to Spelga Dam, near Newcastle, Co Down. The optical illusion explanation seems quite impossible because a side road branches off the main road at about one third of the height from the dam base.   EILY MOUNTFORD, LISBURN, CO. ANTRIM.

This happens at Magnetic Hill, between Ballabeg and the Round Table, on the Isle of Man. It's not, of course, due to magnetism but to the Little People who come out and push the car uphill.

PETER TUCKER, RAMSEY, ISLE OF MAN.

I visited a hill of this type about 20 miles north of Rome last year. A quarter-mile stretch of country lane appears to have a gradient of about one in 12 but to my amazement I witnessed my own car and a large coach full of German sightseers apparently rolling up it.

D. J. EDWARDS, BARKING, ESSEX.

970: Who is the actor who seems to have been Captain Birdseye for ever? What else has he acted in?

The actor who has starred as Captain Birdseye in more than 50 advertisements which have been shown all over the world since 1967 is John Hewer. John was born in London's East End, has been married to Edna for more than 40 years and has two children. After school he had a brief period as a local government welfare officer before beginning a theatrical career at the Players Theatre. During the 1950s he had a number of roles in TV shows, films, cabaret, etc., including West End shows Slings And Arrows, The Two Bouquets, Noel Coward's When In Rome and Norman – Is That You? In 1961 he had set up his own production company producing conferences and industrial shows for large international companies and for 10 years from 1967 he hosted the top TV variety show Pig And Whistle in Canada. In the Seventies he appeared in several pantomimes and musicals such as Kiss Me Kate and in 1982 he played Poo Bah in The Mikado at the Theatre Royal, Plymouth. He has since been involved in several stage shows. His recent TV credits include the BBC's Nicholas Nickleby, The Beryl Reid Show, and The Bill. And, yes, he was a sailor – in the Fleet Air Arm.

LYNDA DA RONAN, RICHARD STONE PARTNERSHIP, LONDON.

Others will no doubt list the talents and career of Captain Birdseye, John Hewer. They may not know that he attended Leyton County High School for Boys which also produced Frank Muir, Derek Jacobi, Jonathan Ross – and the rest of us.

A. J. WELSBY, CRANBROOK, KENT.

John Hewer accompanied the production of The Girl Friend to New York with a virtually unknown leading lady named Julie Andrews.

WILLIAM DAVIS, BIRMINGHAM.

I can confirm that actor John Hewer was a Lieut Observer in the Fleet Air Arm, flying Swordfish planes and a member of my squadron, 836 Squadron, on Atlantic convoy escort duties.

JIM TUKE, SECRETARY, YORKSHIRE FLEET AIR ARM ASSOCIATION.

971: How many English counties can one see from the top of Scafell Pike?

Towering above the crags and ridges at the heart of the Lake District National Park, Scafell Pike is England's highest mountain at 978 metres (3,210ft). It's a long, slow climb, but from the summit on a clear day the views are sensational. But Peter Nattrass, of Lake District Search and Rescue Association confirms that from the top the only English countries on view are Cumbria, North Yorkshire and Lancashire. Northumberland and County Durham are obscured by the height of the Pennines. However, it is possible to see the Isle of Man, Dumfries and Galloway in Scotland and, on an exceptionally clear day, as far as Ireland, as well as Anglesey and North Wales. Anyone who'd like to enjoy the view is advised to wear warm clothing and good boots, know how to use a map and compass, and check with Lake District Weather Line (07687 75757) before setting out.

LORNA VAN HOVE, CUMBRIA TOURIST BOARD, WINDERMERE, CUMBRIA.

When my wife and I last went up there we couldn't see any counties at all because the cloud ceiling was at 2,500ft. I'm told most other walkers experience the kind of very wet conditions we had to endure.

TREVOR DUFFIELD, HEANOR, DERBYSHIRE.

972: The circular UFO which crashed near Romford Brewery during an air raid in World War II was thought to have been a new type of German weapon. The 50-year secrecy ban imposed should have expired by now, so can anyone explain what it was?

The 'new German weapon' probably refers to one of a pair of oil bombs which hit Romford Brewery during the night of October 13, 1940. It failed to ignite and was taken away by military personnel for closer examination. The brewery, now a sales distribution depot for Carlsberg-Tetley, was a popular target for the Luftwaffe. It was hit seven times in air raids between 1940 and 1944, but didn't stop brewing throughout the war. As to aliens, although they might have seen our ads, they can have no justification for attacking the brewery.

IAIN OAG, COMMUNICATIONS MANAGER, CARLSBERG-TETLEY.

I believe British Intelligence ran a misinformation programme to safeguard a Romford factory making vital electric components. The Germans knew the factory was in Romford but not its exact whereabouts. Captured enemy spies were 'turned' by counter-intelligence and instructed to misinform their erstwhile masters in Germany that the factory was hidden in Romford's Ind Coope brewery. The Luftwaffe attacked the brewery many times but its output continued without interruption. The German navy then hatched a desperate plan to send a U-boat on a suicide mission to attack the brewery with ramp-launched torpedoes designed to skim above surface level. The vessel successfully negotiated the Thames and Rom rivers but firing the first torpedo caused the U-boat to founder. The crew scrambled to safety and surrendered to the local police and Home Guard. To keep the enemy guessing as to the outcome of the mission, a cover story was put out to the effect that a U-boat had been sunk off the Essex coast with no precise date given. I have never been able to confirm this story but hope publication of the relevant documents will bear it out.

F. A. BELL, ROMFORD, ESSEX.

973: In which battle were firearms first used?

Gunpowder has been known in Asia since antiquity and widely used in China, India and Turkey as a type of hand-thrown firebomb but there's no evidence of its use in cannon or firearms. The earliest evidence of true firearms is a 1326 manuscript illustration written by Walter de Milemete, chaplain to Edward III, which shows a soldier and a cannon firing a large arrow as opposed to a cannonball. Evidence for the first use of firearms in battle suggests this may have been used with some effect by the English forces fighting the French in the Battle of Crécy, in North-western France in 1346. GRAEME RIMER, ROYAL ARMOURIES, HM TOWER OF LONDON.

The first cannonballs, as opposed to arrows, fired from cannons in battle, were used by the Emperor Maximillian I of Austria, known as the last Knight and first Cannoneer, who died in 1519. His army used both swords and cannon. His cannon founder was the Austrian sculptor Gregor Loeffler, who named the first two cannonballs for use in battle, Weokauf (wake up) and Burlebaus. They were cast at an Alpine castle used by the Emperor as his gunhouse, which in 1855 became the home of my grandmother's family. MISS P. BRADY, COLCHESTER, ESSEX.

974: I am warned that in the interest of safety, I should disconnect my TV set when it is not in use. Why is a similar warning not given in respect of video recorders?

Wherever possible, disconnection of electrical equipment from the mains supply at night or when unattended ensures that no hazard can arise, but we have no reason to believe that continuously connected low-power isolating transformers, as found in TV sets and other electrical equipment such as video recorders, present a fire risk. High power electrical items, such as fires and heaters, should always be disconnected overnight or when not in use.
CATHY WARD, ROYAL SOCIETY FOR THE PREVENTION OF ACCIDENTS (RoSPA), BIRMINGHAM.

975: Why is it that when national dress is required, England does not seem to have one? I am amazed that Wales and Scotland still retain theirs while England appears not to have done.

The lack of our 'traditional' national dress used to be most evident during Miss World contests. The sight of our own nation's hopeful having to wear a beefeater costume always left me in fits of laughter. The plus side is that our constantly evolving approach to clothes shows what an independent lot we really are. THOMAS GRESHAM, LINCOLN.

Our national costume is the smock, worn for many centuries, plain for work and embroidered for best, with needlework and colour indicating regional variations and strapwork – side panels – indicating the trade of the wearer. In countries whose nationality is most threatened, people cling most strongly to their national dress. Perhaps now we are feeling a little uneasy at our apparent merging with Europe it's time to bring out our smocks. I wear mine on St George's Day.

ELIZABETH HORTON, KING'S HEATH, BIRMINGHAM.

English national dress can be seen in our towns and villages around May Day time. Men wear sleeveless coats, full shirts, hose, knee breeches, buckled shoes and cloth cap. For the ladies it is the peasant girl look with a blouse, lace waistcoat, three-quarter length panniered skirt, petticoat, buckled shoes and a bonnet.

CATHERINE STOCK, BRISTOL.

Our national dress has always been regarded by foreigners as pin-striped suit, bowler hat, brogues and umbrella for men and the Mary Poppins look for women. This is now being replaced by the reality these same foreigners see when we visit their countries. The Brit-on-Tour look consists of Union Jack shorts, 'I'm with this idiot' T-shirt, scruffy trainers and knotted hankie for men; sandals, Lycra shorts and football top for women.

TONY YOULTON, HOVE, SUSSEX.

As most national dress is based on a country's climate, may I suggest hooded anorak, waterproof bottoms and green wellies.

JULIE TUCKER, GILLINGHAM, KENT.

Our lack of national costume is something of which we should be proud. Today's national costumes are merely elaborate and fanciful forms of a peasant's dress, mostly created for 19th century tourists. In Scotland, tartans, with four or five exceptions, were the work of designers and entrepreneurs cashing in on the popularity of Sir Walter Scott's novels. England, alone in Europe at that time, had seen her peasants become free, landowning yeomen. No peasantry, no peasant costumes – and no national costume.

J. BRIAN BLACKLOCK, STRADBROKE, SUFFOLK.

This may not be something of which to be so proud. England lost her peasant costume and centuries of culture in the 19th century. Closures of the commons robbed poorer folk of their grazing and fuel, driving them into the towns where they lived in squalor which made them forget their heritage. Then the Industrial Revolution forced them into factories, working hours where even their memories couldn't survive. Those left on the land were too few and too hard driven to keep up their old customs and festivals and the traditional dress was forgotten as well. For women it consisted of a full, mid-calf skirt in any colour except yellow, a laced bodice and a full-sleeved white blouse. A fair representation may be seen on the Yardley lavender bottles. It is overdue for a revival.

B. JENNINGS, COOKLEY, WORCS.

976: When, and by whom, were domestic milking cows introduced into this country?

People have been drinking cow's milk for at least 5,000 years. Middle

Eastern friezes dating from around 3000BC show cows being milked but when the Celtic Shorthorn was originally introduced into Britain from the Eastern Mediterranean during the Early Bronze Age, it was as a draught animal and beast of burden rather than for dairy use. The Romans are generally credited with the introduction of milk drinking in Britain. They were very fond of cheese and brought their dairying skills here, along with their favourite cows. Each time Britain has been invaded, the new arrivals brought their own breeds of cattle. Hornless cattle came from Northern Europe with the Anglo-Saxons and you can still tell where the ancestors of cows in this country originated by their colour. Native Celtic breeds are black, Anglo-Saxon ones usually red and Dutch are piebald.

ANITA BOURNE, NATIONAL DAIRY COUNCIL, LONDON.

977: I have heard that if you move house, you should put butter on your cat's paws to make it return to its new home. What is the origin of this and does it work?

My late father Wally Slemmings was a household removal man, as were my grandfather and greatgrandfather. Wally always kept a wickerwork cat basket on the van and told customers to butter the cat's paws when they arrived at the new house. The theory is that a cat can be very frightened and disorientated by moving and may run off the moment it is let out of the cat basket. By buttering its paws it gets more interested in licking the tasty butter off its feet and by the time it is clean it has calmed down and adjusted. It's worth doing: more than one cat has been let out of a basket and run straight up the nearest chimney.

BARRY SLEMMINGS, ROMFORD, ESSEX.

978: Who wrote the first 'Dear John' letter and which John was the victim?

A 'Dear John' letter is a slang expression for a missive telling somebody their relationship with a wife or girlfriend is over. It entered our language during World War II when, for millions of military personnel on all sides, it was the type of letter they most dreaded. During that war, and in all others before or since, many women couldn't cope with the prolonged separation and uncertainty, and took solace with other men. The term is generally thought to be of British origin, but spread widely through U.S. forces when they entered the war. The first recipient of a Dear John will never be known, though this type of communication must have existed ever since the written word began.

K. P. BARNES, ALDERSHOT, HANTS.

979: If man is descended from the apes, what happened to the intermediate 'higher' species while apes are still swinging in the trees?

There is no missing link between man and ape. About four million years ago, apes evolved from a species called *Australopithecus Afarensis* and from that, a million years later, into *Australopithecus Africanus,* then two million years ago into *Homo habilis* which, 1.8 million years ago, evolved into *Homo erectus.* This species then evolved 150,000 years ago into *Homo sapiens.*

IAN MCCONNELL, EWSHOT, HANTS.

The basic rule of evolution is not survival of the fittest but of the different. If two species have the same lifestyle and live in the same place, one wins and the other becomes extinct. For both to continue, there has to be a difference. Hominids such as Neanderthal Man had the same lifestyle as us but they were not as good at it so they became extinct. Monkeys and apes have a different lifestyle from us, and from each other, so they have continued. The vital difference between us and the apes is in our society. We live in families, they live in polygynous tribes. That difference produced, among other things, our high intelligence. It took brains for couples to pair off and co-operate in rearing children.

FRED CHERRY, WHITEHAVEN, CUMBRIA.

As the first apes came into existence about 28 million years ago and are still with us, we have to consider that the Hominid, which is more in line with our own ancestry and first appeared about 16 to 18 million years later, must be a deviation from the original ape evolutionary pattern. The earliest true member of the next stage, the genus *Homo,* is dated as late as about 2.8 million years ago, a difference of 13 to 15 million years, but the earliest recorded remains of our present species, *Homo sapiens,* come from as recently as between 300,000 and 450,000 years ago, a difference between the last two species in the link of only 2.5 million years. In evolutionary terms this could be considered a huge leap forward in a very short time because the earliest member of genus *Homo,* about 2.5 million years ago, would have looked as much like an ape as a man and yet, within the next half-million years, we arrived. No other creature has evolved or developed in such a short period by a purely evolutionary process.

DAVID HARRIS, SAXMUNDHAM, SUFFOLK.

980: Does the old saying 'Ne'er cast a clout till may be out' refer to the month of May or the may blossom?

The saying refers not to the blossom but to the month of May and is a warning not to leave off warm clothes until the end of that month. The saying is associated most strongly with Scotland and the north of England though the first record of it comes from a 1706 Spanish-English dictionary, written by John Stevens, where the original Spanish saying *'Hasta pasado Mayo no te quites el Sayo'* is translated as 'Do not leave off your coat till May be past.'   JOHN SIMPSON, EDITOR: CONCISE OXFORD DICTIONARY OF POEMS.

981: A great deal of priceless Western art has been acquired by the Getty Museum in California. In the event of a major earthquake, as is often forecast, is there any danger of this treasure disappearing into a hole in the ground?

The J. Paul Getty Museum in Malibu, California, was founded in 1954 in a ranch house behind the present museum, which opened in 1974. The museum, a replica of the Roman Villa dei Papyri built in 200-150BC outside Herculaneum and destroyed by Mount Vesuvius in AD79, cost $17 million to build. Getty himself lived in Surrey and never saw the new museum, as he was apparently afraid of flying. On his death in 1976 the museum was left $700 million to spend on great works of art. A large collection of works has already been amassed and the value of the endowment is about $2.3 billion. Safety and protection is a major concern at the world's richest art collection and the museum is fully prepared for earthquakes. Its design incorporates technology to absorb up to 80 per cent of the energy released by an earthquake in areas where works of art are kept. During the latest major quake the museum suffered only one accident, when the head of a Roman statue fell off. It was easily fixed. Statistics suggest the museum has less likelihood of falling into a hole than the Louvre has of being destroyed by lightning or the Tate Gallery of being blown up by terrorists.   ELIZABETH COBB, EDINBURGH.

982: How much was the single and married couple's pension when introduced in 1908 and what would its relative value be today?

The Old Age Pensions Act 1908 granted non-contributory, means-tested pensions of 5s (25p) per week to males only, over the age of 70, whose total income was less than £21 per year. According to Central Statistical Office figures, 25p per week would in today's terms be worth £13.26. This compares with the present Basic State Pension of £64.45 for a single person and £99.80 for a married couple. Some Senior Citizens also benefit from the State Earnings Related Pension Scheme (SERPS). In 1908, however, company pension schemes were rare.

DAVID EVANS, PENSIONS TECHNICAL MANAGER, PRUDENTIAL, READING.

983: If birds imitate the sounds they hear, how can a young cuckoo 'cuckoo' after never hearing its parents?

Birds sing instinctively and their basic song structure is inherited. This simple inherited song pattern is built into the full song by listening to parents singing and copying it. Cuckoos will never hear their parents, as the female cuckoo lays her eggs in the nests of other birds. But the cuckoo's 'song' is simple and the young have no instinctive drive to elaborate on it. The young cuckoo will probably hear its first 'cuckoo' when it reaches its winter home in Africa – a journey of several thousand miles.

CHRIS HARBARD, ROYAL SOCIETY FOR THE PROTECTION OF BIRDS, SANDY, BEDS.

984: I often hear the phrase 'As the actress said to the bishop', but who were the original actress and bishop and what did they say?

The saying is heard as both 'as the bishop said to the actress' or 'as the actress said to the bishop.' It is Edwardian in origin and is perfect for turning any remark into a double entendre. Unfortunately there were no original bishop and actress to find out what they said. The combination of a bishop, regarded as a person of high principle, and an actress, not the highest of occupations on the Edwardian scale of morality, were perfect examples to use when a person had made a remark that could be taken two ways, especially something with a possible sexual connotation. The saying gained a certain following during World War II but made its mark during the Fifties in programmes such as Educating Archie, with Beryl Reid.

KELVIN GORDON, DUNDEE.

This phrase was often used by The Saint, Simon Templar, in the Leslie Charteris stories I read more than 40 years ago.

FRED VERE, LONDON, SW2.

Some years ago, I was in rep on the Isle of Wight and, wishing to post a letter, I was irritated to find an elderly gentleman having trouble with an odd-shaped package. I said: 'You'd better push it in further and then start wiggling it about – you'll get nowhere with the thing outside.' His lady companion said: 'My dear, that's no way to speak to the Bishop of Winchester.'

PEARL CATLIN, TV PRODUCER, GUILDFORD, SURREY.

985: If dolphins breathe air like us, how do they sleep?

Dolphins do not have regular sleeping/waking patterns linked to night and day but take catnaps whenever they need to rest. It is not possible for dolphins to lose consciousness in the way that we do when sleeping because their breathing is under voluntary control, so only half their brain switches off at a time. The dolphin then floats just below the surface, periodically fanning its fins so that it rises to take a breath. Dolphins may also sleep with one eye open.

M. DODDS, THE MARINE CONNECTION, LONDON.

986: What is the significance of the snake in the centre of the badge of the Royal Army Medical Corps?

In his history of the Royal Army Medical Corp, Not Least In The Crusade, Peter Lovegrove writes: 'The rod and serpent, universally recognised as the symbol of medicine for very many centuries, have their root in both the Bible and mythology. The Old Testament describes how Moses made a serpent of brass, placed it on a rod so that those who were bitten by serpents could look at it and live. From that time the brazen serpent was the Israelites' sign of healing.' The rod around which the serpent is coiled is also the symbol of Aesculapius, the Roman god of medicine, and the official description of the RAMC badge is in fact 'within a laurel wreath surmounted by the crown, the rod of Aesculapius with a serpent entwined.'   K. P. Barnes, former Cpl RAMC, Aldershot, Hants.

The snake or serpent on the RAMC badge denotes the treachery of the medical officers ignoring their Hippocratic oath by being officers first and doctors second.   R. H. Head, Godalming, Surrey.

987: What causes the sting in a stinging nettle and is the dock leaf the best cure?

The stinging nettle (Urtica dioica) is part of the plant family Urticacea whose defence mechanism injects toxins into living creatures. The hairs of a stinging nettle have a protective cap which breaks off when touched, leaving a sharp, bevelled hollow, similar to that made by a hypodermic needle. Plants And The Skin, by Dr Chris Lovell, says the plant secretes a liquid which includes several ingredients which cause irritation to human skin. Stinging nettle effects can last more than 12 hours, depending on how bad a contact was made with the plant. The hairs can get implanted in the skin, causing continuous irritation, but contact is generally more annoying than serious, and squeezing a nettle firmly generally causes less sting. Although the dock leaf has been seen as a natural remedy for the effects of stinging nettles for hundreds of years, no medical proof of its value has yet been found. The treatment recommended by the national poisons unit if you can't find a dock leaf is to soothe stings with cool water.

VIRGINIA MURRAY, NATIONAL POISONS UNIT, LONDON.

It's not necessary to go searching for a dock leaf. The nettle itself carries an antidote if you break the stem and rub the juice onto the sting.

JOHN W. ROSE, PRESTON, LANCS.

988: Active Elder Brethren of the Corporation of Trinity House of Deptford, Stroud, are disqualified from jury service. Who are they and why are they ineligible?

These master mariners, with long experience of command in the Royal or Merchant Navy, are the equivalent of executive directors for the control of the Trinity House Lighthouse Service, the general lighthouse authority for England, Wales, the Channel Islands and Gibraltar. Responsibilities include light vessels and buoys, and dealing with wrecks which might be a danger to navigation or to the lifeboat rescue service. Trinity House is also a maritime charity. Although Active Elder Brethren are exempt from jury service under a Charter of James II, they must, when summoned, sit in the Admiralty Court as nautical assessors in trials involving marine matters. They are, in effect, part of the judicial system.

CAPTAIN MALCOLM EDGE, DEPUTY MASTER, TRINITY HOUSE, TOWER HILL, LONDON.

989: When did clocks first appear? I've been told it was in China.

The earliest mechanical clock was completed in China in AD 725 by Yi Xing and Liang Lingzan. The world's oldest surviving clock is a faceless specimen dating from 1386, or possibly earlier, at Salisbury Cathedral, in Wiltshire. It was restored in 1956, having struck the hours for 498 years and ticked more than 500 million times. Earlier dates have been attributed to the weight-driven clock in Wells Cathedral, Somerset, but only the iron frame is original.

CAROLE JONES, GUINNESS BOOK OF RECORDS, ENFIELD, MIDDLESEX.

990: My husband and I would like to retire somewhere which has a warm (though not hot) climate, no pollution, is not at war, has stable government, a good standard of living and welcomes the British. Does such a heaven on Earth exist?

The requirement of such a climate limits this 'heaven' to certain latitudes. In Europe, these areas include parts of Spain, Gibraltar, the Channel Islands, southern France, parts of Italy and Greece and several Mediterranean islands. On other continents they include the southern tip of South Africa, south-east Australia, most of New Zealand, hundreds of Pacific Islands, parts of the U.S., northern Argentina, Uruguay and several Atlantic islands. The pollution factor eliminates South America, South Africa and some of Europe. The U.S. and Australia have high pollution in certain areas though many countries have policies to reduce it. Though none of these countries is currently directly involved in a war, several are prey to increasing criminal activities. The U.S., Australia, most of mainland Europe and some Mediterranean islands have crime rates at least as high as Britain's. This leaves some islands to choose from, though only a few have stable governments. Added requirements of accepting Britons and possessing a good standard of living mean we are left with Malta, New Zealand, Bermuda, the Channel Islands and a few Pacific islands.   Brian McGovern, Glasgow.

The ideal place would be Alderney in the Channel Islands. The weather is comfortably mild, the air and sea are strikingly clean by mainland standards and the island is a haven for wildlife. Our government is stable and crime almost non-existent. It has safe, sandy beaches, no high-speed roads, friendly natives and activities to suit everyone. There are regular flights from the mainland and other islands, and France is within easy reach. We have our own hospital, two schools, a nine-hole golf course and sailing club and there are no purchasing restrictions on property. You don't have to be a millionaire to live here. Income Tax is 20p in the pound, with no VAT, no Community Charge, Capital Gains Tax or death duties.   Barbara Head, Alderney, Channel Islands.

Bermuda is God's own piece of Earth. The people are friendly and generous, social life is beyond comparison, scenery stunning, golf and sailing superb and the pace of life is reflected by the island's 20 mph speed limit.   A. G. Fletcher, Basildon, Essex.

Try the island of Gozo, off Malta, where they speak English, have good summers, mild winters, 15% taxation and high standards of housing. A stable currency and government are agreeable factors too.

Angela Bowman, Leeds.

The answer can be found 18 degrees west of Greenwich, 33 degrees north of the equator – Madeira. It has year-round springtime, little pollution and endearing natives who speak a little English.

F. Horrigan, Wallasey, Cheshire.

991: Why is the meal served after a wedding called the Wedding Breakfast?

Traditionally, weddings were held very early in the morning. When the British Isles were predominantly Roman Catholic, couples would have a full nuptial mass. They would fast from sundown the day before until after the wedding ceremony so that they could take Holy Communion. The meal that was served afterwards to celebrate the wedding was therefore the first meal of the day and naturally became known as the wedding breakfast.   Kathleen Baird-Murray, You And Your Wedding Magazine, London.

992: Why did the Prime Minister at Commons Question Time often say: 'I refer my/the Honourable Friend/Member to the answer I gave some moments ago,' followed by the questioner asking another question and an answer being given?

Until Tony Blair changed the rules in May 1997, oral questions for reply by the Prime Minister had to be submitted two weeks in advance. At that stage backbench MPs couldn't predict which issues would be topical so they used a standard question, asking the Prime Minister to list his official engagements, which allowed them to introduce a supplementary question to try to catch the PM on the hop. The Prime Minister said 'I refer the Honourable Member to the answer I gave some moments ago' as an acknowledgement of this procedural device before receiving the supplementary or 'real' question.

PUBLIC INFORMATION OFFICE, HOUSE OF COMMONS, LONDON.

993: When I was a police officer, my PC's guidebook said it was against the law to shake doormats outside before 8am. Is this still the case?

This is not quite correct. The offence of shaking a mat, other than a doormat, in the street before 8am was created by the Metropolitan Police Act 1839 within the Metropolitan Police District and the Town Police Clauses Act 1847 outside London. Both acts were torn to pieces by the infamous Police and Criminal Evidence Act 1984 but the relevant sections covering this offence and other minor public nuisances survived and still exist.

D. J. SMITH, PERSHORE, HEREFORD AND WORCESTER.

When I served in the Metropolitan police force, the beating of carpets in the street was prohibited by Section 60 (3) of the Metropolitan Police Act 1839 which stated: 'Every person who in any thoroughfare shall beat or shake any carpet, rug or mat, except doormats, before the hour of eight in the morning shall be guilty of an offence and shall be liable to a penalty of not more than 40 shillings.'

E. W. CHALLANDS, SLEAFORD, LINCOLNSHIRE.

As a police officer on A Division, Whitehall in 1953, I was posted to protection posts outside 10 Downing Street and 1 Carlton House Terrace. Most officers considered these posts boring but I would secrete myself behind the railings of these great houses, ever vigilant to detect and report the honourable occupants or their servants if they shook the wrong mat at the wrong time.

KENNETH EARL, ELTHAM PARK, SOUTH EAST LONDON.

994: It's said that the sun can be seen rising and setting over the sea in Whitby. How is this possible in an east coast town? Are there any other British resorts which share this phenomenon?

Despite being on the east coast, Whitby has a northerly aspect and it's because of this that for two weeks prior to and after the summer solstice (June 21) the sun can be seen rising and setting over the sea. It is generally said that Bram Stoker, author of Dracula, got the idea of the vampire's red eyes while viewing this phenomenon and noticing the reflection of the setting sun in the local parish church windows.

DOROTHY RUSSELL, WHITBY TOURIST INFORMATION CENTRE.

Whitby faces north, not east and has a West Cliff and an East Cliff while Scarborough, just 20 miles to the south, has a North Cliff and South Cliff. I can remember as a child being shown the Durham pitheads which, on a clear day, were just visible on the North Sea horizon from Whitby.

LUCY SUTHERLAND, DORCHESTER, DORSET.

995: In the Forties, my sailor father taught me the game of Crown and Anchor. Does anyone know its origin?

Arthur Taylor's Guinness Book of Traditional Pub Games says Crown and Anchor originated among Royal Navy seamen and fishermen before World War I. Comprising just a board and three dice, it was easily transportable and readily concealed when being played covertly. The board is divided into six squares depicting crown, anchor, heart, club, spade and diamond; the faces of the dice are similarly marked. The player puts his money on his fancied square before the banker rolls the dice, paying evens if one die turns up correctly, 2 to 1 on pairs and 3 to 1 on three of a kind. The Army officially frowned on the game but it was much played by soldiers during the 1914-18 war, when the banker could often be heard calling: 'Lay it down, my lucky lads. The more you put down the more you pick up. You come here on bicycles, you go away in Rolls Royces. The old firm, all the way from 'Olloway. What about the lucky old mud hook? The old mud hook's badly backed. Any more for any more before we turn 'em up? Lay it down, my lucky lads, thick and heavy. Have you all finished, have you all done? Right up she comes. Two jam tarts and the lucky old Sergeant Major.' The 'mud hook' referred to the anchor, 'Sergeant Major' was the crown and the 'jam tarts' were hearts. This patter is still in use some 80 years later.

LAURENCE KING, BLANDFORD FORUM, DORSET.

996: Is it true that Winston Churchill originally showed his Victory V sign with the back of his hand?

After a visit to Coventry on September 26, 1941, Churchill's secretary wrote: 'The PM will keep giving a V sign with two fingers in spite of the representations repeatedly made to him that this gesture has quite another signficance.' (Sir John Colville's Downing Street Diaries, The Fringes of Power: Volume One 1939-1941, published 1985).

Churchill adopted the hand signal with more enthusiasm than worldly wisdom at first but eventually got it right and turned his palm outwards. He popularised but did not invent the V sign.

Victor de Lavaleye, an exiled minister, proposed in a BBC broadcast to Belgium on January 14, 1941, that Belgians defying the Germans with graffiti should chalk 'V' for *vrijheid* (freedom in Flemish) or *victoire* (victory in French). In July the BBC's Colonel Britton (Douglas Ritchie) opened a V for Victory campaign in seven languages, urged listeners to tap out the morse V (dot-dot-dot-dash) as an aural symbol of defiance, represented in BBC news services by the first four notes of Beethoven's 5th symphony, and suggested making a V sign with the fingers.

MAURICE WEDGEWOOD, DARLINGTON.

997: What happened to the Titanic's sister ship, the Olympic?

The Olympic, the first of three ships intended for the North Atlantic service built by Harland and Wolff in Belfast, completed her maiden voyage to New York in June, 1911. After the Titanic sank in April 1912, she spent six months in Belfast having extra lifeboats and a double hull fitted. During the Great War, Olympic carried troops to the Dardanelles and ferried Canadian troops from Halifax to Liverpool, earning her the nickname Old Reliable. In May 1918, one of her propellers sliced through U-boat U130, making her the only big liner to sink an enemy vessel. After the war Olympic returned to the Southampton/New York run for the White Star Line and in 1934, just days after her owners merged with Cunard, she rammed the Nantucket lightship in thick fog, killing seven crewmen. As the Depression continued she lost revenue and made her last transatlantic crossing in 1935 before going to a breakers' yard at Jarrow. For ten days her luxury fittings were auctioned on the quayside. I have a beautiful wardrobe from one of her cabins. The hull of the Olympic was then towed to Fife for final demolition. Her other sister ship, the Britannic, was commissioned in World War I as a hospital ship and sank on November 21, 1916, after hitting a mine in the Aegean.

AIDAN BOWE, LEICESTER.

Part of the dining room panelling from the Olympic now lines the function rooms of The White Swan Hotel in Alnwick, Northumberland.

J. JACKSON, ROCHDALE, LANCASHIRE.

Just three months after her maiden voyage to New York in June 1911, Olympic collided with the cruiser HMS Hawke, near Southampton, sustaining damage to her hull which was opened for some 40 feet. Hawke was severely damaged and in danger of sinking but eventually returned to Portsmouth. The court of appeal held the liner at fault: in command of the Olympic was Captain E. J. Smith. Despite the verdict of the court, and the fact that he was due to retire, the White Star Line gave Smith command of the Titanic for her ill-fated maiden voyage in 1912.

E. T. DASH, HILDENBOROUGH, KENT.

998: Can anyone provide a definition of the recently introduced word 'Yo', and where did it originate?

Used as an exclamation by the younger generation, the word 'Yo' isn't as new as most people believe. It's thought to have been first used by black Americans towards the end of the 19th century, before becoming a part of the language of the American West. First written evidence of the word is from the Western novel Seven Men At Mimbres Springs, by W. Henry, in 1958. The line containing the word reads: 'Let's get out of here, Doc.' 'Yo, Frank.'   RUTH KILLICK, OXFORD UNIVERSITY PRESS, OXFORD.

'Yo' is listed as a usable two letter word in the game of Scrabble with the definition 'a word calling for an accompanying effort.' I suggest it comes from a shortening of the old naval ditty 'yo-heave-ho.'

J. W. E. CARTER, WORTHING, WEST SUSSEX.

There is a Cornish word pronounced 'yo' though spelt 'how' meaning hi or hello, still in common use in Cornwall.   MISS C. SMITH, MULLION, CORNWALL.

In Danish conversation 'jo' is an emphatic 'ja,' meaning 'yes,' equivalent to our own 'absolutely' or 'too true.'   P. GUBI, BATH, AVON.

999: Why did Roy Orbison always wear dark glasses?

Pictures of Roy Orbison taken before 1963 show him with clear lenses or no glasses at all. His dark glasses trademark happened by accident. Flying into Alabama for a performance, Roy left his regular glasses on the plane and didn't realise until the evening that he was still wearing his sunglasses. By then he had no choice; he either had to wear the dark glasses or not see at all. At the last minute he went on stage wearing his sunglasses. The next day, he flew to Britain to join a Beatles' tour and had to continue wearing the sunglasses just to see. Photographs taken of Roy with the Beatles ran in newspapers around the world, showing him in dark glasses. He hadn't planned this new image, but kept it for the next 25 years until his death in December 1988. I wonder if his original glasses were ever found?   ROBERT NIX, LOUTH, LINCOLNSHIRE.

1,000: We used to have our hair singed when it was cut, but hairdressers don't seem to do it now. Why did they do it and when did it stop?

Hair singeing dates from when barbers took on many trades including shaving, dentistry, surgery. etc., as well as cutting hair. Singeing the tips of the hair was thought to keep in its nutrients, preventing the hair from 'bleeding' to maintain and improve the hair's general condition. Singeing was actually supposed to protect the follicles against cold. Once hairdressers became more knowledgeable about the make-up of the hair and scalp and learned that hair doesn't 'bleed', this technique was largely abandoned. But the fashion for singeing hair has clung on in a very small number of hairdressers for people who are still keen on having a wax taper used on the tips of their follicles. BRUCE MASEFIELD, VIDAL SASSOON, MANCHESTER.

On the first day of my hairdressing apprenticeship in 1935, it was drummed into me that singeing was good for the hair. I was told the flame sealed the ends, stopped them 'bleeding' and kept the goodness in, strengthening the hair. This sales patter was put to men whose hair was falling out and who dreaded baldness. Belief in this technique stayed with me for some time, though I knew in my heart that nothing would stop male hair loss, which is hereditary.
GLYN EDWARDS, FORMER HON. SEC. NATIONAL HAIRDRESSERS FEDERATION, AVON.

1,001: Has snow ever fallen at Epsom racecourse on Derby Day? What is the latest date snow has fallen in our English summer?

The Derby usually takes place on the first Wednesday of June. Since it was first run in 1780 there have been, according to my information, only two occasions when an appreciable amount of snow has fallen on the course: 1839, when the winner was Bloomsbury; and 1867 when Hermit won.
JONATHAN LAWRENCE, EPSOM RACECOURSE, SURREY.

My mother used to say the Derby was run in a snowstorm on June 4, 1903, the day my sister was born.
MRS E. M. ONWOOD, SOUTH WOODFORD, LONDON, E18.

My father told me many times of snow at Epsom on Derby day 1932.
GWEN KEMPSTER, AYLESBURY, BUCKINGHAMSHIRE.

The latest date for snow to fall in England this century was recorded by our low ground stations on June 2, 1975. BILL DUNN, LONDON WEATHER CENTRE.

I have a newspaper cutting showing snow at Buxton, Derbyshire on June 7, 1973. MRS I. J. WALTERS, SEAFORD, SUSSEX.

Index